THE 30 DAY MBA

IN INTERNATIONAL BUSINESS

2ND EDITION

For many of the topics in the book there are direct links to the *free* teaching resources of the world's best business schools.

There are also links to hundreds of hours of *free* video lectures given by other distinguished Business School professors, from top schools including Cranfield, Wharton, Chicago, Harvard and CEIBS (China Europe International Business School).

You can download Duke University's top-ranking Fuqua School of Business's lecture material on forecasting; a vital aid to anyone preparing sales projections.

Link into Cranfield's School of Management's Research Paper Series and see the latest insights in global supply chain logistics, or watch Harvard's Professor Michael Porter – a leading world proponent of international business strategy methodology – outline his ideas.

You can find a list of all these resources online and interspersed within the chapters. Visit **http://www.koganpage.com/product/the-30-day-mba-in-international-business-9780749475420**.

THE 30 DAY MBA

IN INTERNATIONAL BUSINESS

2ND EDITION

YOUR FAST TRACK GUIDE TO
— BUSINESS SUCCESS —

COLIN BARROW

KoganPage

LONDON PHILADELPHIA NEW DELHI

First published in Great Britain and the United States in 2011 by Kogan Page Limited
Second edition 2016

Apart from any fair dealing for the purposes of research or private study, or criticism or review, as permitted under the Copyright, Designs and Patents Act 1988, this publication may only be reproduced, stored or transmitted, in any form or by any means, with the prior permission in writing of the publishers, or in the case of reprographic reproduction in accordance with the terms and licences issued by the CLA. Enquiries concerning reproduction outside these terms should be sent to the publishers at the undermentioned addresses:

2nd Floor, 45 Gee Street	1518 Walnut Street, Suite 1100	4737/23 Ansari Road
London EC1V 3RS	Philadelphia PA 19102	Daryaganj
United Kingdom	USA	New Delhi 110002
www.koganpage.com		India

The right of Colin Barrow to be identified as the author of this work has been asserted by him in accordance with the Copyright, Designs and Patents Act 1988.

ISBN   978 0 7494 7542 0
E-ISBN   978 0 7494 7543 7

British Library Cataloguing-in-Publication Data

A CIP record for this book is available from the British Library.

Library of Congress Cataloging-in-Publication Data

Barrow, Colin, author.
  The 30 day MBA in international business : your fast track guide to business success / Colin Barrow. – Second edition.
    pages cm
  ISBN 978-0-7494-7542-0 (paperback) – ISBN 978-0-7494-7543-7 (ebk)   1. International business enterprises–Study and teaching.   2. Personnel management.   3. Industrial management.   4. Master of business administration degree.   I. Title.   II. Title: Thirty-day MBA in international business.
  HD62.4.B35 2016
  658'.049–dc23
                                                            2015034002

Typeset by Graphicraft Limited, Hong Kong
Print production managed by Jellyfish
Printed and bound by CPI Group (UK) Ltd, Croydon CR0 4YY

CONTENTS

LIST OF FIGURES

LIST OF TABLES

Introduction

- What an MBA in International Business knows.
- Why YOU need that knowledge too.
- How to use this book.
- Planning your 30 Day learning programme.

Businesses with a strong international presence have not had a better opportunity to prove their worth and resilience than during the recent worldwide economic downturn. BrandZ (**www.brandz.com**) a research company that studies global brands, has asked over 1.5 million consumers and professionals across 31 countries to compare over 50,000 brands each year since 2005. They rank the top 100 brands every year with such names as Google, Microsoft, McDonald's, IBM, Apple, Coca-Cola, BlackBerry, HSBC, Shell and Walmart regularly heading the list. The share prices of the top 100 brands as identified in the BrandZ study have outperformed the S&P 500 by over 40 per cent over the period 2008–15. In fact, whilst companies in the S&P 500 lost 11.5 per cent in value, those of the top 100 brands gained 18.5 per cent.

It's no coincidence that these same companies are the largest recruiters of MBAs, according to *Fortune* magazine's annual review. There isn't a major listed international company that doesn't employ a clutch of MBAs. Last year McKinsey hired 188, BCG, 138, Deloitte, 119, JP Morgan, 103 and Amazon 94. Further down the league Google took on 63, Microsoft, 54 and Apple, whose founder Steve Jobs famously flunked college, took in 29 MBAs mostly from Duke University's Fuqua School, where Apple's current CEO Tim Cook had earned his MBA.

Apple is by no means an exception in having an MBA for CEO. At the last count, 165 Fortune 500 companies were run by MBAs. John S Watson (Chevron), Jeffrey R Immelt (GE) and Margaret Cushing Whitman (better known as Meg) who runs Hewlett-Packard, and was CEO of eBay for 10 years before that, topped this league. One school alone, the Harvard Business School, produced an incredible 12 graduates who are among the top 50 best-paid CEOs in corporate America last year with an MBA. An impressive 40 of the 100 best-paid CEOs in corporate America last year have an MBA, according to the Forbes list of America's Highest Paid Chief Executives.

The MBA is widely regarded as the solution to the apparent lack of professionalism in many aspects of management as well as providing a recognized qualification for business managers. Accountants, engineers, scientists, actuaries, chemists, psychologists and a host of others in and around the organizational world have a body of knowledge and an accrediting association that ensures those practising in the field meet at least some minimum criteria. The MBA provides business with such a body of knowledge and now over 3,000 institutions around the world turn out hundreds of thousands of MBAs each year.

The MBA has been around for nearly half a century but business schools, where these degrees are minted, have been around a good deal longer. The honour of being the world's first business school is usually said to go to Ecole Spéciale de Commerce et d'Industrie (now ESCP Europe), established in Paris in December 1819, with Jean-Baptiste Say, who coined the word 'entrepreneur' as its first professor of economics. In the United States the first business school is generally accepted to have been Wharton, founded in 1881 by Joseph Wharton, a self-taught businessman. A miner, he made his fortune through the American Nickel Company and the Bethlehem Steel Corporation, later to become the subject of the earliest business case studies. Harvard Business School, a comparative latecomer, opened in 1908 with a faculty of 15 and launched a Management Master's programme two years later. By 1922 Harvard was running a doctoral programme pioneering research into business methods using the case study method, an approach that was to become its trademark and widely emulated throughout the business school fraternity.

The UK was late into the business school game. The Administrative Staff College at Henley, now the Henley Business School, established in 1945 as the civilian equivalent of the Military Staff Colleges, was a business school in all but name. It took a further decade or so before the long-held belief of politicians and business leaders that management was an inherited ability, a view reinforced by the heavy concentration of family-run businesses, diminished. Three Business Schools, each part of a university but with considerable autonomy, were established at Manchester (1965), London (1966) and Cranfield (1967). The Work Study School, which evolved to become Cranfield School of Management, actually opened in 1953.

Aside from ESCP, business schools took a while to catch on in Europe, but they have caught up fast with over 70 institutions offering post-graduate business degrees in Germany alone. ESMT (European School of Management and Technology) in Berlin, Mannheim Business School (MBS) and IESE Business School, Universidad de Navarra, Munich campus are all rated as world-class institutions.

As Table 0.1 shows, the MBA has been embraced with enthusiasm the world over.

With the growing complexity of business it rapidly became apparent that there was a need for a more specialized business degree rather than the all-singing all-dancing general MBA. Although that was fine for giving an overview, anyone wanting to get into the bowels of a particular disciplinary area as a management practitioner needed something with a bit more substance. And so the specialized MBAs were born.

All top business schools have International Business as the focus of their teaching and they strive hard to create an international flavour throughout. Wharton, for example, in their class profile as well as demonstrating their elitism – 862 students enrolled out of 7,493 applicants – claim to have 70 countries represented with international students making up 37 per cent of the class.

INSEAD, based in Fontainebleau just outside Paris has as its mission to bring together people, cultures and ideas from around the world to change lives and transform organizations. An international perspective is reflected in all aspects of their research and teaching. Their 138 faculty members come from 32 countries and in addition they have a campus in Singapore.

Birmingham Business School, who claim to be the UK's first business school – founded in 1902, albeit in a rather different format to the structure generally accepted today – is among a growing band offering a dedicated MBA International Business. The school was ranked by the FT (*Financial Times*) as 13th best in the UK and 95th globally in 2015. IE Business School, based in Madrid, consistently recognized as one of the world's top business schools by the *Financial Times* and *The Economist* rankings among others, offers an MBA International Business taught both in English and Spanish. They boast students from more than 80 countries on their programmes.

What is the content of an MBA in international business and what use will that be to me?

Anyone who wants to play a more rounded role in shaping and implementing the direction of the organization they work in but is inhibited by their lack of detailed international business knowledge will find that reading this book will equip them to take part in the strategic decision making on an equal footing with MBA graduates, while feeling at ease in the process. It places MBA International Business skills within reach of all professionals in large and small organizations in both the public and private sectors, providing them with a competitive edge over less-knowledgeable colleagues.

International Business basically comprises a number of disciplinary areas, each with a number of components. These disciplines in some cases overlap or extend those covered in the general MBA programme. They contain the tools with which you can effectively analyse a business's situation drawing on both internal information relevant to the business and external information on its markets, competitors and general business environment as a prelude to deciding on a course of action.

The emphasis here in the contents of this book is on the terms 'concepts' and 'tools'. The business world is full of conflicting theories and ideas on how organizations could or should work, or how they could be made to work better. They come in and out of fashion, get embellished or replaced over time. A good analogy would be the difference between the limited number of tools a carpenter, for example, has in their toolbox, and the infinite number of products that could be made from those same tools. The ultimate success of the product the carpenter makes is partly down to their skills in using those tools and partly down to the world they find themselves operating in at a particular moment in time. A glance in a carpenter's toolbox will reveal an enduring range of common, robust implements – screwdrivers, pliers, spanners, smoothing planes, saws and hammers.

In business, for example, there is no such thing as the right number of countries or continents to trade in, or whether or not going for an overseas acquisition is a winning strategy. What is best in terms of, say, the ratio of growth generated from existing markets as opposed to, say, that coming from entering new markets varies with the type of organization and the prevailing economic conditions and the competitive environment. That ratio will be different for the same organization at different times and when it is pursuing different strategies. Layering an inherently risky marketing strategy, say, forming a strategic alliance abroad, with a risky financing strategy, using funds that carry currency exposure, creates a potentially more risky situation than any one of those actions in isolation. But whichever of the choices a business makes the tools used to assess business strengths and weaknesses are much the same. This book will explain the concepts and tools that are used in those disciplines. Moreover, it will show you how to use these tools to comprehensively assess a business's situation in an international business environment.

Table 0.1 shows where some of teaching, research and learning resources for this edition have been drawn from.

The MBA International core disciplines

There are a small number of core subject areas that comprise the subject matter of an MBA International programme. For some important areas there is a legitimate debate as to whether or not they should be covered in an MBA programme at all. A prime example is languages. Almost all the top business school programmes are taught in English. In fact, even where the school is based outside the Anglo Saxon sphere, English is used simply because it is the only way to attract an international student body, a vital ingredient to the success of such programmes. EM Lyon, a *grandes école* in France, for example, ranked by *Businessweek* among the Top 25 European B-Schools

TABLE 0.1   Top Ranked World Business Schools FT Global Rankings 2015 and TopMBA 2014 Ranking for International Business (teaching, research and learning resources drawn on for this edition)

School	2015 World Rank (FT)	Country
Harvard Business School	1 (2)	United States
London Business School	2 (4)	United Kingdom
University of Pennsylvania: Wharton	3 (3)	United States
Stanford Graduate School of Business	4 (7)	United States
INSEAD	4 (1)	France
Columbia Business School	6 (11)	United States
MIT Sloan	8 (19)	United States
University of Chicago: Booth	9 (10)	United States
University of California at Berkeley: Haas	10 (17)	United States
IE Business School	12 (5)	Spain
Northwestern University: Kellogg	14 (13)	United States
Yale	17 (41)	United States
IMD	20 (14)	Switzerland
Duke University: Fuqua	21 (28)	United States
Saïd (Oxford)	22 (21)	United Kingdom
Dartmouth College: Tuck	23 (33)	United States
Indian Institute of Management, Ahmedabad	26 (37)	India
SDA Bocconi	26 (16)	Italy
National University of Singapore Business School	31 (30)	Singapore
The Indian School of Business	33 (46)	India

*TopMBA (http://www.topmba.com/mba-rankings/specialization/international-management#)

(in March 2010) states in its MBA prospectus that 'Knowledge of the French language is not required'. But some schools – for example IE, mentioned earlier – teach identical programmes in two or more languages. Cranfield School of Management, ranked 15th in the world in 2010 by the *Economist*, takes a very different approach. They insist that all their students whose first language is English and do not already speak a second language are required to learn French, Spanish or German during part one of the MBA programme. The focus is on spoken rather than written skills and by the end of the course students should be able to understand and hold simple conversations on everyday themes. Languages are not covered in this book; the online resources provide a guide to learning and using foreign languages.

Many Business Schools eschew some vital elements within these disciplines as they are considered either too practical, un-sexy from a research/career prospective or more skill- or art-orientated than academic. A prime example is the field of Selling or selecting overseas sales staff, subjects that fit naturally into the International Business domain but much to the surprise of MBA students often fail to appear on the syllabus. Nevertheless most employers, and students for that matter, feel their MBA's value would be enhanced by a sound grounding in selling and sales management.

The irreducible core MBA International Business syllabus that you will find in the programmes of top business schools is as follows.

Introduction to International Business: A brief history of international business, the rise and rise of the MNE (Multinational Enterprise), the internationalization process – how and why firms move from exporting to players in the global business arena, the benefits and risks to all the key parties to international business, the Globalization Index Rankings – who is who in the international business arena.

The International Business Environment: Political systems, economic climates and systems, social and cultural factors in international business, the Internet and e-commerce infrastructures, technology and knowledge, environmental issues, differing legal frameworks and jurisdictions, international property rights – business and intellectual property protection standards.

Global Business Strategy: focus, differentiation and cost leadership, international market assessment, researching international markets, international market segmentation – methods and procedures, market share, product and service positioning, creating global brands, targeting markets, international competitor analysis, market entry strategies.

International Marketing Strategy: Global product and service offers, defining the product or service, understanding the product/service mix, international product life cycles, quality positioning by market, extending the product service line, launching new products, new product/service adoption cycles. International promotion and advertising: channels, promotional mix, public relations, sales promotion, personal selling, using databases, effective website strategies, measuring advertising effectiveness, marketing channels and direct routes to market, vertical marketing systems (VMS), horizontal marketing systems (HMS), distribution strategy criteria, choosing channel partners, global marketing logistics. Pricing in global markets: value pricing, competition pricing, skim vs penetration strategies, product mix pricing, real-time pricing models, market/country segmented pricing.

Finance and accounting: International sources of finance, FDI (Foreign Direct Investment) and other financial incentives, international and local accounting standards, taxation of multinational enterprises, foreign exchange risk, transfer pricing strategies.

Managing the international organization: Systems and people, structures, the options – functional, matrix and SBU (strategic business unit), country vs region – line and staff relationships, local manufacturing and outsourcing, managing international R&D, the role of headquarters.

Human Resource Management: Recruiting and selecting local staff, using expatriates, compensation strategies, training and development, language and cultural issues, contracts of employment and employment legislation, labour relations practices, repatriation procedures, health care and insurance.

Selecting and maintaining global strategic partners: Mergers, acquisitions and joint ventures, selecting local partners, negotiating alliances, exercising managerial control, reporting procedures and systems.

Ethics and social responsibility in the global market: Corruption in international business, piracy and counterfeiting, smuggling, money laundering, green strategies, ethical responsibility strategies, whistle-blowing, understanding international stakeholder groups.

Entrepreneurship – the global context: Comparative entrepreneurial cultures, cross-border ventures, corporate ventures in the international arena, business incubation.

Preparing the international business growth plan and budget: Setting international goals and objectives, using growth matrices – Ansoff, Boston, GE and others – setting international performance budgets, variance analysis.

Other central subjects: Accounting, statistics, forecasting and decision making tools.

The main uses of MBA International Business knowledge

Most managers whether new or experienced have little knowledge outside their own narrow discipline. Employers have no real incentive to train most of their employees in any subject that doesn't have a reasonably immediate payback. If you want to play a more rounded role in shaping and implementing the direction of the organizations you work in but are inhibited by a lack of fundamental knowledge concerning the implication of decisions on your organization's global competitive position in their industry, then it will be largely down to you to acquire that knowledge.

For example, few managers championing, say, launching a new product or extending a product warranty would be able to put forward a coherent and convincing international business case, appreciate the impact on business operations or understand the significance of the prevailing economic indicators in overseas countries on likely future performance. Worse still they are unlikely to even have sufficient relevant vocabulary to take part in the decision yet alone make it.

Reading this book will equip them to take part in the international strategic decision-making process on an equal footing with their company directors or MBA graduates, while feeling at ease in the process. It places international management skills within reach of all professionals in large and small organizations in both the public and private sectors, providing them with a competitive edge over less-knowledgeable colleagues.

Specialist international business knowledge as covered here in this book or in a business school equips the student to get a thorough understanding of marketing theory and practice and to master the skills needed to use marketing tools essential to implementing, interpreting and influencing marketing performance. With these skills a student will:

- gain the international marketing analysis and strategic perspective they need to interact effectively with top management as a partner in making key global business decisions;
- play a full role in international business planning, control and competitor analysis;
- be able to take part effectively in overseas acquisition strategies, joint ventures and strategic alliances;
- be able to prepare international business plans and financial projections;
- know where to look to find detailed information on any business or market on any continent;
- be able to evaluate and assess the risks associated with trading and operating in different countries, garnering sufficient evidence to choose between competing options or to recommend go or no-go decisions.

MBA International Business knowledge can also open up opportunities for career development and change in a wide variety of areas previously closed. For example, about half of INSEAD's International MBAs work away from their home country on graduation, with Australians, Canadians and Americans most likely to do so and British, Japanese and Russians least likely. Norwegian Helge Lund, an INSEAD MBA and boss of an international Gas group BG, is one such example (see Case Study below). Other career paths for International Business MBAs include consulting, international banking and public services including hospital management, trade bodies, the UN and the World Bank. University of Oxford's Saïd Business School (a top-ranking school whose MBAs' average salary on graduating is $138,000) lists a number of 'tree hugging' destinations for its graduates including running a charity in Africa. The School also offers Skoll

Scholarships, funded by eBay (EBAY) co-founder Jeffrey Skoll that pay the tuition and living expenses for five students each year who are pursuing careers in social entrepreneurship, an increasingly popular destination for MBAs. The list of top employers for International MBAs reads like a who's who of global business: Google, McKinsey & Company, Bain & Company, Goldman Sachs Group, The Boston Consulting Group, Walt Disney, Yahoo and of course Microsoft are all in the frame, as are Nike, JP Morgan, Johnson & Johnson, Deloitte, Procter & Gamble and Amazon.com, in that order.

CASE STUDY Shell bids for BG

On 9 April 2015, Shell announced that it was paying £47 billion for BG, the British multinational oil and gas company headquartered in Reading, United Kingdom. The offer represented a 50 per cent premium to BG's closing share price on the previous day's closing share price. Shell shares closed down more than 4 per cent whilst BG's raced ahead by 38 per cent. Shell claimed that owning BG would allow it to focus on fewer, safer bets and make the most of their mutual assets by integrating gas and deep-water activities whilst pulling back from more risky early stage projects such as the Arctic.

For Helge Lund, BG Group's boss of barely two months, the deal stood to make him up to £32 million of bonuses. For Shell, according to the *Economist*, 'the acquisition will increase its energy reserves by 25 per cent and make it the world's third-biggest producer of liquefied natural gas.'

Lund built his reputation the helm of Norway's Statoil, transforming the company from a small domestic operator into a global business. With an MBA from the INSEAD Lund had a range of opportunities when he decided to quit Statoil, but decided instead to join the much-troubled BG. In 2014 BG's first-half operating profits of $4 billion were sunk by its cash capital expenditure of $4.8 billion. The view on the street was that BG didn't have the operational capacity or financial scale required to realize the potential of its impressive portfolio. In short it was an ideal takeover target.

In a nutshell, in the Shell/BG case example you have all the ingredients that demonstrate the uses of an International MBA: a troubled business with more opportunity than cash, and a giant company with cash and a need to lower risk and milk assets – realize synergy in the MBA jargon of the merger world. Stoke these up with a leavening of ego and personal wealth creation and the stage is set for an MBA to perform to their best on.

How this book is organized and how to use it

Each of the chapters in the book covers the essential elements of each of the core disciplines in a top MBA International Business programme. There are links to external readings and resources, online library and information sources, case examples and self-assessment tests so you can keep track of your learning achievements.

Depending on your knowledge of international business, you should plan to spend about two days on each of the areas. You should draw up a time-table spread over the time period allocated for your 30 day MBA in International Business, say 12, 24 or 36 weeks. Then mark out the hours allocated for each subject, not forgetting to leave an hour or so for the test at the end of each subject. You will also need to build in a couple of days for revision before you take your final exam.

The subject areas within each chapter correspond to what you would find in the syllabus at major business schools in terms of theoretical underpinning and the practical application of that theory that you would pick up from fellow students.

Every MBA student, whether they take a general programme or one that specializes in a particular discipline, as this book does, will be required to have a reasonable grasp of these tools. Depending on your knowledge in these areas you should plan to allocate the remaining six days of your 30 day learning plan to these areas.

The case study method

Pioneered by Harvard and championed by schools such as Cranfield, who host the European Case Study Clearing House, Bocconi (Milan), ESADE (Barcelona) and INSEAD (Paris) the case study teaching method is de rigueur. Business schools use the case study as a vehicle for applying and testing out the theories their students are studying in class. The logic for this is impeccable. By studying a business at a particular moment in time students are forced to grapple with exactly the kinds of decisions and dilemmas managers confront every day. The case study method brings into the classroom the opportunity to analyse a complex situation, where all the relevant facts are not available, and persuade others to your point of view.

Of course if you weren't in the classroom you would be in your own organization, evaluating a business opportunity if you plan to start a business, or looking outside at other enterprises for new career prospects. In short you would have no need of a case study. You would even have to hand an infinite supply of people whose views differed from your own to debate the options with.

This book contains a selection of shorter case studies that will give you a flavour of the case study method. In addition there are links to video case studies at the end of each chapter.

Additional online learning resources

At the end of each chapter you will find two new sections which, if used, will extend and cement your learning. In 'Online video courses and lectures' you will find topical and relevant classroom or lecture theatre presentations and discussions. With a few exceptions these are free and delivered by faculty members of leading business schools. Some of those from business schools are by way of an entire course of anything up to a score or so of lectures. These can comprise everything you would receive had you attended the class in person: teaching notes, handouts and discussion forums using the latest in peer-to-peer social learning tools. Most of the lectures are available all the time, but some of the full courses run periodically, up to four times a year. Some courses will enable you to earn a Certificate of Achievement, or you can just audit the course. Delivery is usually via a virtual 'classroom', open 24/7, where everyone is accepted.

The courses are often delivered on one of the two main MOOCs (Massive Open Online Courses) platforms. These courses are free for everyone but some courses have a fee for verified certificates but are free to audit.

- Coursera (**www.coursera.org**). Founded at Stanford in 2012 their mission is to 'provide universal access to the world's best education.' They are 'an education platform that partners with top universities and organizations worldwide, to offer courses online for anyone to take, for free.' There are over 100 universities offering lecture courses including Stanford, IE Business School, Yale, Princeton, Northwestern, Rutgers, Duke, Copenhagen, Tokyo, HEC Paris, Columbia and Ludwig-Maximilians-Universität München.

- EdX (**www.edx.org**). Founded by the Massachusetts Institute of Technology and Harvard University in May 2012. Over 400 courses are on offer from universities including MIT, Harvard, Berkeley, Caltech, Georgetown, the Sorbonne, Peking, IIT Bombay, Rice, Kyoto, Columbia, Australian National and Cornell. EdX's goal is to 'offer the highest quality courses from institutions who share our commitment to excellence in teaching and learning.'

There are many other MOOC course providers and often universities that participate in Coursera or EdX programmes run their own MOOCs through their university website. It has to be said that such offerings are not easy to find. A better route to further supplementing the lectures and courses offered here is to use the MERLOT 11 (**www.merlot.org**) 'Search Merlot' tab. The letters stand for Multimedia Educational Resource for Learning and Online Teaching. The MERLOT project began in 1997 at the California State University Center for Distributed Learning. For students the search facility is all you really need to know about.

Online video case studies, 80 or so in number, include an eclectic mixture of business school-based presentations, often by entrepreneurs and senior managers of business and other organizations. Some are critiques made by journalists on TV and others are student analysis of business behaviour and performance. Apple's Steve Jobs, Amazon's Jeff Bezos, Airbnb's Nathan Blecharczyk appear here alongside less flattering critiques of Walmart's labour policy, Union Carbide's handling of the Bhopal gas tragedy and Nike defending its position on corporate responsibility. These case studies complement those in the text.

Introduction to international business

- Measuring international trade.
- How it all began.
- Theories of international trade.
- Who benefits.
- Identifying the risks.

International business is both big business and in the hands of big business. The World Trade Organization (WTO), who keep track of the activities of their 160 country members in their latest annual report published in January 2015, note the following:

- China became the world's biggest merchandise trader in 2013, with imports and exports totalling US\$ 4,159 billion. It recorded a trade surplus of US\$ 259 billion, 2.8 per cent of its GDP.
- The United States is the second-biggest merchandise trader, with imports and exports totalling US\$ 3,909 billion in 2013. The US trade deficit was US\$ 750 billion (4.5 per cent of its GDP).
- Germany is in third place, with a trade surplus of US\$ 264 billion in 2013, 7.3 per cent of its GDP.
- Japan ranks fourth, with merchandise trade totalling US\$ 1,548 billion in 2013.It recorded a trade deficit of US\$ 118 billion, 2.4 per cent of its GDP.

Two further revealing facts were that the top 10 countries dealing in merchandise trade accounted for a little over half of the world's total trade in 2013. The 100 or so developing economies accounted for 43 per cent of world merchandise trade in 2013.

The figures for the service sector are similarly polarized. The top 10 traders in world commercial services represent half of the world's total trade in commercial services in 2013. North America alone has a world share of commercial service exports of 16.4 per cent.

World exports of commercial services totalled US\$ 4,645 billion in 2013 with:

- Europe's exports of commercial services grew by 7 per cent in 2013 with very variable rates of growth by member countries. One of the highest growth rates was achieved by the Netherlands (12 per cent) followed by France (10 per cent) and Germany (8 per cent). The United Kingdom saw more modest growth of 2 per cent.
- In North America, exports expanded by 5 per cent.
- Asia's exports grew by 5 per cent, a slightly lower rate than in 2012.
- In Central and South America, exports grew by only 2 per cent.
- In the Middle East, exports rose by 4 per cent, compared with almost 9 per cent the previous year.
- The Commonwealth of Independent States (CIS) recorded the highest growth in exports of commercial services in 2013 (9 per cent), repeating the growth achieved in 2012. This growth was mostly due to Russia's increase in transport exports, which represents the region's most important services sector.
- In contrast, Africa's exports of commercial services contracted by 3 per cent.

A brief history of the instruments of international business

No self respecting MBA student would be without a modest grasp of how international business came about. Although it is tempting to believe that international business is the creation of recent developments, that is not quite so. Improved communication and travel, telephones, the Internet, air and fast sea transport combined with sophisticated financial systems for dealing with foreign exchange and moving money around the globe must surely have given rise to the importance of the sector.

That may well be, but international business and instruments to facilitate its execution have been in place for several millennia and the process of international trade has benefited domestic business from the outset.

Banding together

For thousands of years BC, trade between continents was initiated and in many cases flourished. One example is the Silk Road, so named in 1877 by

TABLE 1.1 Growth in the volume of world merchandise trade 2005–2013 for selected economies (agricultural products, food, fuels, iron, steel, chemicals, office and telecoms equipment, automotive products, textiles, clothing etc)

Exports	Region	Imports
3.5	North America	1.5
0.0	Canada	2.0
4.5	Mexico	4.0
4.5	United States	0.5
1.5	South and Central America	8.0
2.0	Europe	1.0
2.0	European Union (28)	0.5
−1.5	Norway	3.0
2.5	Switzerland	1.5
2.5	Commonwealth of Independent States (CIS)	7.5
6.5	Asia	5.5
3.5	Australia	4.5
11.0	China	10.0
10.5	India	11.0
2.0	Japan	1.0
5.5	Six East Asian traders	3.5

(Hong Kong, China; Malaysia; Republic of Korea; Singapore; Separate Customs Territory of Taiwan, Penghu, Kinmen and Matsu (Chinese Taipei) and Thailand.)
SOURCE: World Trade Organization
(https://www.wto.org/english/res_e/statis_e/its2014_e/its2014_e.pdf)

TABLE 1.2   Growth in the volume of world commercial services 2005–2013 for selected economies (transportation, tourism, insurance, financial services, computer and information services etc)

Exports	Region	Imports
7.0	North America	6.0
5.0	Canada	6.0
8.0	United States	6.0
9.0	South and Central America	14.0
7.0	Europe	6.0
7.0	European Union (28)	6.0
9.0	Switzerland	11.0
14.0	Commonwealth of Independent States (CIS)	14.0
11.0	Asia	10.0

SOURCE: Source: World Trade Organization
(https://www.wto.org/english/res_e/statis_e/its2014_e/its2014_e.pdf)

Ferdinand von Richthofen – the German geographer. From the 2nd century BC to the end of the 14th century AD, this important trade route starting out from Chang'an (now Xian) in the east and ran to the Mediterranean in the west, linking the Roman Empire and China, transferring not only goods, but also informing the cultures of China, India, Persia, Arabia, Greece and the Roman Empire. The tin mines of Cornwall, believed to have been established earlier than 2000 BC, were sought out by metal traders from the Eastern Mediterranean soon after and are thought to be one reason the Romans invaded the British Isles.

From these very early times the effect of international trade on business life in general was disproportionate. From these early trading times to the present day the most popular legal structure under which to operate has been as a sole trader, which in effect means every man for himself. In the beginning merchants always risked their own money, if they had any to invest: if they travelled, as most did, they risked their life on the journey. The caravan trade of Asia, Asia Minor and North and Central Africa ploughed their way through the sands that separated distant cities and seaports. The largest caravans comprised thousands of camels and required careful administration. They also stimulated people to band together in partnerships, pooling protection costs and profits to spread the risks. The partnerships would usually last only for the particular journey. Later on, older merchants who had made money from earlier ventures could join such expeditions by putting up money, without the hardship of making the trip themselves. This could be seen as an early form of limited partnership.

As the ventures became more costly and of longer duration partnership structures of fixed duration between one, three or five years became common, with an ever-increasing range of partners with differing shares in the venture. To add to the complications these partners could join and leave, perhaps for no more sinister reason than death, at different times.

The concept of limited liability, where the shareholders are not liable, in the last resort, for the debts of their business, changed the whole nature of business and risk taking. It opened the floodgate encouraging a new generation of entrepreneurs to undertake much larger-scale ventures without taking on themselves all the consequences of failure. As the name suggests, this form of business liability is limited to the amount you contribute by way of share capital and, in the event of failure, creditors' claims are restricted to the assets of the company. The shareholders of the business are not normally liable as individuals for the business debts beyond the paid-up value of their shares.

The concept itself can be traced back to the Romans where it was granted, albeit infrequently, as a special favour to friends for large undertakings by those in power. The idea was resurrected in 1811 when New York State brought in a general limited liability law for manufacturing companies. Most American states followed suit and eventually Britain caught up in 1854. Today most countries have a legal structure incorporating the concept of limited liability.

Without limited liability international trade could not have flourished, but neither would domestic businesses have had the opportunity to grow and prosper.

Accounting rules

Sometime before 3000 BC the people of Uruk and other sister-cities of Mesopotamia began to use pictographic tablets of clay to record economic transactions. The script for the tablets evolved from symbols and provides evidence of an ancient financial system that was growing to accommodate the needs of the Uruk economy. The Mesopotamian equivalent of today's bookkeeper was the scribe. His duties were similar, but even more extensive. There is detailed evidence that this basic bookkeeping system was common throughout the world. China, during the Chao Dynasty (1122–256 BC), used bookkeeping chiefly as a means of evaluating the efficiency of governmental programmes and the civil servants who administered them. Accounts in ancient Rome evolved from records traditionally kept by the heads of families, where daily entries of household receipts and payments were kept in an adversaria or daybook, and monthly postings were made to a cashbook known as a *codex accepti et expensi*. Up to Medieval times this single-entry system of bookkeeping, divided into two general parts, Income and Outgo, with a statement at the end showing the balance due to the lord of the manor, prevailed in England, as elsewhere. Although these accounts were fairly basic they were sufficient to handle the needs of the very simple business structures that prevailed.

Until Luca Paccioli wrote what was in essence the world's first international accounting book, over 500 years ago, accounting records were maintained in this single-entry format; one event merited one record. This meant that errors could only be prevented by a major duplication of effort, for example by having different people making and counting up parallel records. Paccioli, a mathematician who worked for the Doge of Venice, came up with a system of double-entry bookkeeping that required two entries for each transaction and so provides built-in checks and balances to ensure accuracy. Each transaction requires an entry as a debit and as a credit. Paccioli's genius lay in seeing that the ultimate balancing number in a company's accounts was the profit or loss for the owners of that enterprise. Double-entry bookkeeping was a vital innovation in facilitating the growth of world trade. Long-term ventures with shareholders in different countries and continents could join and leave almost at will, confident in being able to assess, if not always collect, the profit due to them.

Eventually Paccioli's basic rules were augmented by GAAP (Generally Accepted Accounting Practice) and the work of the International Accounting Standards Board (IASB), but the core of his proposition that facilitated world trade for half a millennium remains unchanged.

International law

Business needs law to determine property rights, without which no meaningful enterprise can take place, and to govern the behaviour and responsibilities of buyers, sellers and others involved in any transaction. The laws that govern business behaviour have evolved over thousands of years and from the earliest times it was intended that businesses trading across borders should follow some common rules. The Hammurabi (1795–1750 BC) code of laws is the earliest known example of an entire body of laws, arranged in orderly groups, so that all might read and know what was required of them. The code was carved on a black stone monument, eight feet high, and clearly intended to be in public view, and now resides in the Louvre Museum in Paris.

The code regulates in clear and definite strokes the organization of society in general and commercial dealings in particular. One law states 'if a man builds a house badly, and it falls and kills the owner, the builder is to be slain. If the owner's son was killed, then the builder's son is slain.' Even 4,000 years ago it was considered necessary to protect consumers from shoddy workmanship.

Another law states that 'If, while on the journey, an enemy take away from him anything that he had, the broker shall swear by God and be free of obligation.' This is a forerunner of the term *force majeure*, which under today's international contract law frees both parties from liabilities and obligations.

Hammurabi's code was certainly not the earliest example of international trading law. Traces of preceding sets of law have been found, and Hammurabi's own code clearly implies their existence. He only claimed to be reorganizing a legal system long established.

The origins of international banking

Global banking doesn't have its origins in the 20th century, or even a couple of centuries earlier. The introduction of coined money in about 600 BC by the Greeks first allowed bankers to keep account books, change and loan money, and even arrange for cash transfers for citizens through affiliate banks in cities thousands of miles away.

Despite being remembered mostly for their military prowess during the crusades the Knights Templar became, in part by accident, the first major international banking institution. Their specific forte was in keeping the highways open to allow pilgrims to come to the Holy Land unmolested. This goal inevitably meant the Templars owned some of the mightiest castles, and because of their awesome reputation as fighting men, their castles served as ideal places to deposit money and other valuables. A French knight, for example, could deposit money or mortgage his chateau through the Templars in Paris and pick up gold coins along the route to Jerusalem, and back again if he survived! The Templars charged a fee for both the transaction and for converting the money into various currencies along the route.

Over the years the business grew and eventually the Templars ran a network of full-service banks stretching across Europe from England to Jerusalem. At their maximum strength the Templars employed about 7,000 people and owned 870 castles and fortified houses and were the principal banker to popes and kings.

Free trade

One factor that both facilitates and to a lesser extent inhibits international trade is the presence or otherwise of economic unions and associations designed to ease the flow of goods and services across borders. The EU, founded after the Second World War, is an example of one such association that has gone further than many in that common business and banking laws are enforced. Rules on cross-border mergers and acquisition are enforced and for many member states a common currency, the Euro, elimi-nates currency risk on all inter-state transactions. ASEAN (The Association of South East Asian Nations), BSEC (Organization for Black Sea Economic

Cooperation) and OAS (The Organization of American States) are other examples of cross-border economic cooperation associations.

But some eight centuries earlier, following the ravages of the Black Death in Europe, cities began to grow and prosper as trade increased and small-scale manufacturing revived. In the northern German seaports, merchants and traders sought protection for their business transactions and the transport of their goods. The city of Lübeck had made a treaty with the city of Hamburg in 1230, which established free trade between the two and guaranteed that the road linking the North Sea and the Baltic Sea would be guarded. The absence of a strong central government in Germany allowed the cities to make such treaties, and soon other communities asked to join the arrangement. Riga, Danzig, a trade centre in London in 1266, and Novgorod in Russia all became part of the league's network of 85 cities.

At its peak the league maintained an army and a navy, guarded roads from city to city, kept a fortress and a storehouse in each city, waged war and enforced the merchants' laws at the various fairs.

Global intelligence

Formal methods of conveying intelligence around the world were around long before Marconi and telegraphy entered the vocabulary. The Romans built more than 250,000 miles (400,000 km) of roads to move men, materials and information around their empire. By the 17th century, the British Post Office had a fleet of ships – packet boats – that were sailed out to carry mail, becoming in effect the first international mail forwarding service.

Although governments continued the Roman and British tradition in developing methods of international communication, business-intelligence gathering was the domain of merchants. In 1367, one Hans Fugger started a business weaving fustian, a strong cotton-and-linen fabric, in Augsburg, Bavaria. His sons Andreas and Jacob developed the family textile trade before moving into finance, in Antwerp and Venice. Jacob's sons evolved from trade in textile goods to cotton and spice, and ultimately into mining and processing silver and copper. The family developed a network of trading posts under Jacob's nephew and successor Anton that by 1525 extended from the Mediterranean to the Baltic.

When Anton's nephew Hans Jacob (1516–75) took over he kept control of their holdings through regular reports from their worldwide network of agents. These reports were consolidated into 'Fugger Newsletters' and circulated among their associates. This was one of the first uses of the word 'news' to refer to deliberate attempts to gather the latest intelligence. Three branches of descendants survive today; one of them – Prince Carl Fugger-Babenhausen – re-established the Fugger bank in 1954.

Although there is nothing new about international businesses requiring global intelligence the Internet has speeded up the process, extending the reach and depth of data available while making it available to almost anyone within reach of a Wi-Fi hotspot. But having said all that, the Romans ran their Empire for 1,000 years on what was then state-of-the-art communications technology – good roads.

Why and how businesses become international

The general theory of why and how international trade made businesses become international was once a simple affair. If one country had unique resources, say oil, gold or copper, or its labour costs were low relative to comparable neighbours (as was the case when the iron curtain fell), or if a country's businesses had surplus capacity, then selling that abroad at above its marginal cost – the cost of materials and labour – would create additional profits and so be a worthwhile strategy.

The path to internationalizing a business also followed a steady and predictable pattern. Expansion abroad was usually either opportunistic, say a chance meeting, visit or enquiry, or by virtue of putting a toe in the water in a nearby country. Despite a superficial veneer of hostility, France and Britain for example are major trading partners, mainly inspired by being only 20 or so miles apart. France is the UK's third-largest export market (the second in Europe) accounting for some £20 billion per year, which is nearly 10 per cent of UK visible exports worldwide. France is also the UK's third-largest supplier, shipping in everything from wine, which is in relatively low production, to motor vehicles, which are in abundant supply from local manufacturing facilities of German and Japanese firms in particular. Once a firm had success in one overseas market, it would gradually extend the process to others, often only limited by ambition or cash.

Today the reasons for firms adopting an international approach to business strategy are less predictable and more diverse. Google for example went from taking a cheque for $100,000 from Sun co-founder Andy Bechtolsheim in 1998 to launching 10 language versions of the website in May 2000. The McDonald's case study below is illustrative of a more conventional approach.

CASE STUDY   McDonald's Corporation

In 2015 McDonald's was the leading global foodservice retailer with more than 36,000 local restaurants serving approximately 69 million people in more than 100 countries each day, employing 1.9 million people. In their latest figures they reported $28,106 million sales revenue and net income of $5,586 million. They are the archetypical international business, managed as distinct geographic segments that include the United States, Europe, Asia/Pacific, Middle East and Africa (APMEA) and Other Countries including Canada and Latin America. Its 13-strong board, led by Andrew J McKenna, a graduate of the University of Notre Dame with a degree in Business Administration and Marketing, between them have global experience in companies of world repute such as Aon Corporation, the leading provider of risk management services, insurance and reinsurance, Procter & Gamble, Wells Fargo, Nike, Inc, Wal-Mart Stores, Inc, and Hershey. Unsurprisingly, given the fact that they are the world's biggest property company they also have the non-executive Chairman of Jones Lang LaSalle, the biggest real estate services business, itself employing more than 30,000 people in 750 locations in 60 countries.

The business had an inauspicious start when brothers Richard and Maurice McDonald opened a single restaurant in San Bernardino, California in 1940. The brothers had been in the restaurant business albeit in a modest way since 1937, operating a hamburger stand near the Santa Anita racetrack. By 1948 the McDonald brothers were operating one small chain of carhop drive-ins, with waiting staff delivering food on skates direct to customers' cars, but with consumers becoming more price conscious they decided on a new business model. They set about streamlining the food production and delivery process with staff concentrating on single tasks. Three grillmen did nothing but flip burgers, while two did milkshakes and two french fries. Other staff packed and served on the counter. The McDonald brothers had done for hamburgers what Henry Ford had done for cars by bringing mass production to the restaurant business.

By 1952 business was booming so they ordered eight more mixers for their milkshake production, a purchase that caught the attention of Ray Kroc who sold the Multimixer product the McDonald's had settled on. Kroc, a high-school dropout, had variously worked as ambulance driver, jazz pianist, Florida real-estate salesman, radio station manager and for the Lily Tulip Cup company for several years selling paper cups. It was at Lily Tulip that he hit on the mixer market. The 'Speedee Service System', as it was named, was in Kroc's view ripe for rolling out as a chain. That idea itself was hardly new. White Castle, founded by J Walter Anderson of Wichita, Kansas had operated a chain selling five cent hamburgers along with french fries and colas since 1916, but Kroc had a degree of energy and ambition unknown to the McDonald brothers who preferred a less challenging family life that did not involve travelling the country, yet alone the globe. They were satisfied with the eight outlets they had opened before Kroc came their way.

Kroc persuaded the brothers to let him take on a franchise, which he opened in Des Plaines, Illinois, near Chicago, on 15 April 1955. On the same day he incorporated his company as McDonald's Corporation and, using this as his vehicle, by 1956 he had 12 franchises; two years later there were 34. In 1959 Kroc opened 67 new restaurants and by 1960 the chain was 228 strong. He bought out the McDonald brothers in 1961 for $2.7 million, taking it public in 1965 with his personal stake valued at $32 million.

The corporation's international expansion began in 1967, when the chain opened its first store outside the United States across the border in Canada. By the late 1970s, competition from other hamburger chains such as Burger King and Wendy's intensified and the so-called hamburger wars put such pressure on margins that McDonald's set about penetrating overseas markets with a vengeance. By 1991, 37 per cent of sales came from restaurants outside the United States. Today, McDonald's have more than 32,400 restaurants in more than 100 countries, straddling every continent. Half of the corporation's business is still in the United States.

International trade theory – an A to P

No self-respecting business graduate would settle for mere anecdotes or case examples, however relevant or convincing, as an explanation of how international business came to be such a dominant feature of commercial life. These are the key aspects of the theories and limitations of those theories that underpin the subject of international trade which an MBA needs at least a rudimentary appreciation of.

Absolute advantage

Adam Smith, the Scottish economist whose 'Invisible Hand' saw all economic activity as being subject to the law of unintended consequences, also had a thing or two to say about Mercantilism (see below), the prevailing big idea on international trade. In 1776 in his blockbuster book *The Wealth of Nations* Smith argued that for a country – and by extension the enterprises that make up that country – to simply try always to export more than they imported was both unrealistic and uneconomic. He argued that countries differed in their ability to produce goods efficiently and so had an inherent cost advantage.

Natural advantage

An industry that Smith drew on for his theory was the French wine trade, which due to good soil and a benign climate was the world's most efficient wine industry. Despite shifts in weather patterns, improvements in technology and sheer determination, England's wine industry some 240 years on is still dwarfed by that of France as it makes more and better wine at a lower cost. Other countries, particularly those in the New World – Argentina, Australia, Chile and the United States in particular – have muscled in on the trade, but those countries, too, shared France's natural advantage, in some cases with the added twist of lower costs of either land, labour or both.

Acquired advantage

The French wine industry in Smith's day also had generations of experience in that manufacturing process. This accumulated expertise gave them an acquired advantage. At this time England had the most efficient textile manufacturing industry in the world, courtesy of such innovations as Richard Arkwright's water frame, James Hargreaves's spinning jenny and Samuel Crompton's spinning mule (the spinning jenny and water frame combined, patented in 1769). James Watt's steam engine, patented in 1775, allowed efficient semi-automated factories to operate in places where waterpower was not available, so serving to increase England's acquired advantage in both textiles and other manufactured products.

A more recent example is that of Lean Manufacturing, an approach ascribed to Japanese companies such as Toyota, where they seek to eliminate or continuously reduce waste, which is anything that doesn't add value under such headings as:

- Transport: keep processes close to each other to minimize movement.
- Inventory: carrying high inventory levels costs money and if too low orders can be lost. 'Just in Time' (JIT) manufacturing should be aimed for.
- Motion: improve workplace ergonomics so as to maximize labour productivity.
- Waiting: aim for a smooth, even flow so that men and machines are working optimally, reducing down-time to a minimum.
- Defects: aim for zero defects as that directly reduces the amount of waste.

As a result of this approach many industries in Japan achieved an acquired advantage over those in other countries, allowing them to dominate industries such as motor manufacturing and even to be able to export steel despite having to import iron and coal, its main ingredients.

Comparative advantage

David Ricardo, an English economist, Member of Parliament, businessman, financier and speculator, in his 1817 book, *The Principles of Political Economy*, extrapolated Smith's theory to see what might happen if, as it looked might happen as the industrial revolution developed, one country – England in this case – had an absolute advantage in the production of all goods. Ricardo's conclusion was that a country should concentrate its efforts on those goods it produces most efficiently and be prepared to import goods from other countries even if it could make them more efficiently itself.

Most students and nearly all business managers find this argument counter-intuitive but this example explains the principle. Would a world-class forensic accountant commanding fees of $5,000 a day to unravel the financial mess left behind at Lehman Brothers, who coincidentally is a great bookkeeper, be better off keeping their own books? As even the world's best bookkeeper would be pushed to make $500 a day, clearly a forensic accountant would be better off paying out for a bookkeeper and finding a few more firms like Lehman's to work on.

Gravity Model

The Gravity Model, first used by Jan Tinbergen, the Dutch economist and co-winner of the first Nobel Prize in economics in 1969, postulates that just as Newton's law of gravity draws on distance and physical size between two objects to predict behaviour, trade between countries will be similarly influenced. His theoretical model, developed in 1952, states that the trade between two countries (i and j) takes the form of:

$$F_{ij} = G \frac{M_i M_j}{D_{ij}}$$

Where F is the trade flow, M is the economic mass (GDP) of each country, D is the distance and G is a constant. The mode appears to be empirically reliable and is used by such bodies as the World Trade Organization (WTO) to test the effectiveness of trade agreements. McDonald's choice of Canada as its jumping-off point for international growth supports the distance element of this formula and though not quite in the same economic league it is the 11th richest country in the world.

The Heckscher–Ohlin model

Ricardo (see Comparative advantage) believed that advantage accrued to countries with greater labour productivity. Eli Heckscher and Bertil Ohlin of the Stockholm School of Economics extrapolated this idea by determining that countries are endowed with different factors such as capital, land and labour and it is those that collectively determine cost differences and hence advantage. The Heckscher–Ohlin model (H–O model), as it became known, essentially says that countries will export products that make use of their plentiful and cheap factors of production and import products that use the countries' scarce factors. This theory passes the common-sense test easily.

France, Ireland and the United States are all substantial exporters of agricultural products as they have a relatively high land density (acres per person), while China and South Korea have the advantage when it comes to goods that require an abundance of low-cost labour, such as clothing and footwear. In this latter area China's exports were so high as to attract trade barriers from the EU.

The Leontief Paradox

Economists like the Heckscher–Ohlin model as it mirrors their ideas on how advantage should work in theory. Unfortunately the H–O model is unreliable at predicting trade patterns, less so than the less elegant proposition advanced by Ricardo's Comparative Advantage (see above). Wassily Leontief, a Russian economist, son of a Professor of Economics and a Nobel Prize winner, demonstrated the limitations of the H–O model by showing that since the United States was awash with capital compared to most other countries, with the most sophisticated venture capital and stock markets in the world, they should, in theory, be a major exporter of capital-intensive goods and an importer of labour-intensive goods. Using the 1947 import–export tables covering 200 US industries Leontief showed the reverse to be the case. He postulated that demand and the availability of natural resources might play a greater role than supply in such cases and, as is usual with academics, called for more research to be carried out.

Linder's Income-Preference Similarity Theory

One dominant feature of international business is how much trade is done by virtue of developed countries trading with each other. Table 1.1 earlier in this chapter shows that the top positions, with the partial exceptions of China and India are all held by advanced, developed economies. According to WTO developed economies generate nearly 80 per cent of total world trade. With the exception of commodities, underdeveloped and developing economies, that is those with a per capita income below $12,000 per annum at 2009 levels, account for few exports or imports with more developed economies.

This concentration of trade between developed economies would appear to contradict the Heckscher–Ohlin (H–O) theory which claims that countries are most likely to find trading with those with fundamentally different factor endowments. Staffan B Linder, a Swedish economist, concluded that although the H–O theory may well apply to trade in primary, resource-intensive products including natural resources – oil, agricultural products, metals and so forth – the position with manufactured goods was fundamentally different. He argued that international trade in manufactures takes place largely between developed countries. The WTO statistics would largely support this as Europe and the United States account for 80.5 per cent of world exports of manufactured goods and 74 per cent of imports. Linder's conclusion was that internal demand governs what a country manufactures and they then go on to export those products to countries with a similar need, almost invariably a country with a similar income.

Linder went on to argue that the more similar the demand structure the more intensive the potential for bilateral trade in those manufactures. In 2009 the United States, Europe, Canada, Japan and Australia, all highly developed regions, imported 47 per cent of world output of office and telecom equipment, while they exported 38 per cent. Africa, on the other hand exported just 2.6 per cent, while importing 7.6 per cent. For luxury goods with brand appeal the preference is even more exaggerated – hence the term Income-Preference Similarity Theory.

Mercantilism

This is the granddaddy of all the theories on the subject of international trade. Until the mid-17th century the strategy that dominated English thinking was to stimulate exports by subsidizing them with a range of incentives while restricting imports by imposing tariffs and quotas. As gold and silver were the currency used in international trade, running a permanent trade surplus would ensure England would, as Thomas Mun, an early economic thinker, put it 'increase our wealth and treasure by foreign trade'. The need for all this 'treasure' was to arm to the teeth, in England's and Spain's cases, to build fleets of warships and so be able to literally conquer international markets.

Such was the view until 1630 but even then its central fallacy was evident. When England ran a trade surplus with France, the additional inflow of gold and silver increased the money in circulation so creating inflation that pushed up the prices of the goods England sought to export. Meanwhile in France the opposite was happening; money supply contracted, pulling general prices down. The net effect was that French goods became more attractive for English customers to import while English goods, being more expensive, were less so.

Adam Smith (see 'Absolute advantage' above) and David Ricardo (see 'Comparative advantage' above) went some way to exploding the mercantilists' view that international trade is a zero sum game, with winners (exporters) and (losers) importers. The advantage theories showed that there could be plenty of winners if international trade was encouraged and restrictions reduced or eliminated. The reaction of some countries' leaders after the banking crisis in 2008/09 showed that mercantilist ideas on trade barriers are far from dead, just dormant.

Neo-mercantilism

The thinking behind this theory of international trade is much like that of mercantilism but with a change in emphasis from military development

to economic development. In many ways the idea that a free trade philosophy dominates economic thinking is something of a fallacy: more a pious
hope than a practical reality. Trade barriers abound barring the way to
free trade between nations with many countries seeking (as the mercantilists
did) to export more than they import and to protect their industries from
foreign competition. In fact, at some stage almost every country engages
in neo-mercantilist policies. A glance at the EU website that tracks trade
disputes, reveals claims of unfair practices between half of the WTO member states. The 'General overview of the active WTO dispute settlement cases
as of 16 March 2015' (**http://trade.ec.europa.eu/wtodispute/search.cfm**)
runs to 51 pages. You can see who is disputing with whom using the country
tab on the website.

The arguments advanced for the policy usually revolve around claims
such as:

- Time is needed to let the nation develop its industrial and commercial
  infrastructure to the point where it can compete on equal terms in
  international trade. In effect any country, save perhaps the
  United States, could make such a claim, with some justification –
  and they do.

- Unusual times call for unusual measures. The banking crisis of 2008
  and the years immediately following it saw even the most free-trade-
  orientated countries such as the UK and the United States take
  protectionist measures to save financial institutions. Less committed
  free traders such as the French frequently use this argument too.
  In March 2009 President Nicolas Sarkozy of France granted
  £5.6 billion in soft loans to Renault and Peugeot Citroën in exchange
  for a promise not to shut French plants or axe French jobs. Renault
  promptly announced that Clio Campus cars currently made at the
  Novo Mesto plant in Slovenia would be produced at the Flins plant,
  west of Paris.

National competitive advantage: Porter's Diamond

Michael Porter, a professor at the Harvard Business School, who made his
reputation with his ideas on corporate competitive advantage (see Chapter 3),
turned his hand to trying to establish why some nations were conspicuously more successful than others in the international trade arena. He
had in mind questions such as why does a country like Switzerland do so
well in the pharmaceutical and watch industries, outperforming many other
countries whose resource factors (see the various advantage theories and the
Heckscher–Ohlin model, above) are similar if not better?

Studying 100 industries in 10 countries Porter and his team of researchers
theorized that four national attributes create the local competitive environment for individual businesses, and so in turn promote or limit their advantage in the broader international trade arena.

FIGURE 1.1 The determinants of national competitive advantage: Porter's Diamond

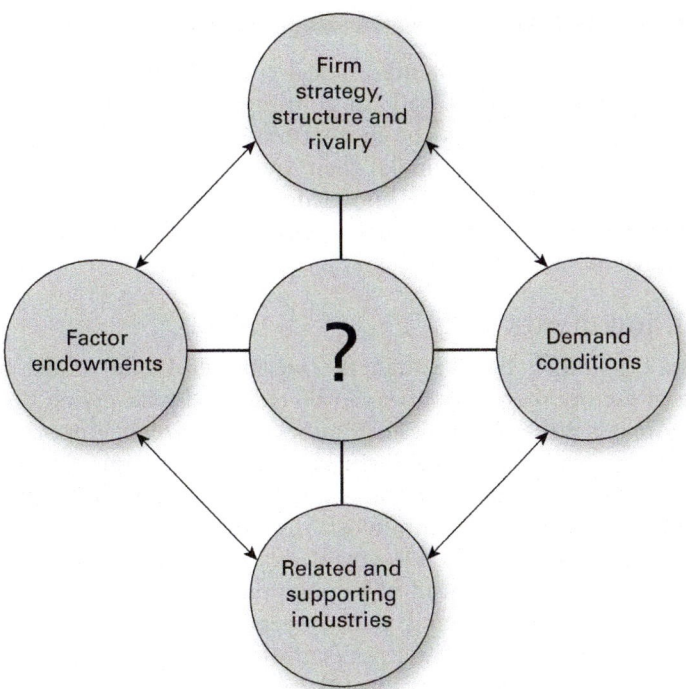

Firm strategy, structure and rivalry

Drawing on his work on the competitive strategy between rival firms within a country Porter identified two elements important to their success or otherwise when operating in the international arena.

- Vigorous rivalry within a country breeds strong firms with a track record in cost cutting and innovation that stands them in good stead when competing abroad. Closed economies with cosseted and protected domestic firms are less likely to create global champions. In Finland, Nokia's success is put down in part to the fact that unlike almost every other country it has never had a national telephone company sheltering behind a monopolistic shield. Nokia entered a market dominated by white-hot competition between 50 rival local companies that put pressure on it to perform from the outset.

- Local management ideologies can profoundly affect performance in the international arena. Porter cites the United States' over-reliance on financially oriented management focused primarily on quarterly earnings reports. This short-term financial emphasis left US firms weak on design and strategies to improve manufacturing processes and so eventually to the opening of their motor market to rivals from Japan and Germany who have carved a swathe through the sector.

Demand conditions

Sophisticated, plentiful and demanding local customers play an important part in keeping businesses focused on continuous development and improvements. Companies tend to be more attentive to their home markets as customers there can quickly make their views known. Porter cited the Japanese consumers' considerable knowledge about cameras and photography and their consequent relentless demand for ever-higher performance that gave the indigenous industry a distinct edge.

Factor endowments

Porter doesn't go much further than the Heckscher–Ohlin model of the importance of factors that a country can be endowed with giving them an edge over those less well-endowed. Porter does emphasize the importance of advanced acquired factors. Citing Japan again, Porter claims that though lacking either mineral resources or arable land, Japan has by dint of producing more engineers per head than almost any other country rival built an enormous manufacturing skills endowment. Also, factors such as telephone and Internet connections per head of population, road density in terms of kilometers per million people and electricity provision measured in kilowatts per head of consumption and per cent of population with provision, can help provide a country with a competitive advantage. For several decades the lack of sufficient electricity 'endowment' was the dominant limiting factor for many Indian companies in achieving success in international markets as they just could not achieve reliable levels of output.

Related and supporting industries

The final strand in Porter's diamond is the presence of suppliers and industries related to those champion sectors, which are also internationally competitive. Pasta, leather and furniture industries in Italy, clothing in China, watches in Switzerland, tyres in Ohio and emerging strengths for industries such as video gaming clustering in the Lyon region (40 per cent of all French companies in the industry and 70 per cent of all employment in the sector). The financial services industry has also emerged as one that can gain world prominence through the presence of related and supporting firms of international stature. The UK has factor endowment, a convenient time zone straddling the East and West, world language (English), well-trained workforce and a dedicated work zone, the City and Docklands. Scotland and Iceland are also countries that played in financial services on the international stage, but were in many ways too dependent on one successful global industry.

New Trade Theory

Paul Krugman, an economics Nobel Prize winner, pioneered an extension of Ricardo's work on comparative advantage generally known as New Trade Theory. Recognizing that economies of scale accrue mostly to big businesses he saw two important factors for firms to keep in mind when developing their international thinking.

1 Firms can use economies of scale to allow them to spread the benefit of low costs across more products while still lowering average costs. This widens consumer choice as the firm can extend the range of products on offer in international markets.

2 If the global market can only support a small number of firms certain product categories may come to be dominated by those that get to market first.

New Trade Theory has been used by governments as the logic for supporting infant industries that might meet this later criteria; for example Denmark, with a high dependency on imported energy, targeted wind power as an industry to support. By 2000 the country's wind turbine firms had captured 60 per cent of a world market estimated at $3 billion a year.

Product Life Cycle Model of International Trade

Raymond Vernon, an American academic, advanced his theory on the subject in an article entitled 'International investment and international trade in the product life cycle', published in the May 1966 edition of the *Quarterly Journal of Economics*. Borrowing from the marketing concept of the product life cycle (see Chapter 4) Vernon suggested that the internationalization process for new innovations followed a broadly predictable path (see Figure 1.2). He drew on the United States for his inspiration as up until that time most of the world's new products had been developed there. However, the principles

FIGURE 1.2   Product life cycle model of international trade

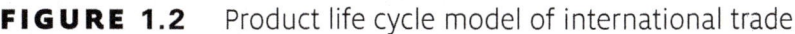
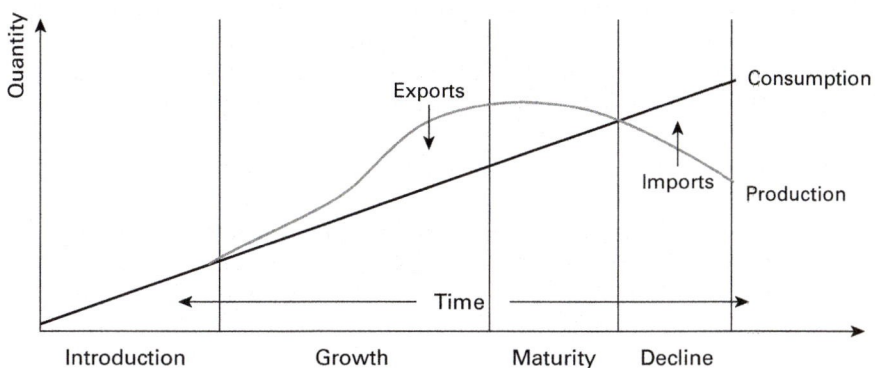

hold good for other countries where innovation is strong. China, which produces 80,000 people a year with higher degrees in computer science or engineering and India, with 70,000, are prime candidates as sources of new innovative industries. So much so that Microsoft's largest R&D centre outside of the United States is in Beijing and Cisco's second global headquarters is in Bangalore.

Vernon argued that most new products are made close to home and consumed largely in that market. The risks associated with anything new made this strategy prudent and in any event looking for low-cost overseas manufacturing was unnecessary as initial demand was unlikely to be based on price factors. Initially during the introduction phase demand would be largely confined to the home market, but later as costs came down growth could be expected from exporting to meet demand in other advanced economies. At first such growth would not warrant those countries establishing their own production but as the product reaches maturity that situation could change. In the final stage in the life cycle – the decline – production in the country in which the innovative new product was created will decrease as cheaper and equally reliable overseas sources come on stream. Though demand will continue to grow, supply will now be met in part by imports. So, according to Vernon, the path from innovator through to exporter and ultimately importer can be traced and to a lesser extent predicted.

The economic, social and enterprise effects of international business

International business and by extension world trade have direct and indirect effects on people and their countries almost everywhere. Not everyone agrees that the effects are universally beneficial, either for corporate enterprises or for the citizens of the countries that host them. There are two broad schools of thought and they are at their most visible during the many protests at the WTO meetings, at IMF, World Bank, G8, G20 and other summits where the conspicuously rich gather to pontificate. The first cluster under the heading known, misleadingly as it turns out, as the Washington Consensus (see below), whose view is broadly that wealth cascades down and free(r) trade between countries is the only way for the poor to get richer. The alternative view is less distinct but shares the view that world trade, as practised by the rich countries, keeps the poor countries in servitude, remaining dependent and pursuing policies that are harmful to the environment. You can see a summary of the thousands of protests against world trade at the Global Issues website (**http://www.globalissues.org/article/45/ public-protests-around-the-world**).

Even the rich nations don't agree that the effects of world trade are universally beneficial to the rich nations themselves, as the Samuelson Critique explains (see below).

Economic and social effects

The following are the key effects claimed for international business on world economies.

Peace

Examples of trade wars that became fighting wars have been a continuing thread through history. The Second World War was in part triggered by the trade wars of the 1930s when countries tried to limit the effects of the great depression, making things worse in the process. Developments after that war, particularly the formation of the EU in Europe and the General Agreement on Tariffs and Trades (GATT) have kept the developed world at least relatively peaceful. Peace since 1945 has not been universal. A glance at this website (**http://wars.findthedata.com**) shows just how prevalent and nasty wars have been since 1945. There is a neat, if macabre, facility on the site to filter the wars by duration and death toll. Plenty of the countries with ongoing wars are active members of the World Trade Organization. Mexico's drug war has claimed 107,000 lives to date and the war in North West Pakistan nearly 80,000. Wars involving major world economic powers have all but vanished.

Freer trade cuts the overall cost of living

According to figures produced by the WTO on protecting agriculture, free trade caused the cost of food to go up – by an estimated $1,500 per year for a family of four in the European Union; by the equivalent of a 51 per cent tax on food in Japan; by $3 billion per year added to US consumers' grocery bills, supporting sugar alone in one year. Removing duties and tariffs has cut the cost of clothing for UK consumers by £500 million a year, while Canadians save around C$780 million and Australians A$300 annually per average family.

Although the big numbers are mostly achieved by the developed countries, overall savings accrue to rich and poor alike. For example, according to the WTO, liberalization in telephone services made phone calls cheaper in the 1990s by 2 per cent per year in advanced economies and by a significantly higher 4 per cent per year in developing countries. The net result was that in the decade to 2000 the cost of making a mobile phone call in China fell by 30 per cent, while in Ghana the drop was 50 per cent.

Deloitte, in a report 'Sub-Saharan Africa (SSA) Mobile Observatory 2012', noted that the number of connections in SSA has grown by 44 per cent since 2000, four times the rate for developed regions, whilst the proportion using mobiles and tablets for web browsing is over five times higher.

Greater consumer choice

Trade in international goods and services widens business and consumer choice exponentially. It's not just end-products that are affected; every element in the process is open to international trade. Motor vehicles, computers, phones, switches and even a McDonald's hamburger (of which 30 per cent of the costs comprise paper and food), can have an imported element. The reverse, of course, is also true when markets are open, providing opportunities for importers to export, too.

This greater choice is not just about making sports shoes or perfume available in new markets. Often bringing new products and services into markets can have dramatic and often unforeseen beneficial economic consequences. For example, the mobile phone has opened up vast swathes of India and China to rapid communication. In Africa the mobile phone has become an essential part of a micro-credit financial system allowing farmers and those in other businesses to transfer small amounts (by Western standards) economically and quickly.

Another facet of choice is that international trade gives consumers the option to buy products out of season. A third of Kenya's flower crop is exported to the UK alone. Some 12 per cent of California's $2 billion all-year strawberry crop is exported, with Canada, Mexico, the United Kingdom, Hong Kong and Japan being the largest importers.

Stimulates growth, creates wealth and spreads democracy

It's an economic fact of life that money passing through an economy has a far greater ripple effect than the initial sum involved, making such activity more important than the sums alone might suggest. Known as the multiplier effect the crude maths state that people will spend most of the money they get. The impact of consumer expenditure on the economy depends on their marginal propensity to consume (MPC) – in other words, how much of their salary they will save and how much they will spend. If we suppose that they will save 10 per cent of salary (the approximate 20-year average), then they will spend 90 per cent. That gives an MPC of 0.9, which is 90 per cent expressed as a decimal:

$$\text{The spending multiplier} = 1 = 10(1 - 0.9)$$

So the effect of £100 million of government spending on the wider economy is 10 × £100 million, or £1,000 million, because each 90 per cent of a worker's income is spent, which in turn becomes someone else's income of which they spend 90 per cent, and so on.

So much for economic theory: the WTO's own estimates for the impact of the 1994 Uruguay Round, a global series of trade negotiations designed to liberalize international trade, were between $109 billion and $510 billion added to world income (depending on the assumptions of the calculations and allowing for margins of error). Using the multiplier effect that figure itself would be increased substantially.

The ranking of liberal and illiberal countries in terms of trading regulation speaks volumes. The world's poorest and most restrictive countries are the least friendly to trade and vice versa. Doing Business (**www.doingbusiness.org/rankings**), a World Bank website, ranks countries on their ease of doing business: the latest data benchmarked to June 2014. The usual suspects, Eritrea, Chad, Myanmar and Bangladesh languish at the bottom with Singapore, New Zealand and Hong Kong as shining beacons at the top. Research by the WTO also shows that those involved in exporting are likely to be better paid. They cite the case of Mexico where in sectors that export 60 per cent or more of their production, wages are 39 per cent higher than in the rest of the economy.

World trade certainly spreads wealth. The growth in economic activity in over 50 so-called developing counties is greater than the average for all countries. Whilst the pace of growth has slowed in the mature parts of the developed world, Europe and the United States, it is accelerating in the developing counties as a result of their international presence. A glance at the new corporate enterprises demonstrates this point. In April 2015 China's oil producer PetroChina was valued at $352.8 billion during trading in Shanghai, surpassing ExxonMobil as the world's most valuable energy company for the first time since 2010. The Banker's Top 1000 put Chinese ICBC in the top spot for the first time in 2014's ranking, joined by China Construction Bank at number two. The capital of Chinese banks overtook that of the United States for the first time ever, at $1190 billion, to make it the largest single banking sector in the world. (**www.thebankerdatabase.com/files/pdf_downloads/Top1000WorldBanks2014.pdf**).

But what is also true is that international trade spreads democracy; that in turn should help the new-found wealth in developing countries become more evenly distributed. Freedom House (**www.freedomhouse.org**), an organization that studies the spread of democracy, listed 44 countries as free in its first report in 1973. Freedom in the World 2015, the latest edition of its annual report on political rights and civil liberties in 195 countries around the globe, rated 89 (46 per cent) as Free, 55 (28 per cent) Partly Free, and 51 (26 per cent) Not Free. This more than doubling of the countries rated as free coincides well with the growth and spread of international trade.

Enhances domestic competitiveness

By virtue of having to defend their native market against the best international companies, local companies and industries become better themselves. The US motor industry is a prime example. Battered by competition from Japanese companies whose vehicles turned out to be more appealing and economic than local products, local market share was dropping fast, even before the credit crunch hit in 2008. In the pickup truck market, a bedrock sector that embodies the American dream of independence and mobility, Ford, with its winning F-150, had the Nissan Titan and Toyota Tundra hot on its tail. Yet by the spring of 2010, albeit with some government help, sales of US models stood at an annualized rate of 11.2 million, up by 10 per cent on the preceding quarter. Ford's latest version of Focus had been designed and engineered as a world product from the outset.

The Samuelson critique

Paul A Samuelson, the Nobel Prize-winning economist and professor emeritus at the Massachusetts Institute of Technology, published an article in September 2004 in *The Journal of Economic Perspectives*, a quarterly put out by the American Economic Association, examining situations where the gains from international free trade no longer outweigh the losses. He cites examples in relation to where call centres had been outsourced to India and the increasing trend due to advances in global communications through use of the Internet to move offshore other service jobs – medical diagnosis, accounting and software development, for example – that were not traditionally internationally mobile. In such cases Samuelson concludes that wages for indigenous workers in the United States will be driven down to the point where gains from international trade are lost. 'Being able to purchase groceries 20 per cent cheaper at Wal-Mart (due to international trade benefits) does not necessarily make up for trade losses.'

The Washington Consensus

This phrase is attributed to John Williamson, an economist from the Peterson Institute for International Economics, an international economic think-tank based in Washington DC. He coined the phrase in 1990 to refer to the lowest common denominator of policy advice being addressed by the Washington-based institutions to Latin American countries as of 1989. The policies advocated contained three big ideas; macroeconomic discipline, a market economy, and openness to the world – all captured in these ten recommendations:

1 Fiscal discipline. This was aimed particularly where countries had run large deficits that led to balance of payments crises and high inflation that hit mainly the poor because the rich could park their money abroad.

2 A redirection of public expenditure priorities away from indiscriminate subsidies toward fields offering both high economic returns and the potential to improve income distribution, such as primary health care, primary education, and infrastructure.

3 Tax reform (to lower marginal rates and broaden the tax base).

4 Interest rate liberalization including instituting a package of measures to remove all undesirable state-imposed constraints on the free working of the financial markets, such as the removal of interest rate ceilings, and loosening of deposit and credit controls.

5 A competitive exchange rate free from artificial state support for the local currency.

6 Trade liberalization provides potential benefits from reforms that can improve trade. For example, Korea has continually reformed its trade logistics environment over the past decade and as a consequence it is a key player in global supply chains, exporting automobiles, mobile

phones and semiconductors around the world. Benefits are not limited to just higher exports. According to a study by the World Bank, Uganda's reforms to improve customs administration and reduce corruption helped increase customs revenue by 24 per cent between 2007 and 2008.

7 Liberalization of inflows of foreign direct investment.

8 Privatization.

9 Deregulation: to abolish barriers to entry and exit and so allow investors to enter and leave markets with minimum constraints.

10 Secure property rights giving title to assets at an acceptable cost quickly.

Enterprise effects

Businesses enjoy some of the benefits of international trade that accrue at the macro level to a country as a whole. Big supermarket chains benefit from being able to sell fresh fruit and flowers to their customers all year round, for example, rather than just when the local climate dictates. Ford (see earlier in this chapter) was able to learn from Toyota and others that important segments of their domestic US market shared the same requirements – economy in particular – as did those in other markets. There are a number of particular benefits and risks a business can expect to encounter in growing on the international arena.

Economies of scale

Selling overseas can lead to higher unit sales. This can in turn result in lower costs brought about in part by the benefits a business gets from repeatedly carrying out the same tasks and as a consequence getting better – the experience curve effect (see Chapter 3). Also, selling more involves buying more, which in turn opens up the possibility of securing lower material costs for all materials involved in both home and overseas sales. Once a business is past break-even, that is the point at which cash generated exceeds costs incurred (see Chapter 12), any extra sales can lead to significant additional levels of profit.

Provide strategic opportunities

Companies, in part as a result of the lower costs achieved when sales are increased, see exporting as an opportunity to sell at lower prices in those markets and so gain market share quickly. Increasing market share leads to a range of advantages that in turn can lead to greater profitability (see Chapter 3). This strategy may not be open to them in their home market as reducing prices may harm an established brand: customers often associate lower prices with lower value. Also there is the real possibility that their competitors will just lower prices too, leading to a price war and lower profits all round.

Following major customers into markets is both an opportunistic and defensive strategy. Following them provides a lower-risk way into a new market, while not doing so opens the way for competitors to do so. Once established as suppliers those competitors could use that relationship to encroach on your home market.

Dampen the effects of cycles and seasons

Economies grow and contract at different paces at different times. For example, while the United States and most of the major European economies were static or contracting between 2008 and 2010, the economies of Australia, China, India and many South American countries were growing, in some cases by near double-digit percentages. That disparity continued through to 2015. China and India, for example, were still growing at around 8 per cent, whilst the United States grew at little more than 3 per cent and Europe as a whole barely managed to hold its ground.

CASE STUDY Unilever

In April 2010 Unilever surprised stock markets by reporting stronger than expected sales, turnover and profits. While analysts were expecting like-for-like sales to grow by 3.2 per cent, they actually achieved 4.2 per cent. Pre-tax profits rose 28 per cent to €1.39 bn (£1.2 bn and $1.84 bn) while total sales rose by 6.7 per cent. What the analysts had failed to recognize was the effect of Unilever's penetration in the emerging markets of Africa, Asia and Central and Eastern Europe. These markets had generally fared better during the economic downturn, so allowing the company to grow sales by 11.2 per cent, while in Western Europe sales actually declined by 0.2 per cent.

Unilever's emerging markets division is their largest operating division and on the back of increased advertising spend to support products such as Domestos bleach, Knorr stock cubes, Marmite, and Lipton tea, they are confident this success will be repeated.

A similar effect arises from seasonal factors, particularly those of climate. So while much of Europe is freezing other countries on other continents are basking in sunshine. Some countries, the United States and China being good examples, have several quite different climate zones operating at the same time. These seasonal differences provide an opportunity to sell a product all year round. In short there will always be somewhere to sell products for the barbeque!

Economic imperatives

Lower costs have forced almost every major apparel manufacturer, clothing and footwear in particular, to relocate or outsource production to lower-cost areas such as China, Sri Lanka, India and Bangladesh. GAP has dozens of factories in India, Nike manufactures in Vietnam and Lacoste in Malaysia. Hundreds of US businesses operate in Mexico, literally on the US border, making products almost exclusively for sale in the United States. Chrysler de México, for example, with a parent company investment of some $2 billion is the company's most important production hub in the North American region. Low-wage Mexican labour is the incentive in such cases, but there are other economic incentives such as lower taxes (UK bankers defecting to Switzerland) or investment incentives (the UK government's £420 million sweetener to Nissan in March 2010 to induce them to make their Leaf electric car in Sunderland in the north of England).

Risks

Along with the above possible benefits of doing business internationally come some certain, probable and possible risks that the firm should take steps to prepare against. In most cases doing business abroad will involve trading in foreign currencies. The American dollar, British pound, Euro, Japanese Yen and Chinese Renminbi have all moved against each other by double digit percentages in the past five years. By a large enough margin in many cases to all but wipe out any prospect of trading profitably. There are ways to limit risk, if not completely eliminate it.

Other risks include political risks where friendly governments fall or become less friendly and change the rules arbitrarily. BP's Russian joint venture TNK–BP gave up after a 10-year battle to develop one of the world's largest gas fields in March 2010. The Kremlin had already taken back ownership of Russia's oil and gas assets, nominally owned by Royal Dutch Shell in its Sakhalin-2 project, so BP could hardly say the writing wasn't on the wall.

The culture and way of doing business also varies from country to country. Although the OECD (Organisation for Economic Co-operation and Development) signed the Anti-Bribery Convention in 1999, topping it up with a Good Practice Guidance to companies in 2009, the problem is still rife. Transparency International's Global Corruption Report 2009 states that 'nearly two in five polled business executives have been asked to pay a bribe when dealing with public institutions. Half estimated that corruption raised project costs by at least 10 per cent. One in five claimed to have lost business because of bribes by a competitor. More than a third felt that corruption is getting worse.'

The difference in the way that business is regulated in different countries varies enormously as does the level of protection awarded by the courts over their assets, both physical and intellectual. Registering business property, for example, requires 14 procedures in Brazil and just one in Norway. The process itself takes two days in New Zealand and 391 in Croatia. The risks are clearly greater the longer and more bureaucratic the procedures are. These and other risks are covered in the relevant chapters that follow.

Online video courses and lectures

Arguments For and Against Free Trade: Professor Kenneth Train, UCBerkeley: **www.youtube.com/watch?v=1lEeb0kBBG8**

Britain's global trade in the Great Days of Sail: Dr John McAleer, Gresham College: **www.youtube.com/watch?v=aNjlcplyVHU**

How Beneficial Is World Trade? Journeyman Pictures: **www.youtube.com/watch?v=xRJZWfqWcs0**

International Relations: An Introduction by Professor William A Callahan, Dr Toby Dodge, Dr Jens Meierhenrich, Professor Iver Neumann, Professor Karen Smith, Dr Stephen Woolcock of LSE: **www.lse.ac.uk/internationalRelations/video/IR-INTRO-video.aspx**

The Heckscher-Ohlin Theorem: Mercatus Center, George Mason University: **www.youtube.com/watch?v=6aCXnbbEMOs**

The International Effects of Growth: Professor Kenneth Train, UCBerkeley: **www.youtube.com/watch?v=24bSk7bFeKI**

The Ricardian Model: Professor Kenneth Train, UCBerkeley: **www.youtube.com/watch?v=pen8EDS5M1M**

Six Valuable Lessons about International Trade: Professor Kenneth Train, UCBerkeley: **www.youtube.com/watch?v=3aimvEc1q98**

Trade and Comparative Advantage: Professor Kenneth Train, UCBerkeley: **www.youtube.com/watch?v=z9YprxAWEuQ**

Online video case studies

Alibaba's Jack Ma: Moving Toward a New Business Paradigm at Columbia Business School: **www.gsb.columbia.edu/video/v/node/4022/video**

East India Company: Audiopedia: **www.youtube.com/watch?v=v1s9T3v9eFY**

How Big Is McDonald's International Reach? Bloomberg: **www.bloomberg.com/news/videos/b/86c7b3f9-d20c-42d6-b75c-acf6ef3d6652**

Tata Motors: Ravi Kant, Vice Chair talks at London Business School: **www.youtube.com/watch?v=A11dxdKz4u8**

Unilever: Path to growth strategy focused on global high-potential brands: **www.unilever.com/aboutus/ourhistory/**

The international business environment

2

- Environment analysis framework.
- Checking out on politics.
- Understanding economic issues.
- Appreciating social dynamics.
- Advancing technology.
- Legal matters.

There is a framework much used by MBAs that, in conjunction with Porter's approach to strategic analysis (see Chapter 3), is used to get a handle on the international business environment. PEST analysis, as this tool is known, categorizes the international external factors that influence business thinking under the headings of political, economic, social and technological forces. Often, two additional factors, environmental and legal, are added, changing the acronym to PESTEL analysis.

This is basically a checklist to ensure that all major factors that could impact on an international business are taken into consideration (see Table 2.1). For example, a real estate business would take into consideration economic factors such as likely local interest rates, as with Greece in 2015 when despite membership of the eurozone its long-term rates soared to 30 times that of Germany and France (**www.ecb.europa.eu/stats/money/long/html/index.en.html**). The availability of funds, changes in capital gains and inheritance taxes brought about by, say, a new government, and potential

TABLE 2.1 PESTEL analysis framework

Factor	Event	Impact	Timing	Proposed response
Political				
Economic				
Social				
Technological				
Environmental				
Legal				

additional streams of income such as with the advent of Home Information Packs in the UK would all be factors to consider. For example, changes in intellectual property rights as in China when its 3rd amendment to the patent law came into effect on 1 October 2009, could also significantly influence a business's view of where to trade. Companies in the home improvements market might recognize opportunities when they see the vigour with which energy audits and compulsory water meters for all homes loom onto the horizon.

CASE STUDY Google fits in

Google China, founded in 2005, was headed by former Microsoft executive, Kai-Fu Lee, until 4 September 2009. His appointment was just the first of a number of serious controversies that beset Google, with Microsoft initially suing both parties for breach of contract only to reach a confidential settlement within months. The Chinese government operated, and still does, a level of censorship on all communication media that is alien to Western culture. To enter the Chinese market Google had to operate a form of self-imposed censorship known as the 'Golden Shield Project'. The effect of this was that whenever people in China searched for keywords on a list of blocked words maintained by the government, google.cn displayed the following at the bottom of the page (translated): In accordance with local laws, regulations and policies, part of the search result is not shown.

Though this form of restriction appeared contrary to Google's culture its management argued that it could be more useful to the cause of free speech by participating in China's IT industry even under such terms than being excluded. In a company statement Google declared: 'While removing search results is inconsistent with Google's mission, providing no information (or a heavily degraded user experience that amounts to no information) is more inconsistent with our mission.' In short Google chose what it saw as the lesser of two evils. Nevertheless, in deciding to launch the censored service Google was attacked on all fronts by free-speech campaigners and accused of 'sickening collaboration' in a Congressional hearing.

By the start of 2010 Google had only a third of the search-engine market in China, a market dominated by local giant Baidu, and though its sales revenues continued to rise it was finding business hard going. On 12 January 2010 Google and more than a score of other US companies recognized that they had been under cyber attack from an organization or organizations based in mainland China. During an investigation into these attacks evidence came to light to demonstrate that the Gmail accounts of key human-rights activists connected with China were being routinely accessed by third parties. Also, attempts over the preceding year were made in China to further limit free speech on the web including the persistent blocking of Facebook, Twitter, YouTube, Google Docs and Blogger.

On 12 January 2010 Google declared it was no longer willing to censor content on its Chinese site after discovering that hackers had obtained proprietary information and e-mail data of some human-rights activists. On 22 March Google decided to stop censoring Chinese Internet searches and shifted its search operations from the mainland to an unfiltered Hong Kong site, in effect reversing its original decision to comply with local conditions. Although this act was criticized as 'totally wrong' by China, to date Google's wider business operations, including its R&D work in China and its sales presence, have been unaffected and allowed to continue.

Political systems

The way a country is governed, shaping both its laws and economic behaviour, is through a political system. Those systems vary between totalitarian regimes – such as communism, which lays greater emphasis on collectivism where society as a whole is at least in theory the most important factor; these are ruled usually by an individual or small opaquely appointed clique – and at the other end of the scale, democracies, where the individual plays the dominant role, usually exercised by some form of election process.

Totalitarian regimes can be capricious and prone to rapid changes of direction that can have a profound effect on the international business enterprise; see BP's experiences in Russia, discussed in the previous chapter. Another example occurred in 2006 when Bolivian President Evo Morales ordered the seizure of the assets of 56 foreign-owned oil and natural-gas production facilities at gunpoint, demanding that these companies renegotiate their operating contracts under threat of forcible eviction from the country. Overall, privately owned corporate assets were appropriated by foreign governments in developing countries more than 100 times over the past two decades. In addition large swathes of industry in totalitarian economies are in state ownership and operate as monopolies.

Democracies are generally more business-friendly in that the rule of law and courts functions effectively, private property rights are universally respected and corrupt practices are relatively rare.

The generally recognized minimum criterion for a functioning democracy is that the principal positions of power are filled through regular free and fair elections. Over 100 countries, many of them in relatively poor, developing nations meet that basic standard. In many of those countries the democratic process is wafer thin at best. While millions risked their lives in Iraq in 2005 to take part in their first free elections for half a century and the population of Zimbabwe have been voting in governments since 1979 with the end of colonial rule, a fully democratic system is clearly not established in either country.

Electoralisms

Electoralism is a term credited to Professor Terry L Karl, Professor of Stanford University, to describe a 'half-way' transition from authoritarian rule toward democratic rule. The regime in question conducts seemingly free and fair elections, often on a monotonously regular basis, as for example in the Philippines where they even have mid-term elections to endorse or repeal their earlier choice of government. But in many countries these elections are accompanied by massive fraud with the process slanted in favour of the incumbent political party. The courts and local media also usually support the government of the day and in many cases, Zimbabwe being a prime example, opposition policies are at best ignored and at worst cast in a negative light. Violence is on the agenda, too. In the Philippines, Comelec, the national election commission, operates a tough gun ban. Candidates can apply to Comelec for up to two armed bodyguards drawn from the police or armed forces. Nevertheless, their past three elections have each seen around 120 candidates, supporters and Comelec officials killed as well as around 250 violent incidents. The police have 68 armed groups on a watch list.

Economic systems

There are clear parallels between the way in which political and economic systems operate. In totalitarian countries where freedom is restricted or non-existent, markets are not allowed much freedom either. In fully democratic countries businesses are allowed to stand or fall on their own merits.

Command economies

Also known as planned economies, this situation describes one where the state regulates the main factors of production – what and how much will be produced; how much labour will be allocated to the provision of various goods and services and what their wage rates will be; what land and other resources will be deployed and for what purpose; and where and how much finance will be extended to such activities.

China and Russia are the best-known examples of centrally planned economies, though both could more accurately be described as mixed economies today. North Korea and Cuba are the two most prominent examples of command economies operating now and these serve as good examples of why the system fell out of favour. Although, theoretically, centrally planned economies should be able to move resources quickly to where they are needed, provide full employment and run a stable economy free of the pain of economic cycles, in practice they don't. In the first place the information flow to allow good decision making was not available in the heyday of this philosophy. Even if data and its processing were up to the job, the job itself was largely subjective. The output of 1 million unmotivated workers is unlikely to match that of a better managed operation. The over-emphasis on quotas ensured that quality was sacrificed routinely so that targets could be achieved. In the command economy corruption was rife, a small number of party officials became very rich, the vast mass of the population lived at or close to poverty and the middle educated class was a relatively unimportant element in the economic equation.

Market economies

The whole of the subject of economics as practised in advanced economies is predicated on the belief that market forces are allowed a large degree of freedom. New firms can set up in business, charging the price they see fit and if their strategy is flawed they will be allowed to fail. Price is allowed to send the important signals throughout the economy apportioning demand and resources accordingly. But perfect competition where price is allowed such freedom is only one of four prevailing market structures; although market economies are dominated by near-perfect competition that is not maintained without a struggle.

The price mechanism

The main concept that underpins market economies is that of the price elasticity of demand. The concept itself is simple enough. The higher the price of a good or service the less of it you are likely to sell. Obviously it's not quite that simple in practice; there's also the number of buyers, their expectations, preference and ability to pay, the availability of substitute products.

Market structures

These are the main economic structures that are at work in market economies, as listed below.

Monopoly

Monopolies exist where a single supplier dominates the market and so renders normal competitive forces largely redundant. Price, quality and innovation are compromised so delivering less value to the end-consumer than they might otherwise expect. Microsoft has a near monopolistic grip on the operating system market, as had Pfizer, the pharmaceutical giant, through its patent on the drug Viagra, and British Airports Authority (BAA), who run Heathrow, Gatwick and Stanstead have a similar hold on London's airport traffic.

Monopolies claim that without being allowed to dominate their market it would be impossible to get sufficient economies of scale to re-invest. That was the argument of the early railway companies and it was BAA's argument in 2008 in defending itself against the prospects of a government-enforced break-up.

In countries where monopolies are seen as being detrimental, bodies exist to regulate the market to prevent them becoming too powerful. The UK has the Competition and Market Authority (**www.gov.uk/government/ organisations/competition-and-markets-authority**), the United States the Federal Trade Commission (**www.ftc.gov**), and the European Union The European Commission (**http://ec.europa.eu/comm/competition/index_en.html**), all keeping monopolies in check. A duopoly is, as the name would suggest, a particular form of monopoly with only two firms in the market.

Oligopoly

This is where between 3 and 20 large firms dominate a market, or where four or five firms share more than 40 per cent of the market. The danger for consumers and suppliers alike is that these dominant firms can control the market to their disadvantage. Supermarket chains in the UK, airlines, oil exploration and refining businesses the world over operate as virtual oligopolies. Frequently, the temptation to act in a cartel to fix prices is too great to resist.

According to the Office of Fair Trading (OFT), between August 2004 and January 2006 British Airways and Virgin Atlantic, the dominant players on the route from London to US cities, colluded with each other to fix the price of fuel surcharges. During that time, surcharges rose from £5 to £60 per ticket. British Airways had to set aside £350 million to deal with fines in the UK and United States.

Perfect competition

This is a utopian environment in which there are many suppliers of identical products or services, with equal access to all the necessary resources such as money, materials, technology and people. There are no barriers to entry so business can enter or leave the market at will and consumers have perfect information on every aspect of the alternative goods on offer.

Competitive markets

Sometimes referred to confusingly as monopolistic competition this rests between oligopoly and, but closer to, perfect competition. Here a large number of relatively small competitors, each with small market shares compete with differentiated products satisfying diverse consumer wants and needs.

Mixed economies

Mixed economies are what it says on the box. Parts of the economy are kept firmly in state control – often such strategic elements as health, education, energy, communications, transport and the media – while other areas are left to private enterprise. In practice pure market or command economies don't exist, although some countries such as the United States (market) and North Korea (command) are clearly close to ends of the spectrum.

Even some advanced economies were late converts to market economies and were well and truly mixed. The French Government owed 25.9 per cent of Renault, the car maker, until 2003. When the going gets tough even countries with reasonably well-developed market economies can swing back to command status. The British Government nationalized Northern Rock, the troubled bank, in February 2008 and took major stakes in RBS (Royal Bank of Scotland) and Lloyds Bank shortly after, to stabilize the financial system during a major global credit crunch.

Privatization

Privatization is the process used to transfer ownership from the state to shareholders of businesses established to run them. The arguments for privatization include: the reduction in national debt, as the government sells off assets; that such enterprises will be run more efficiently when freed from bureaucracy; and that any new capital required will come from private shareholders rather than the state. In Europe many governments owned large swathes of the business world until the 1980s. The process became visible when the German government privatized Volkswagen in 1960. Chile started privatizing in 1974 and under Ronald Reagan and Margaret Thatcher the process gained momentum on both sides of the Atlantic Ocean.

But even in privatized enterprise the state keeps a measure of control. Regulators have replaced the pricing mechanism in setting acceptable levels of price, price increases and hence profitability, in many sectors.

Economic tools to restrain international competition

Even the most open market economies are not free of mechanisms to protect local firms and limit the scope and depth of international competition. These restraints are used by countries to protect jobs and industries either generally or during times of particular difficulty. The WTO (World Trade Organization) and GATT (General Agreement on Trade Tariffs) work hard to eliminate or at least limit the damage to international trade caused by such restraints.

Tariffs

Tariffs are a tax applied on certain imports either ad hoc or for longer periods with the primary aim of raising the price of the products concerned and so protecting domestic enterprises. It also raises revenue for the governments concerned. Consumers invariably lose out as competition is stifled and prices rise. Governments gain as they get extra income and the kudos associated with protecting local jobs.

The arguments advanced for introducing tariffs range from protecting infant or strategically important industries, to plain old tit-for-tat retaliation. Recently, China threatened the EU with a tariff on carbon steel fasteners, in retaliation to an EU import tax on shoes. At about the same time the Chinese government criticized the 'Buy American' aspects of the US stimulus package introduced in 2009 and the 35 per cent import tariff applied to Chinese tyres in September of that year. By December they had responded with duties on speciality steel products from the United States.

Tariffs can be based on value – *ad valorem* – or specific and levied as a fixed charge for each unit, weight or volume. An example of a combined tariff where an *ad valorem* and specific duty rate can also be applied would be breakfast cereals imported into the United States in smaller packages and subject to an *ad valorem* rate of 8.5 per cent and a specific duty rate of 12.6 cents per kilogram.

Research shows that tariffs distort trade and only rarely do any long-term good to the country imposing them. However, particularly with tit-for-tat tariffs the primary goal is political muscle flexing rather than seeking economic advantage.

Licences

Certain products can only be imported when a licence is granted to a business by the government concerned. Food, weapons and medicines frequently fall into the category of goods requiring an import licence as do weapons or military hardware. Dual-use goods such as machine tools, computers and marine equipment designed for civil use but which could have a military application, also are likely to require a licence.

Licences are usually intended to protect consumers, as with foods and medicines where labelling and source of origin are vital pieces of information, or to protect the state as with weaponry. Licensing restricts competition, so increasing prices.

Import quotas

This is a form of licensing where only a certain amount of a particular product can be brought into a country in any one period at a lower duty rate. Products ranging from animal feeds to watch movements can attract import quotas. When an importer puts in a request one of three responses from the relevant authority is possible:

- allowed in full with the whole consignment benefiting from a lower rate of duty;
- partially allowed and only a set amount of the consignment will benefit from a lower duty rate;
- refused, so duty at the higher rate will be applied to the full consignment.

Voluntary Export Restraint (VER)

VER occurs when a country agrees, usually after some arm twisting, to scale back its exports to one or more countries. The most quoted example of VERs is when Japan agreed to limit its auto exports into the United States, the UK and other major European economies. The mid-1970s saw the global car industry come under serious pressure from the weight of Japanese exports combined with a sharp contraction in demand for cars following the 1973 oil crisis. Japan had introduced innovative production methods that made their vehicles better and cheaper than those made anywhere else (see Toyota case study in Chapter 4). Discussions with the Japanese government led to an agreement to limit new car exports to a range between 9 and 11 per cent of total registrations for up to five years. Some countries, France in particular who set the limit at 3 per cent, secured a better deal.

Japanese car companies eventually got round this VER by setting up manufacturing plants in the United States and Europe, effectively attacking the market from within.

Subsidies

Governments can offer local firms low- or no-interest loans, cash grants, tax breaks, employment incentives, or take an equity stake. These all have the effect of giving the indigenous enterprises a cost advantage over imports and a parallel advantage in export markets. Agriculture is one of the largest industries affected, with the EU alone paying out over £60 billion ($92 billion/€69 billion) a year in farm subsidies, originally aimed at boosting production, but since 2006 an entitlement for reducing production.

The EU is hardly unique in this respect. Since the late 1930s, the United States has sought to influence the production and sale of agricultural products by such means as direct cash payments for schemes to discourage idle acreage, for diverting output from one commodity to another, subsidy payments to support alternative uses of farm products, buildings and land, and tax waivers.

Energy is the latest field to be the recipient of massive government subsidies, with incentives to shift from harmful fossil fuels to more environmentally friendly and sustainable sources running at over $300 billion a year, according to OECD figures.

Local content requirements

This requirement specifies that a designated fraction of a good be produced domestically. For example, after the First World War several European countries introduced a system of screen content quotas to protect their film industry from the mass of American films flooding the market. They saw this influx as a double danger; a financial threat to their home film industry and a danger to their cultural expression. This local content rule has extended to cover television and radio. In Canada, for example, French-language radio stations are required to ensure that 65 per cent of the vocal music they broadcast each week, and 55 per cent of vocal music broadcast between 6 am and 6 pm Monday to Friday, is in the French language. Seven per cent of music aired on ethnic radio stations each week must be Canadian.

There is not much evidence that local content requirements achieve much beyond reducing competition and pushing up consumer prices, but they remain popular with governments as a means of appearing proactive without actually having to spend money. Canada, for example, has recently established local content standards to protect its infant wind turbine industry from international competition.

Antidumping

When goods are sold at below their 'cost of production' or 'fair market value' they are considered as being 'dumped' onto the foreign market concerned. Neither 'cost' nor 'fair market value' are terms open to precise definition, but nevertheless countries frequently challenge incidents they believe meet the criteria. The goal of the exporter is to move on excess capacity at any price that will recover some, or ideally all, of their committed costs.

Take the case of a company with a product with a material cost of 50 (£/$/€) and a labour cost of 50 (£/$/€) pouring off the production line at the rate of 1,000 per hour. At the end of each eight-hour day 800,000 (£/$/€) of product cost is sitting in the warehouse. Now if the business has no serious prospect of selling those products costing 100 (£/$/€) in their home market, selling them at ANY price will at least save them warehousing costs and contribute to positive cash flow. In addition the products sold in their home market and anywhere else they can get a reasonable price are getting the benefit of economy of scale from the over-production.

Dumpers try to manipulate their figures to show they are merely recovering full cost but those being dumped on are facing unfair competition. That makes it harder for their domestic producers to compete either at home or in their overseas markets.

Technological effects

Technology and its pace of development continue to have a profound effect on international business development. Computers, the Internet, fast air travel and low-cost mass sea transportation have combined to reshape the commercial environment. Sea cables being laid to the Kenyan coast since 2009 have opened up broadband Internet connection to a section of the African continent hitherto in the near dark ages, in terms of connectivity. The first effect has been a flood of new call centres staffed with well-educated, English-speaking staff eager to work and earn salaries that are competitive with those in other developing countries. Kenya has another advantage in that its time zone fits conveniently with Western Europe.

A phenomena observed in 1965 by Gordon Moore, co-founder of Intel, now universally known as Moore's law is that the cost of almost everything in the communications/IT field falls by 50 per cent, while output power doubles roughly every eighteen months. So fasten your seatbelt as change will only get faster.

Internet

MBAs need a good grasp of how the Internet is currently affecting business operations. Everything from books and DVDs, through computers, medicines and financial services on to vehicles and real estate is being sold or having a major part of the selling process transacted online. Not only are products and services being sold online, they are being supported both technically and commercially and to an increasing extent being fulfilled online too. Software, films and books are just three 'tangible' product categories for which more or less every business operation can be and is being delivered via the Internet. Holidays, airline tickets, training and even university degrees are bundled in with the mass of conventional retailers such as Tesco who fight for a share of the ever-growing online market.

The internet's meteoric rise has been recorded on a country-by-country basis by Internet World Stats (**www.internetworldstats.com/stats.htm**) since 1995, when just 16 million people representing 0.4 per cent of the world's population were online. By the last quarter of 2014 that had grown to 3,035,749,340 users, some 42.3 per cent of the planet's population. Whilst the US still leads the field with 87.7 per cent internet penetration, over a quarter of Africans are now connected, a third of Asians and half of those in the Middle East and Latin America and the Caribbean.

CASE STUDY Match.com

From a seedy corner of the Internet on the fringes of pornography, online dating is now a mainstream business with global reach. Those in search of friendship and more have extended their reach from local classified adverts to stretch out to the furthest continents. People from New York and Boston can hook up with those from Saigon and Manila with as little effort as a stroll to their local newsagent. According to the US Census, some 40 million of the 90 million singles in the United States have tried online dating. YouGov statistics show that one in five relationships in the UK now begins online, and meeting via the internet is the third most popular way to find a date behind 'through friends' or making acquaintance at a pub or bar. Today Match.com generates over $400 million a year in revenue and has 1.8 million paying users.

Gary Kremen, Match.com's founder, started out in a very different field of business. In 1989, the year he completed his MBA at Stanford, he co-founded, Los Altos Technologies (**www.lat.com**), a company that cleaned sensitive data off hard drives for the military and other businesses. Sold to an employee in late 1992, the company is still in business. At LAT, Kremen noticed an important demographic change. New systems such as IBM's Lotus Note enabled administrative staff to send electronic purchase orders without resorting to the assistance of IT staff. That in turn meant an increasing number of women were using these tools to go online for the first time. A user himself of what were known as '1-900 number' services – telephone based dating agencies – in exchange he saw a parallel potential in the small but growing presence of women online.

With Electric Classifieds, founded in 1993, Kremen developed the idea to do classified ads but make it electric, as a test for his idea of doing something similar in the dating market. He saw the mouth-watering revenues that print media made from classified advertising. The *Los Angeles Times* made 40 per cent of their overall revenue from classifieds. A quarter of that was from personal ads.

Two years later, the test proving successful, he unveiled Match.com. Backed with €200,000 of venture finance the company was one of the first sites to use the internet to smooth the progress of dating. The company was among the first to charge money for this service, which in turn put a tremendous pressure on delivering value. In 1995 few people were online and even fewer were women looking for men. Kremen started out by designing the site with women in mind. 'You have to design the whole system for women, not men,' he said. 'Who cares what men think? So things like security and anonymity were important. And little things, like talking about body types, not pounds. Never ask a woman her weight.' But still Match.com struggled to get the numbers to sign up. And online dating is very much a numbers game. Kremen got everyone he knew to sign up as well as getting his employees to create profiles. He and his girlfriend signed up, too, with an unforeseen and unwelcome outcome. Kremen's girlfriend met another man through Match and left him. On the upside at least he had proof positive that the site worked.

Codenamed 'Synapse', Match developed an algorithm that, while taking into account a user's stated preferences, such as desired age range, hair colour and body type, it also learns from their actions on the site. So, if a man says he doesn't want to date anyone older than 30, but often looks at profiles of forty-somethings, Match deduces that he is in fact open to meeting older women. Synapse also uses 'triangulation', looking at the behaviour of similar users and factors in that information, too. Match uses its customer knowledge to operate a readily varied pricing strategy. Match.com operates in a highly competitive and fragmented market, with a low barrier for competition to enter the market. Online dating software is inexpensive; website creation is simple and the market huge. Though their largest age group is between 30 and 49 years old, some 15 per cent of members are 50 years and older, an age group likely to grow fast given high divorce rates and the large number of baby boomers. Nevertheless with an estimated 8,000 competitors worldwide and 1,000 new online dating services opening every year, price is a sensitive issue.

Match spends over $70 million a year in television, radio, and fees to online search engines and distribution partners. That draws people to the website, but pricing strategy is used to pull them in. Match.com's tiered pricing menu reflects price discrimination strategy known in the trade as 'goldilocks'. By offering three price options, potential clients are in effect offered a Good-Better-Best choice. People who are unsure what they want will usually buy the middle, or 'Better' choice out of Good-Better-Best, so providing a middle choice is key to having an acceptable enquiry to conversion ratio. Match.com also uses an à la carte pricing strategy. In addition to the monthly subscription fee, subscribers are offered additional routes of communicating with other prospective dates, through video, voice mail, and text messaging. Once members join as a basic subscriber, Match.com increases revenue by offering premium or supplemental services. Seasonal offers are also made, capitalizing, for example, on the post-Christmas slump as the time to find romance. The period between Boxing Day and the turn of the year is the busiest for online dating sites with some websites reporting a treble digit increase in traffic. In that week alone Match.com has over three million e-mail messages sent by hopefully site users.

Kremen and his board had a number of disagreements resulting in the company being sold in 1998 for $7m to Cendant, a Connecticut consumer-services business. A year later, Cendant sold it to IAC, trading as Ticketmaster, for $50m. Kremen got little from the initial sale; barely $50,000 and a lifetime account on the website, which proved of little value as he met and married his wife in a very low-tech way; through a mutual friend. Kremen's fortune came from a different sort of sex. In 2001 he was awarded $65 million in a dispute over the domain name sex.com, which he registered in the '90s. Then, in 2004, after Electric Classifieds went out of business, Kremen bought the company for $20,000 in order to retrieve its valuable patent, selling it on almost immediately for $1.7 million.

Who is investing most in technology?

One useful indicator of where technological pressures are likely to come from is by noting where patents are coming from and whether the pace of filing is rising (Table 2.2). At the 82 offices monitored by the World Intellectual Property Organization (WIPO) 8.66 million patents were in force in 2014, representing 7.9 per cent more than in 2011. China alone accounted for a quarter of this growth and since 2011 has led the world in this respect when it overtook the United States. Japan has conspicuously stalled in terms of patent applications, where between 2000 and 2005 they saw a growth rate of 37.5 per cent.

Middle-income countries, too, are well represented. Mexico filed 15,314 new patents in the period covered in WIPO's report, a rise of 9 per cent, more than double the rate of the European Union, and Turkey filed 13.4 per cent (4,666) more patents; more than triple the EU growth rate.

TABLE 2.2 World patents applications – top ten

Country	Patent Applications	Annual Growth
China	652,777	+24%
United States	542,815	+7.8%
Japan	342,796	+0.1%
Republic of Korea	188,915	+5.6%
European Patent Office	148,560	+4.0%
Germany	61,340	+3.2%
Russian Federation	44,211	+6.8%
India	43,955	+3.9%
Canada	35,242	+6.2%

SOURCE: WIPO IP Facts and Figures 2014

Environmental factors

Two events on opposite sides of the globe provide a vivid illustration of the dimensions of environmental factors on international business. When Eyjafjallajökull, the Icelandic volcano, erupted in April 2010, air traffic around Europe and across the Atlantic ground to a halt for six days. Airlines lost up to half their annual profits, business passengers were stranded for days, and supply chains shortened by just in time purchasing strategies dried up. Now, arguably, there was little that business could do directly or immediately to mitigate these problems, but the experience served to demonstrate the interconnection of seemingly remote environmental factors and made more obvious and immediate the reasons businesses have to take such issues as climate change seriously. Even if you are in no danger – unlike Lohachara, once island home to 10,000 people, the first inhabited island to be wiped off the face of the Earth by global warming in 2006 – you will eventually be affected by environmental issues.

Another environmental disaster occurred the following month when BP's Deepwater Horizon rig exploded in the Gulf of Mexico killing 11 people and injuring 17. The ecological damage caused by the slick threatened some of the most important wildlife habitats. The cost to BP and its reputation are incalculable, but the stock market took a down payment by wiping £13 billion ($19.9 billion; €15 billion) off its value in two weeks. BP can also expect a big bill for cleaning up the oil as well as damages from the US government for those affected by the catastrophe. Exxon, whose vessel the *Valdez*, spilt 11 million gallons of oil on the Alaskan coast in March 1989, spent an estimated $2 billion cleaning up the spill and a further $1 billion to settle related civil and criminal charges.

Factors the international business needs to keep in mind on environmental issues are:

- environment regulations, which vary from country to country, despite the interconnection between events, as the Eyjafjallajökull eruption showed;
- waste management preventing pollution and dealing appropriately with hazardous substances;
- energy management to reduce carbon emissions;
- efficient use of water resources;
- efficient use of packaging and distribution.

See also Understanding stakeholders in Chapter 9.

CASE STUDY Union Carbide's Bhopal disaster

December 2014 saw the 30th anniversary of what has become known as the Bhopal disaster. It was also the year Warren Anderson, Union Carbide's Chairman and CEO at the time of the gas leak disaster died (29 September). He was charged with manslaughter and placed under house arrest but was later allowed to leave the country and refused to return to face trial. The United States repeatedly turned down India's requests for Anderson's extradition.

Union Carbide set up a pesticide factory in Bhopal, Madhya Pradesh, India in the 1970s, in the belief that India represented a huge untapped market for its pest control products. However, sales failed to meet the company's expectations. Indian farmers had too many more immediate problems to cope with, including droughts and floods, and in any event didn't have the money to buy pesticides. The plant never reached its full capacity and lost money throughout its short life. The Bhopal disaster, which is the town's only enduring claim to fame, took place at around midnight on 2 December 1984. It was attributed in part to a series of failures in the way hazardous substances were stored and handled. That night, water seeped into a tank of methyl isocyanate and the exothermic reaction increased the temperature to over 200°C (392°F). The resulting increase in pressure was such that it forced the emergency venting of pressure from the MIC holding tank, releasing a large volume of methyl isocyanate gas and other toxins into the atmosphere.

Some 2,259 people died immediately, a further 1,500 in the weeks that followed and up to 10,000 more deaths have subsequently been blamed on the disaster. Over 500,000 people were exposed to the chemicals, suffering a range of debilitating illnesses. There had been five previous related incidents in the preceding decade and Union Carbide had been warned of this specific danger by American experts two years earlier. It wasn't until 1989 that Union Carbide, in a partial settlement with the Indian government, agreed to pay out some $470 (£313; €360) million in compensation. The victims ended up with around $400 each (£261; €300). Criminal charges were brought against Warren Anderson, Union Carbide's CEO, eight other executives and two company affiliates. Court cases against various individuals and parties to the disaster were ongoing in 2010.

Legal

Some business schools take law very seriously; for example at Northwestern University's Kellogg School and George Washington University MBA students can take a joint MBA and JD (juris doctor), the basic professional degree for lawyers. Babson in Wellesley, Massachusetts has law as one of its core subjects. Penn State on the other hand offers only an optional module in the second year on 'Business Law for Innovation and Competition'.

Nevertheless lawyers dominate big businesses in the United States and both Congress and the Senate. In the UK around 12 per cent of MPs are either barristers or solicitors, the largest professional grouping in the House of Commons. Other than very large businesses it is not usual to have either a qualified lawyer or a legal department in businesses in the UK. Such services are usually bought in either on a contractual or ad hoc basis. Law is an imprecise field. As Henry L Mencken, the American journalist and critic, so succinctly expressed it, 'a judge is a law student who marks his own examination papers'.

The complexity of commercial life means that, sooner or later, you will find yourself taking, or defending yourself against legal action. It may be a contract dispute with a customer or supplier, or perhaps the lease on your premises turns out to give you far fewer rights than you hoped. A former employee might claim you fired them without reason. Or the Health and Safety Inspector will call and find some aspect of your machinery or working practices less than satisfactory.

Ignorance does not form the basis of a satisfactory defence so every MBA needs to know enough law to know when they might need legal advice, however high their standard of ethics and social responsibility may be.

Types of legal system

While countries generally have a universal legal system that applies throughout its territory and to all of its citizens, in theory at least, there is not one international legal system covering world affairs. Rather there are a set of treaties that govern business and personal behaviour, but not all countries are party to all or indeed any of these agreements. Even those that are party to such treaties don't always apply them. Take the case of Union Carbine (see above); in 1991 the local authorities from Bhopal charged the CEO Warren Anderson with manslaughter. He failed to appear and an international arrest warrant and a US court summons were issued. The Government of India pressed for his extradition from the United States, with whom they had an extradition treaty in place, with no success.

The following are the three main types of legal system and these are applied with variable degrees of fairness. IMD, the Swiss business school, ranks countries on the fairness of their judicial system in their annual *World Competitive Year Book*. On a scale of 1 to 10, where 10 is the fairest, only 20 countries have scores above 8. Countries with very low scores, below three, include such varied countries as Portugal, Indonesia, Mexico, Poland and Russia.

Common law

Based on tradition, custom and practice this system of law has its roots in England and its former colonies, so is to be found as far afield from that land as the United States, Australia and some Asian countries. Judges have the power to interpret the law as it applies to each unique case so creating a precedent, which in turn can be used as guidance in future cases. This makes judgments hard to predict. On the plus side this power to interpret builds flexibility into the judicial process; as against that judges have a large degree of freedom to apply their own prejudices. There are well-established appeal procedures that reduce the impact of any judgments that appear too wide of the mark.

Civil law

Code Napoléon, developed after the *Code Civil des Français*, was not the first civil code; that honour probably goes to the 1760 BC Mesopotamian Code of Hammurabi (see also Chapter 1). But the idea behind the code of civil law has a popular following. The Bavarian *Codex Maximilianeus Bavaricus Civilis*, the Spanish *Código Civil*, the Italian *Codice Civile* and the Portuguese *Código Civil* represent just a handful of the 80 or so countries that operate civil law.

The idea behind civil law is that it is based on very detailed laws organized into codes in an attempt to anticipate and deal with almost every situation. So while in theory the outcome of a case should be more predictable, judges have less room for manoeuvre in trying to accommodate real-world situations that were impossible to anticipate several hundred years ago.

Theocratic law

Theocratic law is based on religious teaching such as Islamic law based on the Koran. Islamic law uses the decisions and the sayings of the Prophet Muhammad as its foundation and is set in stone, theoretically; however, Islamic jurists are always re-interpreting the Koran in an attempt to deal with 21st-century issues.

There is little in the Koran that does not fit comfortably with international business. 'The merit of a man is not measured by the amount of his wealth (nor his poverty, for that matter) but by how he acquired whatever wealth he has and what he shall do with it now that he has it' would fit fine with a Bill Gates or Warren Buffet. In the Muslim era trade was already international.

Islamic law also has concerns over the interpretation of the term *ribâ* (generally translated as usury) and the status of fictitious persons (corporations). There is now widespread acceptance of the idea that fair rates of interest are acceptable and business entities are not fictitious persons; after all business partnerships existed in Hammurabi's time.

Main legal issues for international business

Although there may be differences between legal systems and the way in which laws are applied there is some commonality in terms of the main areas on which the law will routinely impinge.

Corporate structures

As an MBA it is highly likely that you will be working for a conventional company, private or public. These have slightly different names and regulations from jurisdiction to jurisdiction and these are constantly changing. Germany, for example, created a new form of limited liability company reducing one of the highest minimum capital requirements in Europe from €25,000 to €1.

These are the generally accepted distinct forms of which a business can take their choice that depend on a number of factors: commercial needs, financial risk and the need for outside capital.

Partnership

Partnerships (*Offene Gesellschaft* – OG in Austria and *verejná obchodná spoločnosť* in Slovakia) are effectively collections of sole traders and, as such, share the legal problems attached to personal liability. There are very few restrictions to setting up in business with another person (or persons) in partnership, and several definite advantages. By pooling resources you may have more capital; you will be bringing, hopefully, several sets of skills to the business; and if you are ill the business can still carry on.

One possibility that can reduce the more painful consequences of entering a partnership is to form a limited partnership (*Kommanditgesellschaft* – KG in Austria and *komanditná spoločnosť* in Slovakia) combining the best attributes of a partnership and a company. There must be one or more general partners with the same basic rights and responsibilities (including unlimited liability) as in any general partnership, and one or more limited partners who are usually passive investors and are only committed to the amount of their investment.

Limited company

A limited company (*Sabiedrība ar ierobežotu atbildību* in Latvia and *Socitatea cu raspundere limitata* in Romainia) has a legal identity of its own, separate from the people who own or run it. This means that, in the event of failure, creditors' claims are restricted to the assets of the company. The shareholders of the business are not liable as individuals for the business debts beyond the paid-up value of their shares. This applies even if the shareholders are working directors, unless of course the company has been trading fraudulently. Other advantages include the freedom to raise capital by selling shares.

Public limited company (plc)

Plcs (*Aktiengesellschaft* – AG in Austria and *Société anonyme* (SA) in Luxemburg) are companies that can sell shares to the public at large, either through a recognized stock market or by advertising in the press or through intermediaries. They need to fulfil some minimum and often not too onerous conditions in terms of minimum capital, trading history or number of shareholders.

Trading regulations

Organizations are heavily regulated in almost every sphere of their trading operations. Some types of business require a permit before they can even start trading and all business have to comply with certain standards when it comes to advertising, holding information or offering credit. These are the regulations that govern the trading activities of most business ventures:

- Permits or licences: Some businesses, usually those working with food or alcohol, employment agencies, mini-cabs and hairdressers, need a licence or permit before they can set up in business at all.
- Advertising and descriptive standards: Any advertising or promotion you undertake concerning your business and its products and

services, including descriptions on packaging, leaflets and instructions and those given verbally have to comply with the relevant regulations.

- Distance selling and online trading: Selling by mail order either via the Internet, television, radio, telephone, fax or catalogue usually requires that you comply with some additional rules over and above those concerning the sale of goods and services described above. In summary you have to provide written information, an order confirmation, the chance to cancel the contract. During the cooling-off period customers have the unconditional right to cancel within seven working days.

Protecting customer data

If you hold personal information on a computer on any living person – customer or employee for example – then there is a good chance you need to register under the Data Protection Act. The rules state that the information held must have been obtained fairly, be accurate, held only for as long as necessary and held only for a lawful purpose.

Credit licence

If you plan to let your customers buy on credit or hire out or lease products to private individuals or to businesses then you will in all probability have to apply to be licensed to provide credit.

Employment regulations

Employing people full- or part-time is something of a legal minefield starting with the job advert and culminating with the point at which you decide to part company. Things to consider include:

- Advertising the job: this will be governed by the laws on discrimination and equal opportunities.
- Contracts of employment: these must contain all the obvious things such as where the job is to be, what the responsibilities are, pay, holiday entitlement, as well as details on sick pay, pension, period of notice and the grievance and disciplinary procedure need to be given.
- Employment records: these should be maintained noting absences, sickness, disputes, disciplinary matters, accidents, training, holidays and any appraisals or performance reviews.
- Safety at work: employers have a 'duty of care' to ensure anyone working for them is working in a safe environment and is not exposed to possible health and safety hazards.

Intellectual property

The holy grail for international competitive business strategy is to have a product or service with sufficient unique advantage to make it stand out from others in the market. It is equally important that such an advantage cannot be easily copied. In other words there is a barrier to entry preventing others from following the same path to riches. The advantage can be anything from the business name (Body Shop), a catchy slogan (Never knowingly undersold – John Lewis), some technological wizardry (Dolby Noise Reduction), an instantly recognizable logo (Google) or even a jingle such as that used by Microsoft during startup.

The generic title covering this area is 'Intellectual Property', usually shortened by MBAs to IP, and it splits down into a number of distinct areas. Businesses spend a lot of time and money creating and protecting IP, so you need at least an appreciation of the legal issues involved. The case below is an example of how things can go wrong from the outset.

CASE STUDY Facebook

When Mark Zucherberg, then aged 20, started Facebook from his college dorm back in 2004 with two fellow students he could hardly have been aware of how the business would pan out. Facebook is a social networking website on which users have to put their real names and e-mail addresses in order to register, then they can contact current and past friends and colleagues to swap photos, news and gossip. Within three years the company was on track to make $100 million sales, partly on the back of a big order from Microsoft, which appears to have its sights on Facebook as either a partner or an acquisition target.

Zuckerberg wears jeans, Adidas sandals and a fleece and looks a bit like a latter-day Steve Jobs, Apple's founder. He also shares something else in common with Jobs. He has a gigantic intellectual-property legal dispute on his hands. For three years he has been dealing with a lawsuit brought by three fellow Harvard students who claim, in effect, that he stole the Facebook concept from them.

Intellectual property is subdivided into the following broad categories:

- Patent can be regarded as a contract between an inventor and the state. The state agrees with the inventor that if he or she is prepared to publish details of the invention in a set form and if it appears that he or she has made a real advance, the state will then grant the inventor a 'monopoly' on the invention for around 20 years. The inventor uses the monopoly period to manufacture and sell his or her innovation; competitors can read the published specifications and glean ideas for their research, or they can approach the inventor and offer to help to develop the idea under licence.

- Copyright gives protection against the unlicensed copying of original artistic and creative works – articles, books, paintings, films, plays, songs, music, engineering drawings. To claim copyright the item in question should carry this symbol: © (author's name) (date).

- Designs allow you to register the shape, design or decorative features of a commercial product if it is new, original, never published before or – if already known – never before applied to the product you have in mind.

- Trademarks and logos include the symbol by which the goods or services of a particular manufacturer or trader can be identified. It can be a word, a signature, a monogram, a picture, a logo or a combination of these. To qualify for registration the trademark must be distinctive, must not be deceptive and must not be capable of confusion with marks already registered.

- Business names involve choosing an identity so it should reflect:
  - who you are;
  - what you do;
  - how you do it.

Registering domains

Internet presence requires a domain name, ideally one that captures the essence of your business neatly so that you will come up readily on search engines and is as close as possible to your business name. Once a business name is registered as a trademark (see earlier in this chapter) you may (as current case law develops) be able to prevent another business from using it as a domain name on the Internet.

Registering a domain name is simple, but as hundreds of domain names are registered every day and you must choose a name that has not already been registered you need to have a selection of domain names to hand in case your first choice is unavailable. These need only be slight variations; for example, Cobra Beer could have been listed as Cobra-Beer, CobraBeer or even Cobra Indian Beer, if the original name was not available. These would all have been more or less equally effective in terms of search engine visibility.

Help with legal and licence issues

The Doing Business law library operated by World Bank is the world's largest free online collection of business laws and regulations. It links to official government sources wherever possible and is updated regularly. Covering 189 countries, you can find out everything from the rules on opening and closing a business to trading across borders, employment laws, enforcing contracts and much more. (**www.doingbusiness.org/law-library**)

You can get information on business licences and permits on these websites.

- Australia (**www.business.gov.au/registration-and-licences/Pages/ default.aspx**)
- Canada (**www.canadabusiness.ca/eng/page/2843/**)
- New Zealand (**www.business.govt.nz/starting-and-stopping/ entering-a-business/starting-a-business#licenses-consents-permits**)
- South Africa (**http://joburg.org.za/index.php?option=com_ content&task=view&id=416&Itemid=58**)
- UK (**www.gov.uk/licence-finder**)
- USA (**www.sba.gov/category/navigation-structure/starting- managing-business/starting-business/obtain-business-licenses-**)

Online video courses and lectures

Antitrust Regulation: Professor Kenneth Train, UCBerkeley: **www.youtube.com/watch?v=RI6xL2wTlRI**

Democracy – What is Democracy? Critical Productions: **www.youtube.com/watch?v=6GR-9-nB-YE**

Direct Democracy and the (exotic) Swiss political system by Professor Andreas Ladner, at IMD business school: **www.youtube.com/ watch?v=OOH7KGvTMCY**

Karl Marx and Marxism: 1983 British documentary on the basics of Karl Marx and Marxism: **www.youtube.com/watch?v=m8bdndigRA8**

Keynes vs Hayek: Professor George Selgin, Professor Lord Skidelsky, Duncan Weldon, Dr Jamie Whyte at the London School of Economics: **www.youtube.com/watch?v=PLBOKq4On7k**

Monopolistic Competition and Trade: UCBerkeley Professor Kenneth Train: **www.youtube.com/watch?v=SQbxoBSyoew_**

Public Goods: Professor Kenneth Train, UCBerkeley: **www.youtube.com/ watch?v=sDtbbWX5UUU**

Regulation of Natural Monopolies: Professor Kenneth Train, UCBerkeley: **www.youtube.com/watch?v=mt_S0vUvZQ4**

The Rise of China vs the Logic of Strategy: Edward Luttwak at the Institute for International Studies, University of California, Berkeley: **www.youtube.com/watch?v=WejSKbicS00**

The Scope of International Environmental Law: UC Berkeley: **www.youtube.com/watch?v=srVn5lQlh_o&list=PL5A39957CF1E5C676**

Varieties of Authoritarianism: Comparing China and Russia – Talk at USC US-China Institute by Thomas Bernstein who earned his doctorate at Columbia University and taught at Yale and Indiana universities before returning to Columbia: **www.youtube.com/watch?v=9MvACKtx1WA**

When China Rules the World: Martin Jacques, author of the book of this title gives a presentation at The University of Melbourne: **www.youtube.com/watch?v=3G1EyvRZmOs**

Online video case studies

Bhopal gas tragedy: Union Carbide not liable for claims, says US court – NewsX: **www.youtube.com/watch?v=FyHaaAXn0QU**

Dreyer's Grand Ice Cream: T Gary Rogers talks at UC Davis Graduate School of Management about building Dreyer's Grand Ice Cream from a 75-employee company with $6 million in sales to one of the world's largest ice cream companies with more than 9,000 employees: **www.youtube.com/watch?v=NTUfalH2R4Y**

Facebook: ownership contract does not exist; Zuckerberg comments on lawsuit, SmarTrend News: **www.youtube.com/watch?v=rJLjD98QcZ4**

Gulf of Mexico Oil Spill, Legal Liability, Part 1. Witnesses testified on legal liability issues surrounding the Gulf of Mexico oil spill to the House Judiciary Committee. C-SPAN: **www.c-span.org/video/?293754-1/ gulf-mexico-oil-spill-legal-liability-part-1**

Who owns Facebook and its 500 million users? Legal troubles over the ownership of the site. CNBC's Scott Cohn reports: **www.today.com/ video/today/38358645#38358645**

Winklevoss Twins – Facebook was our idea – Tyler & Cameron. ViralFuture: **www.youtube.com/watch?v=KzN6XWDEmXl**

3 Global business strategy

- Assessing international markets.
- Gaining cost leadership.
- Generating differentiation.
- Finding focus.
- Conducting industry analysis.
- Researching and segmenting markets.
- Building brands.

According to the Global Management Education Graduate Survey, 25 per cent of MBAs attend a school outside their countries of citizenship, with the aim of getting a strong international dimension to their learning experience. Even students who don't enrol abroad will expect a strong international flavour to their programme.

Andrew C Inkpen, the J Kenneth and Jeanette Seward Chair in Global Strategy at Thunderbird, gives a definition of the study of international business strategy as succinct as it comes: 'the ability to apply a systematic and replicable methodology to the unique challenges of an organization'. Ranked No 1 in international business by the *Wall Street Journal*, *US News and World Report* and the *Financial Times*, Thunderbird is almost unique in its dedication to producing global leaders. The Thunderbird Learning Consulting Network (TLCN) with its global network ensures strategic thinking is both practical and current.

But Thunderbird is not alone in the international strategy field. University of California at Berkeley's Haas School of Business takes pride in its close ties with Asia. More than 40 per cent of Berkeley's students are Asian or Asian American and the university's schools have strong research ties across the Pacific. Northwestern's Kellogg, University of Southern California's Marshall, and UCLA's Anderson have executive MBA programmes with schools in Asia. IESE Business School at Spain's University of Navarra goes one further and runs its Global Executive MBA with residential modules in the United States, China and India. One of their Professors, Pedro Nueno, helped found the CEIBS, the leading business school in China and probably the whole region.

Strategy, though a core subject in every business school, is less an academic discipline than an ever-shifting appraisal of how an organization should position itself to best meet the challenges it faces. Rather like the quote attributed to one Governor of the Bank of England who said that the true meaning of Christmas would not be apparent until Easter, when it comes to estimating retail sales, successful strategies are often really only recognizable after the event. The case below gives a flavour of the dimensions of how strategy is shaped in an international business; part marketing, part money, part people, part culture and mostly an appreciation of an ever-shifting and developing world.

CASE STUDY Dell strides the world

In a LinkedIn post (**www.linkedin.com/pulse/making-rain-4-steps-happy-successful-salesforce-michael-dell?trk=prof-post**) on 16 March 2015, Michael Dell announced that as usual at the beginning of a new fiscal year 'it's time to rally and align our global salesforce.' Top of his list of key messages was to celebrate. 'Always take time to recognize the successes of your team members. Dell had a great FY15, so we carved out ample time to celebrate together.' In fact the last few years had been tough. Sales had been flat in 2013/4, profits depressed and much time had been spent in fighting off Carl Icahn, the hostile takeover guru, to take the company private in a $25 billion leveraged buyout deal.

The foundations of the company's new-found vigour were set back in 2010 when, gazing around his empire, Dell had plenty to be pleased about. He had come a long way since founding his business from his dorm at the University of Texas nearly a quarter of a century earlier, aged just nineteen. He had turned his $1,000 initial stake into a business generating over $60 billion a year in revenues, making nearly 16 per cent of PCs sold globally. Dell's revenues were growing fast in all its major international markets. Asia-Pacific and Japan (APJ) saw revenue in the latest quarter grow by 28 per cent on a 41 per cent increase in units. Growth was strong across all product categories and led by performance in India, China and Australia/New Zealand, where revenue grew year over year 57 per cent, 32 per cent, and 29 per cent, respectively. Shipments of notebooks increased 71 per cent year over year for the region. Europe, Middle East and Africa (EMEA) revenues increased 8 per cent and shipments were up 14 per cent. Shipments of notebooks increased 36 per cent for the quarter and mobility revenue was up 25 per cent.

Revenue growth in EMEA emerging countries increased more dramatically still, up by some 44 per cent.

It was only in 1980 that he had acquired his first computer, the Apple II, and on founding his company, PC Limited, had as his goal to beat IBM. His first product, The Turbo PC, was supported by a no-quibble returns policy and a unique home-support service. The IPO in 1988 valued his $1,000 business, founded four years earlier, at $85 million. From the outset Dell had three golden rules; disdain inventory, always listen to the customer and cut out middlemen.

An Internet pioneer, the company launched a static online ordering page in 1994, and by 1997 Dell.com claimed to be the first company to record a million dollars in online sales.

Dell since its early beginnings has focused on fundamentally different strategies from its competitors. Unlike Apple they have never tried to design sexy devices or to build a global network of retail outlets. Dell's strategy was to create the leanest possible supply chain direct to the end user while allowing them to choose the features they wanted. They extended that successful strategy across to related products such as servers, printers and storage devices to build a business shipping 140,000 systems a day worldwide – more than one every second – ranking 34 in the Fortune 500 listing of companies and had become one of the world's leading brands.

But just as Dell looked to be in an unchallengeable position the company lost its position as the world's biggest maker of personal computers to Hewlett-Packard (HP), a company founded back in 1939 in a Palo Alto garage. No stranger to setbacks, HP had seen that growth in the PC world had crossed from corporate markets to consumers and from developed economies to emerging markets where people had less access to the Internet and were both more wary and less able to shop online. In addition the competition was hotting up on a new front brought about by past success and galloping innovation with auction sites such as eBay and uBid enjoying flourishing growth rates in PC sales. Dell saw that it had to develop new strategies for the new environment. As well as beefing up its website and launching 'IdeaStorm', a blog that has already pulled in 9,000 customer suggestions for improvements, the company has set up a bulk supply chain alongside its lean customized one and started to design products to hanker after rather than just highly specified black boxes. Dell has also bought up several firms in the IT systems management sector as it sees the shift from product- to service-driven growth as an important factor in the future of its business sector. Dell has had to cut $3 billion of expenses, lay off 8,800 employees and change the mindset of its engineers and designers to reposition it to execute its new strategy.

Strategy has three dimensions; the intellectual analytical and thinking aspect used to devise broad strategic direction; the development and shaping of specific actions in pursuit of those strategies; and the implementation of strategy through the execution of business plans. If an organization gets it wrong in any of these areas the results they are aiming for may not be achieved, they may fall behind others in the market or in the worst case fail altogether. Getting all three areas right can be more of an art than a science, rather like a short-sighted person trying to thread several needles held in parallel by different people in one swift movement.

Devising strategy – the overview

Credit for devising the most succinct and usable way to get a handle on the big picture has to be given to Michael E Porter, who trained as an economist at Princeton, taking MBA (1971) and PhD (1973) at Harvard Business School where he is now a professor. His book, *Competitive Strategy: Techniques for analyzing industries and competitors* (1980, Free Press, Old Tappan, NJ) is in its 63rd printing and has been translated into 19 languages; it sets out the now accepted methodology for devising strategy. As well as being essential reading in most business schools, courses based on Porter's work are taught in partnership with more than 80 other universities around the world using curriculum, video content and instructor support developed at Harvard.

The three generic strategies

Porter's first observation was that three factors above all influenced a business's chances of making superior profits. Firstly there was the attractiveness or otherwise of the country (see Porter's Diamond in Chapter 1), followed by the industry in which it primarily operated. Finally, and in terms of an organization's sphere of influence, more importantly, was how the business positioned itself within that country and industry. In that respect a business could only have a cost advantage in that it could make product or deliver service for less than others. Or it could be different in a way that mattered to consumers, so that their offers would be unique, or at least relatively so. He added a further twist to his prescription. Businesses could follow either a cost advantage path or a differentiation path industry-wide, or they could take a third path – they could concentrate on a narrow, specific segment (see Chapter 4 for more on market segments), either with cost advantage or differentiation. This he termed 'focus' strategy.

Focus strategies can be applied on a country basis or in the international arena. For example, Southwest Airlines, whose mission is 'dedication to the highest quality of Customer Service delivered with a sense of warmth, friendliness, individual pride, and Company Spirit', pioneered low-cost air travel focusing on US destinations only. The airline started up over 38 years ago when Rollin King and Herb Kelleher got together and decided to start a different kind of airline. They began with one simple notion: 'If you get your passengers to their destinations when they want to get there, on time, at the lowest possible fares, and make darn sure they have a good time doing it, people will fly your airline.' This Texas airline has grown to become one of the largest airlines in America flying 3,200 flights a day and carrying over 100 million passengers a year to 66 cities, all in the United States.

Ryanair (see case study) has a similar low-cost strategy, but without any special attempt to foster warmth throughout its customer base. However, Ryanair flies to 150 destinations in 30 different countries.

CASE STUDY   Ryanair: Entering new markets on the back of operating efficiencies

Ryanair's CEO, Michael O'Leary, on his company's corporate website (**http:// corporate.ryanair.com/investors/2015/**) reporting third-quarter 2015 profits of £49 million, went on to state that 'these strong results confirm that our "Always Getting Better" customer programme and our expanded business schedules, coupled with our substantial fare and cost advantage over competitor airlines is drawing millions of new customers to Ryanair.'

The company also announced that the first five of 380 new B737-800 aircraft had been delivered and a new United States Ryanair website was up and running. As Ryanair don't fly to the United States, this represents an interesting approach to global strategy. Thousands of US customers already explore Europe every year on Ryanair's low fares with London, Dublin, Barcelona, Rome and Paris the top five destinations, and the most visitors coming from California, New York, Texas, Florida and New Jersey. The new website aims to make it even easier for US customers to buy tickets.

The paradox surrounding Ryanair's strategy of low cost whilst letting the customer add services on at a cost is that it delivers passenger numbers and profits, whilst leaving customers' opinion of the business languishing in the ratings doldrums. They don't feature anywhere the world ranking of the 100 best airlines as voted for by airline customers around the world (**www.worldairlineawards.com/ Awards/world_airline_rating.html**). The company does however enjoy the title of the world's favourite airline, carrying 80 million international passengers a year, close on double the numbers carried by easyJet, another low-cost airline, according to statistics produced by IATA (**www.iata.org/publications/pages/wats.aspx**).

Ryanair's low-cost strategy allowed it to ride out the global credit crunch. While British Airways was posting its worst-ever financial performance revealing a loss of £401 million and being forced to scrap its dividend, Ryanair posted a reduced quarterly loss of only €11 million against €102 million in the previous year, confirming Ryanair's powerful competitiveness. The average fare was just €34 (£29.70/$44.33) and yields were down only 12 per cent against a feared 20 per cent. Traffic growth was 14 per cent resulting in the airline carrying 66 million passengers as against 65.3 million the year before. But the clincher confirming the company's success in executing its core international competitive strategy was that costs per seat were down 23 per cent, or 4 per cent excluding fuel.

While many airlines were cutting back on routes, Ryanair saw many opportunities to grow. The airline opened new destinations in Eastern European countries – Estonia, Bulgaria and Romania and the Ukraine. The combined population of these targeted countries is over 100 million and a €34 fare makes for a very affordable purchase. Despite the rapid expansion of routes and the addition of hundreds of aircraft Ryanair manages to keep costs down. It uses two strategies to achieve this.

Firstly the average weekly frequency of routes is relatively low, and getting lower. Over the past four years, Ryanair's average weekly frequency across its network has come down to five flights, down from just under nine.

The cost for opening a route is low. Michael Cawley, the former deputy CEO states 'we don't bother trying to analyse the living daylights out of it, we have a look at the demographics, and then make a decision to do it', going on to explain 'we leave routes if we don't make sustainable profits after six months.' Source: anna – Airline Network News and Analysis (**www.anna.aero/2010/02/09/ryanair-reveals-nike-style-approach-to-new-route-planning-says-lets-do-it-for-200-routes-this-year/**).

Cost leadership

Low cost should not be confused with low price. A business with low costs may or may not pass those savings on to customers. Alternatively they could use that position alongside tight cost controls and low margins to create an effective barrier to others considering either entering or extending their penetration of that market. Low-cost strategies are most likely to be achievable in large markets, requiring large-scale capital investment, where production or service volumes are high and economies of scale can be achieved from long runs.

Low costs are not a lucky accident; they can be achieved through these main activities:

- Operating efficiencies: New processes, methods of working or less costly ways of working. Ryanair and easyJet are examples where analysing every component of the business made it possible to strip out major elements of cost (meals, free baggage and allocated seating for example), while leaving the essential proposition – we will fly you from A to B – intact. Internationally both companies make strategic country choices by locating where they can get low operating costs (see Ryanair case).

- Product redesign: This involves rethinking a product or service proposition fundamentally to look for more efficient ways to work or cheaper substitute materials to work with. The motor industry has adopted this approach with 'platform sharing'; that is where major players including Citröen, Peugeot and Toyota have rethought their entry car models to share major components, which has become common.

- Product standardization: A wide range of product and service offers claiming to extend customer choice invariably leads to higher costs. The challenge is to be sure that proliferation gives real choice and adds value. Ford's latest version of Focus had been 'designed and engineered to meet the needs of millions of buyers around the world'. The Focus is at the heart of Ford's new thinking: that car buyers globally share the same priorities in seeking fuel efficiency and cost-effectiveness – the philosophy that underpinned Japanese and European car makers when they launched their assault on the US market decades earlier.

- Economies of scale: This can be achieved only by being big or bold. The same head office and logistics systems can support Tesco's 3,863 stores operating throughout the UK and in Malaysia, Turkey, India, Japan, China, South Korea and the United States, as can, say, the 997 that Somerfield had before they sold out to the Co-operative Group in March 2009. The former will have a lower cost-base by virtue of having more outlets over which to spread its costs as well as having more purchasing power.

The Experience (or Learning) Curve

The fact that costs declined as the output volume of a product or service increased (though well-known earlier) was first developed as a usable accounting process by TP Wright, an American aeronautical engineer, in 1936. His process became known as the Cumulative Average Model or Wright's Model. Subsequently models known as the Unit Time Model or Crawford's Model were developed by a team of researchers at Stanford and The Boston

Consulting Group (BCG) popularized the process with their Experience Curve (Figure 3.1) showing that each time the cumulative volume of doing something – either making a product or delivering a service – doubled, the unit cost dropped by a constant and predictable amount. The reasons for the cost drop include:

- repetition makes people more familiar with tasks and consequently faster;
- more efficient materials and equipment become available from suppliers themselves as their costs go down through the experience curve effect;
- organization, management and control procedures improve;
- engineering and production problems are solved.

BCG was founded in 1963 by Bruce D Henderson, a former Bible salesman and engineering graduate from Vanderbilt University, who left the Harvard Business School 90 days before graduation to work for Westinghouse Corporation. From there he went on to head Arthur D Little's management services unit before joining the Boston Safe Deposit and Trust Company to start a consulting arm for the bank. Naming this the Experience Curve, it was the strategy tool that put BCG on the path to success and has served it well ever since.

The value of the Experience Curve as a strategic process is that it helps a business predict future unit costs and gives a signal when costs fail to drop at the historic rate, both vital pieces of information for firms pursuing a cost leadership strategy. Every industry has a different Experience Curve that itself varies over time. You can find out more about how to calculate the curve for your industry on the Management and Accounting Web (**http://maaw.info/ LearningCurveSummary.htm**).

FIGURE 3.1 The Experience Curve

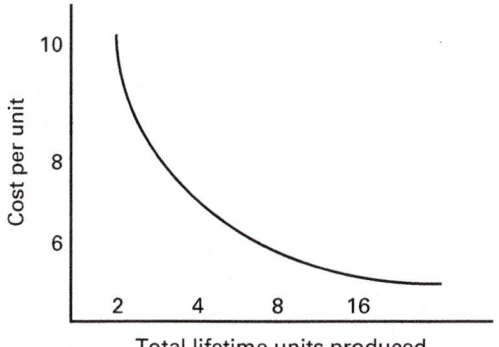

Differentiation

The key to differentiation is a deep understanding of what customers really want and need and more importantly what they are prepared to pay more for. Apple's opening strategy was based around a 'fun' operating system based on icons, rather than the dull MS-DOS. This belief was based on their understanding that computer users were mostly young and wanted an intuitive command system and their 'graphical user interface' delivered just that. Apple has continued its differentiation strategy, but adds design and fashion and ease of control to the ways in which it delivers extra value. Sony and BMW are also examples of differentiators. Both have distinctive and desirable differences in their products and neither they nor Apple offer the lowest price in their respective industries; customers are willing to pay extra for the idiosyncratic and prized differences embedded in their products.

Differentiation doesn't have to be confined to just the marketing arena, nor does it always lead to success if the subject of that differentiation goes out of fashion without much warning. Northern Rock, the failed bank that had to be nationalized to stay in business thought its strategy of raising most of the money it lent out in mortgages through the money markets was a sure winner. It allowed the bank to grow faster than its competitors who place more reliance on depositors for their funds. As long as interest rates were low and the money market functioned smoothly it worked. But once the differentiators that fuelled its growth were reversed, its business model failed.

Focus

Focused strategy involves concentrating on serving a particular market or a defined geographic region. IKEA, for example, targets young, white-collar workers as its prime customer segment selling through 235 stores in more than 30 countries. Ingvar Kamprad, an entrepreneur from the Småland province in southern Sweden, who founded the business in the late 1940s, offers home furnishing products of good function and design at prices young people can afford. He achieves this by using simple cost-cutting solutions that do not affect the quality of products.

Warren Buffett, the world's richest man, who knows a thing or two about focus, combined with Mars to buy US chewing gum manufacturer Wrigley for $23 billion (£11.6 billion) in May 2008. Chigago-based Wrigley, which launched its Spearmint and Juicy Fruit gums in the 1890s, has specialized in chewing gum ever since and consistently outperformed its more diversified competitors. Wrigley is the only major consumer-products company to grow comfortably faster than the population in its markets and above the rate of inflation. Over the past decade or so other consumer-products companies have diversified. Gillette moved into batteries, used to drive many of its products, by acquiring Duracell. Nestlé bought Ralston Purina, Dreyer's (see the video case study in the previous chapter), Ice Cream Partners and Chef America. Both have trailed Wrigley's performance.

Businesses often lose their focus over time and periodically have to rediscover their core strategic purpose. Procter & Gamble is an example of a business that had to refocus to cure weak growth. In 2000, the company was losing share in seven of its top nine categories, and had lowered earnings expectations four times in two quarters. This prompted the company to restructure and refocus on its core business; big brands, big customers and big countries. They sold off non-core businesses, establishing five global business units with a closely focused product portfolio.

First-to-market fallacy

Gaining 'first mover advantage', are words used like a mantra to justify high expenditure and a headlong rush into new strategic areas. This concept is one of the most enduring in business theory and practice. Entrepreneurs and established giants are always in a race to be first. Research from the 1980s which shows that market pioneers have enduring advantages in distribution, product-line breadth, product quality and, especially, market share underscores this principle.

Beguiling though the theory of first mover advantage is, it is probably wrong. Gerard Tellis, of the University of Southern California, and Peter Golder, of New York University's Stern Business School, argued that previous studies on the subject were deeply flawed. In the first instance earlier studies were based on surveys of surviving companies and brands, excluding all the pioneers that failed. This helps some companies to look as though they were first to market even when they were not. Procter & Gamble (P&G) boasts that it created the US's disposable-nappy (diaper) business. In fact a company called Chux launched their product a quarter of a century before P&G entered the market in 1961. Also, the questions used to gather much of the data in earlier research were at best ambiguous, and perhaps dangerously so. For example the term, 'one of the pioneers in first developing such products or services', was used as a proxy for 'first to market'. The authors emphasize their point by listing popular misconceptions of who were the real pioneers across the 66 markets they analysed – online book sales: Amazon (wrong), Books.com (right); copiers: Xerox (wrong), IBM (right); PCs: IBM/Apple (both wrong); Micro Instrumentation Telemetry Systems (MITS) introduced its PC the Altair, a $400 kit, in 1974 followed by Tandy Corporation (Radio Shack) in 1977.

In fact the most compelling evidence from all the research was that nearly half of all firms pursuing a first to market strategy were fated to fail, while those following fairly close behind were three times as likely to succeed. Tellis and Golder claim the best strategy is to enter the market 19 years after pioneers, learn from their mistakes, benefit from their product and market development and be more certain about customer preferences.

First to market – possible international advantages

According to the New Trade Theory of international business (see Chapter 1), in certain cases where the world market will only support a limited number of companies those that are first to market may be a source of enduring competitive advantage. Denmark took that approach with its wind turbine industry as it had few natural sources of energy. Despite being a small country, by 1999 it had captured 60 per cent of the word market for wind turbines. Today, the Danish wind turbine industry accounts for 12,000 jobs in Denmark while component supplies and installation of Danish turbines currently create another 6,000 jobs worldwide.

Companies too, can, for a while at least, establish first-mover advantage in overseas markets by taking their well-established expertise and systems to foreign markets, as the Volkswagen case illustrates.

CASE STUDY   Volkswagen Group China
_____

The Volkswagen Group, headquartered in Wolfsburg, Germany is one of the world's leading automobile manufacturers and the largest carmaker in Europe. In 2014, the Group increased the number of vehicles delivered to customers to 10.137 million (2013: 9.731 million) taking its world market share up to 13 per cent. Their 118 production plants are spread around Europe the Americas, Asia and Africa. Volkswagen's latest accounts show that they sold more cars in China (3,668,433) than in the whole of Western Europe (2,912,905) and that their sales in China grew by 12 3 per cent more than the preceding year, nearly twice the 6.5 per cent growth achieved in Europe.

In 2009 when the China Association of Automobile Manufacturers (CAAM) announced the list of top 10 auto manufacturers, Volkswagen's joint venture headed the pack with sales of over 1.4 million units. Shanghai General Motors Co Ltd and joint ventures from Hyundai, Nissan, Honda and Toyota, along with the BYD Co Ltd. Chery Automobile Co Ltd and Geely Holding Group Co Ltd were also in the top 10. Volkswagen has had the largest share of the Chinese automotive market for more than 20 years.

Volkswagen Group China, often cited as the most visible example of an international business achieving sustained first-mover advantage, was earliest to market, starting its connection with China in 1978. Its first joint venture there was the Shanghai Volkswagen Automotive Co Ltd, established in October 1984, followed in February 1991 by FAW-Volkswagen Automotive Company Ltd, a second joint venture established in Changchun. Growth was slow at first, but by the 1990s the company had sufficient presence to negotiate contracts to provide fleet cars for the Chinese government and taxis for the municipalities of Beijing and Shanghai. Soon Volkswagen Santanas became an everyday scene on streets throughout China. Although the company certainly made superior vehicles, its success in securing these contracts was due in large part to having no serious competition. At one point, Shanghai Volkswagen dominated the Chinese car market, taking a 70 per cent share. The joint venture was named one of the 'Best Companies to Work for in China' in 2007. With its headquarters in Anting International Auto City the company has four vehicle production plants, one engine plant, a technology centre and a design centre. The SVW product range includes a total of 11 models from the Volkswagen brand (Polo Jinqing, Polo Jinqu, Cross Polo, Lavida, Santana, Santana Vista, Passat New Lingyu and Touran) and Škoda brand (Fabia, Octavia und Superb).

Volkswagen's international rivals took another 10 years before they were able to establish a meaningful presence in China. According to Ashok Som, professor at the ESSEC business school in Poitiers and an industry researcher, by 2004 Volkswagen's share of the Chinese car market had fallen to below 20 per cent. Other international players had moved in, while local Chinese car makers had set up shop and were even buying up overseas car firms including MG in the UK, and Volvo, bought from Ford in March 2010. Soon, local manufacturers were undercutting Volkswagen's prices and other international players, such as General Motors, learning from Volkswagen's early difficulties in areas such as sourcing and distribution, eroded market share.

Industry analysis

Aside from articulating the generic approach to business strategy Porter's other major contribution to the field was what has become known as The Five Forces Theory of Industry Structure (see Figure 3.2). Porter postulated that the five forces that drive competition in an industry have to be understood as part of the process of choosing which of the three generic strategies to pursue. The forces he identified are:

- Threat of Substitution: Can customers buy something else instead of your product? For example Apple and to a lesser extent Sony have laptop computers that are distinctive enough to make substitution difficult. Dell on the other hand faces intense competition from dozens of other suppliers with near-identical products, competing mostly on price alone.

FIGURE 3.2   Five forces theory of industry analysis (after Porter)

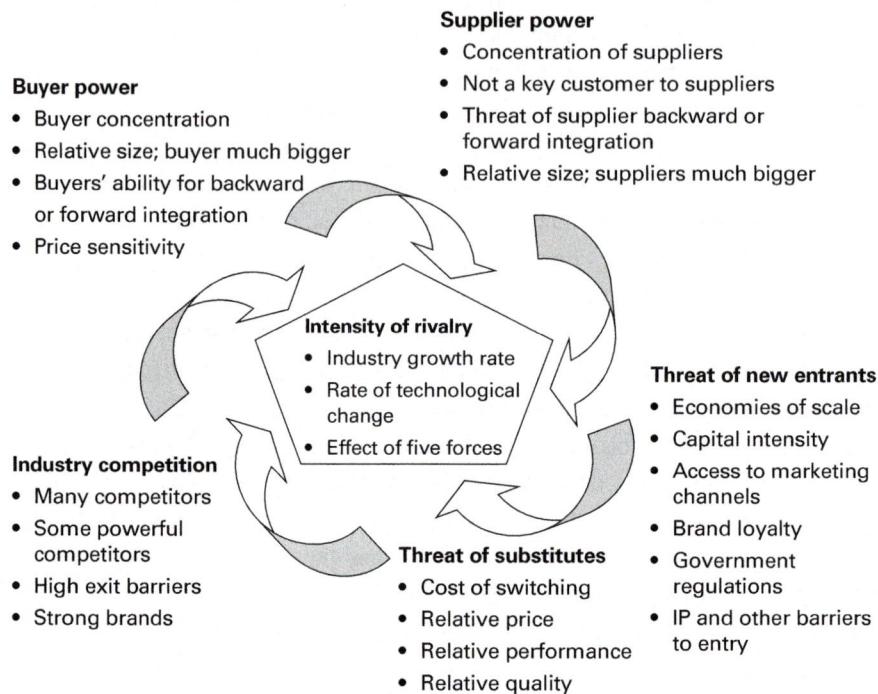

Buyer power
- Buyer concentration
- Relative size; buyer much bigger
- Buyers' ability for backward or forward integration
- Price sensitivity

Supplier power
- Concentration of suppliers
- Not a key customer to suppliers
- Threat of supplier backward or forward integration
- Relative size; suppliers much bigger

Intensity of rivalry
- Industry growth rate
- Rate of technological change
- Effect of five forces

Industry competition
- Many competitors
- Some powerful competitors
- High exit barriers
- Strong brands

Threat of new entrants
- Economies of scale
- Capital intensity
- Access to marketing channels
- Brand loyalty
- Government regulations
- IP and other barriers to entry

Threat of substitutes
- Cost of switching
- Relative price
- Relative performance
- Relative quality

- Threat of New Entrants: If it is easy to enter your market, start-up costs are low and there are no barriers to entry such as IP (intellectual property) protection, then the threat is high.

- Supplier Power: The fewer the suppliers, usually the more powerful they are. Oil is a classic example where less than a dozen countries supply the whole market and consequently can set prices.

- Buyer Power: In the food market for example with just a few, powerful supermarket buyers being supplied by thousands of much smaller businesses they are often able to dictate terms.

- Industry Competition: The number and capability of competitors is one determinant of a business's power. Few competitors with relatively less-attractive products or services lower the intensity of rivalry in a sector. Often these sectors slip into oligopolistic behaviour (see also Chapter 2) preferring to collude rather than compete.

Getting the measure of markets

The starting point in devising a global business strategy is definition of the scope of the market you are either in or aiming for. This comes from the business objectives, mission and vision that form the heart of the strategy of the enterprise. These are topics covered in the business planning section of Chapter 11. For most MBAs for most of the time these will be a 'given' and as such will not inhibit your ability to apply the concepts explored in this chapter. So, for example, if you are working in, say, Toyota, McDonald's, IBM, a major retail chain or an airline, the broad market thrust of your current business will be self-evident. Later you may want or need to change strategic direction, but effective marketing is concerned fundamentally with dealing with a defined product (service)/market scope. These concepts apply to any marketing activity, but you will find that understanding them is made easier by applying them to the business you are in, or have some appreciation of.

Assessing the relevant market

Much of marketing is concerned with achieving goals such as selling a specific quantity of a product or service or capturing market share. MBAs are frequently set the challenging task of measuring the size of the market. Now in principle this is not too difficult. Desk research (see in Market Research later in this chapter) will yield a sizeable harvest of statistics of varying degrees of reliability. Assessing the relevant market then involves refining global statistics down to reach the real scope of your market. Suppose for example you are working in Southwest Airlines in the mid-nineties, on plans to develop an international business strategy. For a start, you know you have a significant cost advantage over full-service airlines such as American Airlines, if for no better reason than because your workforce is more productive. Southwest generates 3.5 million available seat-miles per employee, as compared to 2.5 million at American; by this measure, the productivity of Southwest employees is 40 per cent higher than at American. But American Airways is a global player. They are one of over 2,000 airlines operating more than 24,000 aircraft, providing service to some 4,000 airports. These world airlines fly almost 30 million scheduled flights carrying 2 billion passengers. Over the past 30 years the market has grown on average by 5.5 per cent a year and looks set to double over the next decade or so.

All important information, but Southwest, though the second biggest carrier after Delta, only operates in the United States. That airline industry comprises some 100 certificated passenger airlines with around 12 million flight departures per year, carrying around 750 million passengers. Southwest carried 101 million passengers in 2009, making its share of the US air travel market by passenger at that point 13.47 per cent. Its share of the world market is barely a fraction of 1 per cent, but the world is not its relevant market – only the US market was in its sights.

For Ryanair, a major player in the international arena, its market share has several dimensions. On a passenger basis they have a dominant market share. However, European internal air travel breaks down into a number of sub-markets; for example, countries (Spain, Greece, Germany etc), regions

(Eastern Europe, Scandinavia) and purpose (leisure/business). Ryanair competes with different airlines in each of these markets – Wizz in Eastern Europe, airberlin and easyJet across most of their market. So market share is defined as the share of the market you operate in, and that is not necessarily the whole market for your goods and services. Ryanair have no share of the US internal or international market, but a small and growing share of the market for onward travel by Americans (see case study).

The importance of market share

The relevant market will be shared by various competing businesses in different proportions. Typically there will be a market leader, a couple of market followers and a host of businesses trailing in their wake. The slice each competitor has of a market is its market share. You will find that marketing people are fixated on market share, perhaps even more so than on absolute sales. That may appear little more than a rational desire to beat the 'enemy' and appear higher in rankings, but it has a much more deep-seated and profound logic.

Back in the 1960s a firm of American management consultants observed a consistent relationship between the cost of producing an item (or delivering a service) and the total quantity produced over the life of the product concerned. They noticed that total unit costs (labour and materials) fell by between 20 per cent and 30 per cent for every doubling of the cumulative quantity produced.

So any company capturing a sizeable market share will have an implied cost advantage over any competitor with a smaller market share. That cost advantage can then be used to make more profit, lower prices and compete for an even greater share of the market or invest in making the product better, so stealing a march on competitors (see the Volkswagen Group China case study in this chapter).

Competitive position

It follows that if market share and relative size are important marketing goals you need to assess your product/service/cost positions relative to the competition in your relevant market. The techniques most used to carry out this analysis are SWOT, Perceptual Mapping and Strategic Cost Analysis.

Strengths, Weaknesses, Opportunities and Threats (SWOT)

This is a general-purpose tool developed in the late 1960s at Harvard by Learned, Christensen, Andrews and Guth, and published in their seminal book, *Business Policy, Text and Cases* (Richard D Irwin, 1969). The SWOT framework consists of a cross with space in each quadrant to summarize your observations, as in Figure 3.3.

FIGURE 3.3   Example SWOT chart for a hypothetical Cobra Beer competitor

Strengths	Weaknesses
1. Beginning to get brand recognition 2. Established strongly in Indian restaurants	1. Don't have own production 2. Need more equity finance to be able to advertise more strongly
Opportunities	Threats
1. We could capitalize more on our relationships in Indian restaurants 2. We are only in the UK – so have the world to go for	1. We are vulnerable to a big player targeting our niche 2. Our sector looks like being the target of major tax rises which could reduce overall demand

In this example the SWOT analysis is restricted to a handful of areas, though in practice the list might run to a dozen or more areas within each of the four quadrants. The purpose of the SWOT analysis is to suggest possible ways to improve the competitive position and hence market share while minimizing the dangers of perceived threats. A strategy that this SWOT would suggest as being worth pursuing could be to launch a low-alcohol product (and sidestep the tax threat) that would appeal to all restaurants, rather than just Indian (widen the market). The company could also start selling in India using the international cachet of being a UK brand. That would open up the market still further and limit the damage that larger UK competitors could inflict.

SWOT is also used as a tool in strategic analysis and indeed it was so used by General Electric in the 1980s. While it is a useful way of pulling together a large amount of information in a way that is easy for managers to assimilate it can be most effective when used in individual market segments, as a strength in one segment could be a weakness in another. For example, giving a product features that would enhance its appeal, say, to the retiree market may reduce its appeal to other market segments.

Perceptual mapping

Perceptual or positioning maps are much used by marketing executives to position products and services relative to competitors on two dimensions. In Figure 3.4 the positions of companies competing in a particular industry are compared on price and quality, on a spectrum from low to high.

Similar maps can be produced for any combination of variables that are of importance to customers – availability, product range, after-sales support, market image and so on. The technique is used in a variety of ways including highlighting possible market gaps when one quadrant is devoid of players, suggesting areas to be built on or extended, or where a USP is required to create a competitive edge.

FIGURE 3.4   Perceptual mapping

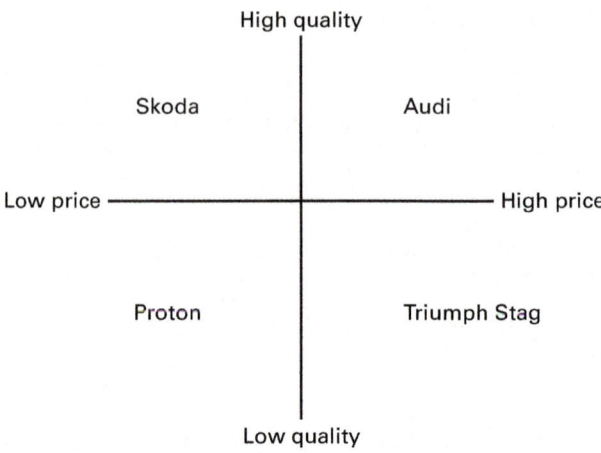

Strategic cost analysis

People often wonder how multimillionaires can still gaze covetously at billionaires. Apparently, and according to a number of seemingly reliably studies, it's not absolute wealth that satisfies; it's being better off than anyone else you know that counts. So it is with costs. If cost competitiveness matters in your industry then you need to keep driving costs down to maintain a leading position (Figure 3.5).

FIGURE 3.5   Assessing your strategic cost position

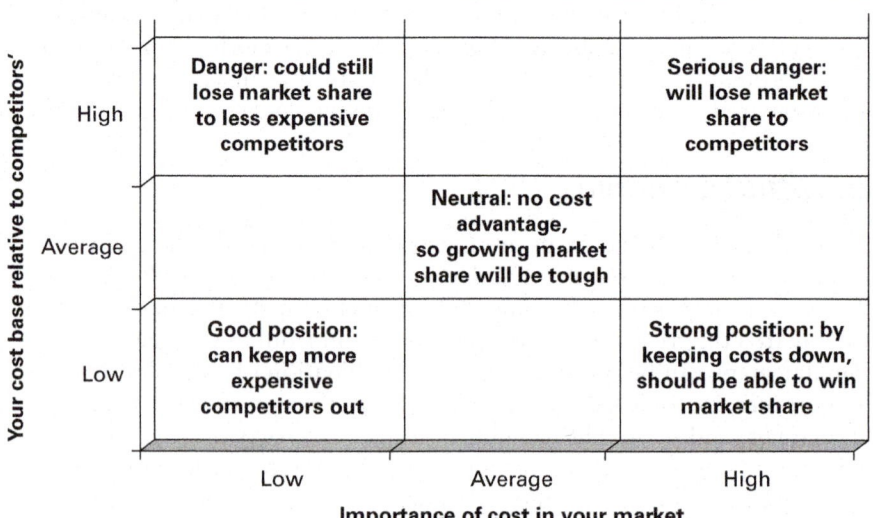

Segmenting markets

Having established that customers have different needs means that we need to organize our marketing effort so as to address those individually. However, trying to satisfy everyone may mean that we end up satisfying no one fully. The marketing process that helps us deal with this seemingly impossible task is market segmentation. This is the name given to the process whereby customers and potential customers are organized into clusters or groups of 'similar' types. For example, a carpet/upholstery cleaning business has private individuals and business clients running restaurants and guest houses.

These two segments are fundamentally different, with one segment being more focused on cost and the other more concerned that the work is carried out with the least disruption to their business. Also, each of these customer groups is motivated to buy for different reasons and your selling message has to be modified accordingly.

Worthwhile criteria

These are five useful rules to help decide if a market segment is worth trying to sell into:

- Measurability. Can you estimate how many customers are in the segment? Are there enough to make it worth offering something 'different'?
- Accessibility. Can you communicate with these customers, preferably in a way that reaches them on an individual basis? For example, you could reach the over-50s by advertising in a specialist 'older people's' magazine with reasonable confidence that young people will not read it. So if you were trying to promote Scrabble with tiles 50 per cent larger, you might prefer that young people did not hear about it. If they did, it might give the product an old-fashioned image.
- Open to profitable development. The customers must have money to spend on the benefits that you propose to offer.
- Size. A segment has to be large enough to be worth your exploiting it, but perhaps not so large as to attract larger competitors.
- Durability. A segment has to have a long-enough life to provide an enduring income stream.

One example of a market segment that has not been open to development for hundreds of years is the sale of goods and services to retired people. Several factors made this a particularly unappealing segment. First, retired people were perceived as 'old' and less adventurous; second, they had a short life expectancy; and finally, the knockout blow was that they had no money. In the last decade or so that has all changed: people retire early, live longer and many have relatively large pensions. The result is that travel firms, house builders, magazine publishers and insurance companies have rushed out a stream of products and services aimed particularly at this market segment.

Segmentation is an important marketing process, as it helps to bring customers more sharply into focus, classifies them into manageable groups and allows you to focus on one or more niches. It has wide-ranging implications for other marketing decisions. For example, the same product can be priced differently according to the intensity of customers' needs. The first- and second-class post is one example, off-peak rail travel another.

It is also a continuous process that needs to be carried out periodically, for example when strategies are being reviewed.

Methods of segmentation

These are some of the ways by which markets can be segmented:

- Psychographic segmentation divides individual consumers into social groups such as 'Yuckies' (young, unwitting, costly kids – who are still at home at 30), 'Yuppies' (young, upwardly mobile professionals), 'Bumps' (borrowed-to-the-hilt, upwardly mobile, professional show-offs) and 'Jollies' (jet-setting oldies with lots of loot). These categories try to show how social behaviour influences buyer behaviour. Forrester Research, an Internet research house, claims that when it comes to determining whether consumers will or will not go on the Internet, how much they'll spend and what they'll buy, demographic factors such as age, race and gender don't matter anywhere near as much as the consumers' attitudes towards technology. Forrester uses this concept, together with its research, to produce Technographics® market segments as an aid to understanding people's behaviour as digital consumers. Forrester has used two categories – technology optimists and technology pessimists – and has used these alongside income and what it calls 'primary motivation' – career, family and entertainment – to divide up the whole market. Each segment is given a new name – 'Techno-strivers', 'Digital Hopefuls' and so forth – followed by a chapter explaining how to identify them, how to tell whether they are likely to be right for your product or service and providing some pointers as to what marketing strategies might get favourable responses from each group.

- Benefit segmentation recognizes that different people can get different satisfaction from the same product or service. Lastminute.com claims two quite distinctive benefits for its users. First, it aims to offer people bargains that appeal because of price and value. Second, the company has recently been laying more emphasis on the benefit of immediacy. This idea is rather akin to the impulse-buy products placed at checkout tills, which you never thought of buying until you bumped into them on your way out. Whether 10 days on a beach in Goa or a trip to Istanbul are the types of thing people 'pop in their baskets' before turning off their computers, time will tell.

- Geographic segmentation arises when different locations have different needs. For example, an inner-city location may be a heavy user of motorcycle dispatch services, but a light user of gardening products.
- Industrial segmentation groups together commercial customers according to a combination of their geographic location, principal business activity, relative size, frequency of product use, buying policies and a range of other factors. Logical Holdings is an e-business solutions and service company that floated for over £1 billion on the London Stock Exchange and TechMark index, making it one of the UK's biggest IT companies.
- Purchasing power segmentation is where the customer's ability or willingness to pay is the dominant criteria for dividing the market. The auto market segmentation in Table 3.1 is one such example.
- Multivariant segmentation is where more than one variable is used. This can give a more precise picture of a market than using just one factor (see Table 3.1).

Market share is a difficult concept to get a handle on. For example, a headline in *Forbes* on 13 December 2012 read 'Microsoft's market share drops from 97 per cent to 20 per cent in just over a decade.' Further down the article came the caveat 'percentage share of a market does depend on what you're defining as being the market.' In this case the market was operating systems in all computing devices. In 2000 when desktop and laptop PCs were dominant Microsoft ruled the market but now that PCs, tablets and smartphones are all part of the computing-device market the situation is rather different. Microsoft's declining share of this vital market explains

TABLE 3.1 Multi-variant segmentation of the auto market

Country	Budget Segment		Compact Segment		Family Segment		Premium Segment		Super Luxury Segment	
	% Size	% Growth	% Size	% Growth	% Size	% Growth	% Size	% Growth	% Size	% Growth
USA										
Middle East										
S Korea										
China										
Russia										
Total										

why they bought Nokia's phone business and licensed its patents for €5.44 billion ($7.2 /£4.92 billion) in 2013. So the rule here is before you cut up the cake, be sure you know what cake you are cutting.

CASE STUDY Nissan Infiniti

When Carlos Ghosn, President and CEO of Nissan Motor Co Ltd, unveiled his company's financial results he had every reason for satisfaction. While most of the US motor industry was sheltering under the protection of bankruptcy, few in the sector were doing more than breaking even; Ghosn announced on 9 February 2010 that in the third quarter, the consolidated net income after taxes totalled 45 billion yen. The company had successfully put in place a series of measures to counter the global financial and economic crisis and had achieved additional sales volume growth in China. Net revenues were 1.9962 trillion yen, increased by 9.9 per cent compared with a year ago. Operating profit was 134.1 billion yen, and the operating profit margin came to 6.7 per cent. Ordinary profit was 112.7 billion yen. Nissan sold 882,000 vehicles worldwide in the October to December 2009 period, a 20.6 per cent increase over the same period in fiscal year 2008. In the nine-month period to December 2009, net income after tax totalled 54 billion yen, up 25 per cent compared with the previous year and globally, Nissan sold 2,505,000 vehicles.

With its global headquarters in Yokohama, Nissan's 224,000 employees, including those acquired when they joined forces with Renault in 1999, work out of regional headquarters, technical and design centres, holding companies, holding and leasing entities all over the world, including one in Russia opened in 2010. One element of the company's success can be traced back to 1985 when the company decided to enter the luxury market segment, dominated by German manufacturers, Audi, BMW and Mercedes. In November 1989 when Nissan was able to launch its new brand, Infiniti, into the US market Japanese rivals Toyota and Honda were already there with their own luxury brands, Lexus and Acura.

Infiniti's market entry was not a success. Their initial advertising campaign using a controversial strategy that involved not actually showing the car was generally viewed a failure. By the late 1990s Infiniti was trailing behind Lexus and Acura in sales and the company as a whole was struggling financially. A major rethink led to the creation of the G35, a sports sedan far exceeding the capabilities of its Nissan Primera-based predecessor (the G20), which became an instant hit and was named Motor Trend Car of the Year in 2003. Also by 2003 the company was establishing a reputation for reliability. That year, while Lexus was the highest-ranking brand in the JD Power and Associates vehicle dependability study, Nissan Motor Co's Infiniti brand was right behind.

By 2008 Infiniti's global operations had grown to include Mexico, the Middle East, South Korea, Taiwan, Russia, China and Ukraine, with more than 230 dealers in 15 countries. At the Geneva Motor Show 2008, Nissan unveiled plans to launch Infiniti in Europe; starting in the autumn of 2008 and phased over a two-year period some 21 European countries would get Infiniti dealer networks, managed from their Europe headquarters based in Rolle, Switzerland.

The company acknowledges it is in for a tough ride in Europe, where the three German manufacturers, BMW, Audi and Mercedes hold 80 per cent of what is now a shrinking market. The market size of this segment has halved to just 2.8 per cent and some big players, Ford and GM in particular, have given up on luxury, offloading Aston Martin and Saab respectively, both well-established and respected brands. Infiniti's strategy is to increase the image of luxury and design. They have added Infiniti's state-of-the-art Connectiviti+ technology package providing a fully integrated navigation, communication and entertainment system including an 11-speaker Bose® Premium Sound System, the Michelin Guide, full iPod connectivity and a 10GB music box with Gracenotes database and a unique Around View Monitor. The goal is to wow would-be Porche Cayenne buyers with a range of in-cabin goodies.

Global Insight, a forecasting service, predicted that sales of luxury cars will never recover, projecting a 3.6 per cent market share in 2013 at about 16 million vehicles. Nevertheless, Infiniti's Europe marketing director Bastien Schupp believed that he could double the company's 2,500 sales in the European market over the coming year or two. His confidence was amply rewarded. Automotive News Europe reported on 27 December 2012 that they had sold 12,500 vehicles in Europe in the preceding year and Renault-Nissan CEO Carlo Ghosn had set a target for Infiniti to boost annual sales in Europe, including Turkey and Russia, to 100,000 vehicles by 2016. To cement this goal Infiniti appointed Johan de Nysschen as President in July 2012. He led Audi in North America, taking Audi's share of the US luxury market to 9.5 per cent, up from 5.3 per cent in 2004. Infiniti's latest figures posted a 13 per cent sales increase to March 2014 and in March 2015 25,000m^2 of new Infiniti production space was opened in Sunderland.

Specifiers, users and customers

When analysing market segments it is important to keep in mind that there are at least three major categories of people who have a role to play in the buying decisions and so whose needs have to be considered in any analysis of a market:

- The user, or end customer, will be the recipient of any final benefits associated with the product.
- The specifier will want to be sure the end users' needs are met in terms of performance, delivery and any other important parameters. Their 'customer' is both the end user and the budget holder of the cost centre concerned. There may even be conflict between the two (or more) 'customer' groups. For example, in the case of, say, hotel toiletries those responsible for marketing the rooms will want high-quality products to enhance their offer, while the hotel manager will have cost issues close to the top of their concerns and the people responsible for actually putting the product in place will be interested only in any handling and packaging issues.
- The non-consuming buyer, the person who places the order, also has individual needs. Some of their needs are similar to those of a specifier except they will have price at or near the top of their needs. A particular category here would be those buying gifts. Once again their needs and those of the recipient may be dissimilar. For example those buying gifts are as concerned with packaging as with content. Watches, pens, perfumes and fine wines are all gifts whose packaging is paramount at the point of purchase. Yet for the user they are often things to be immediately discarded.

Branding

This is considered the holy grail of the product/service aspect of the marketing mix. A brand encompasses not just what a product is or does but all the elements such as logo, symbols, image, reputation and associations. The McDonald's arches represent its brand as a welcoming beacon drawing customers in. Branding is an intangible way of differentiating a product in a way that captures and retains markets through loyalty to that brand. Coca-Cola tastes little different from a supermarket brand, but the promotion that supports the brand confers on the consumer the chance to share the attractive life style of those 'cool' people in the adverts. Apple's iPod is differentiated from just any old MP3 player in much the same way. Intel and Audi are examples of branding designed to reassure consumers in unfamiliar territory that a product will deliver. Body Shop International exudes ethics and concern for the environment, where other cosmetics concentrate on how they will make the wearer look beautiful.

Building a brand takes time and a considerable advertising budget to build. But by creating brand value – that is the price premium commanded by that product over its unbranded or less appealing competitors – a business can end up with a valuable asset. International businesses have dominated the branding world, moving rapidly up the rankings. Tencent, the Chinese social network and Internet portal, led the list of fastest risers so becoming the 14th most valuable global brand and overtaking China Mobile as China's most valuable brand. That puts it ahead of Walmart, Disney and BMW in terms of brand value. The prevalence of valuable brands outside of Europe and the United States has led to BrandZ, a leading brand research company, producing alongside its top 100 world brands, the top 100 Chinese brands and a top 50 for both India and Latin America (**www.millwardbrown. com/mb-global/brand-strategy/brand-equity/brandz**).

Superbrands (**www.superbrands.com**) has a listing of the top brands by country, often with a case study supporting the top brands in any country.

Branding in the Internet

When they work, brands provide benefits for both consumers and suppliers. Customers like brands because it saves them spending time finding out about the features and benefits of all the products and services they buy. A familiar brand reassures the customer that the product or service has certain qualities. The theory then is that the customer is willing to pay a premium for this reassurance. That, then, is the benefit that a supplier could expect. Unfortunately, the theory of brands is proving harder to transpose to the Internet than many hoped. The problem is that 'service' brands, which are really what you will be trying to establish via the Internet, are for the most part invisible. This in turn makes it hard for an Internet brand to deliver one other major benefit consumers hope to get from a brand; the admiration and perhaps even the envy of their peers. The logo on a tee shirt or pair of trainers, clearly marked for all to see, is, for some consumers, the most important value of the transaction. But all the Internet firm may do is deliver a service that no one else can see. Even where a tangible product is delivered, such as a book or record, for example, it will not be obvious to the onlooker who your Internet supplier was. A further problem for the e-business is that information on a competitor's offer is only a click away, making customers even more fickle than ever and much more likely to compare prices each time they make a purchase.

CASE STUDY Amazon.com

On 29th January 2015 Greg Besinger in the *Wall Street Journal* reported on Amazon's results that 'Amazon typically has satisfied investors with rapidly growing sales and investments, even at the expense of profits', going on to note that even when reporting its largest loss since 2000, 'shares rose sharply in after-hours trading, at one point up 14 per cent.' The logic behind the shareholders' euphoria was that sales reached $89 billion, whilst conveniently overlooking the fact that operating expenses at $88.8 billion were a fifth higher.'

Amazon entered the BrandZ™ Global Top 10 for the first time, with a 41 per cent brand value increase to $64.3 billion. For a business that was only started in 1996 and very nearly didn't get off the ground at all that's still quite an achievement. Jeff Bezos, Amazon.com's founder, came up with the idea for selling books online while he was working as a senior vice president of DE Shaw, a New York-based investment management firm charged with coming up with profitable ideas for selling over the Internet. Bezos concluded that online book selling would be a good business because two of the US's largest book distributors already had electronic lists.

Bezos realised that no single bookstore could carry a comprehensive inventory of the books in print. The distributors who carried thousands of titles acted as the warehouse for most stores, particularly smaller booksellers. When customers asked a store for a book it did not have in stock, they filled the customer's order through one of the two largest distributors – Ingram or Baker & Taylor. These companies' inventory lists were digitized in the late 1980s. The online inventory lists would enable Bezos to offer books online through the company he envisioned creating.

Bezos' firm was not willing to invest in the idea. Bezos and his wife then drove across country to Seattle to start the company. Bezos typed the business plan on his computer while his wife drove. Bezos recruited one of the programmers he had met through his investigations for DE Shaw, Shel Kaphan, to become his first employee. Kaphan and a contractor named Paul Barton-Davis built a prototype of the Amazon.com website in a converted garage of a rented home in Bellevue, Washington. Bezos raised the first $1 million of seed capital from 15 wealthy individual investors.

The naming of Amazon.com was based on the importance of its relative size. Bezos reasoned that the Amazon River was ten times as large as the next largest river, which was the Mississippi, in terms of volume of water, and Amazon.com had six times as many titles as the world's largest physical bookstore. Bezos realized early on that not all activities should be conducted online. For example, Bezos decided that Amazon.com should own its own warehouses, so that it could maintain quality control over the packaging and shipping of orders, which he saw as an opportunity to enhance the Amazon.com customer experience and so cement brand value.

Bezos also focused on ways to enhance Amazon.com customers' experiences. He altered the website to make it easier to understand, streamlining the ordering process and responding immediately to each customer question. As Bezos noted, Amazon.com wants people to feel as though they are visiting a place rather than a software application. The heart of the Amazon.com brand proposition is convenient, low-priced, efficient, personalized, and customer-service friendly.

From books Amazon has diversified so as to keep it at the forefront of the online shopping industry and is the first port of call for almost any product. Its reach has been extended by partnerships, collaboration and affiliation with thousands of other companies. Recently it has extended its offer to include a 'Universal Wish List' browser button so you can add items from any website to your Amazon Wish List to keep the product in mind for later purchase. This in effect means that wherever customers are shopping on the web if they are undecided there is always a route back to the Amazon site.

Amazon.com has a brand advantage over physical retail outlets such as Auchan, Tesco and Wal-Mart, other firms with a creditable rating in the top 100 global brands, for several key reasons. Not having the overhead of a physical retail space allows it to excel at competitive pricing. It more than compensates for the lack of in-store customer service by supplying extensive product information, customer ratings and reviews online. And it achieves global reach without a costly, risky roll-out plan of physical storefronts. Amazon.com includes international sites in the United States, UK, Germany, Canada, Japan, France and China.

Amazon.com's customer service continues until the package is in your hands, and their speed of delivery is unsurpassed. Orders can be tracked every inch of the way and their returns process is simple, automated and reliable. This level of service is extended across all products supplied by affiliates, too.

Bezos sustained the Amazon brand through powerful marketing from the outset. Of the $11 million second-round finance he raised from Silicon Valley venture capitalists $8 million went into advertising and marketing. Since then, however, Amazon has stopped big spend advertising on television. This followed a 15-month-long test of TV advertising in two markets – Portland, Oregon, and Minneapolis – to see how much it drove their sales. It worked out that they got more bangs for their buck by investing that money into lower product prices and free shipping, which have significantly accelerated business growth.

Amazon used to put 70 per cent of its energy into shouting about its service and 30 per cent into actually making it great. Bezos believes that sustaining a global internet brand will in future mean inverting that ratio.

Market research

The purpose of market research is to ensure you have sufficient information on customers, competitors and markets so that you can be reasonably confident enough that people want to buy what you want to sell at a price that will give you a viable business proposition.

You do not have to launch a product or enter a market to prove there are no customers for your goods or services; frequently even some modest market research beforehand can give clear guidance as to whether your venture will succeed or not.

Athough big businesses may employ market research agencies to design and execute their research an MBA should both understand the process and be able to carry out elementary research themselves quickly and on a low budget.

The fundamental goals of market research

The purpose of market research from an MBA's perspective is twofold:

1 To build credibility for a business proposition; the MBA must demonstrate first to his or her own satisfaction, and later to their colleagues, superiors and eventually to financiers, a thorough understanding of the marketplace for the new product, service or strategy. This will be vital if resources are to be attracted to execute the proposal.

2 To develop a realistic market entry strategy for the proposed course of action, based on a clear understanding of genuine customer needs and ensuring that product quality, price, promotional methods and the distribution chain are mutually supportive and clearly focused on target customers.

You will need to research in particular:

- Your customers – Who will buy your goods and services? What particular customer needs will your business meet? How many of them are there?

- Your competitors – Which established companies are already meeting the needs of your potential customers? What are their strengths and weaknesses?

- Your product or service – How should it be tailored to meet customer needs?

- What price should you charge to be perceived as giving value for money?

- What promotional material is needed to reach customers; which newspapers, journals do they read?

- Whether or not your operational base is satisfactorily located to reach your customers most easily, at minimum cost.

Seven steps to successful market research

Researching the market need not be a complex process, nor need it be very expensive. The amount of effort and expenditure needs to be related in some way to the costs and risks associated with the proposition. The market research needs to be conducted systematically following these seven stages:

1 Formulate the problem: Before embarking on your market research you should first set clear and precise objectives, rather than just setting out to find interesting general information about the market.

So, for example, if you are planning on selling to young fashion-conscious women, among others, your research objective could be: to find out how many women aged 18 to 28, with an income of over £35,000 a year, live or work within your catchment area. That would give you some idea whether the market could support a venture such as this.

2 Determine the information needs: Knowing the size of the market, in the example given above, may require several different pieces of information. For example, you would need to know the size of the resident population, which might be fairly easy to find out, but you might also want to know something about people who come into the catchment area to work or stay on holiday or for any other major purpose. There might, for example, be a hospital, library, railway station or school nearby that also pulls potential customers to that particular area.

3 Where can you get the information? This will involve either desk research in libraries or on the Internet, or field research, which you can do yourself or get help in doing. Some of the most important of these areas are covered below.

Field research, that is getting out and asking questions yourself, is the most fruitful way of gathering original information that can provide competitive advantage.

4 Decide the budget: Market research will not be free even if you do it yourself. At the very least there will be your time. There may well be the cost of journals, phone calls, letters and field visits to plan for. At the top of the scale could be the costs of employing a professional market research firm.

Starting at this end of the scale, a business-to-business survey comprising 200 interviews with executives responsible for office-equipment purchasing decisions cost one company £12,000. Twenty in-depth interviews with consumers who are regular users of certain banking services cost £8,000. Using the Internet for web surveys is another possibility, but that can impose too much of your agenda onto the recipients and turn them away from you.

Check out companies such as Free Online Surveys (**http:// free-online-surveys.co.uk**) and Zoomerang (**www.zoomerang.com**) who provide software that lets you carry out online surveys and analyse the data quickly. Most of these organizations offer free trials.

Doing the research yourself may save costs but may limit the objectivity of the research. If time is your scarcest commodity, it may make more sense to get an outside agency to do the work. Using a reference librarian or university student to do some of the spadework need not be prohibitively expensive. Another argument for getting professional research is that it may carry more clout with investors.

Whatever the cost of research, you need to assess its value to you when you are setting your budget. If getting it wrong would cost £100,000, then £5,000 spent on market research might be a good investment.

5 Select the research technique: If you cannot find the data you require from desk research, you will need to go out and find the data yourself. The options for such research are described later in this section, under 'Field research'.

6 Construct the research sample population: It is rarely possible or even desirable to include every possible customer or competitor in your research. Instead you would select a sample of people who represent the whole population being surveyed. You need to take care and ensure you have included the Innovator and Early Adopter segments in your research sample. These will be discussed later, in Chapter 4, but they are particularly important to Internet and other highly innovative product categories of firm, whose entire first year's sales could be confined to these groups.

The accuracy of your survey will increase with the sample size. This subject is discussed in Chapter 12.

7 Process and analyse the data: The raw market research data needs to be analysed and turned into information to guide your decisions on price, promotion and location, and the shape, design and scope of the product or service itself.

Desk (or secondary) research

The business world is awash with information on almost every aspect of business, covering everything from what people buy, why and when they buy and how satisfied they are with their purchase. The challenge for an MBA is how to tap into that information. These are the essential starting points.

Libraries

Aside from visiting a library you can identify what information is available in your local library without scouring the shelves. WorldCat (**www.worldcat.org**) claims with some justification to be the world's largest network of library content and services, letting you search the collections of libraries in your community and thousands more around the world. Entering the term 'market research' into the site's search pane yielded over 1.1 million sources in barely half a second with some 100,000 of those in a downloadable format. Narrowing that down to 'sources of marketing information' delivers 114,000 items, with 5,000 in a downloadable format. WorldCat results often include a direct link to the 'Ask a Librarian' help feature of a library's website. You have to be a member of that library to use that resource.

Major country national libraries often have dedicated business research resources. For example the British Library has a Business and IP Centre (**www.bl.uk/bipc/#**) where they have put together workshops such as 'Beginners Guide to Business Information' and 'Qualitative and Quantitative Research' as well as links to organizations to help you make the most of market research. Courses here range from free to around £25.

Business Insider has a directory of the greatest libraries (**http://uk.businessinsider.com/18-of-the-worlds-greatest-libraries-2014-12**).

Online Newspapers

Online Newspapers (**www.onlinenewspapers.com**). Newspapers and magazines are a source of considerable information on companies, markets and products in that sphere of interest. Virtually every online newspaper in the world is listed here. You can search straight from the homepage, either by continent or country. You can also find the 50 most popular online newspapers from a link in the top centre of the homepage. There is also a separate site for online magazines (**www.onlinenewspapers.com/SiteMap/magazines-sitemap.htm**).

Using the internet

The internet is a rich source of market data, much of it free and immediately available. But you can't always be certain that the information is reliable or free of bias, as it can be difficult if not impossible to always work out who exactly is providing it. That being said, you can get some valuable pointers as to whether or not what you plan to sell has a market, how big that market is and who else trades in that space. The following sources should be your starting point:

- Google Trends (**www.google.com/Trends**) provides a snapshot on what the world is most interested in at any one moment. For example, if you are thinking of researching the restaurant market, entering that into the search pane produces a snazzy graph showing how interest measured by the number of searches is growing (or contracting) since January 2004 when they started collecting the data.

- Google News (**www.google.com**), which you can tap into by selecting 'News' on the horizontal menu at the top of the page under the Google banner. Here you will find links to any newspaper article anywhere in the world covering a particular topic over the past decade or so listed by year. Asking for information on baby clothes will reveal recent articles on how much the average family spends on baby clothes, the launch of a thrift store specializing in second-hand baby clothes and the launch of an organic baby clothes catalogue.

Harvard has a useful guide to using web information. (**http://usingsources. fas.harvard.edu/icb/icb.do** > Evaluating Sources > Evaluating Web Sources)

Field research

Field research, also known as primary research, is the activities associated with generating specific and timely information relating directly to those business issues and problems being addressed by an organization at a particular time. Most fieldwork carried out consists of interviews, with the interviewer putting questions to a respondent. The more popular forms of interview are currently:

- personal (face-to-face) interview: 45 per cent (especially for the consumer markets);
- telephone, e-mail and web surveys: 42 per cent (especially for surveying companies);
- post: 6 per cent (especially for industrial markets);
- test and discussion group: 7 per cent.

Personal interviews, web surveys and postal surveys are clearly less expensive than getting together panels of interested parties or using expensive telephone time. Telephone interviewing requires a very positive attitude, courtesy, an ability not to talk too quickly and listening while sticking to a rigid questionnaire. Low response rates on postal services (less than 10 per cent is normal) can be improved by accompanying letters explaining the questionnaire's purpose and why respondents should reply, by offering rewards for completed questionnaires (small gift), by sending reminder letters and, of course, by providing pre-paid reply envelopes. Personally addressed e-mail questionnaires have secured higher response rates – as high as 10–15 per cent – as recipients have a greater tendency to read and respond to e-mail received in their private e-mail boxes. However, unsolicited e-mails ('spam') can cause vehement reactions: the key to success is the same as with postal surveys – the mailing should feature an explanatory letter and incentives for the recipient to 'open' the questionnaire.

There are basic rules for good questionnaire design, however the questions are to be administered:

1 Keep the number of questions to a minimum.

2 Keep the questions simple! Answers should be either 'Yes/No/Don't know' or offer at least four alternatives.

3 Avoid ambiguity – make sure the respondent really understands the question (avoid 'generally', 'usually', 'regularly').

4 Seek factual answers, avoid opinions.

5 Make sure that at the beginning you have a cut-out question to eliminate unsuitable respondents (eg those who never use the product/service).

6 At the end, make sure you have an identifying question to show the cross-section of respondents.

Sample size is vital if reliance is to be placed on survey data. How to calculate the appropriate sample size is explained in Chapter 12 in the section headed 'Surveys and sample size'.

Testing the market

The ultimate form of market research is to find some real customers to buy and use your product or service before you spend too much time and money in setting up. The ideal way to do this is to sell into a limited area or small section of your market. In that way if things don't quite work out as you expect you won't have upset too many people.

This may involve buying in a small quantity of product as you need to fulfil the order in order to fully test your ideas. Once you have found a small number of people who are happy with your product, price, delivery/execution and have paid up then you can proceed with a bit more confidence than if all your ideas are just on paper.

On the international scene it is usual for a company to trial new products and services in one market, often though not always their home market, before going for a wider launch. Amazon tested AmazonFresh, offering free same-day and early morning delivery on orders over $50 including thousands of Amazon items, fresh grocery and local products in its hometown of Seattle for five years, using its own fleet of trucks, before moving further afield. They took the same approach with their colour tablet, selling it exclusively in North America for over a year before crossing the Atlantic. Amazon is now planning to expand its grocery business outside Seattle.

Online video courses and lectures

Business Strategy: Professor Carlo Alberto Carnevale Maffe of SDA Bocconi School of Management, Milan: **www.youtube.com/watch?v=a_1O-3xhKm4**

The Five Competitive Forces That Shape Strategy: Professor Michael Porter, interviewed for the Harvard Business Review: **www.youtube.com/watch?v=mYF2_FBCvXw**

How to Build a Strategy for 'the Long Game': Paul Schoemaker, research director for Wharton's Mack Institute for Innovation Management: **http://knowledge.wharton.upenn.edu/article/how-to-build-a-strategy-for-the-long-game**

The Importance of Urgency: Professor John Kotter, Harvard Business: **http://freevideolectures.com/Course/2526/Strategy/7**

Introduction to Strategic Management, by Professor David Kryscynski of Goizueta Business School, Emory University, Atlanta, Georgia: **www.youtube.com/watch?v=rJ2tmqRkiCM**

Porter's Five Forces of Analysis: How to Determine the Attractiveness of an Industry: Alanis Business Academy: **www.youtube.com/watch?v=uvwjip3CTMA**

Transforming Giants: Professor Rosabeth MossKanter, Harvard Business: **http://freevideolectures.com/Course/2526/Strategy/8**

What is strategy? Professor Michael Porter of Harvard University's School of Business discusses competitive strategy at UNC-Chapel Hill: **www.youtube.com/watch?v=KvYwKM5bY0s**

Online video case studies

Airbnb: Nathan Blecharczyk – CTO and Co-founder talks about their strategy to reach customers located in 192 different countries: **www.akamai.com/html/customers/testimonials/airbnb.html**

Apple's acquisition strategy: CNBC's Josh Lipton and USA Today San Francisco Bureau Chief Jon Swartz discuss what Apple's acquisition plans say about its hardware business: **http://video.cnbc.com/gallery/?video=3000296348**

Building a Global Brand, One Banjo at a Time: Greg Deering, founder talks about his company's 38-year history from a small family-owned business to a global leader in banjo sales at USD School of Business Administration: **www.youtube.com/watch?v=Ba6L7PiH0rk**

Discovery Communications: John Hendricks, founder talks to Inc about avoiding 'brand drift' while growing into an international, multi-channel business: **www.inc.com/lewis-schiff/john-hendricks-discovery-building-global-brand.html**

Patrón Spirits International: John McDonnell, COO explains to Harvard Business Review how his company grew beyond the domestic market: **https://hbr.org/2013/02/building-a-global-brand.html**

Southwest Airlines: Strategy Genius or Common Sense? (**https://www.youtube.com/watch?v=Szn-TbvEL2I**) and Colleen Barrett, Southwest Airlines president at the Wharton Leadership Conference on how the airline has posted profits for 35 consecutive years: **www.youtube.com/watch?v=6TgR95vnM0c**

Trouble at Tesco Documentary 2015. Panorama: **www.youtube.com/watch?v=JlubbsWNmnY**

Why hate Ryanair? Panorama: **www.youtube.com/watch?v=JkD3JDzj33Y**

4 International marketing strategy

- Mixing markets.
- Defining products and services.
- Understanding promotion and distribution.
- Getting the measure of the price/quality equation.
- Marketing on the Internet.
- Marketing mix
- Social media

Business schools didn't invent marketing but they certainly ensured its pre-eminence as both an academic and practitioners' discipline. *Principles of Marketing* and *Marketing Management*, seminal books on the subject by Philip Kotler (*et al*) of Kellogg School of Management at Northwestern University have been core reading on management programmes the world over for decades. Kotler's books have been written with an international audience in mind as his co-authoring team straddle several key cultural areas. The school's marketing department has rated at the top in all national and international ranking surveys conducted during the past 15 years, knocking Harvard and Wharton into 2nd and 3rd place respectively in 2015.

Extending the marketing concept to the international arena has attracted a prolific range of academics, too. Professor Capon, the RC Kopf Professor of International Marketing at Columbia Business School in New York, who has also served as a Visiting Professor at INSEAD (Fontainebleau, France), The Hong Kong University of Science and Technology, and the China Europe International Business School (CEIBS) (Shanghai) and is the Distinguished

Visiting Professor at Manchester Business School (Great Britain) is at the forefront of thinking in the field.

Marketing, whether international or parochial, is defined as the process that ensures the right products and services get to the right markets at the right time and at the right price. The devil in that sentence lies in the use of the word 'right'. The deal has to work for the customer because if they don't want what you have to offer the game is over before you begin. You have to offer value and satisfaction otherwise people will either choose an apparently superior competitor, or if they do buy from you and are dissatisfied they won't buy again. Worse still they may bad-mouth you to a whole mass of other people. For you, the marketer, being right means there has to be enough people wanting your product or service to make the venture profitable; and ideally those numbers should be getting bigger rather than smaller.

So, inevitably, marketing is something of a voyage of discovery for both supplier and consumer from which both parties learn something and, hopefully, improve. The boundaries of marketing stretch back from inside the mind of the customer, perhaps uncovering emotions they were themselves barely aware of, out to the logistic support systems that get the product or service into customers' hands. Each part of the value chain from company to consumer has the potential to add value or kill the deal. For example, at the heart of the Amazon business proposition are a superlatively efficient warehousing and delivery system and a simple zero-cost way for customers to return products they don't want and get immediate refunds. These factors are as important as elements of Amazon's marketing strategy as are its product range, website structure, Google placement and its competitive pricing (see Amazon case study in Chapter 3).

Marketing is also a circuitous activity. As you explore the topics below you will see that you need the answers to some questions before you can move on, and indeed once you have some answers you may have to go back a step to review an earlier stage. For example, your opinion as to the size of the relevant market may be influenced by the results achieved when you segment the market and assess your competitive position.

The marketing mix

Marketing mix refers to the mix of ingredients with which marketing strategy can be developed and implemented. The ingredients, originally referred to as the 4Ps are; price, product (or/and service), promotion and place. This is now extended to 7Ps, adding people, process and physical evidence to accommodate the increasing emphasis on customer focus in business. Just as with cooking, taking the same or similar ingredients in different proportions can result in very different 'products'. The ingredients in the marketing mix represent only the elements that are largely, though not entirely, within a firm's control. Uncontrollable ingredients include the state of the economy, changes in legislation, new and powerful market entrants and rapid changes in technology.

Origins

The term 'marketing mix' has a pedigree going back to the late 1940s when marketing managers referred to mixing ingredients to create strategies. James W Coulton, a Harvard Business School professor, made the earliest recorded reference to the term 'mix' in this context in an article, 'The management of marketing costs' (Division of Research, Graduate School of Business Administration, Harvard University, 1948). In this study of manufacturers' marketing costs Coulton described the business executive as a 'decider, an artist – a mixer of ingredients, who sometimes follows a recipe prepared by others, sometimes prepares his own recipe as he goes along, sometimes adapts a recipe to the ingredients immediately available, and sometimes experiments with or invents ingredients no one else has tried.'

A Harvard colleague of Coulton, Neil Borden, liked his idea of calling a marketing executive a 'mixer of ingredients', one who is constantly engaged in fashioning creatively a mix of marketing procedures and policies in his efforts to produce a profitable enterprise. He introduced the term 'marketing mix' in his 1953 American Marketing Association Presidential Address, and went on to summarize his ideas on how to use the concept in 1964 in his paper, 'The concept of the marketing mix' (*Journal of Advertising Research*, 4 (2), pp 2–7).

By the time Borden's work was published a rash of academics had arrived on the scene. Verdoorn, P J (1956) 'Marketing from the producer's point of view' (*Journal of Marketing*, 20 (January), pp 221–35) and Frey, Albert W (1956) 'The effective marketing mix: programming for optimum results' (Hanover, NH: The Amos Tuck School, Dartmouth College) were just two of the many influential works on the subject.

Early proponents of the marketing mix advanced a variety of checklists of decision variables, given a variety of different forms. It was down to a relative latecomer, E Jerome McCarthy, a marketing professor at Michigan State University to coin the expression, the four Ps: product, price, place and promotion – which became the most popular. In his 1960 book, *Basic Marketing: A managerial approach* (Homewood, IL: Richard D Irwin), McCarthy suggested that 'it is useful to reduce the number of variables in the marketing mix to four basic ones – Product, Place, Promotion, Price.'

Mary Jo Bitner (Arizona State University) and Bernard H Booms (Washington State University) in a 1981 paper (Marketing strategies and organization structures for service firms, in Donnelly, J H and George, W R (eds) *Marketing of Services*, Chicago: American Marketing Association) modified and expanded the traditional marketing mix elements from 4Ps to become 7Ps by adding three new Ps – people, process and physical evidence. The authors had in mind the unique problems in marketing intangible services; however, as almost every 'product' has a major service element, the 7Ps have been adopted in mainstream marketing mix analysis.

Using the Marketing Mix

A change in the way the elements in the marketing mix are put together can produce an offering tailored to meet the needs of a specific market segment. For example, a hardback book is barely more expensive to produce than a paperback. However, with a bit of clever publicity, bringing a hardback out a few weeks before the paperback edition, and a hefty price hike, an air of exclusivity can be created which satisfies a particular group of customers. A similar effect can be achieved by carefully timing the launch of an e-version (Kindle *et al*), shortly after the paper version.

In the e-business world the same rules apply. You can take almost any business proposition and change the ingredients in the marketing mix to appeal more specifically to one of the target **market segments** you have identified as being worth pursuing. Take an online share-dealing business, for example. Their key market segments may include such diverse groups of clients as day traders, novice share clubs and sophisticated private investors. The company's core 'product', which consists of providing information to enable investors to make choices and so place orders, can be altered along with other elements of the marketing mix, to appeal more to a certain segment.

Using the marketing mix successfully in your organization can help your organization to:

- Get a better fit between your product service offer and your customer segment's requirements. Often organizations spend more time looking in than out. As a consequence much of what they do is to meet their needs rather than those of the customers. Using the elements of the marketing mix to produce a product or service that delivers more value at the same or a lower cost is a key benefit that arises from analysing your marketing.

- Make more profit. It follows that if you are better at meeting a particular customer segment's needs through changing elements in the marketing mix you should be able to command a better price or capture a larger market share.

- Improve the efficiency of your marketing efforts. Analysing the elements of the marketing mix and the extent to which they matter to your customers will help improve the way you deal with your customers. If, like the example with IBM, your customers want a price quote faster than you currently provide, than that is the element of 'price' you need to examine. If certain important customer segments want products in a different size, as with all liquid containers destined for cabin luggage on flights post 9/11 then there is an opportunity to produce toiletries in containers smaller than 100ml.

- Provide new product opportunities. British American Tobacco (BAT), the world's second-biggest tobacco company, saw its sales slump to 332 billion cigarettes in the first half of 2013, against 344 billion in the first half of 2012, as mature markets proved less lucrative. The company, which owns Lucky Strike, Dunhill, Kent and Pall Mall, revealed revenues of £7.57 billion in the first half of 2013, up 2 per cent on last year and pre-tax profits were up slightly too. Smokers were paying on average 7 per cent more for cigarettes than a year ago, due in part to price increases and to consumers upgrading to premium brands. They decided on an aggressive expansion of their nascent electronic cigarettes business in an effort to counter declining sales, using some of their profits from conventional cigarette sales. In August 2013 BAT started selling its Vype e-cigarette brand over the internet in Britain with a roll out to other European countries and the United States scheduled to follow soon after. Kingsley Wheaton, BAT's director of corporate affairs announced it to be their 'declared intent to be the leading player in that business. The market is currently small and fragmented but showing movement, creating a buzz.'

- Develop specific product features. The iPhone 4S is a case in point. Launched in October 2011 and sandwiched between the 4 that came on stream in June 2010 and the 5 that arrived in September 2012. The iPhone 3 was introduced in 2008 so the 4S represented a minor product adjustment to the marketing mix, launched the day before Steve Jobs, Apples co-founder and the inspiration behind Apple's iPhone and a host of other iDevices, died. The new feature introduced in the 4S was a new voice-activated assistant, called 'Siri.'

- Introduce new service options. Service can be one of the quickest and cheapest elements of the marketing mix to change. Live traffic avoidance systems offered by brands such as TomTom (HD Traffic) and Garmin (3D Traffic Live) on their mid-range and high-end sat-navs are examples of how the market leaders keep a healthy distance between themselves and their less nimble competitors.

- Build an optimal distribution strategy. The classic route to market with the birth of the internet was to move from 'bricks to clicks', taking a physical presence and putting the offer online. Amazon and Ocado are relative oddities in going the other way. Another group that are going from online beginnings to a physical presence in their efforts to build the best route to market is Connections Academy. Launched in the United States in 2001 with 400 students, they offered a complete, full-time education online for kindergarten through 12th-grade students. Their target market was those who for reasons of work, health or ability wanted or needed to learn at home rather than in a school setting. However, Connection's Executive Vice President Steven Guttentag, recognizing that though a life saver for some students, it was always going to be a 'drop in the bucket'. Connections had 30,000 of the country's 50 million potential students and could see a total market of two million. Blended learning with online material delivered from a physical premises where students could have PE, lunch and contact time with teachers on school campus was the key to tapping into a much larger market. In 2005 they set up their first school, in 2009 they partnered with an all-boys school in Texas and are now setting up their own blended or hybrid schools, and applying for a hybrid charter.

● Optimize product pricing. Price is the easiest element of the marketing mix to change quickly and can deliver some stunning results in terms of increased sales volume and profit. Booking.com, the hotel booking website, changed its flat commission pricing model to one of bidding for a place on the first page of a destination. Priceline, Bookings.com's parent company saw revenues explode from \$3,084 million in 2010 to \$5,261 million in 2012.

FIGURE 4.1   International marketing mix

	Product	Place	Price	Promotion
North America				
W Europe				
Asia				
E Europe				
Africa				

Products and services

A product or service can be defined as anything offered to a market for acquisition, attention, use or consumption that might satisfy a need or a want. Generally the terms product and service will be used synonymously in this part of this chapter.

Products, and services for that matter, can be offered in different shapes and forms in different geographic areas. Tata, the Indian conglomerate that took over Jaguar and Land Rover, launched its Nano, the 'People's Car' in 2008, in basic form aimed at the local and Chinese markets. Models with air conditioning and a range of extras that would double its price were scheduled for its launch on the European market at a later date. Nissan attacked the market from the opposite end and didn't even offer its Infiniti product range in Europe until a decade after its launch in North America (see case study in Chapter 3).

The bundle that makes up a successful product includes the following physical and service elements:

- **Colour/flavour/odour/touch.** These are the sensory elements, which for cosmetics are vital, but even more prosaic products such as computers can be endowed with additional value by the judicious use of colour.

- **Payment terms.** The use of credit can prove a vital element in a product's 'availability'. Motor vehicle sales slumped during and immediately after the credit crunch due first to the global lack of credit finance and later because of its excessive cost.

- **Specification and functionality.** This describes the functionality of whatever your product is. For example you could not offer a computer for sale without providing details of its memory, processor speeds and so forth. An Internet recruitment business would include details on how it sources candidates, how it interviews and evaluates them and then matches them to job opportunities in the 'specification' of its offer.

- **Features and benefits.** The product or service is what people use, but what they buy are the underlying benefits it confers on them. Business people usually define their products in terms of features. Customers on the other hand are only interested in what it does for them. Compare a Bic with a Parker pen. Basically they perform identical functions when it comes to writing. The Parker also confers intangible benefits such as 'status' on its user. It is for those benefits the customer pays the majority of the price difference, not the relative writing qualities.

- **Design.** This is the element of the product that is the hardest to describe yet in many ways the most tangible to its intended target market. The Apple Mac, for example, promotes both its funky design and its advanced graphics capability. Apple see their product as appealing particularly to creative people who would see value in having something other than a plain PC box on their desk. So they make their product visually distinctive as a way of emphasizing its difference as a product. You need to consider what your product should look like visually and the chances are your website will be the first and main opportunity to do so. We will look at website construction later.

- **Branding.** Usually aligned with design, this involves giving the product or service a distinct identity (see the Toyota case study in this chapter).

- **Quality** is another complex area and is usually seen as one that can be traded off against price. While that may be true to a certain extent, everything you do, within a product range, needs to be of similar quality otherwise your brand will become devalued. Mercedes have small and less expensive cars on the market, but they come up to the same finish quality as the largest cars in their range. Quality on the Internet is as much about the visual elements of your website as its functionality and the way you deal with customer support. A slow response to complaints or cries for help tends to tarnish the image of quality.

- **Packaging** is the wrap around your product. It can be thought of as whatever the customer opens first to get at what they have bought. So again you can see that for many Internet businesses the website performs the function that packaging usually does for a tangible product. Software sold on the Internet but delivered to your door, needs a packaging that protects, informs and gives a sense of value.

- **Guarantee.** This is what gives people comfort that in ordering over the Internet they will get their product and get it on time, that it will do what it says it will do, and if it doesn't perform they will get their money back. Customers also want to feel secure in making their financial transaction online. Buying offline, customers have fewer concerns. Often they can see the product or even try it out. They can go round to the place they bought from and either get help or exchange or return the product.

- **After-sales service.** The whole area of customer support has become one of the most important aspects of any product offering. The virtual nature of the Internet makes customer support an even greater issue for people buying online. By helping your customers get their questions answered quickly and their problems resolved you can build customer loyalty and competitive advantage. As well as having a good online support service of your own, you can pool the expertise and experiences of your other customers.

- **Performance and reliability**. This covers the whole field of the product's or service's ability to sustain its functionality. Failure or usage rates, for example, are a standard feature of many product propositions. Motor tyres are usually affixed with a mileage duration stating how far you can expect to travel on them.

- **Safety.** Customers want to be reassured that the product or service has no unknown harmful side effects – pharmaceutical products are a case in point. Cross-border commercial sale of medicines that don't conform to The United States Federal Food, Drug, and Cosmetic Act (Act) (21 USC section 331) is illegal. They also must have proper labelling that conforms to the FDA's requirements.

- **Availability.** For some products lack of availability is a plus. Mercedes, Morgan and other luxury or specialist motor brands often invite you to 'queue' for a delivery date and perhaps visit the factory and see your car being made. All part of the brand mystique.

But generally, customers, say, for chewing gum, cigarettes or wine, will expect the products to be on the shelf.

- **Delivery.** This covers how the product or service will reach the customer. Many customers, especially those whose entire family is out or working during the day are irritated by those firms who will only indicate that a delivery will be made between 8 am and 6 pm, or at best a half-day within that period, likewise when Amazon changed over to a delivery service that requires customers to sign for receipt of goods. If you are not in at the time, the product delivery has to be rescheduled at best or at worst collected from an often inaccessible office.

The principle tools that marketing managers use to manage product issues follow.

Product categories

There are two broad categories of product or service on offer on the international market.

Consumer products and services

Consumer products, where the buyer and consumer are either the same or closely associated and the entire value proposition in the acquisition process rests with them. Consumer products can be further subdivided as follows:

- Convenience products are mostly frequent purchases bought on a regular basis where availability and price are more important than most other factors. Most food and basic clothing fit into this category.

- Loss leaders and special purchases are products that purport to offer exceptional value and are only available for a limited period of time. Their goal is to tempt customers into a store or onto a website. Sellers need to be sure that they can keep such products distant from their more conventional products so as not to destroy their value.

- Shopping products are those that a customer buys less frequently, paying more attention to brand values and carrying out some research at the minimum to ensure products meet their specification, are reliable and good value for money. Clothing, furniture, computers and hi-fi equipment are all products that fit into this category. Shopping services include such items as insurance or a holiday.

- Speciality products are usually higher-priced goods such as designer clothing, branded watches, cars, furniture and white goods – such as TVs, washing machines, dishwashers – and medical or legal services. Consumers will carry out lots of research to ensure they get the product or service that meets their needs and they will demand strong after-sales support.

Industrial products and services

Industrial or business products are those that are usually bought as part of a process to add value for some future end-consumer. These include:

- Capital items such as equipment, machinery and buildings required as part of a production process. International capital services include such items as: specialist tax advice where important differences exist between countries; corporate finance assistance in raising capital; localized advice acquisitions; and help with securing intellectual property. These are relatively infrequent purchases made usually by the board of directors with specialist staff support, typically those with MBA-type training. All are areas where customs, practice and the law vary greatly around the world.

- Materials, supplies and parts. These are the raw ingredients of the production process, are consumed over relatively short periods of time and as such are a frequent purchase.

- Supplies, services and utilities. These don't usually end up as part of the finished product, though they play a key part in the process. Nothing much could be made and sold, for example, without telephone services or stationery. Internet Service Providers (ISP), advertising agencies and business consultants are all providers of such supply services.

Product/service life cycle

The idea that business products and services have a life cycle as much as any being was first seen in management literature as far back as 1922, when researchers looked back to the growth of the US automobile industry and observed a bell-shape pattern for the sales of individual cars. Over the following four decades various practitioners and researchers adding, substituting and renaming the stages in the life cycle, arrived at the five steps shown in Figure 4.2 and carried out further work. The length of a product's lifetime can be more than a century, as with, say, Oxo, or just weeks or months in the case of fads such as the hula-hoop or Rubik's cube.

Marketing in the international arena adds a further twist in that a product or service can have its life significantly extended as it enters different geographic areas, as Figure 4.2 illustrates.

Stages in the product life cycle

Products typically go through six distinct stages over their life from birth to death, or re-launch if that proves to be a viable marketing strategy:

- Research and development: This stage is typified by cash outlays only and can last decades in the case of medical products down to a few months or even weeks to launch a simple consumer product.

FIGURE 4.2 International product life cycle strategies

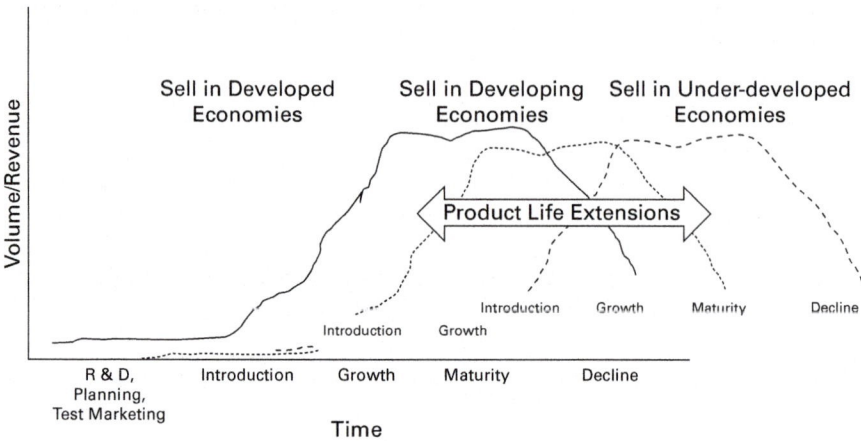

- Introduction: Here the product is brought to market, perhaps just to one initial segment and it may comprise little more than a test marketing activity. Once again costs are high; advertising and selling costs have to be borne up front and sales revenues will be minimum.
- Growth: This stage sees the product sold across the whole range of a company's market segments, gaining market acceptance and becoming profitable.
- Maturity and saturation: Sales peak as the limit of customers' capacity to consume is reached and competitors or substitute products enter the market. Profit starts to tail off as prices drop and advertising is stepped up to beat off competitors.
- Decline: Sales and profits fall away as competition becomes heavy and better and more competitive or technologically advanced products come into the market.

The usefulness of the product life cycle as a marketing tool is as an aid to deciding on the appropriate strategy to adopt. For example, at the introduction stage the goal for advertising and promotion may be to inform and educate; during the growth stage differences need to be stressed to keep competitors at bay; during maturity customers need to be reminded you are still around and it's time to buy again. During decline it's probable that advertising budgets could be cut and prices lowered. As all major costs associated with the product will have been covered at this stage this should still be a profitable stage.

These of course are only examples of possible strategies rather than rules to be followed. For example many products are successfully re-launched during the decline stage by changing an element of the marketing mix or repositioning into a different marketplace. Cigarette manufacturers are responding to declining markets in the developed economies by targeting markets such as Africa and China, even setting up production there and buying up local brands to extend their range of products.

Product range

Being a single-product business is generally considered too dangerous a position except for very small or start-up businesses. The two options to consider are:

- Depth of line. This is the situation when a company has many products within a particular category. Washing powders and breakfast cereals are classic examples of businesses that offer scores of products into the same marketplace. The benefits to the company are that the same channels of distribution and buyers are being used. The weakness is that all these products are subject to similar threats and dangers. However 'deep' your beers and spirits range, for example, you will always face the threat of higher taxes or the opprobrium of those who think you are damaging people's health.
- Breadth of line. This is where a company has a variety of products of different types, such as Marlboro with cigarettes and fashion clothing, or 3M with its extensive variety of adhesives extending out to the Post-it Note.

Product/service adoption cycle – who will buy first?

Customers do not sit and wait for a business to launch new products or enter new markets. Word spreads slowly as the message is diffused throughout the various customer groups. Even then it is noticeable that generally it is the more adventurous types who first buy from a new business. Only after these people have given their seal of approval do the 'followers' come along. Research shows that this adoption process, as it is known, moves through five distinct customer characteristics, from Innovators to Laggards, with the overall population being different for each group (see Table 4.1).

One further issue to keep in mind when shaping your marketing strategy is that Innovators, Early Adopters and all the other sub-segments don't necessarily use the same media, websites, magazines and newspapers or respond to the same images and messages. So they need to be marketed to in very different ways.

Quality

As well as using efficient marketing operation and control procedures an organization has to deliver a quality product or service. Quality in marketing does not carry quite the same meaning as it does in, say, production,

TABLE 4.1   The product/service adoption cycle

Innovators	2.5% of the overall market
Early adopters	13.5% of the overall market
Early majority	34.0% of the overall market
Late majority	34.0% of the overall market
Laggards	16.0% of the overall market
Total market	100%

where it signifies something of a high standard. In marketing quality means that something meets a customer's needs and performs as expected. In other words promises are made and kept. But quality is also part of the efficiency equation too. Quality below standard can lead to high waste, disrupted schedules and lost orders, all factors that directly impact on the marketing side of the enterprise.

The product/quality/price proposition

There are nine strategic marketing options when it comes to positioning a product or service in relation to its quality and price. Any strategy pursued here has to be consistent with the rest of the marketing mix and the individual elements of the product construction. For example, a premium product would be expected to have premium packaging and strong after-sales support. But sometimes companies try to set a high price for a relatively low-quality product; some brands of watches, for example, attempt to occupy this space. They attempt to compensate with excessive and high-quality packaging, but rarely does this achieve either satisfaction or the all-important customer referrals.

Figure 4.3 shows the position of the Tata Nano in terms of its quality price propositions in its home market and in Europe. These are very different and the other elements of the marketing mix need to be adapted to support such a proposition.

Inspection

Frederick W Taylor in his book *The Principles of Scientific Management* stated that one of the clearly defined tasks of management was to ensure that no faulty product left the factory or workshop. This led to a focus on

FIGURE 4.3 The international product, price quality proposition

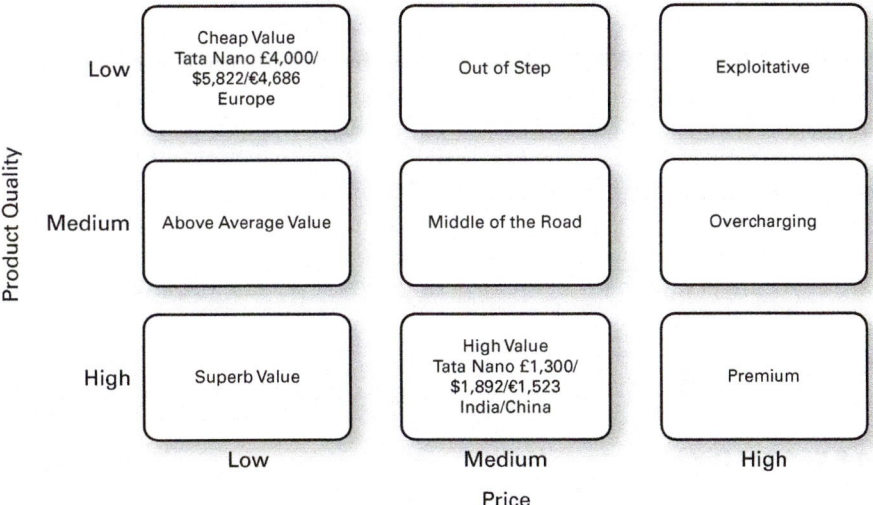

the detection of problems in the product testing of every item to ensure that it complied with product specifications. The task was carried out at the end of the production process using specially trained inspectors. The 'big idea' emerging from this approach was defect prevention as the means to ensure quality control. Inspection still plays a part in modern quality practices, but less as an answer and more as one tool in the toolkit.

The philosophy behind quality

W Edwards Deming (**www.deming.org**), an American statistician and member of the faculty at the New York University Graduate School of Business and Columbia University, where he taught until 10 days before his death in 1993, is considered as the founder of modern quality management. He took the inspection aspect of quality control a stage further with the introduction of statistical probability techniques. His view was that quality should be designed into products and processes and that mass inspection was redundant as statistical sampling that uses control charts will signal when a process is out of control.

Deming is remembered most for his 14-point 'System of Profound Knowledge'. In this he explains that becoming a quality-driven organization requires everyone, starting with top management, 'to fully embrace a new way of thinking that involves seeking the greater good for everyone involved and implementing continuous improvement'. He wanted slogans, targets and numerical targets removed and to emphasize to all employees in the company that if change is to be made and processes are to be continuously improved it's down to them to achieve it. Deming's ideas were adopted enthusiastically by the Japanese, whose economy having been crippled by the Second World War were ready to embrace radical change. It was not until the Japanese motor industry was cutting deep into their home market that US industry woke up to Deming's message on quality. Total Quality Management, Quality Circles and Six Sigma have become buzzwords for variations and extensions of Deming and other pioneers' work on quality. The later term was in use in the 1920s where mathematicians used it as a symbol for a unit of measurement in product quality variation. But it was not until the mid-1980s that engineers in the US company Motorola used 'Six Sigma' first as an informal name – later as a brand – for their initiative aimed at reducing defects in production processes. The name Six Sigma was chosen because mathematically it represents 3.4 parts – or defects – per million, an extremely high level of quality.

CASE STUDY Toyota

In February 2015 Toyota said it expected to post an operating profit of ¥2.7 trillion ($23 billion) in the fiscal year ending in March, up 17.8 per cent from a year earlier. True volume had not grown but as the *Financial Times* quoted Toyota managing officer Takuo Sasaki: 'We made efforts during the strong-yen era to firmly cut costs and improve per-vehicle profitability and as a result, we have built a leaner structure that does not rely on sales increase and the currency.' (*Financial Times*, 4th February 2015). This was a far cry from January 2010, when Toyota announced a recall of up to 1.8 million cars across Europe, including about 220,000 in the UK, following an accelerator problem. At the same time the US Transportation Department opened an investigation into brake problems in a number of Toyota vehicle ranges. Company share price sagged by $25 billion (£15.9 billion) when the news broke. There was nothing especially new in vehicle recalls. GM had recalled nearly 6 million of its cars back in 1981 due to a defective bolt in the front suspension and Ford had pulled in nearly 8 million vehicles in 1996 due to a faulty ignition switch that could catch fire. Ford also recalled 4.5 million cars in 2009; this time it was the cruise control that could potentially overheat and catch fire.

What hit Toyota so badly was that its heritage, strategy and brand value proposition were linked inexorably to product quality. Since 1890 when one Sakichi Toyoda invented a wooden handloom, to which he gave his name, the company has been in the reliability business. In the decades that followed Toyoda added a number of related innovations including the non-stop shuttle change-type automatic loom. In 1929 while on a trip to Europe and the United States, Toyoda transferred the patent rights to his automated loom to the British company Platt

Brothers and began his investigations into the latest product to hit the headlines in the world of mass production, the automobile. By 1933 an automobile department had been established in Toyoda Automatic Loom Works, Ltd and in 1935 Hinode Motors (currently Aichi Toyota) started operations. Vehicles were initially sold under the family name 'Toyoda' and in September 1936 the company ran a competition to design a new logo. Out of nearly 30,000 entries the three Japanese katakana letters for 'Toyoda' in a circle, were chosen. However, Risaburo Toyoda, an adopted son of the founder, preferred a runner up, 'Toyota', because it took eight brush strokes (a fortuitous number) to write in Japanese and was visually simpler. Toyota also helped distance the company from its past association with old-fashioned industries. Since 'Toyoda' literally means 'fertile rice paddies', changing the name also helped to distance the company from associations with old-fashioned farming. The word 'Toyota' was trademarked, the company was registered in August 1937 as the 'Toyota Motor Company' and it began operations in a dedicated facility, the Koromo Plant (currently Honsha Plant).

Toyota Motor Corporation introduced TQC (Total Quality Control) in 1961, and in 1965 were awarded the Deming Application Prize, named after the American quality guru, W Edwards Deming, whose teachings had inspired the company. The Toyota route to product quality is enshrined in their five principles:

- Challenge
- Kaizen (improvement)
- Genchi Genbutsu (go and see)
- Respect
- Teamwork.

Toyota was also an early adopter of 'Lean Manufacturing' and Just In Time Production, both aids to delivering value products of superior quality.

The company's quality problems have, according to Akio Toyoda, the company's current president, been caused by its growth outstripping the speed with which it could develop the appropriate technical expertise. He went on to say that the company's priorities, traditionally ranked as safety, quality and volume, had become confused, with the last moving to a higher position.

In February 2010 when the latest ranking of the world's most valuable brands was published Toyota was still ranked as the top motor brand and tenth overall in the top 500 companies across all industries. Mercedes and BMW were ranked third and second respectively in motor brands. The question now is will the Toyota brand survive the crisis?

Advertising and promotion

Advertising is to some extent an intangible activity, although the bills for it are certainly not. It is, as Lord Bell, formerly of Saatchi & Saatchi, has described it, 'essentially an expensive way for one person to talk to another!'

Advertising and promotion, A&P for short, has been around in a form that would be easily recognizable by today's marketers for nearly four centuries. In 1631 *La Gazette*, a French paper, printed the first classified advertisements and just under 80 years later the world's first magazine, *Tatler* was launched. A&P was mainstream enough by 1841 for Volney B Palmer, the first ad agency, to open their doors in Philadelphia. By 1892 Sears, the US mail order giant, had launched its first direct-marketing campaign, sending out 8,000 handwritten postcards and getting over 2,000 orders for its pains. In 1905 Fatty Arbuckle, a silent movie star, became the first recorded celebrity endorsement, supporting Murad, a cigarette brand, claiming it to be 'the natural preference of cultivated men'.

The business school world was quick to recognize the subject as an important sub-division of marketing and professors of the subject quickly sprang up. CEIBS (China Europe International Business School) recruited Robert F Lauterborn to a visiting chair. He is the James L Knight Chair Professor of Advertising at the University of North Carolina, backed by a million-dollar grant from the Knight Foundation 'to improve the teaching of advertising'. Columbia, Tennessee, Michigan and Ball State Universities all have designated professors in advertising or related fields such as consumer psychology.

A leading French business school, Reims Management School, has gone one step further and appointed a professor to research the promotion of champagne. Major champagne houses, including Moët & Chandon, Veuve Clicquot, Ruinart and Krug (all owned by LVMH), Laurent Perrier, Nicolas Feuillatte and Pommery, have clubbed together to fund the chair.

The mediums used by A&P professionals have expanded exponentially and their relative importance is constantly being influenced by changes in technology.

At the time of writing, print media still had the largest share of advertising spend, while advertising online looked set to overtake TV to become the biggest non-print advertising sector. But just as the pundits were predicting that it was only a matter of time before e-advertising becomes the largest advertising medium, television, by virtue of digital Internet delivery, is making a comeback.

Advertising rules

The answers to these five questions underpin all advertising and promotional strategies:

- What do you want to happen?
- If that happens how much is it worth?

- What message will make it happen?
- What media will work best?
- How will you measure the effectiveness of your effort and expense?

What do you want to happen?

Do you want prospective customers to visit your website; phone, write or e-mail you; return a card; or to send an order in the post? Do you expect them to have an immediate need to which you want them to respond now, or is it that you want them to remember you at some future date when they have a need for whatever it is you are selling?

The more you are able to identify a specific response in terms of orders, visits, phone calls or requests for literature, the better your promotional effort will be tailored to achieve your objective, and the more clearly you will be able to assess the effectiveness of your promotion and its cost versus its yield.

How much is that worth to you?

Once you know what you want a particular promotional activity to achieve, it becomes a little easier to estimate its cost. Suppose a £1,000/$1,468/€1,161 advertisement is expected to generate 100 enquiries for your product. If experience tells you that on average 10 per cent of enquiries result in orders, and your profit margin is £200/$294/€232 per product, then you can expect an extra £2,000/$2,936/€2,936 profit. That 'benefit' is much greater than the cost of the advertisement, so it seems a worthwhile investment. Then with your target in mind decide how much to spend on advertising each month revising that figure in the light of experience.

Deciding the message

Your promotional message must be built around facts about the company and about the product. The stress here is on the word 'fact', and although there may be many types of fact surrounding you and your products, your customers are only interested in two: the facts that influence their buying decisions, and the ways in which your business and its products stand out from the competition.

These facts must be translated into benefits (see also 'Features and benefits' on page 106). There is an assumption sometimes that everyone buys for obvious, logical reasons only, when we all know of innumerable examples showing this is not so. Do people only buy new clothes when the old ones are worn out? Do bosses have desks that are bigger than their subordinates' because they have more papers to put on them?

The message should follow the AIDA formula: get Attention, capture Interest, create Desire and encourage Action.

Choosing the media

Your market research (see Chapter 3) should produce a clear understanding of who comprise your potential customer group, which in turn will provide pointers as to how to reach them. If a consumer already knows what they want to buy and are just looking for a supplier then, according to statistics, around 60 per cent will turn to print, eg Yellow Pages (or similar); 12 per cent will use a search engine; 11 per cent will use telephone directory enquiries; and 7 per cent will use online Yellow Pages. Only 3 per cent will turn to a friend. But if you are trying to persuade consumers to think about buying a product or service at a particular time then a leaflet or flyer may be a better option. Once again it's back to your objectives in advertising. The more explicit they are the easier it will be to choose media.

Above or below the line Advertising media are usually clustered under two headings; above the line and below the line. It has to be said that the line is becoming increasingly indistinct but it is still a term that is part of the lexicon in setting the advertising budget.

Above the line Above the line (ATL) involves using conventional impersonal mass media to promote products and services, talking at the consumer. Major above-the-line techniques include:

- TV, cinema and radio advertising. The vast array of local newspapers, TV channels and digital radio stations can make this a more targeted advertising strategy than has been the case.
- Print advertising in newspapers, magazines, directories and classified ads. Print of all forms has the merit of having a long life so it can be used for handling more complex messages than, say, radio or TV.
- Internet banner ads, which act as a point of entry for a more detailed advert.
- Search engines. Search engine advertising comes in two main forms. PPC (Pay Per Click) is where you buy options on certain key words so that someone searching for a product will see your 'advertisement' to the side of the natural search results. Google, for example, offers a deal where you only pay when someone clicks on your ad and you can set a daily budget stating how much you are prepared to spend, with $5 a day as the starting price.
- Podcasts. This is where Internet users can download sound and video for free and they are now an important part of the e-advertising armoury.
- Posters and billboards.

Below the line Below the line (BTL) talks to the consumer in a more personal way using such media as:

- Direct mail – leaflets, flyers, brochures. Response rates are notoriously low, often less than 1 per cent resulting in sale, but it has the merit of being a proven method of reaching specific targeted market segments.

- Direct e-mail and viral marketing. The latter is the process of creating something so hot the recipients will pass it on to friends and colleagues, creating extra demand as it rolls out. Examples include jokes, games, pictures, quizzes and surveys.

- Sales promotions, including point-of-sale material. Activities carried out in this area include free samples, try before you buy, discounts, coupons, incentives and rebates, contests and special events such as fairs and exhibitions.

- PR (Public Relations). This is about presenting yourself and your business in a favourable light to your various 'publics' – at little or no cost. It is also a more influential method of communication than general advertising – people believe editorials. There may also be times when you have to deal with the press; anything from when you are trying to get attention for a new product, to handling an adverse situation – say, if your product has to be recalled for quality reasons, or worse (see Toyota case study in this chapter).

- Letterheads, stationery and business cards. These are often overlooked in the battle for customer attention, but are in fact often the first and perhaps only way in which a business's image is projected.

- Blogs, where the opinions and experiences of particular groups of people are shared; using online communities such as MySpace, for example is an extension of this idea. Neilson NetRatings reported in 2015 that over 4 billion community sites are viewed every month in the UK alone.

Push or pull Like above or below the line, push and pull are different advertising strategies used for achieving different results. Pull advertising is geared to draw visitors into your net if they are actively looking for your type of product or service. Search engines, listings in on- and offline directories, Yellow Pages and shopping portals are examples here.

Push advertising tries to get the word out to groups of potential customers in the hope that some of them will be considering making a purchase at about that time. Magazines, newspapers, TV, banner ads and direct mail both on- and offline are examples here.

As with above and below the line the distinctions are fast becoming blurred, but the message used in your advertising will be different. With pull there is the assumption that people want to buy, they just need convincing they should buy from you. Push calls for a different message convincing them of their need and desire in the first place.

Measuring results

This is the area most neglected by most advertisers. It is, however, one area in which an MBA can bring their skills to bear with good effect. The key term to keep in mind is ROI (Return on Investment). Although marketers know that they have to advertise, most of them (69 per cent) do not measure it in any way, according to a new study by Forrester Research. But once you have determined your objective and decided how much achieving that is worth, the ROI is just a matter of simple maths. The real problem is that few A&P campaigns start out with measurable goals.

Selling

Marketing is the thinking process behind selling; in other words finding the right people to buy your product or service and making them aware that you are able to meet their needs at a competitive price. But just because customers know you are in the market is not in itself sufficient to make them buy from you. Even if you have a superior product at a competitive price they can escape your net.

Getting customers to sign on the dotted line almost invariably involves selling. This is a process that business people have to use in many situations other than in persuading customers to buy. MBAs have to 'sell' to a bank manager the idea that lending their business money is worthwhile; to share-holders that they should invest; to employees that by working for them they are making a good career move; or to their boss that they should back one of their proposals.

Although essential, selling on its own is an inefficient method of getting potential customers to the point of buying. Understanding the 'Ascending Ladder of Influence', as marketers call it, puts the salesperson's role in perspec-tive. This is a method to rank the 'warm bodies' a customer will encounter in the selling process in the order in which it is most likely to favourably influence your customers. At the top of the scale is the personal recommen-dation of someone whose opinion is trusted and who is known to be unbiased. An example here is the endorsement of an industry expert who is not on the payroll, such as an existing user of the goods or services who is in the same line of business as the prospective customer. Although highly effective, this method is hard to achieve and can be expensive and time consuming. Further down the scale is an approach by you in your role as a salesperson. While you may be seen to be knowledgeable you clearly stand to gain if a sale is made; so you can hardly be unbiased. Sales calls, however they are made, are an expensive way to reach customers, especially if their orders are likely to be small or infrequent.

Pricing strategy

Near-identical commodities, seemingly the most difficult to differentiate in terms of value, in fact can be made to vary dramatically from country to country. Nearly 3 billion cups of coffee are consumed daily, making it the fifth most widely traded commodity in the world. Millions of people depend directly or indirectly on coffee for their livelihoods and according to The World Bank some 95 developing countries out of a total of 141 depend on exports of commodities such as coffee for at least 50 per cent of their total export earnings. The main buyers of raw coffee beans are the largest multinational buyers, dominated by four firms: Nestlé, Kraft, Procter & Gamble and Sara Lee. However, according to Mercer, the HR consulting firm who surveys among other things the cost of living around the globe, a near-identical cup of coffee can cost as little as $1.60 (£1.09/€1.26) in Johannesburg compared to some $6.92 (£4.71/€5.47) in Moscow.

CASE STUDY Hourly Nerds

Rob Biederman, Peter Maglathlin and Patrick Petitti co-founded Hourly Nerd in 2013 whilst finishing off their MBA programme at the Harvard Business School.

The limiting factor in demand from top consultancy practices such as Bain, McKinsey and the Boston Consulting Group is the exorbitant fee structure. Only the biggest organizations with the most serious of issues to address are willing and able to fork out for advice from serious consulting firms. Hourly Nerds, set up by three Harvard MBAs aims to disrupt this market place and change the price/demand curve radically. Essentially Hourly Nerds runs a 'marriage bureau', matching up MBA students from the top 20 business schools with small business in need of some consulting. Quality is assured as these 'consultants' have all been in effect vetted by the universities through their rigorous admissions standards.

The average pay has been $35 an hour, for projects requiring 10 to 15 hours of work. In the first six months more than 500 MBA students and 45 small businesses with projects in mind have registered on the site so far. Hourly Nerd holds the client's money, only paying the student when the project is completed to the small business person's satisfaction.

Their projects include a small Spanish manufacturer whose objective is to enter the US market and needs pricing information and primary research for construction bricks, glazed bricks, klinker bricks and facing bricks. They are paying $2,500 for this work. A small private equity firm has budgeted $5,000 to fully research and collect data in order to write a business plan. An online e-commerce portal for attracting digital content from elite contributors and selling the same to elite niche target audience has set $20,000 aside for this project.

The company has raised $750,000 in a first round of seed capital finance, over half from a business owner who is on record as saying that getting an MBA is 'an absolute waste of time'.

Business schools, as you might expect, take the subject of pricing very seriously; their elevated fee structures confirm this. None more so than at the Wharton School, University of Pennsylvania, where Jagmohan S Raju, a leading authority on competitive pricing strategy resides as Joseph J Aresty Professor. Here students spend the equivalent of four full days systematically studying pricing strategies designed to capture maximum value, under all types of market conditions. These include complex situations such as pricing new products, products with short life cycles, dynamic pricing, and where products and services are bundled together into a single proposition. Professor Raju contrasts the systematic approach he and professors at other business schools take with the ad hoc or trial-and-error approach to pricing taken by most businesses, which his research shows can significantly reduce a firm's bottom line.

For the MBA student pricing straddles a number of academic disciplines. Economics provides the big picture, macro, external overview of factors that affect demand, including the nature of the market/competitive structure the firm faces. Accountancy provides the micro framework for understanding the characteristics of a firm's cost structure, how that changes with changes in volume and consequently how to set target prices to achieve desired profit goals.

Pricing in economic theory

The main economic concept that underpins almost the whole subject of pricing is that of the price elasticity of demand. The concept itself is simple enough. The higher the price of a good or service the less of it you are likely to sell. Obviously it's not quite that simple in practice; the number of buyers, their expectations, preference and ability to pay, the availability of substitute products all have to be taken into account. Figure 4.4 is that of a theoretical demand curve showing the different economic characteristics in different markets.

The figure shows how the volume of sales of a particular good or service will change with changes in price. The elasticity of demand is a measure of the degree to which consumers are sensitive to price. This is calculated by dividing the percentage change in demand by the percentage change in price.

FIGURE 4.4   The demand curve for different international markets

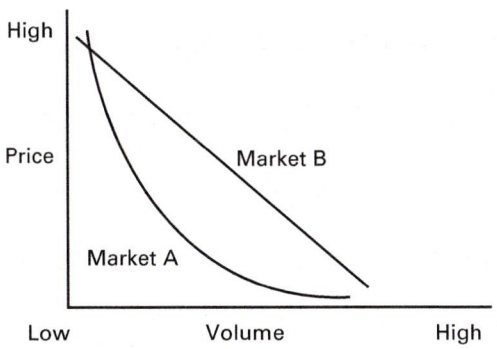

If a price is reduced by 50 per cent (eg from £100 to £50) and the quantity demanded increased by 100 per cent (eg from 1,000 to 2,000), the elasticity of demand coefficient is 2 (100/50). Here the quantity demanded changes by a bigger percentage than the price change so demand is considered to be elastic. Were the demand in this case to rise by only 25 per cent, then the elasticity of demand coefficient would be 0.5 (25/100). Here the demand is described as being 'inelastic' as the percentage demand change is smaller than that of the price change.

Having a feel for elasticity is important in developing a business's marketing strategy, but there is no perfect scientific way to work out what the demand coefficient is; it has to be assessed by 'feel'. Unfortunately the price elasticity changes at different price levels. For example, reducing the price of vodka from £10 to £5 might double sales, but halving it again may not have such a dramatic effect. In fact it could encourage one group of buyers, those giving it as a present for example, to feel that giving something that cheap is rather insulting. The additional twist in international markets is that the elasticity and the demand coefficient will be different in different markets. So reducing or increasing the price will have very different effects from country to country as well as from time to time.

Pricing strategies – the marketing options

Seemingly the simplest of the marketing choices, it is often the most agonizing decision that MBAs are faced with. The subject transcends almost every area of a business. The economists get the ball rolling with ideas around the elasticity of demand. Set too high a price and no one comes to the dance; too low and your sales could go right off the Richter scale, generating plenty of cost but very little profit. The accounts and production teams are concerned that sales will at least be sufficient to reach break even in reasonable time.

The strategists are worried about the signals in terms of corporate positioning that prices can send. However profitable a certain price may be for the business it may just be so low that it devalues other products in your range. Apple, for example, has a position fairly and squarely at the innovator end of the product adoption cycle. Their customers expect to pay high prices for the privilege of being the first users of a new product. The iPod was positioned above the Walkman in price terms, though as the market for pocket sound devices was already mature there was scope to come into the market lower down the price spectrum.

Skim vs penetrate

Two generic pricing strategies need to be decided between before you can fine-tune your plans. Skimming involves setting a price at the high end of what you believe the market will bear. This would be a strategy to pursue if you have a very limited amount of product available for sale and would rather 'ration' than disappoint customers. It is also a way to target the 'innovators' in your market who are happy to pay a premium to be among the first to have a new product. To be successful with this strategy you would need to be sure competitors can't just step in and soak up the demand that you have created. Penetration pricing is the mirror image; prices are set at the low end, while being above your costs. Prices are competitive with the deliberate intention of eliminating your customers' need to shop around. Slogans such as 'everyday low prices' are used to emphasize this policy. The aim here is to grab as much of the market as you can before competitors arrive on the scene and hopefully lock them out. The danger here is that you need a lot of volume either of product or hours sold before you can make a decent profit. This in turn means tying up more money for longer before you break even.

Danger of low pricing

Aside from the obvious possible problems of the cash flow implications of stretching out the break-even horizon and quality/image issues, it is an immutable law that raising prices is a whole lot more difficult than lowering them. It is less of a problem if the market as a whole is moving up, but raising a price because you set it too low in the first place is a challenge, to say the least.

Value pricing

Another consideration when setting your prices is the value of the product or service in the customer's mind. His or her opinion of price may have little or no relation to the cost, and he or she may be ignorant of the price charged by the competition, especially if the product or service is a new one. In fact, many consumers perceive price as a reliable guide to the value they can expect to receive. The more you pay, the more you get. With this in mind, had Dyson launched his revolutionary vacuum cleaner, with its claims of superior performance, at a price below that of its peers, then some potential customers might have questioned those claims. In its literature Dyson cites as the inspiration for the new vacuum cleaner the inferior performance of existing products in the same price band. A product at six times the Dyson price is the one whose performance Dyson seeks to emulate. The image created is that, although the price is at the high end of general run-of-the-mill products, the performance is disproportionately greater. The runaway success of Dyson's vacuum cleaner would tend to endorse this argument.

Real-time pricing

The stock market works by gathering information on supply and demand. If more people want to buy a share than sell it, the price goes up until supply and demand are matched. If the information is perfect (that is, every buyer and seller knows what is going on), the price is optimized. For most businesses this is not a practical proposition. Their customers expect the same price every time for the same product or service – they have no accurate idea what the demand is at any given moment.

However, for businesses selling on the Internet, computer networks have made it possible to see how much consumer demand exists for a given product at any time. Anyone with a point-of-sale till could do the same, but the reports might come in weeks later. This means online companies could change their prices hundreds of times each day, tailoring them to certain circumstances or certain markets, and so improve profits dramatically. Easyjet.com, a budget airline does just this. It prices to fill its planes, and you could pay anything from £30 to £200 (including airport taxes) for the same trip, depending on the demand for that flight. Ryanair and Eurotunnel have similar price ranges based on the basic rule – discounted low fares for early reservations and full fares for desperate late callers!

Internet auction pricing

Once the prerogative of the fine art and antiques markets, auctioning is a fast-growing pricing strategy for a whole host of very different types of business. The theory of auctioning is simple. Have as many interested potential buyers as possible see an item, set a time limit for the transaction to be completed and let them fight it out. The highest bidder wins and in general you can get higher prices than by selling through traditional pricing strategies. eBay was a pioneer in the new auction house sector and is still perhaps the best-known. But there are dozens of other auction houses you can plug into:

Pay what you like pricing

This strategy is based on the auction concept but buyers set their own price. The twist is that there is no limit on supply, so everyone can have one at the price they want to pay. Radiohead, the band, released its seventh album *In Rainbows* in October 2007 as a download on its website where fans could pay what they wished from nothing to £99.99. Estimates by the online survey group comScore indicate that of the 1.2 million visitors to Radiohead's website three out of five downloaders paid nothing; the payers averaged £3 per album so allowing for the freeloaders the band realized £1.11 per album. The band reckon that was more than they would have made in a traditional label deal. In fact the version of the album released in this way was not the definitive one; that was released three months later in CD format debuting at No 1 in the United States and the UK.

Place

'Place' is the fourth 'P' in the marketing mix. This aspect of marketing strategy is about how products and services are actually got into customers' hands. In the online world this is sometimes known as 'the last mile', originally used to describe the final leg of delivering connectivity from a communications provider to a customer, but now used more generally. The whole chain from seller to consumer is itself dynamic and changes to reflect market conditions and a firm's strategy. A case in point is Amazon, who until 2010 had confined its distribution to some 30 state-of-the-art giant fulfilment and warehousing operations stretching from Arizona to Beijing, passing through Ontario, Bedford (UK), Orléans (France) and Leipzig (Germany) en route. At \$50 million a pop these represent a colossal strategic commitment to a particular route to market. Yet in the spring of 2010 Amazon was rumoured to be searching UK high streets for retail outlets. They would only be following a strategy adopted by Argos who claim that nearly a fifth of products bought online are actually collected in store by customers who are either too impatient to wait, or who don't want the hassle of waiting at home to sign for deliveries. Lastminute.com, too, has changed from Internet-only as a route to market and is opening kiosks in train stations to support its late-booking service for hotels, travel and holidays.

On the academic front Martin Christopher, Emeritus Professor of Marketing and Logistics at Cranfield School of Management, is the leading light in the field of logistics and supply chain management. In the United States the Supply Chain & Logistics Institute (SCL) at Georgia Tech provides global leadership for research and education in supply chain management, which they define as 'the application of scientific principles to optimize the design and integration of supply chain processes, infrastructure, technology and strategy'.

Channel structures

A marketing channel is a set of businesses that are involved in making a product or service available for use or consumption by a business or another end-user. Such businesses may be independent, owned by others in the channel, they may co-exist, compete or collaborate in a wide variety of ways.

The members of a channel carry out some or all of the following functions:

- promotion and contact including advertising, creating awareness and providing contact resources;
- information on the product or service;
- matching the product or service to specific customer requirements;
- risk-sharing in elements of the transaction;
- negotiation in setting the terms of trade and price;
- financing the cost of the transaction, say by providing credit;
- physical distribution of the product or execution of the service.

There are four main types of channel, as listed below.

1 Conventional

This is when each link in the chain is independent of the other and in effect competes for a slice of the value in getting the end product to the end consumer or user. There are usually four links in the chain (see Figure 4.5); however, on occasion one link will leapfrog over the other.

FIGURE 4.5   International marketing channels

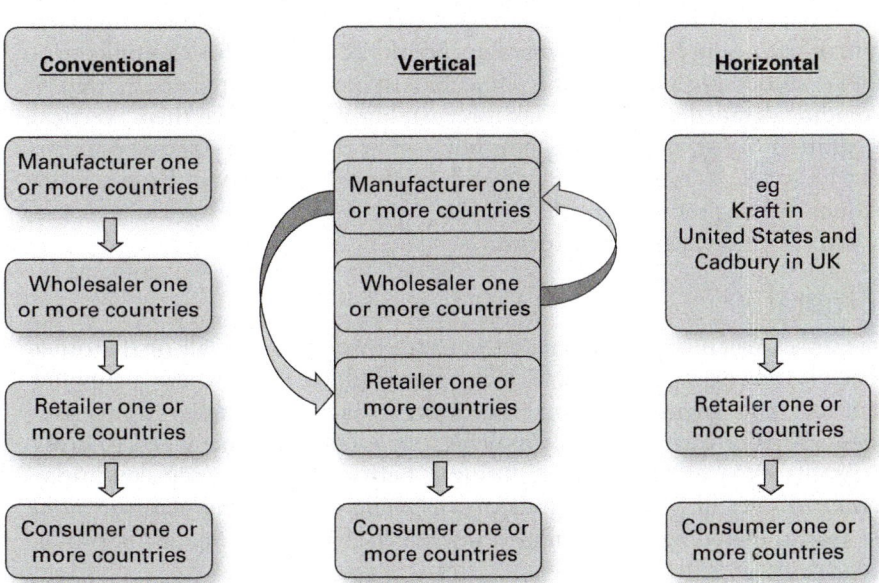

2 Horizontal Marketing Systems (HMS)

This occurs where two or more non-competing businesses at one level in the chain combine together to market an existing product, or create a new channel to market because they lack physical or capital resources, an established brand name or to secure economies of scale. The music partnership started by Apple and Starbucks in 2007 is one such example. The aim was to allow Starbucks' customers to wirelessly browse, preview, buy and download music from iTunes Music Store onto anything running iTunes. Apple's brand leadership in digital music combined with Starbucks' loyal customer base was expected to create a win–win situation for both parties. Apple hoped to sell a million songs in the first six months but passed that threshold in six days. Starbucks benefited from higher sales and even stronger customer loyalty.

This strategy works particularly well in global distribution strategies. For example, one goal of US giant Kraft in making its bid for British firm Cadbury's in January 2010, was that becoming a part of Kraft means that Cadbury's products will go through a far bigger global distribution network. Products such as Creme Eggs and Fruit and Nut will be introduced to two of the superpowers of the 21st century – Russia and China – where, as an independent company, Cadbury has made little impact and Kraft has a strong presence. Kraft in return expects increased penetration in Western Europe.

3 Vertical Marketing Systems (VMS)

This strategy integrates producer, wholesalers and retailers working in one unified system. The goal of vertical marketing is to eliminate unnecessary competition between chain participants as occurs, say, when producers and retailers slug it out to get better prices from each other. VMS give all those involved control but not necessarily ownership. Marks & Spencer, for example, provides considerable amounts of technical assistance to its suppliers, as well as providing detailed sales and stock forecast, but does not own them. Vertical integration is a strategy that is best pursued at the mature stage of the product life cycle, as at earlier stages each part of the chain will have a more distinct role to perform.

VMS itself comes in three forms.

Corporate

This arises when one member of the chain owns some or all of the other elements. For example 'forward' integration, which arises where a supplier such as Apple owns its own retail outlets. 'Backward' integration arises when a retailer owns its own suppliers. Coca-Cola, who managed to grow its profits by over 50 per cent during a period of near slump conditions thanks to sales in China and India, owns some 400 bottling plants around the world, including one launched in Malaysia in 2011. Spanish clothing chain Zara out-flanks its competitors such as Gap and Benetton by having control over almost every element of the supply chain from design and production (it makes nearly half of all the fabrics it uses itself) through to worldwide distribution and retailing. Zara can get a new line to market in just one month, some nine times faster than the industry average, which gives it a significant market edge in a fashion-dominated industry.

Contractual

This is where independent firms at different levels of the distribution chain agree to cooperate in return for specific advantages. Retail cooperatives are one example of CVMS, where independent retailers band together to increase their buying power, improve their operating systems or to create distinctive brands. The International Cooperative Alliance, the trade body representing this sector, has 230 member organizations from 92 countries active in all sectors of the economy. Japan is home to the No 1 ranked coop, Zen-Noh, a national federation of agriculture and food cooperatives with revenue of over $60 billion.

Franchising

Franchising is the most prevalent form of CVMS operating in hundreds of business sectors, providing both service – such as advertising, accounting and web design – as well as products – Ziebart in car protection and the near-ubiquitous McDonald's (see case study in Chapter 1). The International Franchise Association Educational Foundation's report, Franchise Business Economic Outlook for 2015 confirms that there are just short of 800,000 franchise outlets in the United States alone, employing nine million people generating $890 billion in sales (**http://emarket.franchise.org/FranchiseBizOutlook2015.pdf**).

The franchisor supplies the product or teaches the service to the franchisee, who in turn sells it to the public. In return for this, the franchisee pays a fee and a continuing royalty, based usually on turnover. They may also be required to buy materials or ingredients from the franchisor, giving them an additional income stream. The advantage to the franchisee is a relatively safe and quick way of getting into business for themselves, but with the support and advice of an experienced organization close at hand.

The franchisor can expand his distribution with the minimum strain on his own capital and have the services of a highly motivated team of owner-managers.

4 Administered

Administered Vertical Marketing Systems are those where one or at most a few members dominate the distribution chain and use that position to coordinate the other members' activities. Any part of the chain can dominate. Big retailers such as Wal-Mart, Sainsbury's, Toys R Us and Carrefour can leverage their strength on manufacturers to such an extent they can make them bid for shelf space. Giant consumer firms with strong brands – Procter & Gamble, Kraft, Coca-Cola, for example, can exert a similar pressure on retailers. Firms away from the fast-moving consumer sector such as Sony and Samsung also exert power over the distribution chain. Samsung achieved its strong position by ditching their dozen or so subsidiary brands – Wiseview, Tantus and Yepp, none of which meant much to consumers – to put all its resources behind the Samsung name.

Multiple channels

Major companies almost invariable use several channels to market, most noticeably clicks and bricks (see Amazon, above, for example). There are significant benefits to using more than one route to market if they deliver superior benefits to a particular market segment and don't erode the brand value. Dorling and Kindersley – prior to their acquisition by Pearson plc, part of the Penguin Group – had a party plan operation promoting their books along the lines of Avon and other multi-level marketing companies. Pearson, however, cut out this channel immediately post-acquisition as it did not correspond with the image of their high street branding.

Selecting distribution channels

These are the factors you should consider when choosing channels of distribution for your particular business:

1 Does it meet your customers' needs? You have to find out how your customers expect their product or service to be delivered to them and why they need that particular route.

2 Will the product itself survive? Fresh vegetables, for example, need to be moved quickly from where they are grown to where they are consumed.

3 Is it compatible with your image? If you are selling a luxury product, then door-to-door selling may spoil the impression you are trying to create in the rest of your marketing effort.

4 How do your competitors distribute? If they have been around for a while and are obviously successful, it is well worth looking at how your competitors distribute and using that knowledge to your advantage.

5 Will the channel be cost-effective? A small manufacturer may not find it cost-effective to sell to retailers over a certain distance because the direct 'drop' size – that is, the load per order – is too small to be worthwhile.

6 Will the mark-up be enough? If your product cannot bear at least a 100 per cent mark-up, then it is unlikely that you will be able to sell it through department stores. Your distribution channel has to be able to make a profit from selling your product too.

7 Push–pull. Moving a product through a distribution channel calls for two sorts of selling activity. 'Push' is the name given to selling your product in, for example, a shop. 'Pull' is the effort that you carry out on the shop's behalf to help it to sell your product out of that shop; that pull may be caused by your national advertising, a merchandising activity or the uniqueness of your product. You need to know how much push and pull are needed for the channel you are considering. If you are not geared up to help retailers to sell your product, and they need that help, then this could be a poor channel.

8 Physical distribution. The way in which you have to move your product to your end customer is also an important factor to weigh up when choosing a channel. As well as such factors as the cost of carriage, you will also have to decide about packaging materials, warehousing and storage. As a rough rule of thumb, the more stages in the distribution channel, the more robust and expensive your packaging will have to be.

9 Cash flow. Not all channels of distribution settle their bills promptly. Mail-order customers, for example, will pay in advance, but retailers can take up to 90 days or more. You need to take account of this settlement period in your cash flow forecast.

Logistics

The goal of a marketing logistics system is to manage the whole process of getting products to customers in an efficient and cost-effective manner to meet marketing goals; and to get faulty or unwanted products back. This interfaces with a host of related areas of business including physical transportation, warehousing, relationships with suppliers and inventory and stock management. Some important considerations in logistics include:

- Just in Time (JIT), which aims to reduce the need for warehousing through accurate sales forecasting. All parties in the distribution channel carry minimum stock and share information on demand levels.

- Vendor Managed Inventory (VMI) and Continuous Inventory Replenishment Systems (CIRS), which require customers to share real-time data on sales demand and inventory levels with suppliers.

Both supplier and customers while benefiting from cooperation have mutually conflicting goals in that they want to shift costs onto the other party. Their capacity for doing so depends on their relative strengths. For example, giant retailers such as Tesco and Marks & Spencer have been very successful in getting their suppliers to carry a major part of the cost of stockholding.

Marketing in the Internet era

Exactly when the Internet was born, like so many enabling technologies – steam, electricity and the telephone, for example – is a subject for conjecture. Was it 1945 when Vannevar Bush wrote an article in *Atlantic Monthly* concerning a photo-electrical-mechanical device called a Memex, for memory extension, which could make and follow links between documents on microfiche? Or was it a couple of decades later when Doug Engelbart produced a prototype of an 'oNLine System' (NLS) that did hypertext browsing, editing, e-mail and so on? He invented the mouse for this purpose, a credit often incorrectly awarded to Apple's whizz-kids.

Some date the birth as 1965 when Ted Nelson coined the word 'Hypertext' in 'A File Structure for the Complex, the Changing, and the Indeterminate', a paper given at the 20th National Conference, New York, Association for Computing Machinery. Others offer 1967 when Andy van Dam and others built the Hypertext Editing System.

The most credible claim for being the Internet's midwife probably goes to Sir Tim Berners-Lee, a consultant working for CERN, the European Organization for Nuclear Research. In June–December of 1980, he wrote a notebook program, 'Enquire-Within-Upon-Everything', that allowed links to be made between arbitrary nodes. Each node had a title, a type and a list of bidirectional typed links. 'ENQUIRE' ran on Norsk Data machines under SINTRAN-III. Berners-Lee's goal was to allow the different computer systems used by the experts assembled from dozens of countries to 'talk' to each other both within CERN itself and with colleagues around the globe.

The record of the Internet's meteoric growth has been tracked by Internet World Stats (**www.internetworldstats.com/emarketing.htm**) since 1995. Then just 16 million people, representing 0.4 per cent of the world's population were online, mostly using slow and very limited connections with modest bandwidths – the measure of how much data can be moved and how fast it can travel. The amount of goods and services being sold over the internet is at best an estimate. The simple fact is that the rate of growth in terms of reach and richness (see later in this chapter) is moving too fast to count with any degree of accuracy. The best you can do is check the date of any figure you are given and add 20 per cent a year to that.

In March 2015 the best guess was that 40 per cent of internet users had bought something online. As nearly half the world's population has an internet connection that amounts to between 2 and 3 billion customers. Clearly that's nothing like the penetration of a corner shop, but that model has been around for thousands of years. The internet is at best three decades old. But don't ditch the bricks route in your strategy. Britain's oldest shop has been standing for 600 years and over the centuries it has been a butcher's, grocer's, ironmonger's, draper's and for the past 50 years a general store and post office and the model still endures. So much so that the internet pioneers are looking for ways back. In February 2015 Amazon opened its first staffed pick-up and drop-off location that is a shop in all but name at Perdue University in the United States. They are expected to follow this by opening university shops across America starting in California and Massachusetts. They are rumoured to be looking for a bricks-and-mortar chain to buy to jump-start their strategy to set up pick-up and drop-off points everywhere. In March 2015 Google got in on the retail act too, opening its first ever bricks-and-mortar store, inside a Currys PC World on London's Tottenham Court Road. It follows the Apple Store model with products on wooden tables and staff on hand to guide users through their hardware and software letting them try before they buy.

Richness vs reach

The Internet has largely changed the maths of the traditional trade-off between the economics of delivering individually tailored products and services to satisfy targeted customers and the requirement of businesses to achieve economies of scale. The near impossible to find second-hand book that had to be tracked down laboriously and at some cost, is now just a mouse click away. The cost of keeping a retail operation open all hours is untenable but sales can continue online all the time. A small business that once couldn't have considered going global until many years into its life, today, thanks to the Internet, can sell its wares to anyone anywhere with a basic website costing a few hundred dollars and with little more tailoring than the translation of a few dozen key words or phrases and a currency

FIGURE 4.6   Richness vs reach – globalizing industries

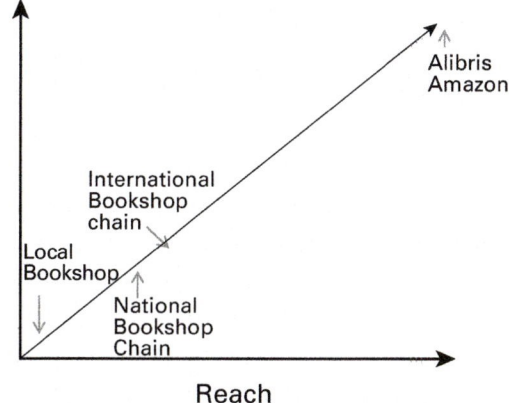

Richness

- Bandwidth or amount of data that can be transmitted
- Ability to customize product or service to an individual buyer's needs
- Interactivity between 'buyer' and 'seller'
- Reliability of the service
- Security of data and transaction processes, including payment systems
- Currency – how current the data is
- Operating hours 24/7
- Ease with which languages can be added to facilitate global reach

Reach

- Number of people/customers who can be approached
- Geographic spread
- New intermediaries in the distribution channels

widget that handles its payments. Internet has made real what in the 1970s Marshall McLuhan, a Canadian visionary of marketing communications, called the 'Global Village'.

The book business is a powerful illustration of the way a product and its distribution systems endure in principle while changing in method over the centuries. From 1403 when the earliest known book was printed from movable type in Korea, through to Gutenberg's 42-line Bible printed in 1450, which in turn laid the foundation for the mass book market, the product, at least from a reader's perspective, has had many similarities. Even the latest developments of in-store print-on-demand and ebook delivery such as that by Amazon's Kindle look like leaving the reader holding much the same product. What has, however, transformed the book business is its routes to market, the scope of its reach and the new range of business partnerships and affiliate relationships opened by the Internet. The Alibris case is a powerful example of how the Internet has affected the way in which marketing strategy is developed and implemented.

CASE STUDY Alibris.com

Alibris is one of the premier rare and out-of-print book sites on the internet. Started in 1998, they were a pioneer in the field of bringing first editions, signed books and other rare and antique treasures to a wider market via their website using their network of trusted sellers from around the world. By 2015 the company was still vibrant, but in a fiercely competitive marketplace. Amazon raised the stakes when in December 2008 they bought out AbeBooks, founded three years before Alibris, by two couples from Victoria. AbeBooks remains a stand-alone operation with headquarters in Victoria, British Columbia, Canada, and a European office in Dusseldorf, Germany.

Unsurprisingly, Alibris took corporate shelter too and on 23 February 2010 sold up to Monsoon, Inc, an Oregon-based marketplace selling-solutions company. The deal was for a combination of cash and stock in Alibris Holdings. Oak Hill Capital, a private equity firm, acquired Alibris Holdings in 2006. Oak Hill also provided funding for the transaction along with additional bank financing from Square 1 Bank. After the merger the intention is that Alibris and Monsoon will continue to operate as separate businesses under their existing names.

Alibris is an online marketplace for sellers of new and used books, music and movies that connects people who love books, music and movies to the best independent sellers from 45 countries worldwide. They offer more than 100 million used, new and out-of-print titles to consumers, libraries and retailers, which include Amazon.com, Barnes & Noble, Borders and eBay.

Alibris was founded in 1998 out of the germ of an idea that had been bugging Richard Weatherford, a bookseller who loves old books and new technology. After teaching college for a number of years, Dick turned to selling antiquarian books via specialized catalogues from his home near Seattle, a city that would also become home to Amazon. Realizing that computer databases had a lot to offer the antiquarian book business, in 1982 he wrote a business plan for a company that would build an online database for antiquarian booksellers. He called the company Interloc because it would serve as a 'go-between' helping sellers to locate hard-to-find books from the 11,000 or so rare book dealers operating in the United States at the time. Unfortunately start-up capital was hard to find, in part because personal computers were still scarce, expensive, and difficult to connect as the Internet was still in its infancy.

But by 1998 the growth of the Internet had radically altered the business environment. With financial resources totalling more than $60 million in venture capital, Alibris was launched with a daring national advertising campaign aimed at building a mighty brand on the spines of old books. Alibris's eye-catching ads have propelled the company to the forefront. The ads promote not leather-bound first editions of Charles Dickens but what might best be described as baby-boomer classics – books that were hugely popular somewhere between 35 and 50 years ago and whose covers, hard or soft, are invoked to trigger Proustian memories.

One early Alibris ad featured a battered copy of Lewis Padgett's 1950s-vintage science fiction book *Mutant*. The ad reads: 'April 11, 1977. Freaked you out so bad you had to bury it. Jan 25, 2000. Unearth on Alibris for son who shares your sci-fi gene.' Other ads featured titles ranging from Jack Kerouac's *On the Road* to *Phyllis Diller's Housekeeping Hints*. Martin Manley, Alibris's first chief executive, set out to spend at least $100 million to market its titles. Manley, a former McKinsey & Co management consultant, sought-after turnaround expert, and Assistant Secretary of Labour for Bill Clinton had some experience of raising and spending such sums.

Alibris is a business that could only exist in the Internet era. The richness of information on hard-to-find second-hand books and its global reach marrying tens of thousands of sellers with hundreds of millions of buyers can only be delivered online. The company built specialized, sophisticated low-cost logistics capabilities from the start to allow orders to be consolidated, repackaged, custom invoiced, or shipped overseas at low cost. Because Alibris collects a great deal of information about book buying and selling, the company came to be able to offer both customers and sellers essential and timely market information about price, likely demand and product availability. The eight new business partnerships (Akademos, Better World Books, BookRenter, Buy.com, Chegg, Coutts, eBay and Waterstone's) launched by Alibris in 2009 bring the total partner count to 16 and confirm its place as the premier marketplace for sellers of new, used and out-of-print books, music items and movies, and the world's most advanced online media marketplace provider.

By 2015 Alibris had assembled a galaxy of stars in their business partner network. All the usual suspects – Amazon, Barnes & Noble, Blackwell, Follett and Foyles – alongside a score of names known mainly to the rare book-buying aficionados.

CASE STUDY dunnhumby

Clive Humby and Edwina Dunn, founders of dunnhumby, came up with their entire business proposition based on understanding buyer behaviour. Their concept involved retaining and analysing customer data based on behaviour, which would enable companies to deliver marketing that was more relevant to their customers. They approached their employer (the geo-demographics firm CACI) with the idea but they were not willing to invest their profits in this new concept. Clive was adamant this idea should be pursued and his disappointment in the company's lack of vision led him to resign from the business in order to pursue the vision on his own. As Edwina, who was married to him, recalls, 'I was literally fired 10 minutes later as they felt I would be competing with their business.' She received a substantial payout – enough to dissuade her from claiming unfair dismissal. The result was a new player in the market, dunnhumby, which left CACI playing catch-up in a market they could have dominated from the outset.

The company undoubtedly made its mark when it took on Tesco as a client. The top handful of multinational retailers, Walmart, Metro, Groupe Carrefeur, Ahold and Tesco all slug it out around the globe with the all-important aim of capturing a few additional percentage points of market share. To win that extra share retailers have to know more about their markets than their competitors. Tesco's growth in stores in the early years was more art than science. But to be absolutely fair the other retailers operated in much the same way. Jack Cohen, Tesco's founder, based his initial strategy on operating from market stalls which made it easy, cheap and quick to follow his customers rather than requiring them to come to him. But if you want the customers to come to you the strategy has to be based more on science than art. A $130,000ft^2$ supermarket costs around £45 million to build and before you get to lay the first brick getting planning and other approvals can set a major retailer back many millions more. So it was hardly surprising for Tesco to want to find ways to understand their customers and encourage their loyalty when so much investment was at stake. Tesco liked dunnhumby so much they bought it out for £100 million, leaving the pair to move on to pastures new.

In 2014 they raised £4.7 million ($7.5 million) to fund Starcount (**www.starcount.com**), aiming to do for celebrities on social media what their previous company did for Tesco's Clubcard.

Viral marketing

This term was coined to describe the ability of the Internet to accelerate interest and awareness in a product by rapid word-of-mouth communications. To understand the mathematical power behind this phenomenon it is useful to take a look at recent communications networks and how they work. The simplest are the 'one to one' broadcast systems such as television and radio. In such systems the overall value of the network rises in simple relationship to the size of the audience; the bigger the audience the more valuable your network. Mathematically the value rises with N, where N represents the size of the audience. This relationship is known as Sarnoff's Law, after a pioneer of radio and television broadcasting. Next in order of value comes the telephone network, a 'many to many' system where everyone can get in touch with anyone else. Here the mathematics are subtly different. With N people connected, every individual has the opportunity to connect with $N-1$ other people (you exclude yourself). So the total number of possible connections for N individuals $= N(N-1)$. Or N^2-N. This relationship is known as Metcalf's Law, after Bob Metcalf, an inventor of computer networking. The size of a network under Metcalf's law rises sharply as the value of N rises, much more so than with simple one-to-one networks. The Internet, however, has added a further twist. As well as talking to each other, Internet users have the opportunity to form groups in a way they cannot easily do on the telephone. Any Internet user can join discussion groups, auction groups, community sites and so on. The mathematics now becomes interesting. As David Reed, formerly of Lotus Development Corporation demonstrated, if you have N people in a network they can in theory form 2^N-N-1 different groups. You can check this formula by considering a small N of, say, 3 people; A, B and C. They can form three different groups of two people: AB, AC and CB and one group of three people, ABC, making a total of four groups as predicted by the formula. As the value of N increases the size of the network explodes (see Figure 4.7).

The birth of viral marketing using the power of Reed's Law to the full, has been attributed to the founder of Hotmail, who insisted that every

FIGURE 4.7   The mathematics of Internet networks

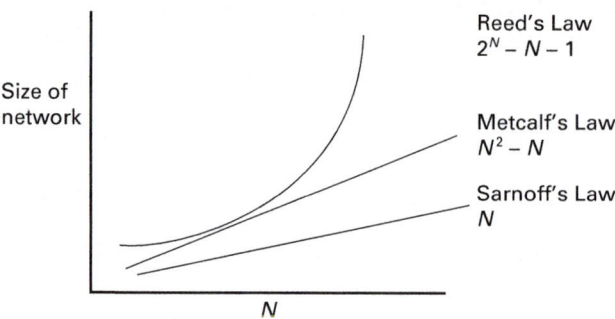

e-mail sent by a Hotmail user should incorporate the message: 'Get your free web based email at Hotmail'. By clicking on this line of text, the recipient would be transported to the Hotmail home page. Whereas this e-mail sent by the company itself would not have had much effect, at the foot of an e-mail sent by a business colleague or friend it made a powerful impact. The very act of sending a Hotmail message constituted an endorsement of the product and so the current customer was selling to future customers on the company's behalf just by communicating with them. The recipient of a Hotmail message learnt that the product works, but also that someone they respect or like is a user. You only have to see how quickly a harmful computer virus can spread in hours and days to cover the whole world, to see the potential of viral marketing. For a small firm this technique has the added advantage of being inexpensive and easy to execute. Just look at some major sites on the Internet to get ideas. Book e-tailers all have links for you to e-mail a friend about a book you have 'stumbled' across on their site. Travel sites encourage you to e-mail to a friend any of their special offers that you don't plan to take up yourself. However, the beauty and limitation of viral marketing is that it only works when you are talking about a good product. No one recommends something they don't like using themselves.

New world – new threats

Even if a firm thinks that e-business offers few advantages, they could find themselves facing a range of new threats. For example, it is probable that the competitors an offline business currently face are small and big firms in their own country or area, and international firms from elsewhere in the world. With the Internet they could now have small firms similar to themselves, but based anywhere in the world, entering their market. Potentially this could put them up against hundreds of new competitors.

Also, their more nimble or forward-thinking smaller competitors could add to their apparent value, in their customer's eyes at least, by having an

Internet presence. This could be true even if the proportion of business or other activities conducted on the Internet is small. Customers are often favourably influenced by irrelevant benefits, which they nevertheless think they may one day take advantage of. A vivid example of this phenomenon has been 24-hour retail shopping. Few people actually shop for groceries in supermarkets at two in the morning, but by having a sign saying the shop is open all the time customers will be more inclined to use it anyway, than a shop with more conventional opening hours.

So all businesses face new dangers as a consequence of the Internet:

- They will have a range of new competitors of all sizes from around the world that can attack their market using the Internet.

- An Internet presence is now almost mandatory, as is the cost that goes with it. Firms without a presence may appear old-fashioned and out of date compared with other firms who do have websites.

- Firms without an Internet strategy and presence will miss out on some business that may only go to firms with an Internet presence. This is particularly true of rural markets, where the Internet has offered a degree of choice that is otherwise only available in major cities.

- The staff they employ may leave in search of more stimulating places to work. They will miss out on the operational cost saving that can be made using e-business, which may make them uncompetitive and so lose out to other firms.

Websites and Internet presence

Many businesses have poor and ineffective websites, largely because the site is static and in effect an online brochure; or because it is designed to be visually exciting and commissioned by managers with a limited grasp of how Internet visibility works. For an international business a website is both mandatory and potentially the most powerful and valuable marketing tool. This is an area that the MBA should be able to have an impact on quickly and senior managers will expect them to at least have a better grasp of the subject than them. Good website design is essential if your Internet presence is to be fully effective. Short loading time (use graphics, not photographs), short and sweet, legible text and an attractive layout are important features of a user-friendly website. Research indicates that 'within three clicks, visitors must be captivated or they will leave'. So, clear signposting is necessary, including a menu on every page so that visitors can return to the homepage or move to other sections in just one click.

Promote your website by acquiring links on other commercial websites, using key words to ensure you can be found and by promoting outside the Internet – feature your website address on all products and publications. Fill your homepage with regularly updated 'success stories', give discounts to first-time buyers, ask customers to 'bookmark' your site or add it to their list of 'favourites' on their browser. You could also try partnering with manufacturers and distributors in related business fields.

To get some idea of what to include and exclude from your website check out your competitors' websites and those of any other small business that you rate highly.

Getting seen

Nine out of 10 visitors reach Internet sites via a search engine or equivalent so you need to fill the first page with 'key terms' that search engines can latch on to.

This process is known as SEO (Search Engine Optimization), where your website is 'optimized' so that it improves its position in search engine rankings. This involves the frequent use of the key words that searchers are most likely to use when browsing on the Internet for your types of product or service. As a rule of thumb for every 300 words you need a key word or phrase to appear between 10 and 15 times. Search engines thrive on content so the more relevant content the better. You can use products such as that provided by Good Keywords (**www.goodkeywords.com)**, who have a free Windows software program to help you find words and phrases relevant to your business and provide statistics on how frequently those are used. Keywords Gold is their paid-for product; priced at $49, which has several additional filters and tools to help you refine your key word lists.

Measuring marketing effectiveness on the Internet

Seeing the value from Internet advertising can be a difficult proposition. The first difficulty is seeing exactly what you are getting for your money. With press advertising you get a certain amount of space; on TV and radio you get airtime. But on the Internet there are at least three new ways to measure viewer value, as listed below, aside from the largely discredited 'hits', used only because there was no other technique available. ('Hits' measure every activity on the web page, so every graphic on a page as well as the page itself counts as a hit.)

- Unique Visitors: This is more or less what it says – new visitors to a website. What they do once there and how long they stay is not taken into account, so it's a bit like tracking the number of people passing a billboard. Could be useful, but perhaps they just stumbled across the site by accident. Also if users clear their cookies and clean up their hard drives there is no way to identify new and old visitors.

- Time Spent: Clearly if a visitor stays on a website for a few minutes they are more likely to be interested or at least informed about your products and services than if they were there for a second or two.

- Page Views: Much as in hard copy, a page on the web can now be recognized and the number of viewers counted.

Nielsen, a market-leading audience and market-research measurement company, suggests that 'Time Spent' is the best way to measure advertising effectiveness, other of course than actual sales if you can trace them back to their source. The order of the worldwide top websites is changed radically using this measure. For example, in January 2008 Google ranked first for Unique Visitors and Page Views, but only third for Time Spent.

The Internet Advertising Bureau (**www.iabuk.net**) has a wealth of further information on Internet advertising strategies as well as a directory of agencies that can help with some or all of these methods of promoting your business.

These are some of the services that are used to track website activity.

Google Analytics. The basic version is free and will deliver most of what you need to get a strategic view of what is happening on your website. This is rated the most comprehensive of website tracking tools. It helps you paint a complete picture of your audience and their needs, wherever they are along the path to purchase, from just viewing a page to shortlisting options or comparing prices. Traffic Sources and Visitor Flow, two of the Analytics tools, help you track the routes people take to reach you, and the devices they use to get there – PC, tablet or smartphone. In-Page Analytics, another tool in the service, lets you make a visual assessment of how visitors interact with your pages and what they're looking for and what they seem most interested in about your proposition based on viewing time. Mobile App Analytics covers all the same ground letting you know who uses your apps, on what devices, and where they come from. Custom reports can be set up to track specific advertising campaigns. Visit **www.google.com/analytics**.

Sitemeter. This service delivers 'the Who, What, When and Where' of your online traffic. They can't tell you specifically who is visiting your site, but are able to record a list of visitors with general geographic location information for each visitor. So you could establish that 'x' per cent of visitors to your site come from Athens, Berlin or Sofia, for example and using the 'Referring URL' report you could see a large number of these visitors have an '**.edu**' or '**.ac.uk**' extension, indicating an occupation in the education sector. SiteMeter can provide you with a list of your site's most visited pages, what times of the day are your busiest and any season trends or patterns. Site Meter Basic provides all the essential data, statistics, and reports needed to know who is visiting your site, how many pages have been viewed, and detailed information about each individual visitor. Site Meter Premium, at a modest monthly cost of around £7, offers additional statistics including ranked reports, more historical data and the ability to export data on recent visitors. Visit **www.sitemeter.com**.

AWStats. This log analyser shows you all possible information your log contains, in a few graphical web pages covering information such as:

- authenticated users, and last authenticated visits;
- days of week and rush hours (pages, hits, KB for each hour and day of week);

- domains/countries of hosts visitors (pages, hits etc);
- hosts list, last visits and unresolved IP addresses list;
- HTTP errors (Page Not Found with last referrer, etc);
- most viewed, entry and exit pages;
- number of visits, and number of unique visitors;
- search engines, keyphrases and keywords used to find your site from the 115 most prominent search engines;
- visits duration and last visits;
- visits of robots (319 robots detected);
- worms attacks (5 worms families).

AWStats is free, but if you want to support future development you can make a donation. Visit **www.awstats.org**.

StatCounter: This is a free service that lets you drill down into the data about visitors to your website to see what are your most popular pages, which sites people reach you from, the pages visitors enter and exit your site, visitor paths, length of time at each stage, keyword analysis and recent keywords used. Visit **http://statcounter.com/features**.

Social media strategy

The Oxford Dictionary has a suitably pithy definition of social media – 'websites and applications that enable users to create and share content or to participate in social networking'. Social media can be seen as a collection of online communications channels dedicated to community-based input, interaction, content-sharing and collaboration. Social media was in its infancy when the first edition of *The 30 Day MBA* was being written in 2008, but in just a few short years has become prolific, influential and now occupies half the promotional world space. The notion that using social media for business has become a mainstream activity is evident in the fact that the options are numerous and expanding fast. Aside from the usual suspects – Facebook, LinkedIn and Twitter – hundreds of sector-specific sites exist. Pinterest, for example, is a tool for collecting and organizing pictures of things that inspire you. YouTube provides a forum for people to inform billions of people around the world by distributing videos for free. eHarmony, Match.com and 6,000 other dating sites aim to help the lonely find love. Social bookmarking sites, including Digg, Delicious, Newsvine, and Reddit allow users to recommend online news stories, music and videos. Then you have word-of-mouth forums including blogs, company-sponsored discussion boards and chat rooms, and consumer product or service ratings websites and forums like Skytrax airlines rating, TripAdvisor and local-business review site Yelp. Social media sites make up at least half of the top 20 websites in most regions of the world.

Today even the smallest business can incorporate social media into their promotional plan, and it is essential for the prospective MBA marketer to have a reasonable grasp of the basics of the subject and the benefits that knowledge can bring to his or her organization. Stanford's 'Social Media Use Among Directors and Senior Managers' report suggests that this is fertile ground for an MBA to sow the seeds of fast-tracked career progression. Whilst 80 per cent of senior managers had a LinkedIn account, only half used it regularly. Forty per cent had a Twitter account but less than 10 per cent actually used it. Around a fifth of those they surveyed – typically in their mid-50s – across a broad set of industries – manufacturing, utilities, banking, and services – and from fairly large companies ($500 million in revenue), didn't access social media. (**www.gsb.stanford.edu/sites/default/ files/13SocialMedia.pdf**)

Different social media reach different audiences. Facebook, for example, dominates in the B2C space (67 per cent of marketers select it as their number one choice). However, in B2B, LinkedIn and Facebook are in joint first place at 29 per cent each. Blogging and Twitter play a much more important role for B2B marketers – 19 per cent and 16 per cent respectively – whilst for B2C the shares are 11 per cent and 10 per cent. Companies such as Ning (**www.ning.com**) and engagor (**http://engagor.com**) will let you create and cultivate your own custom social network as well as being able to measure, monitor and manage all your social media activity. Both these sites offer a free trial.

Key uses of social media include:

Improve market intelligence

Social media has fundamentally transformed the way people exchange information. Today people with similar interests band together in different online communities sharing information and exchanging views on blogs and forums, both excellent sources of continuous information on industry issues, customers and competitors. Bloggers are no longer inhibited if they are not a recognized expert in the field. Anyone and everyone can and does express their comments and views through blogs and forums. The quality of information can be variable and there are often many blogs, sometimes hundreds, on any topic. Alternatively you can create a blog or forum on your own website. You can use information on blogs to arrive at a crowd forecast, that is one which relies on the 'wisdom of the crowd' effect to get a feel for what people are feeling. The term refers to the phenomenon that the average of estimates provided by a group of individuals is more accurate than most of the individual estimates. The idea that the combination of many forecasts usually performs better than the forecast of a single person, however expert, was spread by the lead story in James Surowiecki's 2005 book, *The Wisdom of Crowds* (Abacus; New edition). The story tells of a 1906 contest to guess the weight of an ox. The analysis of the 787 usable entries found that the sample average of 1,197 pounds was extraordinarily close the actual weight of 1,198 pounds. Crowd forecasting allows you to balance expert perspectives with that of a wider audience for a more representative view of where a trend is heading.

Enhance company profile

Most company websites are used as marketing tools used to draw in more prospective customers or to maintain relationships with current buyers. The corporate image is developed by public relations by way of press releases announcing expansion, new strategic partnership and new products and services; and by journalists reading, analysing and commenting on company financial results. Two social media routes are open to help cultivate a particular type of image, over which a company has some editorial control:

- Wikipedia. This site now gets of 600 million visitors a month, putting it up alongside Google. Companies can have their own Wikipedia page created putting their own slant on the information. Information on their site must be verifiable and fair comment can be made by anyone, which is a risk. For example Kerry Group, a food ingredients and flavours business quoted on the Dublin and London stock markets, devotes a substantial portion of its page to its acquisition history. A clear indication that they are in the market for businesses for sale (**http://en.wikipedia.org/wiki/Kerry_Group**).

- LinkedIn. This is the social media site of choice in the corporate world. There is virtually no editorial control over this site so almost anything legal can be published. Once again you can put your own spin on the facts. Kerry Group's LinkedIn profile again emphasizes its acquisitive nature. 'The Group has grown organically and through a series of strategic acquisitions in its relatively short history,' is the second sentence on the page. An advantage of LinkedIn is that you can alert your followers (in Kerry Group's case 32,624 of them) to anything you feel useful. On 24 February 2015 they let them know that their latest interim accounts were available. LinkedIn can also be used for precision B2B targeting of messages by job title and function, by industry and company size, by seniority and geography.

CASE STUDY   Caterpillar

You couldn't get a more conservative company than Caterpillar. Started in 1925 the company has grown to become the world's leading manufacturer of construction and mining equipment, diesel and natural engines and industrial gas turbines. In 2015 their worldwide sales exceeded US$ 56 billion. It is a name associated with yellow bulldozers and building sites. Caterpillar recognizes the power of the big three social media platforms – Facebook, Twitter, and YouTube – but is also exploring other platforms that are used in specific areas of the world as well as social media tools such as Foursquare, Facebook Places and Gowalla.

The company even has a dedicated Digital Marketing Manager, Kevin G Espinosa, and a social media strategy based on what they describe as their four pillars: social listening, customer support, promotion and thought leadership. All of their social media activities fall under these pillars. For thought leadership, Espinosa states they 'want to provide our customers the information they need to become better in their job and be seen as an industry leader when it comes to construction equipment, and we have a lot of knowledge to share.' They are using social listening 'to understand what people are saying about our products, the issues they have, where they are saying it, and who the key influencers are.'

Caterpillar is an active participant in social media channels, seeing them as powerful tools that allow them to connect with their customers, investors, potential employees and fans.

The Social Media section of their website (**www.caterpillar.com/en/news/social-media.html**) lists their areas of interest such as Cat Auction Services, a partnership of Cat Dealers, providing both buyers and sellers with a better heavy equipment auction experience and Caterpillar Safety Services advising on the right Personal Protective Equipment. With these separate areas the company has 23 different Facebook sites for different aspects of their business, five blogs and Google + sites as well as dedicated links to YouTube, Instagram, Vimeo, SoundCloud and Pinterest.

Process

This element of the marketing mix is concerned with the customer's experience of its dealings a supplier. Essentially this is bringing the service element of a company's offer into sharper relief. Process can spread across every aspect of the customer/supplier relationship. For example a recent Nespresso offer, the £25 Club Reward on a Nespresso Machine from March 2015, was made somewhat less attractive by the *process* of redeeming the reward:

How to participate in this offer

1 *Purchase a Nespresso coffee machine*. Purchase any Nespresso coffee machine from **www.nespresso.com** and register with the Nespresso Club, where you will receive a Nespresso Club Member Account Number.

2 *Receive your machine and apply for your £25 Nespresso Club Reward.* Once you have received your machine you must apply for your Nespresso Club Credit online at **www.nespresso.com/ UKpromotion**. You will be required to upload a copy of your proof of purchase and input the 19-digit serial number of your machine. Alternatively you can download an application form from **www.nespresso.com/UKpromotion,** attach a photocopy of your proof of purchase and return to us at the address found on the application form by the stated closing date.

Websites and mobile apps are another source of potential customer dissatisfaction with a firm's process. Google has introduced a 'Mobile-Friendly Test' that will analyze a URL and report if the page has a mobile-friendly design. Visit **www.google.co.uk/webmasters/tools/mobile-friendly.**

With myriad rating services and the National Cross-Industry Benchmarks of Customer Satisfaction for the United States and the UK (**www.theacsi.org**) measuring the satisfaction of household consumers with the quality of products and services offered by both foreign and domestic firms' business products, services and processes are being put under the spotlight as never before. The Industry Benchmarks annual studies involve roughly 70,000 customers in the United States and 30,000 in the UK being surveyed about the products and services they use the most. The survey data benchmarks customer satisfaction with more than 300 companies in 43 industries and 10 economic sectors, as well as various services of national and local government agencies.

Note: 'People', the final P in the marketing mix, is covered in Chapter 7, Human Resource Management.

Online video courses and lectures

14 ways to raise your prices (and keep your customers): Part of the Business Essentials series from Hixsons Chartered Certified Accountants and Business Advisors, produced in conjunction with Bournemouth & Poole College: **www.youtube.com/watch?v=adpn8AeObXU**

7Ps of Marketing: Physical Evidence. Once a day marketing: **www.youtube.com/watch?v=zbW4GGf8JU0**

Advertising, Professor Kim Donahue, Kelley School of Business: **www.youtube.com/watch?v=NroY4SSrjL8**

Amazon FBA Pricing Strategies: Pricing High and Still Making the Sale: **www.youtube.com/watch?v=_iUudUP7LcM**

Distribution and Logistics Management: London School of Business and Finance: **http://freevideolectures.com/Course/2749/Marketing-Management/4**

Fedex Case Study: Rod McNealy, Johnson & Johnson Marketing Executive, Wharton Lecturer, presenting the Federal Express (Fedex) Case Study on Strategic Pricing to Princeton audience: **www.youtube.com/watch?v=B2rF3cTg0Mc**

How to Develop Breakthrough Products and Services: Professor Eric von Hippel of MIT in a series of four lectures with accompanying notes: **http://ocw.mit.edu/courses/sloan-school-of-management/15-356-how-to-develop-breakthrough-products-and-services-spring-2012/**

Introduction to Managing Price: London School of Business and Finance: **www.youtube.com/watch?v=k-MjWF2I428**

Introduction to Marketing: This course covers topics including branding strategies (eg, brand positioning, brand communications) and customer-centric marketing strategy. Wharton Online Learning: **http://online.wharton.upenn.edu**

Marketing Channels & Their Functions: Professor Kim Donahue, Kelley School of Business: **www.youtube.com/watch?v=fifM5-qBH5E**

Personal Selling: Professor Kim Donahue, Kelley School of Business: **www.youtube.com/watch?v=cOkycHYyz5k**

Philip Kotler 'Marketing': Talking at Anaheim University: **www.youtube.com/watch?v=84PewDOi5AY**

Pricing Objectives and Strategies: Alanis Business Academy: **www.youtube.com/watch?v=gPAGip9GOIU**

Pricing Tactics & Strategies: Professor Kim Donahue, Kelley School of Business: **www.youtube.com/watch?v=0U_6Huw2gFo**

Product Category: Professor Reibstein David at Knowledge Wharton: **http://kwhs.wharton.upenn.edu/term/product-category/**

Product Lifecycle: Professor Mogilner Cassie at Knowledge Wharton: **http://kwhs.wharton.upenn.edu/term/product-lifecycle/**

Product Loyalty: Professor Reed Americus at Knowledge Wharton: **http://kwhs.wharton.upenn.edu/term/product-loyalty/**

Social Media, Search-Engine Optimization: Ohio Wesleyan University: **www.youtube.com/watch?v=yWkQIIrQjlA**

Supply Chain Distruptions and Humanitarian Logistics: Professor Yossi Sheffi, MIT: **www.youtube.com/watch?v=ky_h4YB_O4U**

Supply Chain Management Masterclass: Dr Sinéad Roden, Cass Business School: **www.youtube.com/watch?v=nmO-y0q8sdl**

The Future of Logistics and Trade: Scott Davis, CEO UPS talks on MIT Global Leadership Lecture: **www.youtube.com/watch?v=wQrltY2K6bs**

Online video case studies

Amazon's Seventh Generation Fulfilment: CBS 60 Minutes: **www.cbsnews.com/news/amazons-jeff-bezos-looks-to-the-future/**

Andrew Masanto, one of the Founders of Higher Click SEO Company, talks at Harvard: **www.youtube.com/watch?v=Op28m1wnqu0**

Apple: Think Different ad (1997) (**www.youtube.com/watch?v=nmwXdGm89Tk**) and Steve Jobs talking about how the advertising campaign was developed at an internal meeting the same year (**www.youtube.com/watch?v=9GMQhOm-Dqo**).

Desigual Fashion, Warehouse Logistics and Distribution: Desigual operates 157 stores worldwide and annually provides 10 million garments: **www.youtube.com/watch?v=9I6HPpDUR-s**

Ford Motor Company's European Supply Chain Case Study: Penske Logistics: **www.youtube.com/watch?v=KWABT48wTFw**

How P&G tripled its product innovation: Harvard Business Review: **https://hbr.org/2011/06/how-pg-tripled-its-innovation-success-rate**

Kalashnikov launches fashion line: The Age: **http://media.theage.com.au/news/world-news/kalashnikov-launches-fashion-line-6060738.html**

P & G: Supply Network Operations (Logistics) at Procter & Gamble, Graeme Carter, Associate Director, Supply Network Operations: **www.youtube.com/watch?v=GEceq7MOSs0**

Sichuan Garden: Harvard Business School professor Ben Edelman was overcharged four dollars for his Chinese food takeout order and went to battle with the restaurant over the mix-up: **www.youtube.com/watch?v=RPf_Lf83rJo**

Sony Playstation price war with the Xbox 360: Cnet: **http://video.cars.aol.co.uk/the-xbox-360-vs-the-ps3-price-war-260107988**

Finance and accounting

5

- Accounting uses.
- The difference between debt and shareholder's investment.
- Sources of debt.
- Sources of equity.
- Dealing with foreign exchange.
- Planning for taxes.
- Understanding FDI (Foreign Direct Investment).

The dividing line between Accounting and Finance is blurred. In basic terms accounting is considered to be everything concerned with the process of recording financial events and ensuring such recordings are in compliance with the prevailing rules. Finance is the area concerned with where the money to run a business actually comes from in order to be accounted for. In order to be able to understand and interpret the accounts using such tools as ratios you need a reasonable grasp of both these areas, though the ratios themselves are generally considered to be in the accounting domain.

In many business schools you will find an array of options in addition to the core elements of this discipline. At the London Business School, for example, you will find Asset Pricing, Corporate Finance, Hedge Funds, Corporate Governance, Investments, Mergers and Acquisitions, Capital Markets, and International Finance on the menu. Members of the Finance Group also run the BNP Paribas Hedge Fund Centre; Centre for Corporate Governance; Private Equity Institute; and the London Share Price Database. At Cass Business School, City of London you will find options on Behavioural Finance, Dealing with Financial Crime, and Derivatives.

The basic finance and accounting that every MBA should have an appreciation of are contained in Chapter 12, The Core. In this chapter there are the elements of finance and accounting peculiar to the international organization.

Accounting

Accounting is the process of recording and analysing transactions that involve events that can be assigned a monetary value. By definition financial information can only be a partial picture of the performance of an enterprise. People, arguably a business's most valuable asset, don't appear anywhere in the accounts, except for football clubs and the like where people are the subject of a transaction.

Although accounting has become more complex, involving ever more regulations and has moved from visible records written in books to key strokes in a software program the purpose is the same:

- to establish what a business owns by way of assets;
- to establish what a business owes by way of liabilities;
- to establish the profitability, or otherwise, at certain time intervals, and how that profit was achieved.

An MBA in Finance is unlikely to be required to perform the recording side of the accounting process, except in the very smallest of organizations, or if the venture is their own. But it is only by knowing how accounts are prepared and the rules governing the categorizing of assets and liabilities, about which more in Chapter 12, that they can gain a good understanding of what the figures really mean. For example, it is not obvious to the uninitiated that a company's shares are classed as a liability and it is extremely unlikely that the assets as recorded will realize anything like the figures shown in the accounts, audited or not. That Bear Stearns, an 85-year-old investment bank, was sold for $2 a share to JP Morgan Chase in 2008 – roughly $236 million for a business that was worth $20 billion only a few weeks previously – provides a vivid insight into the gap between reported and realizable figures in the accounting world.

Nevertheless, accounting reports do provide a valuable insight into business performance and in any event are a basic requirement for shareholders and regulators alike.

Who uses accounting information and why

The aim of all accounting information is to provide the particular user with relevant and timely data to make decisions. Who are these users of accounting information and what decisions do they need to take? Possible users are an extensive group, who require the information to be impartial, accurate and timely:

- Shareholders of limited companies will be influenced in their decision to remain investors or to increase/decrease their holding by receiving information about the financial performance and financial position of their company. This usually occurs twice a year in the form of a profit and loss account and a balance sheet relating to the first half-year and, later on, the full year.

- Owner-managers of non-incorporated businesses will require the above information but they will also be privy to more detailed and more frequent information about the business's financial affairs.

- Management in companies range from director level down to supervisor level. Each person requires accounting information to help them in their role. Supervisors may be concerned with operating costs for a very small part of the undertaking. Directors need to control the overall performance of the company and make strategic financing and investment decisions. Middle management need feedback on whether they are meeting their financial targets.

- Suppliers need to assess the creditworthiness of potential and existing customers when setting the amount and period of credit allowed. This will partly, if not mainly, be based on the financial history of each customer so the supplier's accountants will assess the latest profit and loss account and balance sheet. Other data on payment history may be obtained from credit agencies – for example, Dun & Bradstreet – to assist in this decision.

- Customers also need to be reassured, in this case to minimize the risk of their supplies drying up and disrupting their own output. Firms entering into a joint venture will also need mutual reassurance. Similar checks to those outlined above for suppliers will need to be carried out.

- Employees and their representatives have a vested interest in the financial health and future prospects of their employer. They rely on an assessment of the published accounts by experts for this.

- Government levies tax on the profits earned by businesses and value added tax (or sales tax) on the sales value of most industries. Tax authorities rely on the information provided by companies for these purposes.

- Competitors can make some comparisons, for example, sales, profit or asset utilization per employee, from published accounting data in a process known as benchmarking. This may provide clues to areas where performance may be improved, particularly if explanations of differences in operating systems can be obtained.

- Lenders need to be confident that their capital is safe and that the borrowing company can service the loan or overdraft adequately, so again the financial statements of profit and loss account and balance sheet will be examined from this viewpoint.

- Partners need to keep track of business performance in much the same way as shareholders and to ensure appropriate and fair treatment by their fellow partners.

- Special interest groups ranging from Friends of the Earth, Sierra Club (environment), National Right to Life (anti-abortion), Common Cause (campaign finance reform) and PETA (ethical treatment of animals), track the accounts of companies operating in their sectors to monitor and comment on their behaviour, usually adversely.

Accounting branches

Different users of accounting information will require different information and use it for different purposes. Accounting can be broken down into three main branches, with some overlap between, particularly in smaller enterprises where in effect all three areas will be the responsibility of a single person or department:

- financial accounting;
- management accounting;
- financial management.

Financial accounting is concerned with preparing financial statements summarizing past events, usually in the form of profit and loss accounts and balance sheets. These historic statements are mainly of interest to outside parties such as investors, loan providers and suppliers.

Management accounting involves assembling much more detailed information about current and future planned events to allow management to carry out their roles of planning, control and decision-making. Examples of management accounting information are product costs and cost data relevant to a particular decision, say, a choice between make or buy. Also included in management accounting are preparing and monitoring budgeted costs relating to a product, activity or service. Management accounting information is rarely disclosed to outside parties, though bankers and private equity providers often ask for monthly management accounts as a condition of funding.

Financial management covers all matters concerned with raising finance and ensuring it is used in the most efficient way. For example, it would be financially inefficient to raise a long-term loan or sell shares just to finance a short-term increase in sales. It would be the role of financial management to select and use a more cost-effective funding source such as an overdraft. The cost of capital is influenced by both the capital structure adopted as well as the riskiness of the investments undertaken.

Within these three broad areas of accounting there may be further subsets of accounting relating either to one specific activity, or across the whole spectrum. Examples of these are:

- treasury;
- taxation;
- audit;
- forensic.

Treasury is a finance function usually only found in a very large company or group of companies. For example, the managing of bank balances to get the maximum interest on positive balances, or minimize the payment of interest on negative balances would be a typical treasury task. This might involve lending money overnight on the money markets. Treasury activity would also be concerned with managing of exchange risk where financial transactions in foreign currencies are involved.

Taxation in a small company will be included in the duties of the financial accountant who may need to call on outside professional advice from time to time. Corporation tax on company profits is not straightforward and the system of capital allowances can be complex for some large companies, groups of companies, or multinational companies. The ramifications of value added tax (VAT), sales tax where it applies, employee tax and other related deductions such as National Health Insurance and director benefits in kind, often call for the services of a specialist accountant, or team of accountants. Large companies usually use the services of such firms to minimize the pain and maximize the gain from such taxes and allowances.

Audit is another accounting function mainly found in larger organizations. Internal auditors monitor accounting procedures, documents and computerized transactions to ensure they are carried out correctly. This work is additional or complementary to that undertaken by external auditors who take a broader approach in providing an independent report to shareholders in the annual report.

Forensic accounting is exclusively working from the outside and looking in. Forensic accounts are described on the ACA website as 'the detectives of the finance world and help investigate fraud and other financial misrepresentation.' Their work is to aid lawyers, insurance companies and their clients to resolve disputes. They have to look beyond the bare numbers and analyse, interpret and summarize complex business and financial issues. Equally important is being able to communicate clearly and succinctly under pressure in a court of law.

International accounting standards

Experience and common sense have taught business and financial professionals that uniform financial reporting standards and methods are critical in a free-enterprise, private, capital-based economic system. A common vocabulary, uniform accounting methods, and full disclosure in financial reports are the goals. But it would be misleading to suggest that anything approaching accounting uniformity exists. The world can be broadly divided into five accounting zones:

1 Anglo Saxon: In these countries the accounts are orientated towards the needs of investors and creditors. This approach incorporates the most widely accepted financial statement and financial reporting standards and rules in the international business arena, known as

generally accepted accounting principles (GAAP). This describes the basic methods to measure profit and to value assets and liabilities, as well as what information should be disclosed in those financial statements released outside a business. Variations on GAAP, which is the gold standard for accounting reports in the United States include UK GAAP and the International Financial Reporting Standards (IFRS). International standards sound like a great idea, especially with the introduction of a single European currency and the emergence of pan-European equity markets. You could ask if the move to IFRS is such a big deal. In reality, this programme is not an accounting revolution, but a journey from one comprehensive basis of GAAP to another. GAAP remains the preferred option for the majority of the 1.4 million private companies and 3 million partnerships and sole traders in the UK. Only the 3,500 or so companies listed on UK stock markets are changing to IFRS. The countries in the Anglo Saxon camp include the United States and the UK, of course, but also over 70 other countries ranging from Australia to Zimbabwe, while roping in Canada, India, Australia, Malaysia and South Africa along the way.

2 Continental: Accounting here is highly conservative and is orientated towards a strict legal code. Most of Europe, except for the UK and the Netherlands, follow this standard, as do many Francophile countries such as Algeria and Egypt. Japan is also a surprise addition to the 30 countries adopting continental standards.

3 South American Zone: As you might expect, this covers the continent and, as a consequence of its economic experience, features routine adjustments for inflation. Although that helps render current accounts more meaningful, historic figures are virtually meaningless without major adjustments.

4 Transitional Economies: These include most of Eastern Europe, Russia, Georgia, China and Ukraine. Here the accounting standards vary according to the ownership type. Some are more closely allied to the Anglo Saxon model with investors' and creditors' needs being paramount. In others where the state dominates profits and liabilities alike reside with the country and are of limited importance to managers in terms of information.

5 Centrally Planned Economies: Cuba, North Korea and Vietnam are the last remaining countries in this accounting camp. Shareholders in any meaningful way don't exist, so the accounts are not concerned with their needs.

CASE STUDY HP versus Autonomy

In the spring of 2015 the financial press both sides of the Atlantic had headlines on the legal battle between Hewlett Packard and Autonomy, the company it had acquired four years earlier. HP paid its lawyers an US$18 million retainer and up to US$30 million more in contingency fees, depending on how much money HP is able to recover from Autonomy executives and advisors. The dispute lies somewhere on a continuum with variations in accounting methods between the UK and United States at one end and fraud uncovered by forensic accounting at the other.

When HP, the Silicon Valley giant founded in 1935 by Bill Hewlett and Dave Packard, electrical engineering graduates from Stanford University, bought Autonomy, founded in 1996 in Cambridge, England, by Dr Mike Lynch and Richard Gaunt, for $11.1 billion (£7.4 bn) it was seen as great deal – for Autonomy shareholders at least. Autonomy, a pioneer in creating search software that can make sense of complex, unstructured information was unique in being virtually the only UK technology player operating on a worldwide stage. HP, run by Meg Whitman, a Harvard MBA from the class of 1979, was reported in the *Financial Times* as having just 'revealed disappointing quarterly earnings along with plans to spin off its personal computer business. It also said it was cancelling its attempt to compete with Apple iPad.' Whitman needed corporate noise to drown out the bad news and Autonomy, although a relative minnow with sales of $870.4 million (£583.4 million) and 1,878 employees to HP's net revenue of $119 billion and 331,800 employees seemed a good fit. Autonomy was a rising star having won the Queen's Award for Enterprise and Management Today's 'Britain's Most Admired Companies' award for the software sector, positive messages that HP hadn't seen in the press for a long time. Autonomy's shares rose 79 per cent on the day the bid was announced, a staggering premium for a company whose earnings grew by just 6 per cent in the first half of the year in question. Whitman had only been HP's CEO since September 2011, the year of the Autonomy acquisition, but she had sector experience from her time on the board of eBay and HP had made some 100 acquisitions over the preceding four decades, albeit none the size of this deal.

The dispute between HP and the directors on Autonomy with whom the deal was struck started on 20 November 2012, when Whitman stunned the business world by declaring that HP would take a $8.8 billion write down on its $11.1 billion acquisition of Autonomy with $5 billion of that write down related to accounting irregularities at the UK software group. HP's advisors claim that Autonomy booked phantom sales where no money changed hands so inflating their sales revenue and as a consequence, the value of the company. Sushovan Hussain, Autonomy's former chief financial officer claims the differences in HP's interpretation of Autonomy's financial status were based only on transatlantic differences in accounting standards.

Why a reliable common accounting standard matters

Suppose you're reading the financial statements of a business. Managers in international businesses get paid to make profit, and they should be very clear on how profit is measured and what profit consists of. The amount of profit a business makes depends on how profit is defined and measured. For example, a business records the purchase of products for resale at cost, which is the amount it paid for the products. Inventory/stock are the names given to products being held for sale to customers. Examples include clothes in a department store, fuel in the tanks in a petrol station, food on the shelves in a supermarket, books in a bookstore, and so on. The cost of products is put in the stock asset account and kept there until the products are sold to customers. When the products are eventually sold, the cost of the products are recorded as the cost of goods sold expense, at which time a decrease is recorded in the stock asset account. The cost of products sold is deducted from the sales revenue received from the customers, which gives a first-step measure of profit. (A business has many other expenses that need to be factored in, which you can read about in Chapter 12.)

Now, assume that before the business sells the products to its customers, the replacement cost of many of the products being held in stock awaiting sale increases. The replacement cost value of the products is now higher than the original, actual purchase cost of the products. The company's stock is worth more, is it not? Perhaps the business could raise the sales prices that it charges its customers because of the cost increase, or perhaps not. In any case, should the increase in the replacement cost of the products be recorded as profit? The manager may think that this holding gain should be recorded as profit. But GAAP accounting standards say that no profit is earned until the products are sold to the customers.

What about the opposite movement in replacement costs of product when replacement costs fall below the original purchase costs? Should this development be recorded as a loss, or should the business wait until the products are sold? The accounting rule that applies here is called lower of cost or market, and the loss is recorded. So the rule requires one method on the upside but another method on the downside. You can see why business managers and investors in international ventures need to know something about the rules under which the accounts they are trying to interpret have been prepared.

The basic idea behind GAAP is to measure profit and to value assets and liabilities consistently from business to business and to establish broad-scale uniformity in accounting methods for all businesses. The idea is to make sure that all accountants are singing the same tune from the same songbook. The purpose is also to establish realistic and objective methods for measuring profit and putting values on assets and liabilities. GAAP also include minimum requirements for disclosure, which refers to how information is classified and presented in financial statements and to the types of information that have to be added to the financial statements in the form of footnotes.

Taxsites.com (**www.taxsites.com/Associations2.html**) provides a link to the websites of most of the accountancy bodies and regulatory authorities around the world, who are responsible for setting and maintaining the standard of accountancy reports.

Protecting investors

When confidence in US businesses was rocked badly with a series of high-profile financial frauds, Enron and Worldcom for example, the US government introduced the Sarbanes–Oxley Act, known less commonly but better understood as The Public Company Accounting Reforms and Investor Protection Act – 2002. The act's purpose is to close the loopholes opened up by creative accountants, who are always devising ways to overstate profits and understate liabilities, and so make it easier for shareholders to see how profitable a business really is. The act doesn't just apply to US companies; any businesses with shares listed on an American stock market that does business in the United States is swept into the net. Check out **www.soxlaw.com** for the lowdown on that act.

The UK version is The Companies (Audit, Investigations and Community Enterprise) Act. You can read up on the UK rules at **www.legislation.gov.uk/ ukpga/2004/27/pdfs/ukpga_20040027_en.pdf**.

Sources of funds

There are many sources of funds available to businesses; however, not all of them are equally appropriate to all businesses at all times. These different sources of finance carry very different obligations, responsibilities and opportunities for profitable business. Having some appreciation of these differences will enable managers and directors to make an informed choice.

Most businesses initially and often until they go public, floating their shares on a stock market, confine their financial strategy to bank loans, either long-term or short-term, viewing the other financing methods as either too complex or too risky. In many respects the reverse is true. Almost every finance source other than banks will to a greater or lesser extent share some of the risks of doing business with the recipient of the funds.

Debt vs equity

Despite the esoteric names (debentures, convertible loan stock, preference shares), businesses have access to only two fundamentally different sorts of money. Equity, or owner's capital, including retained earnings, is money that is not a risk to the business. If no profits are made, then the owner and other shareholders simply do not get dividends. They may not be pleased, but they cannot usually sue, and even where they can sue the advisors who recommended the share purchase will be first in line.

Debt capital is money borrowed by the business from outside sources; it puts the business at financial risk and is also risky for the lenders. In return for taking that risk they expect an interest payment every year, irrespective of the performance of the business. High gearing is the name given when a business has a high proportion of outside money to inside money. High gearing has considerable attractions to a business that wants to make high returns on shareholders' capital.

How leverage/gearing works

Table 5.1 below shows an example of a business that is assumed to need $/€/£60,000 capital to generate $/€/£10,000 operating profits. Four different capital structures are considered. They range from all share capital (no gearing) at one end to nearly all loan capital at the other. The loan capital has to be 'serviced', that is, interest of 12 per cent has to be paid. The loan itself can be relatively indefinite, simply being replaced by another one at market interest rates when the first loan expires.

Following the table through you can see that return on the shareholders' money (arrived at by dividing the profit by the shareholders' investment and multiplying by 100 to get a percentage) grows from 16.6 to 30.7 per cent by virtue of the changed gearing. If the interest on the loan were lower, the ROSC, the term used to describe return on shareholders' capital, would be even more improved by high gearing, and the higher the interest, the lower the relative improvement in ROSC. So in times of low interest, businesses tend to go for increased borrowings rather than raising more equity; that is money from shareholders.

At first sight this looks like a perpetual profit-growth machine. Naturally shareholders and those managing a business whose bonus depends on shareholders' returns would rather have someone else 'lend' them the money for the business than ask shareholders for more money, especially if by doing so they increase the return investment. The problem comes if the business does not produce £10,000 operating profits. Very often a drop in sales of 20 per cent means profits are halved. If profits were halved in this example, the business could not meet the interest payments on its loan. That would make the business insolvent and so not in a 'sound financial position'; in other words, failing to meet one of the two primary business objectives.

TABLE 5.1   The effect of gearing on shareholders' returns

	No gearing N/A	Average gearing 1:1	High gearing 2:1	Very high gearing 3:1
Capital structure	$/€/£	$/€/£	$/€/£	$/€/£
Share capital	60,000	30,000	20,000	15,000
Loan capital (at 12%)	–	30,000	40,000	45,000
Total capital	60,000	60,000	60,000	60,000
Profits				
Operating profit	10,000	10,000	10,000	10,000
Less interest on loan	None	3,600	4,800	5,400
Net profit	10,000	6,400	5,200	4,600
Return on share capital	= 10,000	6,400	5,200	4,400
	60,000	30,000	20,000	15,000
	= 16.6%	21.3%	26%	30.7%
Times interest earned	= N/A	10,000	10,000	10,000
		3,600	4,800	5,400
	= N/A	2.8 times	2.1 times	1.8 times

Bankers tend to favour 1:1 gearing as the maximum for a business, although they have been known to go much higher. As well as looking at the gearing, lenders will study the business's capacity to pay interest. They do this by using another ratio called 'times interest earned'. This is calculated by dividing the operating profit by the loan interest. It shows how many times the loan interest is covered, and gives the lender some idea of the safety margin. The ratio for this example is given at the end of Table 5.1. Once again rules are hard to make, but much less than 3x interest earned is unlikely to give lenders confidence. (See Chapter 12 for more on ratios.)

Debt (borrowings)

Debt finance and the regulation of such transactions is hardly new and its practice stretches far before the arrival of such firms as Banca Monte dei Paschi di Siena S.p.A. (MPS) in 1472, though that is now the oldest operating bank.

Banks

Towards the lower risk end of the financing spectrum are the various organizations that lend money to businesses, in particular banks, which between them put up nearly two-thirds of all business funds. Banks try hard to take little or no risk, but expect some reward irrespective of performance. They want interest payments on money lent, usually from day one, though sometimes they are content to roll interest payments up until some future date. While they hope the management is competent, they are more interested in securing a charge against any assets the business or its managers may own. At the end of the day they want all their money back. It would be more prudent to think of these organizations as people who will help you turn a proportion of an illiquid asset such as property, stock in trade or customers who have not yet paid up, into a more liquid asset such as cash, but of course at some discount.

Bankers like to speak of the 'five Cs' of credit analysis; factors they look at when they evaluate a loan request. When applying to a bank for a loan, be prepared to address the following points:

- Character. Bankers lend money to borrowers who appear honest and who have a good credit history. Before you apply for a loan, it makes sense to obtain a copy of your credit report and clean up any problems.
- Capacity. This is a prediction of the borrower's ability to repay the loan. For a new business, bankers look at the business plan. For an existing business, bankers consider financial statements and industry trends.
- Collateral. Bankers generally want a borrower to pledge an asset that can be sold to pay off the loan if the borrower lacks funds.
- Capital. Bankers scrutinize a borrower's net worth, the amount by which assets exceed debts.
- Conditions. Whether bankers give a loan can be influenced by the current economic climate as well as by the amount.

Bonds et al

Bonds, debentures and mortgages are all kinds of borrowing with different rights and obligations for the parties concerned. For a business a mortgage is much the same as for an individual. The loan is for a specific event, buying a particular property asset such as a factory, office or warehouse. Interest is payable and the loan itself is secured against the property, so should the business fail the mortgage can substantially be redeemed.

Companies wanting to raise funds for general business purposes, rather than as with a mortgage where a particular property is being bought, issue debentures or bonds. These run for a number of years, typically three years and upwards, with the bond or debenture holder receiving interest over the life of the loan with the capital returned at the end of the period.

The key difference between debentures and bonds lies in their security and ranking. Debentures are unsecured and so in the event of the company being unable to pay interest or repay loans they may well get little or nothing back. Bonds are secured against specific assets and so rank ahead of debentures for any payout.

Unlike bank loans that are usually held by the issuing bank, although even that assumption is being challenged by the escalation of securitization of debt being packaged up and sold on, bonds and debentures are sold to the public in much the same way as shares. The interest demanded will be a factor of the prevailing market conditions and the financial strength of the borrower.

Categories of bond

There are several general categories of bond that companies can tap into:

- Standard bonds pay interest, a coupon, half-yearly on the principal amount, known as the face or par value. At the maturity date the principal is repaid. The value of bonds fluctuates dependent on market condition, the length of time to maturity and the likelihood of the borrower defaulting. None of these matters are of immediate concern to the recipient of the funds, as long as they can service the interest. The risk is for the bondholder who can see the value of their investment alter over time.

- Zero coupon bonds pay no interest over their life but pay a lump sum at maturity equivalent to the value of the interest such an investment would normally bear. The buyer of the bond receives a return by the gradual appreciation of the bond's price in the marketplace. This could be an attractive financing strategy for a business making an investment that itself will not bear fruit for a number of years.

- Junk bonds are bonds usually subordinated to, that is put below in the pecking order of who gets paid in tough times, other regular bonds. Such bonds carry a higher interest burden.

- Callable bonds are used when an issuer wants to retain the option to buy back their bonds from the public if general interest rates fall sharply after the issue date. The issuer notifies bondholders that after a certain date no further interest will be paid, leaving the holders with no reason to keep the bond. The company issuing the bond can then go out to the market and launch a new bond at a lower rate of interest and so lower its cost of capital. This process is also known as refinancing.

Commercial paper

Banks and big companies such as General Electric Co and AT&T Inc regularly raise cash for operations by issuing paper to investors that often matures in six months or less. Private investors, especially money-market funds, buy this debt because as well as being very safe it pays an interest rate slightly higher than comparable US Treasury notes or UK Government Gilts. Although Commercial Paper is technically repayable in under six months, in practice the corporate borrower repays investors by issuing more paper, effectively paying back investors with more borrowed cash. The attraction to the borrower over other forms of lending is that as long as it matures before nine months (270 days) it doesn't have to be registered with any regulatory body, making it in effect 'off balance sheet', which in turn reduces gearing. (see pp 158–59 for more on gearing and financial risk). The exception to this rule is if the proceeds from this type of financing are to be used for anything other than current assets (inventories, debtors etc); for example fixed assets, such as a new plant. In such cases the relevant regulatory body has to be informed. However, in practice business funds tend to go into a pot and tracing where a particular sum of money came from and what was done with it is virtually impossible.

Syndicated loan

This is a loan offered by a group of lenders (a syndicate) who work together to provide funds, usually, though by no means always, for a single borrower. The borrower could be a business, a large project or a government. The loans are usually so large as to be potentially fatal to any single lender in the event of a default – hence the syndication. Borrowers who need a sophisticated facility or multiple types of facility find that using a syndicated loan agreement simplifies the borrowing process by using a single agreement covering the whole group of banks and different types of facility rather than entering into a series of separate bilateral loans. A syndicated loan agreement could contain a fixed term or revolving facility, which is in effect permanent; or they can contain a combination of both or several of each type (multiple-term loans in different currencies and with different maturity dates are fairly typical of the more complex syndicated loan). The syndicated loan can be for one borrower, a group of borrowers or even allow for new borrowers to join in under certain circumstances from time to time. Four important pieces of documentation accompany syndicated loans.

- Term Sheet: This sets out the terms of the proposed financing, the parties involved, their expected roles and the key features of the loan, including: the type of facilities, the amounts, the pricing, the term of the loan, and the covenant (any conditions and restrictions).

- Information Memorandum: This contains a commercial description of the borrower's business, management and accounts as well as details of the proposed loan facilities required. This document contains more information than is usually in the public domain so potential lenders will be expect to sign a confidentiality undertaking.

- Syndicated Loan Agreement: The Loan Agreement sets out the detailed terms and conditions on which the facility is made available to the borrower.

- Fee Letters: The borrower pays fees to those banks in the syndicate who have performed additional work or taken on greater responsibility in the loan process, including the Arranger, the Agent and the Security Trustee. Details of these fees are usually put in separate side letters to ensure confidentiality. These fees are in addition to paying interest on the loan and any related bank expenses.

Payment-in-Kind (PIK)

A PIK loan usually doesn't require any cash payment of either capital or interest until it matures. Such loans are typically unsecured with maturity dates usually exceeding five years. These loans usually carry a detachable warrant, that is the right to purchase a certain number of shares at a given price for a certain period of time, or some such mechanism. This allows the lender to share in the future success of the business, by way of compensation for their risk.

PIKs are something of a controversial debt structure and can ratchet substantial amounts of interest every year that can ultimately destroy a company. Paramount Restaurants, the owner of Chez Gerard and Caffè Uno, is an example of the distress this form of finance can cause. In March 2010 the company saw its PIK notes stand at over £78 million, up from £51.5 million three years earlier. The debt was provided by Silverfleet, which backed a £107m buy-out. The PIK element was rolling up a crippling 15.5 per cent interest annually.

Paramount's bankers, including Royal Bank of Scotland, HSBC and Barclays had to take over the company from Silverfleet, taking a 60 per cent equity stake in the business themselves, in an effort to save the business from failure.

Letters of credit and bills of exchange

Until the 19th century the branch banking system was fairly limited and postal services relatively slow. A system of transferring money, particularly between countries, but also within countries was established. Initially under the general heading of 'bills of exchange' these financial instruments were in effect promissory notes, much like the modern-day cheque, drawn up by one party who promises to pay another a certain sum on a certain day. Variations on this theme also became established, letters of credit being one of the most common. These were and to some extent still are used for buyers and sellers of international goods to transfer money to facilitate transaction. These letters can be irrevocable, that is payment must be made if all conditions are met; revocable – these can be cancelled or amended without prior notice; or transferrable where the letter concerned and the money attached can be passed to another party, usually a 'middleman' or agent. An MBA needs only a nodding acquaintance with these types of financial instruments and when you need to know more read up on them at Gov.UK (**www.gov.uk/letters-of-credit-for-importers-and-exporters**), and for the US the Export-Import Bank of the United States (**www.exim.gov/products/exportcreditinsurance/letter-of-credit.cfm**) where you will find a series of checklists to guide you through the maze.

Export/import government-backed finance

Many countries have their own government-backed scheme to support international trade via bank guarantees and insurance. Typical examples are: the Export Import Bank, Exim (**www.exim.gov**) in the United States; the UK has its Export Credits Guarantee Department (**www.ecgd.gov.uk**) based in the Department for Business, Innovation and Skills; The Export Credit Guarantee Corporation of India (**www.ecgc.in**); and Instituto de Resseguros do Brazil (**www.irb.gov.br**).

These organizations do not usually compete with banks and other domestic financial institutions. Rather they step in to areas in which such institutions either don't operate or see as too risky. Their support comes usually in the form of insurance covering both political risk and the possibility of default by a customer. Armed with such insurance a business can usually negotiate an additional banking facility.

Countertrade

This is a form of trade between parties where some or all of the transaction is in the form of a swap of products or services. The most common form of countertrade and the best known is barter, a process also well established in domestic markets. Barter involves direct and usually simultaneous trade. Russia and China have traded military equipment with resource-rich countries such as Indonesia and Saudi Arabia.

Three variants of basic countertrade are described here. Counterpurchase, which adds the element of time to the equation allowing one party to spread its 'payment' by allowing the recipient to call off deliveries to suit its needs. Offsets allows one party to 'earn' its way to paying for the goods in question.

An American aircraft manufacturer sold planes to several small European countries allowing them to pay nearly half the bill in return for making parts of those aircraft themselves. Buybacks, the last of the countertrade variations, occurs frequently in major capital projects. Here the supplier of the facility – say, a steelworks – agrees to take some of the output as payment at a future date.

The very nature of this type of transaction makes it difficult to estimate its significance as a financing tool for international trade. However, some researchers put it down as accounting for nearly one in five international transactions. Companies such as 3M have a dedicated business operation, in their case 3M Global Trading Inc (**http://solutions.3m.com/wps/portal/3M/ en_US/GlobalTrading/Inc/**), that handles their countertrade operations.

Equity

This is the generic name for money put into a business by shareholders, who are in turn the ultimate owners of the business. Whilst there are many sources of equity finance, personal contacts or semi-formal groups of private investors such as business angels or online bodies including crowdfunding associations, these are not likely to be players in funding international business. The three likely sources are stock markets, venture capital providers and corporate ventures funds. You may well be expected to know something about business angels and crowdfunding, as their reach and scope is being greatly enhanced by the Internet.

Stock markets

Stock markets are the place where serious international businesses raise serious money. It's possible to raise anything from a few million to tens of billions; expect the costs and efforts in getting listed to match those stellar figures. The basic idea is that owners sell shares in their businesses that in effect bring in a whole raft of new 'owners' who in turn have a stake in the business's future profits. When they want out they sell their shares on to other investors. The share price moves up and down to ensure that there are as many buyers as sellers at any one time.

As well as the practical issues around getting listed and dealing with shareholders an MBA would be expected to have some historical perspective of the subject. The need for stock exchanges developed out of early trading activities in agricultural and other commodities. During the Middle Ages, traders found it easier to use credit that required supporting documentation of drafts, notes and bills of exchange. The history of the earliest stock exchange, the French stock exchange, goes back to the 12th century when transactions occurred in commercial bills of exchange. To control this budding market, Phillip the Fair, of France (1268–1314) created the profession of *couratier de change*, which was the predecessor of the French stockbroker. At about the same time, in Bruges, merchants began gathering in front of the house of the Van Der Buerse family to engage in trading. Soon the name of the family became identified with trading and in time a 'bourse' came to signify a stock exchange. At the same time, stock exchanges began to materialize in other trading centres such as the Netherlands (Amsterdam Bourse) and Frankfurt (the Deutsche Stock Exchange, formerly the Börse).

The world's stock markets

How many stock exchanges are there? All you may have heard of are the LSE (London Stock Exchange) and NYSE (New York Stock Exchange), with the more informed adding Frankfurt, Tokyo and perhaps Paris. Those guessing five, or even 10 or 20, are way off. The answer is around 200. The big markets compete with alternative platforms, brokerage networks for market share and about a third of equities trading occurs off-exchange.

You can find out more about most of the world stock markets on the University of Chicago website (**http://guides.lib.uchicago.edu/stock_exchanges**) where exchanges are listed by continent and country. The World Federation of Exchanges (**www.world-exchanges.org/**) is useful source for facts and figures on these markets.

Junior stock markets

Many countries have experimented with introducing stock markets with less onerous entry conditions than those required by main markets. These usually require shorter trading histories and less rigorous regulations. Arguably the most successful of these is AIM (Alternative Investment Market) where since its launch in 1995, over 3,000 companies from across the globe have raised billions.

Towards the other end of the scale Nigeria's Alternative Securities Market (ASeM) has just 12 companies listed (**www.nse.com.ng/Listings-site/listing-your-company/asem**). There are dozens of junior markets to choose from including Entry Standard Deutsche Boerse, Alternext at Euronext NYSE, First North and New Connect in Warsaw. EY (Ernst & Young), the global accounting firm has a guide, 'Choosing a junior market' (**www.ey.com/UK/en/Services/Strategic-Growth-Markets/EY-ipo-leaders-insights-sebastian-lyczba**)

Venture capital

Venture capitalists (VCs), sometimes unflatteringly referred to as 'vulture capitalists', are investing other people's money, often from pension funds.

They have a different agenda from that of business angels, and are more likely to be interested in investing more money for a larger stake. In general, VCs expect their investment to have paid off within seven years, but they are hardened realists. Two in every 10 investments they make are total write-offs, and six perform averagely well at best. So, the one or two stars in every 10 investments they make have to cover a lot of duds. VCs have a target rate of return of 30 per cent plus, to cover this poor hit rate.

Raising venture capital is not a cheap option and deals are not quick to arrange either. Six months is not unusual, and over a year has been known. Every VC has a deal done in six weeks in its portfolio, but that truly is the exception. Fees will run to hundreds of thousands of pounds, the sweetener being that these can be taken from the money raised.

E&Y's latest take on the venture capital industry reports that the US economy accounts for 68 per cent of the $48 billion (£33 billion) of total global VC activity. Europe accounts for just 15 per cent of the VC capital and China just 7 per cent, down from a pre-financial crisis level of 11 per cent. Though important, it is helpful to put VC activity in perspective. Just 3,400 deals are done each year in the United States, 1,400 in Europe, 300 in China and 200 in India. Israel, an over achiever in this respect, sees 166 deals signed off, an impressive performance bearing in mind its comparative size. (**www.ey.com/Publication/vwLUAssets/Global_venture_capital_insights _and_trends_2014/$FILE/EY_Global_VC_insights_and_trends_report_2014.pdf**)

The National Venture Capital Association has directories of international of venture capital associations both inside and outside the United States (**www.nvca.org/Resources**).

You can see how those negotiating with or receiving venture capital rate the firm in question at The Funded website (**www.thefunded.com**) in terms of the deal offered, the firm's apparent competence and how good it is at managing the relationship. There is also a link to the VCs website. The Funded has 20,572 members.

CASE STUDY　Meraki: Corporate venture multi-million dollar pay day

---

Meraki (may-rah-kee), a Greek word that means doing something with passion and soul, could soon stand for how to make a billion in under a decade. Meraki was formed in 2006 by three PhD candidates from MIT, Sanjit Biswas, John Bicket and Hans Robertson; all currently on leave from their degree programmes.

Meraki, according to its website, 'brings the benefits of the cloud to edge and branch networks, delivering easy-to-manage wireless, switching, and security solutions that enable customers to seize new business opportunities and reduce operational cost. Whether securing iPads in an enterprise or blanketing a campus with WiFi, Meraki networks simply work'. With over 10,000 customers worldwide ranging from the English public school Wellington College to fast-food chain Burger King, Meraki was initially backed by Californian venture capital firm Sequoia Capital and Google, two early venture investors. Rajeev Motwani, the Stanford University professor who taught Google co-founders Larry Page and Sergey Brin made the necessary introductions.

Payday came on 19 November 2012 when Cisco, who had been in exclusive talks since September with Meraki bought the company for $1.2 billion (£754 million). The founders had been considering a flotation and at first rejected Cisco's overtures. Analysts think Cisco has overpaid, but with their greater market presence and cash resources the company is confident it will be able to expand Meraki's technology using their global networks. Cisco has included a retention package to keep Meraki's co-founders at Cisco to consummate the deal. Sujai Hujela, an executive at Cisco, also stated: 'We are making sure we want to preserve and pollinate the culture (at Meraki) into Cisco.'

Corporate venturing

Venture capital firms often take a hand in the management of the businesses they invest in. Another type of venturer is also in the risk capital business, without it necessarily being their main line of business. These firms, known as corporate venturers, usually want an inside track to new developments in and around the edges of their own fields of interest.

Sinclair Beecham and Julian Metcalfe, who started with a £17,000 ($27,000/€20,000) loan and a name borrowed from a boarded-up shop, founded Prêt a Manger. They were not entrepreneurs content with doing their own thing. They had global ambitions and it was only by cutting in McDonald's, the burger giant, that they could see any realistic way to dominate the world. They sold a 33 per cent stake for £25 million ($40/€29.5 million) in 2001 to McDonald's Ventures LLC, a wholly-owned subsidiary of McDonald's Corporation, the arm of McDonalds' that looks after its corporate venturing activities. They joined forces with the corporate venturing arm of a big firm.

They could also have considered Cisco, Apple Computers, IBM and Microsoft, which also all have corporate venturing arms. Other corporate venturers include Deutsche Bank, which set up DB eVentures to get a window on the 'digital revolution'. Reuters Greenhouse has stakes in 85 companies and even the late and unlamented Enron had venture investments (totalling $110/£176/€130 million). For an entrepreneur, this approach can provide a 'friendly customer' and help open doors. For the 'parent' it provides a privileged ringside seat as a business grows and the opportunity to decide if the area is worth plunging into more deeply, or at least provides valuable insights into new technologies or business processes.

According to Global Corporate Venturing (**www.globalcorporateventuring.com**) some 47 of the 100 biggest US companies are involved in venture investing. In the United States Google leads the field with 121 investments worth $5 billion. Elsewhere, the main action is in China and India where the values of corporate venturing investments made were $10 billion and $3 billion respectively.

CASE STUDY Innocent

April 2015 was a busy month for Innocent Drinks. The last couple of years following its 2013 record year – turnover £196.4 million ($283/€270.5 million) up from £150.8 million ($219/€208 million) and profits were up almost 200 per cent to £12 million ($17.5/€16.5 million) – had been difficult to say the least. The company invested heavily in rolling out its products across 14 European countries and saw profits crash to less than £1 million ($1.46/€1.38 million). But the company reckons its bet on Europe is paying off. With revenues from the continent of just over £100 million they have become the market leader in smoothies in Germany, with strong juice sales in France and Scandinavia. April 2015 also saw the launch of Innocent Bubbles, a blend of sparkling water and natural fruit juice, aimed as an alternative to sugary soft drinks. This Innocent sees as a way to capture a bigger market share in the competitive drinks sector.

The company had come a long way since the summer of 1998 when Richard Reed, Adam Balon and Jon Wright, Innocent's founders, had developed their first smoothie recipes. They were still nervous about giving up their jobs, when they bought £500 ($800/€590) worth of fruit, turned it into smoothies and sold them from a stall at a London music festival. They put up a sign saying, 'Do you think we should give up our jobs to make these smoothies?' next to bins labelled 'YES' and 'NO', inviting people to put the empty bottle in the appropriate bin. At the end of the weekend the 'YES' bin was full, so they went in the next day and resigned. The rest, as they say, is history. Virtually a household name, the business has experienced a decade of rapid growth. But the business stalled in 2008, with sales slipping back and their European expansion soaking up cash at a rapid rate.

The founders, average age 28, decided that they needed some heavyweight advice and talked to Charles Dunstone, Carphone Warehouse founder, and

Mervyn Davies, chairman of Standard Chartered. The strong advice was to get an investor with deep pockets and ideally something else to bring to the party to augment the youthful enthusiasm of the founders. They launched their search for an investor the day that Lehman Brothers filed for bankruptcy. In April 2009 the Innocent team accepted Coca-Cola as a minority investor in their business, paying £30 million ($48/€35 million) for a stake of between 10 and 20 per cent. They chose Coca-Cola because as well as providing the funds, it can help get their products out to more people in more places. Also, with Coca-Cola having been in business for over 120 years, there will be things they can learn from it.

Crowdfunding

Crowdfunding business finance is a new game-changing concept that puts the power firmly into the hands of entrepreneurs looking to raise finance. Instead of one large investor putting money into a business, larger numbers of smaller investors contribute as little as £10 each to raise the required capital. Crowdcube, the first UK-based crowdfunding website, has now teamed up with Startups.co.uk so entrepreneurs will be able to both access information on raising finance and have direct access to an innovative way to solve the problem from one site (**www.crowdcube.com/partner/startups**).

Crowdcube was the first crowdfunding website in the world to enable the public to invest in and receive shares in UK companies, and has more than 10,000 registered members currently seeking investment opportunities. The platform has already raised more than £3 million for small businesses through its principal site, and hosted the world's first £1 million crowdfunding deal in November 2011. The range of businesses that have used this financing method is wide and getting wider. Darlington Football Club raised £291,450 from 722 investors over 14 days through Crowdcube to help fend off closure after going into liquidation. Oil supplier Universal Fuels has raised £100,000 through Crowdcube, making founder Oliver Morgan the youngest entrepreneur to successfully raise investment through the process.

CASE STUDY Chilango – how the Burrito Bond was born

When former Skype employees Eric Partaker and Dan Houghton started Chilango they had in mind supplying mouth-watering Mexican food, something of a rarity when they launched seven years ago. Eric developed an appetite for tacos, burritos and the like in his native Chicago, but when he came to work in London was faced with a veritable Mexican cuisine desert. When Eric met Dan, by coincidence also a Mexican food fanatic, the pair made it their mission to plug what they saw as a gap in the market.

Eric, an American and Norwegian national, graduated from the University of Illinois at Urbana-Champaign with a Bachelor of Science degree in Finance, and is also an alumnus of Katholieke Universiteit Leuven, Belgium, where he studied History, Philosophy, and Literature. Dan is a Cambridge mathematics graduate, leaving with a First. They met up in 2005 when they were both on the new business ventures team reporting to the CEO of Skype Technologies.

By 2014 with seven London Mexican food outlets open, one opposite the Goldman Sachs headquarters, they had proved there was an appetite for their business model. But with each new restaurant costing around £500,000 to launch opening they discovered another gap – an urgent need for cash to achieve their goal to launch six new Chilango restaurants around London quickly.

In 2014 they hit the headlines for financial rather than culinary innovation. Using the Crowdfunding website they set out to raise £1 million in two months offering 8 per cent interest with the capital to be repaid in four years. With the minimum investment set at £500, those putting up £10,000 get free lunch once a week at one of their restaurants. Hence the name 'Burrito Bond' was born.

One day after books on the bond opened, investments had already been received from executives in the food and drinks business, including the chief executive officer and chief financial officer of café-chain Carluccio's, the former CEO of Domino's Pizza UK and the former CEO of Krispy Kreme UK, according to the prospectus website. By 3 July 2014, according to information on the Crowdfunding website the company had received £1,140,500 from 344 investors.

Business angels

These are private individuals with their own funds, and perhaps some knowledge of the type of business in which they are looking to invest. In return for a share in the business, such investors will put in money at their own risk. They have been christened 'business angels', a term first coined to describe private wealthy individuals who back a play on Broadway or in London's West End.

Most angels are determined upon some involvement beyond merely signing a cheque and may hope to play a part in your business is some way. They are hoping for big rewards – one angel who backed Sage with £10,000

($16,000/€12,000) in its first round of £250,000 ($500,000/€295,000) financing saw his stake rise to £40 ($64/€47) million.

These angels frequently operate through managed networks, usually on the internet. The World Business Angels Association (**www.wbaa.biz** > Members) provides links to angels and angel associations around the globe. The UK Business Angels Association (**www.ukbusinessangelsassociation.org.uk**) has an online directory of UK business angels. The European Business Angels Network (eban) has directories of national business angel associations both inside and outside of Europe at (**www.eban.org** > About EBAN > Members Directory) from which you can find individual business angels.

Foreign Direct Investment (FDI) incentives

Primary incentives to attract FDI lie largely in creating a benign business environment, security of title to assets, transparent and robust accounting procedures and prevalence of the rule of law. Some countries – and indeed, at some time or other, most – indulge in a little sweetening of the pill, either by way of compensation for a deficiency in one or more of the primary incentives, or to deal with a particular economic problem such as low growth or high unemployment. Such incentives represent a source of free or relatively free funds to international businesses.

Table 5.2 shows the top ten destinations for FDI comparing 2010 with 2014. Major shifts in the pattern of international business are revealed in these bare statistics. In 2010 China ranked 14th and four years later had overtaken the United States. If you add in Hong Kong you can see clearly the shift of trade from West to East.

Incentive categories

Incentives for FDI are policed by the OECD (Organisation for Economic Co-operation and Development) who have agreed on a checklist for assessing FDI incentive policies. The checklist serves as a tool to assess the costs and benefits of using incentives to attract FDI; to provide operational criteria for avoiding wasteful effects; and to identify the potential pitfalls and risks of excessive reliance on incentive-based strategies.

The OECD divides FDI incentives into three broad categories: regulatory, financial and fiscal incentives financed wholly or in part by the host country.

Regulatory FDI incentives

These are policies of attracting foreign-owned enterprises by offering them exemptions from local rules and regulation such as easing the environmental, social and labour-market rules and regulations or other related employment requirements.

TABLE 5.2 Top 30 destinations for FDI (2010)

	2010		2014
1	United States	1	China
2	France	2	Hong Kong
3	United Kingdom	3	United States
4	Germany	4	Singapore
5	Netherlands	5	Brazil
6	Hong Kong	6	United Kingdom
7	Switzerland	7	Canada
8	Japan	8	Australia
9	Belgium	9	Netherlands
10	Spain	10	Luxembourg

Financial FDI incentives

These include some or all of the following:

- infrastructure subsidies, for example by increasing the attractiveness of an area by providing physical infrastructure (roads, railways, ports, airports) or communications generally;
- job training subsidies particularly when investors are faced with a shortcoming of qualified labour;
- relocation and expatriation support including grants to help meet removal costs of individual members of staff, as well as family-related expenses of expatriate members of staff;
- administrative assistance, eg carrying out a range of tasks such as applying for permissions that would otherwise have fallen on the investor;
- temporary wage subsidies.

Fiscal FDI incentives

Examples include:

- Credits to investors such as soft loans, interest subsidies or loan guarantees.
- Real estate support by, for example, selling land or buildings to foreign investors at below market values.
- Cost participation, helping investors cover their start-up costs.
- Reduced taxation, including lower corporate income tax, tax holidays, special tax-privileged zones, investment allowances, tax credits and reduced rates of withholding tax on remittances to home countries. Some countries use lower sales taxes and VAT reductions as an incentive, while others offer property tax reductions.
- Reduced taxation of employees can also be used as an inducement; for example by offering lower personal income tax or social security reductions for expatriate executives.

Sources of data on FDI

United Nations Conference on Trade and Development (**www.unctad.org**) produces comprehensive statistics on the pattern of Foreign Direct Investment and the incentives on offer to international businesses to locate in a particular country or region.

CIA World Fact Book (**www.cia.gov/library/publications/the-world-factbook** > Guide to country comparisons > Economy) provides rankings by country on a year-by-year basis.

Taxing international enterprises

One reason a business produces accounts and reports is to enable internal staff to keep track of performance, but although that is an important reason it is neither the only one nor the most important. It is the parties external to the business, shareholders and government authorities in particular, that have specific expectations and requirements that must be adhered to. Furthermore it's the responsibility of the directors, and by extension their advisors – accountants, MBAs and legal staff – to keep the business on the straight and narrow.

Some business schools take tax and reporting very seriously indeed. California State University, Northridge (CSUN) has offered a Master's of Science in Taxation since autumn of 2007, consisting of eight courses aiming to provide students with an in-depth knowledge in all the key areas of taxation. The University of Southern Maine's MBA Program offers a number of specializations in taxation including Advanced Business Taxation, as well as providing the opportunity for an internship in taxation.

Double taxation agreements

International businesses are usually taxed on their worldwide profits in the country in which they are domiciled. It is nevertheless possible for a business to incur a tax liability in more than one country. Most countries have 'double taxation' agreements to help make sure that tax isn't paid on the same taxable event twice, once in a foreign country and again at home.

Transfer pricing

International firms have a degree of flexibility as to where they incur charges and make profits if they have operations in more than one country. For example, if a company buys in components in one country, manufactures in another and has a marketing or administrative function in a third country, which is itself incurring cost and adding value, a business has a range of options on where it takes its final profits. By paying a subsidiary a high price for elements of their activities it is possible to lower taxable profits in the company's domestic market. This is not a strategy that appeals much to tax authorities, who work hard to limit the scope of such activities.

Sources of advice on international tax

Doing Business (**www.doingbusiness.org**) is a Word Bank Group service where you can see the full details of the tax regime for a specific country, the total number of taxes paid, the time it takes to prepare, file and pay (or withhold) the relevant tax, the value added tax/sales tax and social security contributions (in hours per year), and total amount of taxes payable by the business. You can sort the relevant data to show, for example, which country has the highest or lowest taxes, requires the most or least time to deal with or involves the most or fewest separate tax payments.

The International Tax Planning Association (**www.itpa.org** > The ITPA Green Book) is a directory of tax advisory organizations searchable by jurisdiction. Worldwide Tax (**www.worldwide-tax.com**) as well as showing tax rates and comparisons has a narrative explaining recent and imminent international tax changes.

Foreign exchange

It is almost inconceivable that an MBA will be working in a company that has no dealings with either overseas customers or foreign suppliers. This in turn means handling money in at least two currencies; your own and the country you will trade in or with. Many countries have their own currency, but not all currencies are equally stable. The less stable the currency the more cost and risk is involved in any transaction.

Key factors to consider about foreign currencies

There are four types of foreign currencies and each have very different risk profiles and need to be managed accordingly:

- Not fully convertible, which means that the government of the country concerned exercises political and economic control over the exchange rate and the amount of its currency that can be moved in or out. China and India are among many countries that fall into this category. These currencies can be very volatile and you will need permission to repatriate money.

- Pegged. The most favourable way to obtain currency stability has been to peg the local currency to a major convertible currency, such as the Euro or Dollar. This means that while the local currency may move up and down against all other world currencies, it will remain or at least attempt to remain stable against the one it is pegged against.

- Dollarized, which is a slight misnomer as the term is used to describe a country that abandons its own currency and adopts the exclusive use of the US dollar or another major international currency, such as the Euro.

- Fully convertible and so stands on its own two feet and fluctuates as the country in question succeeds or fails. Russia, for example, lifted currency controls in July 2006 as a sign of economic confidence, making the rouble fully convertible.

Types of foreign exchange risk to be managed

A business has two distinct types of foreign exchange risk to consider when it comes to considering which, if any, risk management strategy to pursue.

Transaction exposure

Transaction exposure occurs when a business incurs costs or generates revenues in any currency other than the one shown in its filed accounts. Two types of event can lead to an exchange rate risk: there is a mismatch between cost of sales (manufacturing etc) incurred in one currency and the actual sales income generated in another; any time lag between setting the selling price in one currency and the date the customer actually pays up. As it is unlikely that there will have been no movement in exchange rates, transaction risk is real and potentially could have serious consequences.

Translation exposure

Translation exposure refers to the effects of movements in the exchange rate on the balance sheet and profit and loss account that occur between reporting dates on assets and liabilities denominated in foreign currencies. In practice any company that has assets or liabilities denominated in a currency other than the currency shown on their reported accounts will have to 'translate' those back into the company's reporting currency when the consolidated accounts have to be produced. This could be up to four times a year for major trading businesses. Any changes in the foreign exchange rate between the countries involved will cause movements in the accounts that have nothing to do with the underlying economic performance of the company.

Help with managing foreign exchange risk

These organizations can help an MBA keep on top of foreign exchange matters:

- HiFX plc (**www.hifx.co.uk**). The Reuters Forex Poll ranks HiFX plc within the top three most accurate foreign exchange forecasters globally, beating many of the world's leading banks.
- OANDA (**www.oanda.com**) were first to market in making comprehensive currency exchange information available over the Internet, and now licence out to hotels and airlines providing exchange-rate information on their websites.
- The Financial Markets Association (**www.aciforex.com** >ACI in your country). From here you will find links to the websites of some 90 country-affiliated associations, listed by continent. The country associations contain directories of members.

Online video courses and lectures

Capital structures in major corporations: Discussion at Columbia Business School by visitors and faculty: **www7.gsb.columbia.edu/video/v/node/1363?page=1**

Corporate Finance Essentials: Prof Javier Estrada of IESE Business School offers this course each year. It consists of six sessions requiring no previous knowledge or preparation. Each session will consist of a video lecture of around 45–60 minutes and one or two recommended readings: **www.coursera.org/course/corpfinance**

Exchange Rates and Balance: Professor Kenneth Train, UCBerkeley: **www.youtube.com/watch?v=_KljHF8nn-U**

Financial Risk Management: Peter Levene, chairman of Lloyd's of London talks at Berkeley-Haas: **www.youtube.com/watch?v=cM40cJNZ9A4**

Forward Contract: Investopedia: **www.investopedia.com/video/play/forward-contract/**

How Do Futures Contracts Work? Investopedia: **www.investopedia.com/video/play/futures-contract-explained/**

Interest Rate Risk: Investopedia: **www.investopedia.com/video/play/ interest-rate-risk/**

Introduction to Leverage: Khan Academy: **www.khanacademy.org/ economics-finance-domain/core-finance/money-and-banking/banking- and-money/v/banking-10-introduction-to-leverage-bad-sound**

Managing Risk and Cash Flow in International Trade: Delivered by Export Development Canada: **www.youtube.com/watch?v=XRNxSZ7Ry7Y**

Mastering the VC Game: How to Raise Your First Round of Capital with Jeff Bussgang, Senior Lecturer in Entrepreneurship at HBS and a General Partner at Flybridge Capital Partners: **www.youtube.com/ watch?v=aNfB4sBBwEc**

The Debt To Equity Ratio: Investopedia: **www.investopedia.com/ video/play/debt-to-equity-ratio/**

US GAAP – Revenue Recognition: Krista Pound from KPMG's US Accounting & Reporting Group: **www.youtube.com/ watch?v=nCrqktx-b38**

What are US GAAP and IFRS: Kevin Kimball, Brigham Young University– Hawaii: **www.youtube.com/watch?v=qxGbbtroDwg**

Online video case studies

BP: Risk management failure at BP. QBE Insurance Europe Ltd: **www.youtube.com/watch?v=mGq2kVPVuig**

Challenger – A Case Study in Risk Management: History Channel: **www.youtube.com/watch?v=mG8BPB_oPlg**

Crowd-funding Case Studies with Fundit.ie: **www.youtube.com/ watch?v=phX1q9CHmkY&feature=iv&src_vid= CejPet3MiMs&annotation_id=annotation_165899**

Endeca. Co-Founders Steve Papa and Pete Bell simulate the founding and early growth of their company, walking through key terms and legal due diligence. Harvard i-lab. Strategy: **www.youtube.com/ watch?v=0QTProGpc1o**

Funding Strategies at Apperian. Mark Lorion, CMO of Apperian, talks about his company's funding strategy at the Harvard i-lab: **www.youtube.com/watch?v=5CtUNS5kERw**

HP-Autonomy debacle: In the Boardroom from Reuters. Lucy Marcus looks at the fall-out: apportioning blame, audit committees & board responsibility: **http://uk.reuters.com/video/2012/11/21/in-the- boardroom-hp-autonomy-debacle?videoId=239296266**

Meraki: Co-founder and CEO, Sanjit Biswas presents the history of the company, from its roots at MIT in Cambridge, MA to February 2012, immediately prior to the deal with Cisco: **www.youtube.com/ watch?v=-btH98nZVE8**

Profit Pollution and Deception BP and the Oil Spill BBC Documentary: Best Documentaries: **www.youtube.com/watch?v=8zGFvzMMO9w**

Royal Dutch Shell – How management accountants manage risk: Simon Henry, CFO: **www.youtube.com/watch?v=rKNv2hVCfNU**

Innocent Drink's: Richard Reed Innocent co-founder talks about rejection from banks and others: **http://startups.co.uk/richard-reed-on-struggling-to-find-investment-video/**

Netstore: Founder Paul Barry-Walsh on not risking his house when raising a loan: **http://startups.co.uk/netstore-founder-paul-barry-walsh-on-not-risking-his-house-video/**

6 Managing the international organization

- Structural options.
- Line and staff relationships.
- Building and leading teams.
- Outsourcing.
- Understanding the composition of an international board of directors.

Managers in international businesses often believe that the most important challenges lie in areas such as finding markets they can quickly dominate, sources of significant FDI (Foreign Direct Investment) or countries with a low-cost, well-educated, under-employed workforce, as with Kenya's foray into the call-centre business arena (see Chapter 2). Not to denigrate these factors in any way, but the single most prevalent reason for a firm's international business strategy failing lies in its implementation and, by extension, it is the people that carry out business tasks and the way in which they are organized that contribute most to success. Stated like that it sounds a fairly simple task. Just work your way through those headings and any MBA worth their salt should be able to get the desired results. Unfortunately, people both individually and collectively are rarely malleable and organization structures have a knack of getting in the way of performance at every level. The famous German military strategist Moltke's statement that 'No campaign plan survives first contact with the enemy' applies here if the word enemy is replaced by organization.

HRM (Human Resource Management) is the subject of Chapter 7. This chapter considers the options for how those 'humans' should be organized. By understanding and applying the following principles and concepts the MBA student can improve an organization's chances of achieving its objectives.

International business strategy vs structure, people and systems

This is the 'which came first' question akin to that of the chicken and the egg. Unless you are starting up a new international organization on a greenfield site with no people other than you and a pile of cash, every business situation involves some compromise between the ideal and the possible when it comes to people and structures.

The theory is clear. An organization's strategy, itself a product of its business environment, determines the shape of the organization structure, the sort of people it will employ and how they will be managed, controlled and rewarded. But in the real world the business environment is constantly changing as economies fluctuate, competitors come and go and consumer needs, desires and aspirations alter. In any event a business is limited in its freedom of action. However violent and essential a change in strategy, a business will rarely be free to hire and fire staff at will simply to change direction. The exception is in the case of a complete closure or withdrawal from an activity such as that of Marks & Spencer's controversial closure of its French outlets in 2001. This move was considered vital to the survival of the whole business and despite May Day protests in France the company's shares rose 7 per cent on the announcement.

Figure 6.1 is a useful aid to understanding how to approach organizational development. The concentric circles are a metaphor to remind us of

FIGURE 6.1   A framework for understanding organizational behaviour

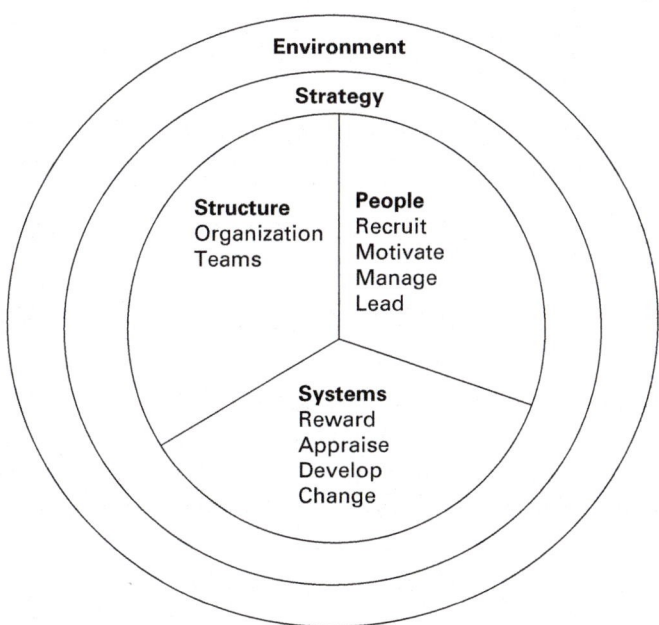

the circular nature of the subject. You can't just tackle one area without having an impact on others.

Structures – the options

Just as the skeleton is the structure that holds a body together, a business and its various departments, including marketing, also have their framework. The goal of any framework is to provide some boundaries while at the same time allowing the whole 'body' flexibility to respond to go about its business. Whereas human bodies keep a very similar skeleton to the one they start out with a business has a number of very different organizational structures to choose from. Also it is unlikely that any one structure will be appropriate throughout an organization's life.

For an organization a structure has to perform the following functions:

- show who is responsible for what and to whom;
- define roles and responsibilities;
- establish communication and control mechanisms;
- lay out the ground rules for cooperation between all parts of the organization;
- set out the hierarchy of authority, power and decision making.

There are two major building blocks used in shaping an organization's structure beyond the level of the individual:

- the organizational chart;
- team composition.

There is nothing permanent about the organization of the marketing function, as the Cisco case illustrates.

CASE STUDY Cisco Systems – organizational evolution

On 11 February 2015, John Chambers, Cisco chairman and CEO, reported that Q2 Revenue for their current financial year was $11.9 billion, an increase of 7 per cent year over year, no mean achievement for what the company acknowledged as 'a volatile economic environment.' Chambers, who obtained his MBA from Kelley School of Business, Indiana University, joined Cisco in 1983 as senior vice president, Worldwide Sales and Operations, as part of the team responsible for the start-up. The CEO continued in his Q2 statement to emphasize that 'our strong momentum is the direct result of how well we have managed our company transformation over the last three-plus years.' Cisco's organizational evolution had been going on for much longer than three years. Barely a decade after husband and wife Len Bosack and Sandy Lerner, both working for Stanford University, invented the technology to enable them to e-mail each other from different buildings on the campus, the company was already embarking its first major structural change.

Cisco Systems is a world leader in networking for the Internet, with over 75,000 employees in more than 115 countries. Today, Cisco solutions are the networking foundations for service providers, small to medium business and enterprise customers who include corporations, government agencies, utilities and educational institutions. Since starting it has undergone several major changes in organizational structure, the latest being:

- In April 1997 Cisco structured its products and solutions into three customer segments: enterprise, small/medium business, and service provider. The organizational structure was altered to address two major new market opportunities: the service provider migration to IP services and the adoption of IP products by small and medium-sized businesses through channel distribution. To that point Cisco had a product-focused structure.

- In August 2001 Cisco announced a transition from its three lines of businesses – enterprise, service provider and commercial – to allow the company to focus specifically on technology areas such as: Access, Aggregation, Internet Switching and Services, Ethernet Access, Network Management Services, Core Routing, Optical, Storage, Voice and Wireless.

- In December 2007 Cisco announced a new organizational structure to position itself for growth in new markets and cater to the demands of new and emerging markets in China, Brazil and India. The new structure also set out to address the challenges imposed by the next phase of Internet growth centred on the demands of growth in video and collaborative and networked Web 2.0 technologies.

- In December 2012 Cisco announced a global strategy – Tomorrow Starts Here – designed to position them for the next 10 years as a global leader in connecting the previously unconnected 'Internet of Everything'. A company spokesperson said 'transforming Cisco requires making tough, tough decisions', whilst announcing 12,000 people would go as part of 'reallocation of resources.'

Chambers, in a recent interview with McKinsey and Company, the US management consultancy company, explained that to move the company from one that 'sold plumbing and routers' to becoming 'the most trusted business advisor as well as the most trusted technology advisor' required a change in organization structures. Cisco's future, Chambers claims, requires 'collaboration and teamwork, with a structured process behind it. And that's the key.'

Organizational charts

Daniel C McCallum is generally credited with developing the first systematic set of organizational charts in 1855 to organize railroad building on an efficient basis. The trigger for his innovation was the discovery that the building costs per mile of track did not drop with the length of line being built, contrary to logic. The inefficiencies were being caused by poor organization.

Basic hierarchical organization

This simple structure has everyone or every part of the organization reporting to one person. It works well when the organization is small, decisions are simple or routine communications are easy.

FIGURE 6.2   Basic hierarchical organization chart

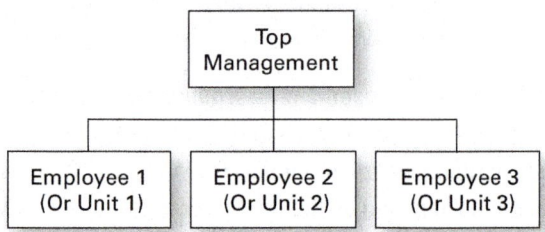

This basic structure can be based around one of several groupings including:

- functions such as sales, new product development, market research, PR or advertising;
- geography such as country or region;
- product or service and product or service groups;
- customer or market segment such as trade, consumers, new accounts or key accounts.

Span of control

The number of people a manager can have reporting to them in a hierarchy is governed by the span of control. Where fewer people are reporting, the span of control is termed as narrow and more is wide.

A narrow span of control means any one manager has fewer people reporting to them so communications should be better and control easier; however, as the organization grows, it usually means creating more and more layers of management so it negates any earlier efficiency.

A wide span of control, also known as a flat management structure, involves having many people or units reporting to one person. This usually means having fewer layers of management, but it does call for a greater level of skill from those doing the managing. The nature of the tasks being carried out by subordinates will limit the capacity to run a flat organization. For example, a regional manager responsible for identical units such as a branch of a supermarket chain supported by good and well-developed control systems may be able to have 10 or more direct reports. But if the organization comprises very different types of unit – for example, retail outlets, central bakeries, garages, factories, accounts departments and sales teams – the ability of any one manger to handle that diversity will be limited.

A further factor to take into account is the skill level of both managers and managed. A higher-skilled workforce can operate with a wider span of control as they will need less supervision and a higher-skilled manager can control a greater number of staff.

Line and staff organization

One way to keep an organization structure flat as the enterprise gets bigger and more complex is to introduce staff functions that take over some of the common duties of unit mangers. For example, a marketing manager could probably handle their own recruitment, selection and training of staff while they have a dozen or so people in their domain. Once that expands to hundreds, and if growth is also impacting on other management areas such as sales and marketing, then it may be more efficient to create a specialist HR unit to support the line marketing managers.

Staff positions support line managers by providing knowledge and expertise but the buck ultimately stops with the line manager. Three types of authority are created in a line and staff organization, so alongside some efficiencies lies the possibility for conflict.

- Line authority goes down the chain of command giving those further up the right and responsibility to instruct those below them to carry out specific tasks.

- Staff authority is the right and responsibility to advise line managers in certain areas. For example, an HR staffer will advise a line marketing manager on redundancy terms, conditions of employment and disciplinary issues.
- Functional authority or limited line authority gives a staff person the ultimate sanction over particular functions such as safety or financial reporting.

There are possibilities for conflict in the relationship between line and staff but these can be minimized in two ways. In the first instance staff people report to their own superiors who have line authority over them. Secondly, line and staff personnel can be organized into teams with shared goals and objectives.

FIGURE 6.3   Line and staff organization chart

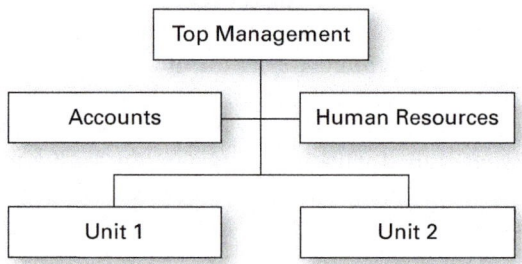

Functional organization

In a functional organization the staff and line managers all report to a common senior manager. This places more of a burden on senior management who have a wider span of control and a greater variety of tasks to take responsibility for. However, this structure concentrates all responsibility in one person and so minimizes the area for conflict. It may also deny an organization the high level of expertise that comes with having a professional staff function. For example, this would leave the onus for being fully conversant with current employment law on a production manager, rather than giving them access to staff advice. They can of course read up on the law themselves, but that is not quite as good as having it as part of an everyday skill and experience base.

Matrix organization

A matrix organization gives two people line authority for interlocking areas of responsibility. In Figure 6.5 below you can see that a manager is

FIGURE 6.4 Functional organization chart

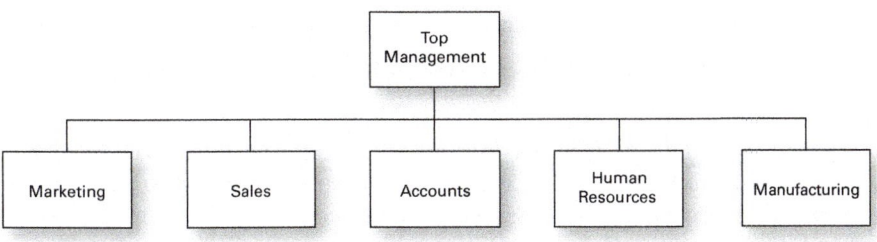

FIGURE 6.5 Matrix organization chart

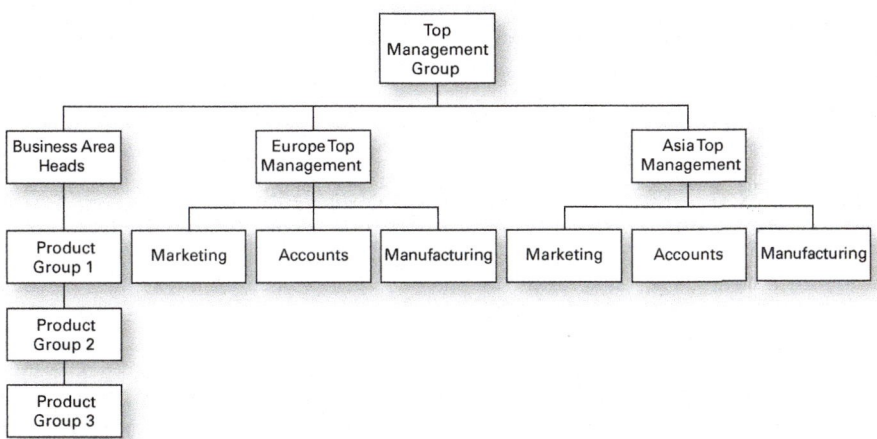

responsible for sales of product group 1 in both Europe and Asia. However, a manager is also responsible for the sales of all product groups within their continent.

The aim of a matrix structure is to ensure all key areas in an organization have a line manager responsible for championing them. There is still the possibility for conflict of interest. For example, the person responsible for a product group may try to get more attention for their product in a particular market than it really warrants. In theory the managers in matrix organizations are senior enough to iron out their differences. That is not always the case in practice and in such cases their mutual boss has to resolve the issue.

Matrix organizations in the overseas operations of an international firm, as with other uses of the matrix structure, are not without weaknesses. There is always a danger of ambiguity especially when managers of different nationalities are in competition for common resources against one another. The potential for cultural bias if allowed to get hold and result in favouritism could destroy or at least seriously erode any potential benefits.

Strategic Business Unit (SBU)

SBUs are in effect separate enterprises (Figure 6.6) with full responsibility for their own profit or loss, either right down to the net profit level or as far back as the marketing margin (see Chapter 12 'Tests of profitability' section for more on margins). In a business where most of the costs are in service, advertising, branding or Internet fulfilment it would be quite possible for this type of SBU to be virtually a stand-alone venture, excepting for treasury, accounting and tax functions. They may themselves be organized in any one of the above structures. If they don't have their own specialist staff function they may buy it in from the parent company when required. This maintains the concept of full profit accountability.

SBUs are further divided into those who simply have control over current revenue and expenditure and those 'Investment Centres' that can make capital expenditure decisions such as investing in new product research and development or buying into joint ventures and other strategic relationships (see also the Bayer case study in Chapter 9).

FIGURE 6.6 Strategic business unit organization chart

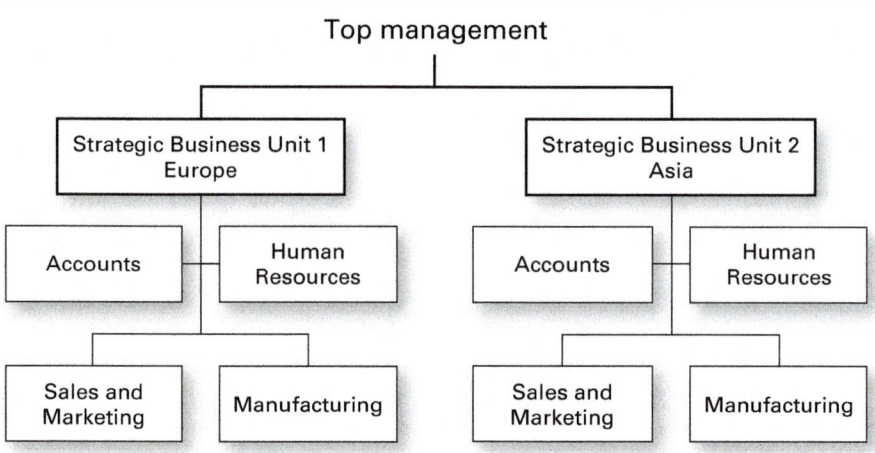

Succession planning

No general would fight a battle without having a reserve force ready to plug gaps that appear either in the front line or are caused by casualties in key staff. Perhaps the most spectacular military example was the rapid deployment of Montgomery to head the 8th Army when Churchill's own preferred candidate, 'Strafer' Gott, was killed flying back to Cairo.

For business and other organizations this reserve is usually limited to the process of identifying future potential leaders to fill key positions when staff leave or are themselves promoted. A subsidiary but nonetheless important role of any organization chart is to facilitate this planning.

Elements to consider in this area include:

- broadening existing managers' competencies by lateral moves in the organization;
- training and development across a wider skill base than is required for current roles;
- having a database of outsiders who can rapidly be approached by headhunters (specialist recruitment consultants) when the need arises.

Teams

Teams are the component parts of a business's structure and their effective creation and operation are a key way to get exceptional results from an organization. A group of people, even if they work together, are not necessarily a team; look at Figure 6.7 below, which compares some of the characteristics of a sports team with those of a random collection of people that meet for a game. You can see immediately what needs to be done to weld people into a team.

Successful teams have certain features in common. They all have strong and effective leadership; have clear objectives; appropriate resources; the ability to communicate freely throughout the organization; the authority to act quickly on decisions; a good balance of team members; the ability to work collectively; and a size appropriate to the task.

FIGURE 6.7 Groups are not the same as teams

Sports team	Sports club
- Has the right number of players for the game	- Just the number of people who turn up
- Everyone has a clearly defined role	- Positions of players decided on the day
- Concrete and measurable objectives	- Often the aims have never been explained and where they have, different people have different aims
- An obvious competitor for the team to unite against	- Sometimes the internal competition is more important than winning a game
- A coach to train and improve players' game	- Training is ad hoc
- Right equipment for the game	- The right equipment is sometimes missing and not all players have the right equipment

Team types

Teams can be made up of anything from 5 to 20 people. Anything above 20 is usually too unwieldy and will take up more resources than an organization can afford to devote to one aspect of the business.

Business teams

These are a group of people tasked with managing functions and achieving specific results over the longer term. In our example there are three of these covering sales, administration and warehouse/dispatch. So, for example, the sales team is expected to meet sales targets and the dispatch team to get goods to customers on time. In practice every firm will have its own definition of business functions.

Project teams

These are often cross-functional, made up of people from different areas. These can be assembled for any period of time to look at a particular project. In this example we have assumed that each of these teams has been asked to look at how each function could be made more efficient. The value of having someone from other functions in these teams is to ensure that too parochial a view is not taken.

Taskforce teams

These are short-term bodies put together quickly to look at one narrow issue or specific problem. For example, if you proposed changing your working hours a taskforce could look at the implications for everyone inside and outside the firm and report back. Then a decision can be made based on the best information provided by people most affected by the change.

Team roles

However talented the soloists are in an organization in the end it's orchestras that make enough 'noise' to make things happen. But teams don't just occur naturally. The presumption that people are going to work together is usually a mistake. Chaos is more likely than teamwork.

Cultures in businesses have very different pedigrees and can pull the organization in very different directions. Take one successful new Internet business for example, where people came from financial services, retail and more recently technology. The company's roots were in financial services. Their competitors were banks and brokerage firms and their employees had moved around the sector in search of the ultimate accolade, to become a vice-president. The focus was inward towards 'hierarchy and title'. Their second cohort of employees came from retailing, the staff of their one-time expanding branch network. For retailers the focus is outwards towards the customer. Their success was measured in the market and the best salesmen had the greatest respect and power. The third group, and the most recent, was the technologists. For these people success was measured by technical expertise. Titles were irrelevant and their main concern was for the completion of the project. Their loyalty was not to the hierarchy but to the principles of the project itself, and to their team.

Putting people with disparate cultures into teams because of their particular professional or job skills can cause problems but if the team is to function effectively the balance of behavioural styles has to mesh too. Although there are other methods of categorizing team roles, the following – identified by Meredith Belbin while a Research Fellow at Cranfield (**www.belbin.com**) – are the key roles that need to be taken if a team is to work effectively:

- Chairman/team leader. Stable, dominant, extrovert. Concentrates on objectives. Does not originate ideas. Focuses people on what they do best.
- Plant. Dominant, high IQ, introvert. A 'scatterer of seeds' who originates ideas. Misses out on detail. Thrustful but easily offended.
- Resource investigator. Stable, dominant, extrovert and sociable. Lots of contacts with the outside world. Strong on networks. Salesperson/diplomat/liaison officer. Not an original thinker.
- Shaper. Anxious, dominant, extrovert. Emotional and impulsive. Quick to challenge and to respond to a challenge. Unites ideas, objectives and possibilities. Competitive. Intolerant of vagueness.
- Company worker. Stable, controlled. A practical organizer. Can be inflexible but likely to adapt to established systems. Not an innovator.
- Monitor evaluator. High IQ, stable, introvert. Goes in for measured analysis not innovation. Unambiguous and often lacking enthusiasm. But solid and dependable.
- Team worker. Stable, extrovert, but not really dominant. Much concerned with individuals' needs. Builds on others' ideas. Cools things down when tempers fray.
- Finisher. Anxious introvert. Worries over what could go wrong. Permanent sense of urgency. Preoccupied with order. Concerned with 'following through'.

Building and running a team

The following are the five essential elements to establishing and running effective teams.

1 Balanced team roles

You have to start building a team by recognizing that people are different. Every team member must not only have their 'technical' skills such as being an accountant or sales person, they must also have a valuable team role.

Experts in team behaviour have identified the key team profiles that are essential if a team is to function well. Any one person may perform more than one of these roles. But if too many people are competing to perform one of the roles or one or more of these roles are neglected, the team will be unbalanced. They will perform in much the same way as a car does when a cylinder misfires.

2 Shared vision and goal

It is essential that the team has ownership of its own measurable and clearly defined goals. This means involving the team in marketing planning and strategy. It also means keeping the communication channels open as the business grows. The founding team knew clearly what they were trying to achieve and as they probably shared an office they shared information as they worked. But as the group gets larger and new people join, it will become necessary to help the informal communication systems to work better. Briefing meetings, social events and bulletin boards are all ways to get teams together and keep them facing the right way.

3 Have a shared language

To be a member of a business team people have to have a reasonable grasp of the language of business. It's not much use extolling people to increase market share or reduce debtor days if they have only the haziest notion of what those terms mean, why they matter or how they can influence the results. So you need to develop rounded business skills across all the core team members through continuous training, development and coaching.

4 Compatible personalities

While having different Belbin team profiles is important it is equally vital to have a team who can get on with one another. They have to be able to listen to and respect other people's ideas and views. They need to support and trust one another. They need to be able to accept conflict as a healthy reality and work through it to a successful outcome.

5 Good leadership

First-class leadership is perhaps the most important characteristic that distinguishes winning teams from the also-rans. However good the constituent parts, without leadership a team rapidly disintegrates into a rabble bound by little but a pay cheque. (See the 'Managing change' section later in this chapter for more on leadership.)

Managing a global team

Multi-site global businesses can present some difficulties when it comes to teamwork. If your team is scattered around five continents and a dozen time zones you could spend more time at airports than with your team. These are a few ways to work around this difficulty and so bridge the gap between the times when face-to-face visits are possible.

Skype and video conferencing: Skype with its Internet chat and phone functions brings back the real-time aspect, and to a certain extent the spontaneity if people leave Skype running at their workstations. Video conferencing using the inbuilt camera on a PC notebook is another way to recoup some of the impulsiveness inherent in MBWA (Management by Walking Around). Neither Skype nor video conferencing are quite as effective as a heart-to-heart around the coffee machine, but from time to time they are a reasonable approximation.

Project and function management software tools (eg Basecamp, Salesforce): Structured project and function management is necessary, even when MBWA is being used. Web-based solutions like Basecamp and Salesforce have the advantage of being central repositories for information, event scheduling and progress reports whilst being visible to you as the manager. But whilst you can see what is happening with your team anywhere anytime, such software does not readily provide the insights or opportunities to develop the trusting relationships that MBWA can offer.

Google Docs – real-time work collaboration: Tools such as Google Docs let teams work together from different geographical locations, producing documents and commenting on them. Despite different time zones for example, executives can 'visit' projects to add their own remarks. However, with no real-time or face-to-face contact whilst exposing an employee's work to constant management scrutiny of the executive, it reduces spontaneity and can be demoralizing.

The board of directors

One team stands apart from all the others within an organization – the Board of Directors, usually reduced to the title 'The Board'. It is the team every MBA needs to know and understand and to aspire to joining its ranks. Directors in major or public companies have a role outside that of simply heading up a function, even one as important as marketing. There is often confusion as to where the ultimate power rests in a company; with the directors or the shareholders. In private companies they are often one and the same body but in public companies even where family ties remain they are distinct and separate. In law a company is an entity separate from both its shareholders and directors. According to a company's articles of association some powers are exercised by directors, certain other powers may be reserved for the shareholders and exercised at a general meeting. If the powers of management are vested in the directors, then they and they alone can exercise these powers. The only way in which shareholders can control the exercise of powers by directors is by altering the articles, or by refusing to re-elect the directors of whose actions they disapprove. Some of a director's duties, responsibilities and potential liabilities are:

- to act in good faith in the interests of the company – this includes carrying out duties diligently and honestly;
- not to carry on the business of the company with intent to defraud creditors or for any fraudulent purpose;
- not knowingly to allow the company to trade while insolvent – directors who do so may have to pay for the debts incurred by the company while insolvent;
- not to deceive shareholders and to appoint auditors to oversee the accounting records;
- to have regard for the interests of employees in general;
- to comply with the requirements of the Companies Acts, such as providing what is needed in accounting records or filing accounts.

Composition of the board

The board is made up of two types of directors, internal and external, and typically the board would exercise major decisions through a number of committees:

- Internal directors: Usually headed up by a chairman who runs board meetings, a CEO (Chief Executive Officer) or Managing Director who runs the operating business and a number of other directors.
- External directors: Known as non-executive directors, usually people of stature and experience who can act as both a source of wise independent advice and a check on any wilder elements on a board.
- International directors: Shell, a global group of energy and petrochemicals companies with around 101,000 employees in more than 90 countries and territories has a main board reflecting that diversity. The chairman is Finnish and his deputy is British and a former Ambassador to the United States. Other directors include a German national who is also on the board of Deutsche Bank AG, an American who formerly headed up DuPont, a former Dutch prime minister, a Frenchwoman who was previously chief executive of Société Générale de Belgique, and a Swiss CEO who has held a variety of finance and business roles in Switzerland, the UK, Argentina and Chile.
- Local country/region boards: Shell, for example, has local boards of directors in Hong Kong, Ireland, Pakistan, Canada, Oman, Malaysia, Australia, the United Kingdom and a whole host of other countries.
- Committees: The main board committees are those that oversee remuneration (particularly for directors), auditing, social responsibility (and 'green' matters), mergers and acquisitions and regulatory affairs.

Outsourcing

Outsourcing, a key feature of most international business strategies, is the activity of contracting out the elements that are not considered core or central to the business. It is an important logistics and distribution strategy open to a business that will help it to lower costs and hence be more competitive and to move elements of production or service delivery to a more effective point in the value chain. There are obvious advantages to outsourcing; the best people can do what they are best at. But the approach can get out of hand if left unmanaged. In 2008 IBM completed a major overhaul of its value chain and for the first time in its century-long history created an Integrated Supply Chain (ISC) – a centralized worldwide approach to deciding what to do itself, what to buy in and where to buy in from. Suppliers were halved from 66,000 to 33,000; support locations from 300 to 3 global centres – Bangalore, Budapest and Shanghai. Manufacturing sites were reduced from 15 to 9, all 'globally enabled' in that they can make almost any of their products at each plant and deliver them anywhere in the world. In the process IBM has lowered operating costs by more than $4 billion a year.

Outsourcing became formally recognized as a business strategy in the late 1980s. Then as organizations began to focus more on cost-saving measures, they started to outsource those functions necessary to run a company but not deemed to be mission critical, to countries with a lower cost base. Many US and European firms outsourced accounting, bookkeeping, telemarketing and more recently IT and software writing to the Indian sub-continent. Almost the entire garment industry was outsourced to Asia. The speed of technological change, intense competition and the increasing expertise and specialization required for different operational activities has made it impossible for one organization to maintain competitive advantage across every aspect of its operation.

Even Apple, a pretty big business in its own right, has outsourced all of its PowerBook, iBook, MacBook Pro and MacBook Air to Taiwan-based Quanta Computer, the largest notebook computer company in the world. One out of every three laptop PCs in the world is manufactured by Quanta and the top 10 PC companies in the world all use Quanta as their ODM (Original Design Manufacturing) partner. Quanta has the double benefit or operating in a low-wage environment, with operations on the Chinese mainland, and economies of scale in that it makes many more laptops than any of its partners do individually.

Setting the boundaries

The starting point in outsourcing is to decide what you are good at then consider outsourcing everything else. Focus your company on your core competency, and stick to the knitting. There are some things that are central to your business that you should probably not outsource at the outset.

Start small, cutting your teeth on something that if things go wrong you can survive a failure. In 2000 Boeing set out to turn its Seattle aircraft factory from a manufacturing unit to becoming a simple assembly plant putting aeroplane kits together from modules designed and produced elsewhere. Until this new outsourcing strategy was introduced, Boeing provided parts subcontractors with detailed blueprints, but now it planned to give suppliers less detailed specifications from which they had to create their own blueprints. The strategy began to unravel almost from the outset. One major supplier didn't even have an engineering department when it won its contract and had to outsource the work itself. Some of the pieces manufactured halfway around the globe didn't fit together and some outsourcing partners couldn't meet their output quotas. In 2009, Boeing had to stump up $1 billion in cash and credit to take over the underperforming fuselage manufacturing plant of Vought Aircraft Industries and go back into the aircraft manufacturing business itself.

Online video courses and lectures

The Benefits of Teams: Alanis Business Academy: **www.youtube.com/ watch?v=tBC4JsaBYkl**

Introduction to Operations Management. Key topics include: Process analysis, Productivity, Responsiveness and Quality and Product variety. Taught four times a year by Wharton's faculty: **www.coursera.org/ course/whartonoperations**

Managing Global Virtual Teams: Programme director Erin Meyer and participants of INSEAD's Managing Global Virual Teams programme discuss the challenges faced by global teams and how you can leverage your team's cultural diversity: **www.youtube.com/ watch?v=Y1YokiumAkQ**

The Management Hierarchy: A Look Into the Different Levels of Management: Alanis Business Academy: **www.youtube.com/ watch?v=UJS9JrFDuRo**

Operations Management: Delivered by Professor Gopesh Anand, University of Illinois at Urbana-Champaign. This course will be broken up into 4 weekly modules covering the following topics: Week 1: Operations Strategy and Process Configurations. Week 2: Operations Metrics and Process Maps Week 3: Inventory and Supply Chain Management. Week 4: Statistical Process Control and Process Capability. Runs once a year in the autumn: **www.coursera.org/course/operationsmanagement**

Restructuring your organisation for the digital age: Adobe Summit 2014: **http://tv.adobe.com/watch/adobe-summit-2014-emea/restructuring- your-organisation-for-the-digital-age/**

Supply Chain Distruptions and Humanitarian Logistics: Professor Yossi Sheffi, MIT: **www.youtube.com/watch?v=ky_h4YB_O4U**

Supply Chain Management Masterclass: Dr Sinéad Roden, Cass Business School: **www.youtube.com/watch?v=nmO-y0q8sdl**

Teamwork and communication: Lauren Rodda and Amanda Mok, MIT Open Courseware: **http://ocw.mit.edu/high-school/humanities-and-social-sciences/leadership-training-institute/video-lectures/lecture-4/**

Online video case studies

Amazon's Seventh Generation Fulfilment: CBS 60 Minutes: **www.cbsnews.com/news/amazons-jeff-bezos-looks-to-the-future/**

Cisco CEO John Chambers talks on Teamwork and Collaboration to Harvard Business Review: **https://hbr.org/2008/10/cisco-ceo-john-chambers-on-tea**

Desigual Fashion, Warehouse Logistics and Distribution: Desigual operates 157 stores worldwide and annually provides 10 million garments: **www.youtube.com/watch?v=9I6HPpDUR-s**

Ford Motor Company's European Supply Chain Case Study: Penske Logistics: **www.youtube.com/watch?v=KWABT48wTFw**

Lee Kuan Yew speaking at INSEAD in 2007 on leadership and global politics: **www.youtube.com/watch?v=LvBlzDz9ttM**

Lufthansa Outsourcing Deal With IBM: Daily Motion: **www.dailymotion.com/video/x2crelq_eu-clears-lufthansa-outsourcing-deal-with-ibm_news**

Mighty River Power: Doug Heffernan, Chief Executive delivers 'Financial Results – Analyst Presentation': **www.youtube.com/watch?v=EzNPBvSyYUI**

Starbucks: Tom Peters returns to his favourite topic from In Search of Excellence, Managing by Wandering Around, as exemplified by Howard Schultz, Starbucks CEO: **www.youtube.com/watch?v=2UIY0Vykc_Y**

7 Human resource management

- Understanding culture.
- Leadership styles.
- Appointing expatriates.
- Motivating staff.
- Developing people.
- Handling employment law.
- Managing change.

If structures (see Chapter 6) are the skeleton of an organization, people are its blood and guts. Douglas McGregor, a founding faculty member of MIT's Sloan School of Management began his management classic *The Human Side of Enterprise* (published in 1960) with the question: 'What are your assumptions (implicit as well as explicit) about the most effective way to manage people?' This seemingly simple question led to a fundamental revolution in management thinking. McGregor went on to claim 'The effectiveness of organizations could be at least doubled if managers could discover how to tap into the unrealised potential present in their workforces.'

Finding the right people, keeping them onside, motivating, managing and rewarding them are the defining distinctions between the most successful organizations and the mediocre. Over the past 30 years or so organizations have acquired centralized HR (Human Resources) departments whose purpose is to facilitate people issues, as they often quaintly term their work. McGregor anticipated their arrival with this pithy quote: 'It is one of the favourite pastimes of management to decide, from within their professional ivory tower, what help the field organisation needs and then to design and develop programs for meeting these needs. Then it becomes necessary to get the field organisation to accept the help provided. This is normally the role of the Change Manager; to implement the change that no-one asked for or wants.'

None of this is to suggest that HR departments can't contribute to helping with 'people issues'. It's just that people issues are too important to exclude their immediate superiors from. At the very least MBA skills include a sound grasp of the key tasks that the HR department is charged with performing.

Culture

Culture is the defining issue for HR management in the international business. A company operating with most of its key employees born, educated and domiciled in one country or region can reasonably expect to build its HR strategy in terms of recruitment, motivation and management within the scope of a single dominant culture. That is certainly a belief that no international business could or should share.

Geert Hofstede, a sometime Visiting Professor at INSEAD Business School in Fontainebleau near Paris, France, and a Fellow of the Academy of Management, conducted research with IBM starting in the 1960s, to survey and analyse information about the cultures from some 70 countries. His definition of culture derived from social anthropology and refers to the way people think, feel and act. Hofstede defined it as 'the collective programming of the mind distinguishing the members of one group or category of people from another'. The 'category' can refer to nations, regions within or across nations, ethnicities, religions, occupations, organizations or genders. A simpler definition he offers is 'the unwritten rules of the social game'. He identified four main dimensions of a nation's culture that the international business person needs to come to grips with to understand culture.

- Power Distance – A high power distance ranking indicates a society with inequalities of power and wealth, and where significant upward mobility of its citizens is not possible. A low power distance ranking indicates that the society promotes equality and opportunity for everyone.
- Individualism versus Collectivism – A high individualism ranking indicates that individuality and individual rights are paramount within the society, encouraging the forming of a large number of loose relationships. A low individualism ranking typifies societies of a more collectivistic nature, which have close ties between individuals and everyone takes responsibility.
- Uncertainty Avoidance – A high uncertainty avoidance ranking indicates that a country has a low tolerance for uncertainty and ambiguity, necessitating a rule-orientated society. A low uncertainty avoidance country is less rule-orientated, more readily accepts change, and takes more and greater risks.
- Masculinity versus Femininity – A high masculinity ranking indicates that the country experiences a high degree of gender differentiation;

with females being controlled by male domination. A low masculinity ranking indicates that the country has a low level of differentiation and discrimination between genders; females and males are treated equally in society.

Hofstede's scores for his dimension study, a portion of which is shown in Table 7.1, reveal a clear difference between say the United States where individualism is highly rated and in Japan where teams are more important. France and the United Kingdom are at opposite ends of the spectrum when it comes to the potential for upward mobility.

Hofstede's is not the only system used to get a measure of cultural difference. SH Schwartz, who studied at Columbia University, has developed the SVI (Schwartz Value Inventory) studying 10 value categories (**http://changingminds.org/explanations/values/schwartz_inventory.htm**) and Fons Trompenaars teamed with Charles Hampden-Turner to produce their Seven Cultures of Capitalism analysis (**http://changingminds.org/explanations/culture/trompenaars_culture.htm**). MBAs should have at least a nodding acquaintance with all three of these international culture analysis tools.

Why understanding culture matters

Until the Convention of Kanagawa (31 March 1854) Japan's international trade was conducted by the Sakoku policy, a word that describes a literally locked country, or chained country. No foreigner could enter or leave the country on penalty of death. Japan traded with different countries through four gateways. The goal was to ensure that cultural pollution was restricted and controlled. It wasn't until 1860 that Japan opened an Embassy in the United States. China to some extent operated a similar policy using entry points such as Macau and Hong Kong, transferred to China as recently as 1997.

TABLE 7.1   Selected country scores for Hofstede's culture dimensions

Country	Power distance	Individualism	Uncertainty	Masculinity
United States	40	91	46	62
United Kingdom	35	35	89	66
France	68	86	71	43
Japan	54	46	92	95

Today, international business is a more open affair and business people need a greater understanding of the behaviour and mores of those they are trading with. Cultural norms vary greatly from country to country. An American, British or German executive kept cooling their heels waiting for a Spaniard or South American to show up for an appointment may feel irritated. Time matters more to the former group, while the latter may feel completing a discussion more important than the consequences of cutting it short. In the Western world time has a more precise definition than in Arab or Mediterranean cultures.

People accept differences in power in very different ways. In China the meaning has to be inferred or implied while Americans use direct language. It's not that one culture is evasive and the other rude; that's just the way they are. If you are working in the international arena having an appreciation of these differences is vital to successful business relationships.

What determines culture?

Culture is shaped by a number of factors, of which the following are generally accepted as the most important:

- Religion. These are beliefs shared about leading a particular way of life considered to be 'good'. The main religions include Christianity, where one god is accepted, and which is the world's largest religion. Protestantism, a branch of Christianity, is credited by some as the centre of the 'spirit of capitalism' through the endorsement of hard work. Other major religions include: Islam, to whom worldly gain and power are illusions and to be ranked below leading a good life; Hinduism, a religion that believes in spiritual progression through reincarnation; Buddhism, where the stress is asceticism rather than wealth creation; and Confucianism, until 1949 the official ethical system in China, calling for loyalty and high moral behaviour. Unlike other religions Confucianism is not much concerned with life after death.

- Language: Both verbal and non-verbal language – facial expressions and hand gestures and the like are a further defining way in which a culture is shaped and groups of people are bound together. English, though not exactly as spoken in England, is the most prevalent spoken tongue in business, although Chinese Mandarin has roughly twice as many speakers. Hindustani, the primary language in India accounts for half-a-billion people, followed by Spanish with around 400,000. China, Germany and France have all made efforts recently to expand the presence of their language and culture. FRANCE 24, a 24/7 international news channel is one example of such initiatives. Launched in December 2006, its mission is to cover international current events from a French perspective and to convey French values throughout the world.

- Education: The extent and depth of a country's education plays its part in cultural development. From an international business perspective the availability of well-educated customers or employees presents important opportunities or challenges. Call centres and outsourced Internet, web and e-learning products are all available from the Indian subcontinent courtesy of an improving education system and having English as a near-mother tongue.

CASE STUDY IKEA

In January 2015 IKEA released its yearly summary for the financial year 2014, showing a net income of €3.3 billion, up by 6 per cent on the preceding year. There were 716 million visits to the IKEA Group stores and more than 1.5 billion visits to IKEA.com. The IKEA Group with 147 000 employees, has 315 stores in 27 markets and operations in more than 40 countries. Their websites generate online sales in 13 markets. Peter Agnefjall, who studied business at the Linköping University in central Sweden, is company's fifth chief executive in its 70-year history. His appointment continued the trend of Ikea chief executives having been an assistant to its founder, Ingvar Kamprad.

IKEA was founded by Ingvar Kamprad when he was just 17, having cut his teeth on selling matches to his nearby neighbours at the age of five, followed by a spell selling flower seeds, greeting cards, Christmas decorations and eventually furniture. IKEA targets young, white-collar workers as its prime customer segment, selling through 315 stores in more than 40 countries. Kamprad, an entrepreneur from the Småland province in southern Sweden, offers home furnishing products of good function and design at prices young people can afford. He achieves this by using simple cost-cutting solutions that do not affect the quality of the products.

IKEA's entry into the international arena was not without its problems. Its launch in the US market hit a cultural barrier from the outset. IKEA does not give employees job titles or precise job descriptions. This arises from the founder's no-nonsense personal culture. Worth £16 billion, Kamprad is the world's seventh richest man, but lives frugally, in keeping with the functional nature of the IKEA brand. He lives in a bungalow, flies easyJet and drives a 15-year-old Volvo. When he arrived at a gala dinner recently to collect a business award, the security guard turned him away because they saw him getting off a bus. He and his wife Margaretha are often seen dining in cheap restaurants. He does his food shopping in the afternoon when prices are lower and even then haggles prices down.

Many of IKEA's new recruits in the United States quit after a few months because there was a gulf between the company's values and the culture and expectations of US employees, who were used to clear roles and responsibilities. The ensuing high turnover rate forced IKEA to review its selection criteria. Rather than just going for candidates with the best qualifications and experience the recruiters highlighted IKEA's culture and values, so letting those applicants who were going to be uncomfortable in that environment elect to withdraw early in the process. This saved the company the cost of high staff turnover and prevented the company from being saddled with a hire and fire reputation.

IKEA has a distinctive employee culture stating on their website: 'We believe in people! It takes a dream to create a successful business idea. It takes people to make dreams a reality'. That distinction extends to calling everyone in the firm a co-worker rather than an employee. (**www.ikea.com/ms/en_GB/about-the-ikea-group/working-at-the-ikea-group/**).

This approach certainly seems to pay off. In 2015, not a great year for many retailers, the IKEA Group gained market share in almost all markets and entered a new country – Croatia. The largest markets in terms of sales were Germany, the United States, France, Russia and the UK.

Expatriates

An expatriate is simply defined as a citizen of one country working in another. Hiring an expat is one way that international organizations seek to widen the field of potential applicants while limiting the risk of failure. Making appointments, particularly with senior appointments, is a hazardous and costly business so hiring people from their own country or culture, or with a background the hirer feels some affinity with is perceived to be a lower-risk recruitment strategy. According to the UN some 200 million people live in a country other than their own. Clearly only a small proportion of those are in the market for being hired by international organizations. Mercer (**www.mercer.com**), the international HR and recruitment consultancy, who routinely survey the expat sector, reckon that the market is growing with over 40 per cent of firms who use expats planning to hire more.

Expatriate categories

There are three broad categories of expatriate employee. The smallest of these groups is those professional expats who stay in a country for between one and five years, moving from country to country on a more or less permanent basis. The next largest group comprises people selected for their specific technical or managerial skills who go on a single assignment, usually for between two and five years, returning to their home country, though often not to a job in their parent company. A third category of expatriate is made up of temporary staff, usually relatively junior, who relocate for up to a year to assist with a specific assignment or task. A large group of expats comprises junior staff placed abroad as part of their training and development programme. Johnson & Johnson, for example, operate an IRDP (International Recruitment and Development Programme) and their job offers include an individual development plan for each new hire that includes a 'rotation' in a Johnson & Johnson overseas host company during the first 12 months of employment. A final, large and fast-growing expatriate population is the virtual expat. A recent PwC (PricewaterhouseCoopers) study indicated that this is the fastest-growing sector, for reasons at least partly based on cost.

CASE STUDY Cisco Systems and the virtual expat

Cisco, a Fortune 100 transnational and the worldwide leader in providing hardware, software, and service offerings that provide networking solutions for the Internet, is always striving to build lower costs into its product offerings. Unsurprisingly the company is an enthusiastic consumer of its own products. They use wikis, social networking and other low-cost, web-based collaboration services, all enabled by their routers. But it is TelePresence, developed over a seven-year period while economies were booming, that Cisco believes to be a long-term winner. TelePresence is a video conferencing system that captures subtle nuances such as body language and tone of voice and gives users the real feeling of being in the same room together. Cisco use TelePresence as a key resource for their international team of virtual expatriate managers. Some 5,500 TelePresence meetings take place throughout Cisco worldwide every week, enabling their key staff to operate out of almost any location in any country. As well as improving the efficiency of their expat operations it has enabled them to cut their annual travel budget by $290 million (£175 million) – just over 50 per cent.

Advantages and disadvantages of using expatriates

The key advantages in employing expats are that the recruitment process widens the pool of potential applicants and it should be possible to take on staff with a closer cultural fit to those at HQ. Also you can appoint managers from within the organization with known abilities and a proven track record, who know your systems. Additionally it can be a valuable training and development tool for HiPo (High Potential) managers.

There are, however, some considerable disadvantages. Taking an overseas assignment is less popular than you might think as not everyone shares an MBA's ethos when it comes to acquiring new experiences. The PwC survey referred to above also found that in 80 per cent of the 270 companies approached employees had refused overseas appointments, generally citing family commitments as a reason for their reluctance. Studies of the sector also reveal that between 20 and 40 per cent of expats hired to go to developing countries return early. The failure rate in expats sent to developing countries is even higher, with in excess of 60 per cent returning home early. The cost of these failures is often high when resettlement expenses are taken into account. The most successful countries from an expat employment prospect are Germany, followed by Canada and Spain. In these countries, expatriates tend to make local friends, learn the language and generally integrate with their community. They and their spouse and children mostly end up speaking two or more languages. The expat experience in the United Arab Emirates and China, for example, is almost the opposite, where most find it hard to integrate or make local friends. One further disadvantage is that the pay rate for expats and locals will be very different and may lead to resentment among employees of the host country. Russian HR departments sidestep this problem by the judicious use of typical Soviet-era practices. So the use of supplementary words or references to grades that appear to differentiate positions, such as 'senior', 'chief', or 'grade A', can be built into job descriptions to emphasize differences and to explain salary discrepancies.

Improving the odds of making a successful expat appointment

As an MBA it's quite likely that you will be looking to take on the challenge of an overseas assignment yourself and perhaps also be involved in recruiting others for such positions. Most expat appointments are men – a recent study carried out by Cranfield revealed that only 9 per cent of 3,620 expatriates surveyed were women and only 5 per cent of those in management roles were female – it is usual in the case of married men that their families will accompany them. The primary reason for expat appointments failing is the inability of the spouse or children to adjust to the host country. It follows that this has to be an area to probe during the selection process.

The expat's personal or emotional maturity and their consequent ability to cope with larger overseas responsibilities are also high on the list of reasons for appointments failing. Here the use of psychometric testing can reduce the incidence of failure. A survey of International Assignment

Practice showed that only 8 per cent of international organizations use any form of psychological testing during the selection process.

Training and preparation play an important part in ensuring success, as with any appointment.

Two tests most MBAs will come across both at business school and in job and promotion interviews that can be used in staff selection are:

The 16PF (Personality Factor) Questionnaire
(www.psychometrictest.org.uk/16pf-test)

Developed in 1949 by Raymond Cattell, this test sets out to measure the whole of a human personality using a structure questionnaire assessed against a normative sample reflecting current census statistics on sex, age and race. The scores enable employers, among others, to predict human behaviour.

The 16PF Questionnaire measures levels of: warmth; reasoning; emotional stability; dominance; liveliness; rule consciousness; social boldness; sensitivity; vigilance; abstractedness; privateness; apprehensiveness; openness to change; self-reliance; perfectionism and tension.

The Myers-Briggs Type Indicator
(www.myersbriggs.org)

This is a personality inventory based on the psychological types described by C G Jung explaining how seemingly random variations in behaviour are actually normal, and due to basic differences in the ways people choose to use their perception and judgement. Developed by Katharine Briggs and her daughter, Isabel Myers, the indicator was initially created during the Second World War to help women working in industry for the first time find the sort of war-time jobs where they would best fit in.

The indicator uses a battery of questions to identify how a person fits in with the 16 distinctive personality types.

Learning the language

There are two schools of thought on language in the international business world. In many countries aside from the obvious ones, Malaysia, Malta, the Caribbean and Cyprus and in much of Africa for example, English is widely spoken. Even where it is not, English is often the working language. But in most non-English-speaking countries few people outside of the major cities speak much English. If you are doing business being able to negotiate or at least follow a discussion in the local language is an advantage and as an expat without that skill you will find your relationships limited to fellow expats. Some parts of the world have other dominant languages that may be as useful as learning the local language itself. In Eastern Europe some 300 million people in 18 countries including Ukraine, Belarus, Poland, the Czech Republic, Bulgaria, Serbia and of course Russia itself all have languages that are similar to Russian. Indeed many of the citizens of these countries speak Russian as their second language. French is widely spoken in the parts of Africa that don't speak English, as well as in Morocco, Algeria, Equatorial Guinea, Haiti, the Quebec province of Canada and Egypt and it is even used extensively in two areas in the United States: Louisiana and New England.

Repatriation

That the expat executive is a valuable resource after a successful stint overseas is not in doubt. What is less obvious is that the organization they are returning to knows how to tap into those skills. Some 60 per cent of international businesses have no specific plan to deal with repatriated employees and have no plan as to where to place them in the organization. This has a demoralizing effect, particularly as the expat in all probability had a position of relative importance in their overseas role and has returned to relative obscurity. Not surprisingly, nearly a fifth leave within a year and 40 per cent do so within three years.

A planned programme covering not just expenses, but accommodation, career progression and assistance on issues relating to spouses and children will go far in mitigating such problems.

Compensation strategies

Although pay is an important part of any compensation strategy there is much more to the subject than that. A benefit to any organization is that much of the compensation package can comprise soft elements such as frequent appraisals, feedback and empowerment. Some of it can be of direct benefit to the organization, such as training and development, which as well as being motivational, should result in better performance and a cadre of staff to fill more senior appointments around the whole international business structure.

Two factors stand out as problems for the international business: compliance with local regulations and laws and compensation equity.

Compliance

A recent Ernst & Young survey on Managing Global Compensation found that '59 per cent of respondents have experienced local tax authority audits or queries over non-compliance.' The report went on to note that tax authorities are placing greater emphasis on payroll compliance and this may result in a significant revenue stream. In effect this can be seen as something akin to speed cameras; an easy source of revenue that doesn't upset the general population too much. E&Y observe that as this is a money spinner the audits are more likely to increase in frequency. They also note that as well as fines some countries are using payroll irregularities as a reason to create additional complications in areas such as visa and immigration approval. Their order of which countries were the greatest challenge in this area was as follows:

1 United States
2 United Kingdom
3 Germany and India (joint third)
4 China
5 Australia, France and Russia (joint fifth)
6 Asia as a whole, Brazil and Switzerland (joint sixth)

E&Y went on to single out India and China as areas where tax and social security laws have changed significantly and are likely to cause more problems for international employers in the future. In terms of annual cost to the business of these compliance failures, 68 per cent had not quantified the costs, whilst 10 per cent put the bill somewhere between $1.5 million (£1 million) and $4.5 million (£3 million) and 5 per cent as more still.

Compensation

This is a difficult enough field in one country, but transplanted to the international field it has the potential to be a minefield. Set the pay level too high and locals may be dissatisfied; too low and mobility of talented staff may become constrained. One of the advantages an international firm expects from its global reach in terms of markets is to get the same access to a global talent pool.

Carlos Rodriguez, a Harvard MBA and President and Chief Executive Officer of ADP (**www.adp.com**), a cloud-based Human Capital Management (HCM) solutions business that brings HR, payroll, talent, time, tax and benefits administration into one package, reckons he has the ideal proposition for international business. With 610,000 clients he probably has a point. His view is that 'the more you add or relocate employees to multiple locations around the world, the more obvious the need for a globally consistent platform for compensation becomes.' With a sound, merit-based global employee compensation solution in place, your organization benefits by:

- clearly tying individual employee performance to goals, demonstrating how actions and outcomes impact rewards such as promotions, compensation and other incentives;
- adhering to corporate procedures and policies – in every department, in every country;

- creating a global pay-for-performance culture and improving employee engagement and morale in the process.

Payscale.com (**www.payscale.com/rccountries.aspx**) pitches this question at prospective employers on its website: 'Today's job candidate, armed with data, knows what he's worth and will expect a fair salary offer or pay rise. Are you ready?' Payscale, run by CEO Mike Metzger who has his MBA from Tepper School of Business at Carnegie Mellon University, is a sensible starting point to check out your compensation strategy. They claim to have the 'largest, most detailed salary dataset,' covering over 180 countries, with everything from salaries by occupation to cost of living comparisons.

Appraisals

An appraisal is almost certainly an MBA's first point of contact with an organization's systems and the most likely one to cause dissatisfaction and frustration; although supposedly not about blame, reward or even praise, that's how it ends up. Its output is a personal development plan to help everyone perform better and be able to achieve career goals. When carrying out appraisals in international organizations the appraiser should not assume that concepts or terminology have equivalent or even similar meanings in different cultures or ethnic groups. Hofstede (see under Culture in this chapter) says that 'culture is the collective programming of the mind that distinguishes the members of one group or category of people from others'. So every culture imbues its citizens with different ways to process concepts and ideas, leading to very different behavioural norms. For example, an appraiser from a culture that leans towards dependency and teamwork appraising an employee from a highly individualistic culture where autonomy and independence are fostered, could result in the opinion that the employee is weak and may need help in this respect. One of the appraiser's first tasks is to try to understand why and how such differences occur and to what extent they need to be addressed. No checklist guides to cross-cultural appraisal exist, but you have to assess and appraise people taking cultural issues into account. A useful chapter by Walter J Lonner and Farah A Ibrahim, 'Appraisal and Assessment in Cross-Cultural Counseling', can be downloaded at this link (**www.sagepub.com/upm-data/15655_Chapter_3.pdf**). There you will also find a sound bibliography of reference works on the subject.

There are plenty of standard appraisal systems and procedures; many are little more than a tick boxes and rating process; others are built around buzzwords such as '360 degree appraisals', meaning that staff below, above, as well as peers have an input into the process.

There are really only four ground rules for successful appraisals, outside of the problems and issues associated with cross-cultural factors. These are:

- The appraisal needs to be seen as an open two-way discussion between people who work together rather than simply a boss/subordinate relationship and prepared for in advance. Discussion should be focused on achievements, areas for improvement, overall performance, training and development and career expectations – not salary (that's for a separate occasion).

- It should be results-orientated rather than personality-orientated. The appraisal interview starts with a review against objectives and finishes by setting objectives for the next period.

- Appraisals should be regular and timely; at least annually, perhaps more frequent in periods of rapid change. New employees should be appraised in their first three months.

- Sufficient time should be allowed and the appraisal needs to be carried out free from interruptions.

Development

If an organization is only as effective as the people it employs it follows that the money invested in developing them and improving their skills should translate into improved results for the business as a whole. The statistics support the argument that money spent wisely on development pays dividends, so as a task it forms a major part of the Human Resources department's workload.

Two acronyms an MBA will find useful to prime any development plan are:

KSAs (knowledge, skills and attitudes): Development programmes have learning objectives in each of these three areas and all three aspects need to be addressed for development to have the greatest impact.

- Knowledge, described as perception, learning and reasoning, has been subdivided by HR and learning gurus into these three areas: declarative knowledge or factual information; procedural knowledge, ie understanding how and when to apply the facts; and strategic knowledge used in planning and evaluating.

- Skills are concerned with a proficiency level; for example using a software application such as Excel, making a presentation, operating equipment, closing a sale or negotiating a deal.

- Attitudes are the positive, negative or neutral feelings arising out of opinions and beliefs concerning actions that affect motivation levels, which in turn influence a person's behaviour.

TNA (Training Needs Analysis): This process identifies the gap between the skills an organization needs to achieve its strategic and tactical goals and those that employees currently have. Employee surveys, management observations, customer comments and appraisal are all among the tools used to gather information to identify training needs. (See the worksheet in Table 7.2 below.)

TABLE 7.2 Training needs analysis worksheet

Development area	Gap identified	Action to be taken to address the gap	Date action to be achieved by
Knowledge			
Skills			
Attitudes			
Learning options			

Preparing for development

To make sure you get the best out of investment in development follow these guidelines.

- Introduce a routine that ensures all employees attending training are briefed at least a week beforehand on what to expect and what is expected of them.
- Ensure that all employees discuss with their manager or supervisor what they got out of the training programme – in particular, did it meet both parties' expectations. This should take place no later than a week after the programme.
- Managers should check within a month and then again at regular intervals to see whether skills have been improved, and that those skills are being put into practice.
- Evaluate the costs and benefits of your training and development plans arriving at a financial ratio such as return on investment and use this information to help set next year's training budget.

Labour relations, practices and law

International firms have to be aware of and sensitive to the practices, procedures and the law related to employing staff in the countries in which they operate. Getting things wrong can be an expensive procedure, especially if the wronged parties choose to pursue their case in the parent companies' home legal environment where penalties can be punitive. Abercrombie and Fitch, the US fashion retailer is a case in point. In 2003 A&F were embroiled in a series of issues after they had launched a series of T-shirts with slogans such as 'Wong Brothers Laundry Service: Two Wongs Can Make It White', featuring two slant-eyed caricatures in coolie hats. Hampton Carney, an A&F representative claimed, 'We personally thought Asians would love this T-shirt', but a backlash quickly forced A&F to pull the products from shelves. More seriously the company was sued by Asian and Mexican store employees claiming that A&F generally refuses to hire Asians and Latinos and banishes African Americans to behind the scenes jobs in the stockroom ensuring that their visible staff mirrors the white Caucasian models in its quarterly catalogue.

The Equal Employment Opportunity Commission alleged that Abercrombie & Fitch violated Title VII of the Civil Rights Act of 1964 by maintaining recruiting and hiring practices that excluded minorities and women and by adopting a restrictive marketing image, and other policies, which limited minority and female employment. The company agreed to pay $50 million to resolve the lawsuit along with two private class action suits. It was a condition of the settlement that A&F appoint a Vice President of Diversity, employ 25 diversity recruiters, implement new hiring procedures, introduce diversity training, monitor and report on compliance and ensure that minorities and women were promoted into manager-in-training and manager positions without discrimination. The judgment in effect became the firm's diversity strategy.

It is beyond the scope of this book to do more than flag the dangers and pitfalls of employing an international labour force. HG.org (**www.hg.org/employ.html**) provide a comprehensive directory to international labour associations, organizations and to articles written by attorneys and experts worldwide discussing legal aspects related to employment and labour including: discrimination, employee benefits, employee rights, ERISA, human resources law, labour relations, outsourcing, sexual harassment, whistle-blowers, workers' compensation and wrongful termination.

Monitoring staff morale

One way to keep track of how effective your HR policies and practices are is to carry out regular surveys of employee attitudes, opinions and feelings. HR-Survey (**www.hr-survey.com** > Employee Opinions) and Custom Insight (**www.custominsight.com** > View Samples > Sample employee satisfaction survey) provide fast, simple and easy-to-use software to carry out and analyse human resources surveys. They both have a range of examples of surveys that you can see and try before you buy, which, who knows, might just be enough to stimulate your thinking.

Organizational behaviour

Organizational behaviour, usually shortened to OB, is the whole, rather amorphous area that deals with people, why they behave the way they do and how to create, lead and manage an organization that can achieve the goals set for the business. As one cynical CEO summarized, the task is 'to get people to do what I want them to do because they want to do it'. Leadership exists to a greater or lesser extent in all societies and is essential to the effective functioning of their organizations; however, different cultural groups are likely to have a different understanding of what leadership should entail.

Russian employees expect an autocratic leadership style whereas a US employee expects to be involved in decision-making. International leadership can involve more subtle variations than that of the stark gulf between Russian and US positions. A study by Alexander Ardichvili and K Peter Kuchinke, University of Illinois at Urbana-Champaign ('Leadership styles and cultural values among managers and subordinates: a comparative study of four countries of the former Soviet Union, Germany, and the US', *Human Resource Development International*, 2002, 5 (1), pp 99–117), gives an insight into the issues. This survey-based study addressed the cultural values and leadership styles of some 4,000 managers and non-managers in 10 business organizations in six countries. Using Hofstede's framework (see Chapter 7 for an explanation of this framework and the terms used below) they concluded that far from presenting a homogeneous picture, the four former USSR countries, as might be expected from their history, differed from each other in substantial ways. Georgia ranked lowest with respect to power distance, followed by Russia, Kazakhstan and Kyrgyzstan. All four countries ranked substantially lower on this dimension than Germany or the United States, indicating a much higher level of egalitarianism and the expectation that positions of social power be distributed equally or, at a minimum, within reach of everybody.

The single most prevalent reason for a strategy failing lies in its implementation; the analysis and planning behind a proposed course of action are rarely the root of the problem. That is more likely to lie in the selection of the people to implement strategy, their leadership management, motivation, rewards and the way in which they are organized and led. Stated like that it sounds a fairly simple task. Just work your way through those headings and any MBA worth their salt should be able to get the desired results. Unfortunately, people both individually and collectively are rarely malleable and infinitely variable in their likely responses to situations. The famous German military strategist Moltke's statement that 'No campaign plan survives first contact with the enemy' applies here if the word enemy is replaced by organization. However, by understanding and applying a number of principles and concepts on the typical MBA syllabus you can improve an organization's chances of achieving its objectives.

The structure of the organization is a subject covered in Chapter 6, as it applies particularly to the international organization. What follows are the other elements in the core of OB that the MBA will be expected to have an appreciation of.

Motivation

As a subject for serious study, motivation is a relatively new 'science'. Thomas Hobbes, a 17th-century English philosopher suggested that human nature could best be understood as self-interested cooperation. He claimed motivation could be summarized as choices revolving around pain or pleasure. Sigmund Freud was equally frugal in only suggesting two basic needs; the life and the death instinct. These ideas were the first to seriously challenge the time-honoured 'carrot and stick' method of motivation that pervaded every aspect of organizational life from armies at war to the weavers in Britain working through the Industrial Revolution.

The first hint, in the business world, that there might be more to motivation than rewards and redundancy came with Harvard Business School Professor Elton Mayo's renowned Hawthorne Studies. These were conducted between 1927 and 1932 at the Western Electric Hawthorne Works in Chicago. Starting out to see what effect illumination had on productivity Mayo moved on to see how fatigue and monotony fitted into the equation by varying rest breaks, temperature, humidity and work hours, even providing a free meal at one point. Working with a team of six women Mayo changed every parameter he could think of including increasing and decreasing working hours and rest breaks; finally he returned to the original conditions. Every change resulted in an improvement in productivity, except when two ten-minute pauses morning and afternoon were expanded to six five-minute pauses. These frequent work pauses, they felt, upset their work rhythm.

Mayo's conclusion was that showing 'someone upstairs cares', engendering a sense of ownership and responsibility were important motivators that could be harnessed by management. After Mayo came a flurry of theories on motivation. William McDougall in his book *The Energies of Men* (1932, Methuen) listed 18 basic needs that he referred to as instincts (eg curiosity, self-assertions, submission). HA Murray, assistant director of the Harvard Psychological Clinic, catalogued 20 core psychological needs including achievement, affiliation and power.

The motivation theories most studied and applied by business school graduates are those espoused by Maslow and these below.

Theory X and theory Y

Douglas McGregor, an American social psychologist who taught at two top schools, Harvard and the Massachusetts Institute of Technology (MIT), developed these theories to try to explain the assumptions about human behaviour that underlie management action.

Theory X makes the following assumptions:

- The average person has an inherent dislike of work and will avoid it if possible. So management needs to put emphasis on productivity, incentive schemes and the idea of a 'fair day's work'.

- Because of this dislike of work, most people must be coerced, controlled, directed and threatened with punishment to get them to achieve the company's goals.

- People prefer to be directed, want to avoid responsibility, have little ambition and really want a secure life above all.

But, while theory X does explain some human behaviour, it does not provide a framework for understanding behaviour in the best businesses. McGregor, and others, have proposed an alternative.

Theory Y has as its basis the belief that:

- Physical or mental effort at work is as natural as either rest or play. Under the right conditions hard work can be a source of great satisfaction. Under the wrong conditions it can be a drudge, which will inspire little effort and less thought from those forced to participate.

- Once committed to a goal most people at work are capable of a high degree of self-management.

- Job satisfaction and personal recognition are the highest 'rewards' that can be given, and will result in the greatest level of commitment to the task in hand.

- Under the right conditions most people will accept responsibility and even welcome more of it.

- Few people in business are being 'used ' to anything like their capacity. Neither are they contributing creatively towards solving problems.

A typical theory-X boss is likely to keep away from their employees as much as possible. However small the business they may, for example, make sure they have an office to themselves, and its door is kept tightly shut. Contact with others will be confined to giving instructions about work and complaining about poor performance. A theory-Y approach will involve collaborating over decisions rather than issuing orders, and sharing feedback so everyone can learn from success and failures, rather than just reprimanding when things go wrong.

Hygiene and motivation theory

Frederick Hertzberg, Professor of Psychology at Case Western Reserve University in Cleveland, discovered that distinctly separate factors were the cause of job satisfaction and job dissatisfaction. His research revealed that five factors stood out as strong determinants of job satisfaction.

Motivators

- Achievement. People want to succeed, so if you can set goals that people can reach and even better they will be much more satisfied than if they are constantly missing targets.
- Recognition. Everyone likes their hard work to be acknowledged. Not everyone wants that recognition made in the same way, however.
- Responsibility. People like the opportunity to take responsibility for their own work and for the whole task. This helps them grow as individuals.
- Advancement. Promotion or at any rate progress are key motivators. In a small firm providing career prospects for key staff can be a fundamental reason for growth.
- The Attractiveness of work itself (Job Interest). There is no reason why a job should be dull. You need to make people's jobs interesting and give them a say in how their work is done. That will encourage new ideas on how things can be done better.

When the reasons for dissatisfaction were analysed they were found to be concerned with a different range of factors, as follows.

Hygiene factors

- Company policy. Rules, formal and informal, such as start and finish times, meal breaks, dress code.
- Supervision. To what extent are employees allowed to get on with the job, or do people have someone looking over their shoulders all day?
- Administration. Do things work well, or is paperwork in a muddle and supplies always come in late?
- Salary. Are employees getting at least the going rate and benefits comparable with others?
- Working conditions. Are people expected to work in substandard conditions with poor equipment and little job security?
- Interpersonal relationships. Is the atmosphere in work good or are people at daggers drawn?

Hertzberg called these causes of dissatisfaction 'hygiene factors'. He reasoned that the lack of hygiene will cause disease, but the presence of hygienic conditions will not, of itself, produce good health. So the lack of adequate 'job hygiene' will cause dissatisfaction but hygienic conditions alone will not bring about job satisfaction; to do that you have to work on the determinants of job satisfaction.

Leadership vs Management

However great the employees are unless a business has effective leadership nothing of great value can be made to happen. While the boss may have a pretty clear idea of what the business is all about and what makes it special and different, it may not be so clear to those who work further down. Employees often just keep their heads down and get on with the task in hand. Although that's a useful trait it is not sufficient to make a business a great place to work. To make that happen the boss has to have a precise idea of where the business is heading and use their leadership skills to achieve results. (See the discussion on strategy later in this chapter.)

Leadership and management are not the same thing, but you need both. A leader challenges the status quo, while a manager accepts it as a constraint. A boss usually has to be both a leader and a manager. Dozens of catchy titles such as bottom up, top down, management by objectives, and crisis management have been used to describe the many and various theories as to how to manage.

American engineer, Frederick Winslow Taylor (circa 1911), who is credited with coining the phrase 'time is money' was one of the pioneers of the search for the 'one best way' to execute such basic managerial functions as selection, promotion, compensation, training and production. Taylor was followed by Henri Fayol (1919), a successful managing director of a French mining company, who developed what he called the 14 Principles of Management, recognizing that his list was neither exhaustive, nor universally applicable. He also set out what he saw as the five primary functions of a manager. Nearly a decade later Luther Gulick, an American and Lydnall Urwick, a founder of the British management consultancy profession, expanded Fayol's list to seven executive management activities summarized by the acronym POSDCORB:

- Planning: determine objectives in advance and the methods to achieve them.
- Organizing: establish a structure of authority for all work.
- Staffing: bring in and train staff, and maintain favourable conditions of work.
- Directing: make decisions, issue orders and directives.
- Coordinating: interrelate all sectors of the organization.
- Reporting: inform hierarchy through reports, records and inspections.
- Budgeting: depend on fiscal planning, accounting and control.

By 1973 Canadian academic Henry Mintzberg, now Professor of Organizations at INSEAD in France, had further expanded the manager's tasks and responsibilities into 10 areas:

1 Figurehead: performs ceremonial and symbolic duties as head of the organization.
2 Leader: fosters a proper work atmosphere and motivates and develops subordinates.

3 Liaison: develops and maintains a network of external contacts to gather information.

4 Monitor: gathers internal and external information relevant to the organization.

5 Disseminator: passes factual and value-based information to subordinates.

6 Spokesperson: communicates to the outside world on performance and policies.

7 Entrepreneur: designs and initiates change in the organization.

8 Disturbance handler: deals with unexpected events and operational breakdowns.

9 Resource allocator: controls and authorizes the use of organizational resources.

10 Negotiator: intermediates with other organizations and individuals.

All of these attempts at formulating an overarching and universal approach to arriving at a single best definition of the role of management foundered on the limitations of the information flow from the front line upwards. Two management theorists, Tom Peters and Nancy Austin, suggest that managers in effective companies get the information they need by getting out of their offices and talking with people – employees, suppliers, other managers and customers They coined the approach as 'management by walking around', or 'MBWA' (T Peters and N Austin, *A Passion for Excellence: The leadership difference*, Collins, 1985).

Today the view of the role of manager is best described as being contingent on the internal and external circumstances they find themselves in. Expanded into the rather grandiose title of 'Contingency Theory' its exponent Fred Fiedler, a business and management psychologist at the University of Washington, first introduced what he called the contingency modelling of leadership in 1967.

Managing change

The story told in business schools to illustrate the dangers of ignoring the need for change is that of the hypothetical frog dropped into a pot of boiling water. The immediate impact of a radically different environment spurs the frog into action, leaping out of the pot. The same frog placed in the same pot, where the initial temperature is much lower will happily allow itself to be boiled to death, failing to recognize the danger if the process is slow enough.

Managing change for any business is difficult but for the international business it is doubly so. Country culture and norms need to be factored into any attempts at change. A recent report, 'The World's Most Repressive Regimes Resistant to Change' by Freedom House (**www.freedomhouse.org**), an independent watchdog organization that supports the expansion of freedom around the world, listed the 17 regimes most resistant to change of any sort. Belarus, Burma, China, Cote d'Ivoire, Cuba, Equatorial Guinea, Eritrea, Laos, Libya, North Korea, Saudi Arabia, Somalia, Sudan, Syria, Turkmenistan, Uzbekistan and Zimbabwe unsurprisingly were all on that list. But even in less-hostile regimes a degree of cultural awareness is essential if change is to be induced. For example, in Mexico workers often have more respect for their peers than for their managers. Therefore, Ford sends operatives from its US plants to its Mexican operations when it wants to introduce new working methods.

The first task of a leader is to define an organization's purpose and direction. This inevitably means changing these in response to changing circumstances.

Why change is necessary

The need for change comes from two main directions; either a new impetus from outside or inside of the organization, or from the natural evolution of the organization itself.

Impetus-driven change

These are the primary sources of the impetus for change that disturb the equilibrium of an organization.

- New management. This doesn't always trigger change but the temptation to tamper with even the best of organizations is usually too much for a 'new broom'. The person appointed almost invariably will want to put their stamp on strategy and structure; if all was really so hunky-dory why appoint them in the first place?

- Competitor behaviour. This can be either new entrants or existing players changing the dynamics in your markets by competing with better products, lower prices or smarter operations.

- Technology. Changes here can hit whole business sectors. For example, the advent initially of online DVD services and more recently of broadband delivery has profoundly changed the environment for the retail video rental business.

- Economic, political or legal environment. These include such factors as: business cycles altering demand levels radically; changes of government with consequent shifts in expenditure and taxation; and regulatory changes such as those affecting the tobacco industry and its ability to promote its wares.

Natural evolution

Organizations are in some ways like living organisms and have a natural progression from birth through childhood, adolescence, adulthood, senility and death. Some stages in the process for an organization are easily recognizable. All have a start and finish date and although their lifespan varies, for businesses the average is around 35 to 38 years. Some last much longer; there is a small club for businesses who have been around for over 250 years (Japan's 1,400-year-old Kongo Gumi may be the oldest business enterprise, but guns (Beretta), banking (Rothschild) and booze (The Gekkeikan brewery founded in 1627) also feature strongly).

The phases of growth

Larry Greiner, a Harvard professor, identified the key phases an organization has to go through on its path to maturity (see Figure 7.1 below). Churchill and Lewis (NC Churchill and VL Lewis (1983) 'The five stages of Small Business Growth', *Harvard Business Review*, May/June) refined this for small businesses.

Each phase of growth calls for a different approach to managing the organization. Sometimes strong leadership is required; at others a more consultative approach is appropriate. Some phases call for more systems and procedures, some for more cooperation between staff. Often, leaders

FIGURE 7.1 The five phases of growth

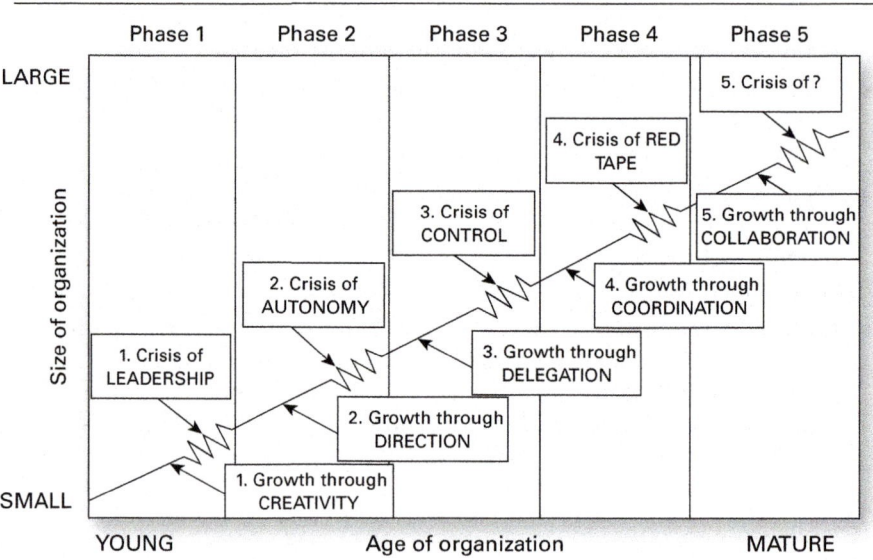

SOURCE: LE Greiner, *Harvard Business Review*, July/August, 1972

believe taking on another salesperson, a few hundred thousand square metres of space or another bank loan can solve the problems of growing up. This approach is rather like suggesting that the transition from infancy to adulthood could be accomplished by nothing more significant than providing larger clothes.

Managing the process

Because change is inevitable and unpredictable in its consequences doesn't mean that it can't be managed as a process. These are the stages in managing change.

- Tell them why: Change is better accepted when people are given a compelling business reason. Few bankers would question the need for change after the 2008 debacles at Bear Stearns, SocGen and Northern Rock.

- Make it manageable: Even when people accept what needs to be done, the change may just be too big for anyone to handle. Breaking it down into manageable bits can help overcome that issue.

- Take a shared approach: Involve people early – asking them to join you in managing change gives key participants some say in shaping the change right from the start. This will reduce the feeling that change is being imposed and more brains will be brought to bear on the problem.

- Reward success early: Flag up successes as quickly as possible. Don't wait for the year-end or the appraisal cycle. This will inspire confidence and keep the change process on track. Also you should make the reward appropriate to the country in which you are introducing change. Peru, the world's largest silver producer, second in zinc, and sixth in gold production has seen an influx of global mine developers including BHP Billiton, Freeport-McMoRan Copper & Gold, Pan American Silver, Southern Copper, Hochschild Mining and Teck Resources, in a frenzied quest for high-quality mineral investment opportunities. In some instances international companies have found it easier to encourage a local workforce to accept change by donating sheep, than by offering cash.

- Expect resistance: Kurt Lewin, a German-born professor at the Massachusetts Institute of Technology (MIT) was one of the first researchers to study group dynamics and how change can be best effected in organizations. In 1943 in an article entitled 'Defining the field at a given time', published in the *Psychological Review*, Lewin described what is now known as Force Field Analysis. This is a tool that you can use to anticipate resistance to change and plan to overcome it.

- Recognizing change takes longer than expected: Three researchers explained in *Transition: Understanding and managing personal change* (J Adams, J Hayes and B Hopson, 1976, Martin Robinson, London) the seven stages that people go through when experiencing change and hence the reason the process takes so long. The stages are; immobilization or shock, disbelief, depression, acceptance of reality, testing out the new situation, rationalizing why its happening and then final acceptance. Most major changes make things worse before they make them better. More often than not the immediate impact of change is a decrease in productivity as people struggle to cope with new ways of working while they move up their own learning curve. The doubters will gloat and even the change champions may waver. But the greatest danger now is pulling the plug on the plan and either adopting a new plan or reverting to the status quo. To prevent this 'disappointment' it is vital to both set realistic goals for the change period, and to anticipate the time lag between change and results.

Online video courses and lectures

Douglas McGregor's Theory X & Theory Y: Alanis Business Academy: **www.youtube.com/watch?v=kQp9zFHgimU**

Employee Motivation & Behavior: Alanis Business Academy: **www.youtube.com/watch?v=ymW8gaO3UiM**

Forget big change, start with a tiny habit: BJ Fogg, director of the Persuasive Tech Lab at Stanford University, talks to TEDx: **www.youtube.com/watch?v=AdKUJxjn-R8**

Frederick Winslow Taylor's Scientific Management: Alanis Business Academy: **www.youtube.com/watch?v=dsnMjVBYNE8**

Harvard: James 'Jamie' Dimon, chairman and CEO of JPMorgan Chase & Co, address to HBS MBA Class of 2009 on Leadership: **www.youtube.com/watch?v=9T9Kp4NE5I4**

IMD: Martha Maznevski, Professor of Organizational Behavior and International Management delivers MBA – Organisational Behaviour Class: **www.youtube.com/watch?v=CAfFyBZSdPo**

Leadership skills: Lauren Rodda and Amanda Mok, MIT Open Courseware: **http://ocw.mit.edu/high-school/humanities-and-social-sciences/leadership-training-institute/video-lectures/lecture-5/**

Leadership: Alanis Business Academy: **www.youtube.com/watch?v=bnmqxW8GzV8**

Lewin's Force Field Analysis: Alanis Business Academy: **www.youtube.com/watch?v=tRAKmzsYLG8**

London Business School: **http://freevideolectures.com/Course/2750/ Organisational-Behaviour**. There are 17 lectures in this series including panel discussion and case studies.

Make Meaning in Your Company: Guy Kawasaki, founder and Managing Director of Garage Technology Ventures talks at Stanford: **http://ecorner.stanford.edu/authorMaterialInfo.html?mid=1171**

Maslow's Hierarchy of Needs: Alanis Business Academy: **www.youtube.com/watch?v=wx3qR3gLh60**

Mintzberg's Managerial Roles: Alanis Business Academy: **www.youtube.com/watch?v=NgkQYRqxKTs**

Prepare Your Brain for Change: Margaret Moore, CEO of Wellcoaches Corporation talks to Harvard Business Review: **https://hbr.org/2013/04/ prepare-your-brain-for-change/**

Professor Blake explains the Grid he co-developed at Scientific Methods, Inc.: **www.gridinternational.com/news/grid-theory-reviewed-by-co-founder-dr-robert-r-blake**

The Benefits of Teams: Alanis Business Academy: **www.youtube.com/ watch?v=tBC4JsaBYkl**

The Hawthorne Effect: Why Workers Respond to More Than Just Money: Alanis Business Academy: **www.youtube.com/watch?v=EEwCWR5Vkpw**

The Management Hierarchy: A Look Into the Different Levels of Management: Alanis Business Academy: **www.youtube.com/ watch?v=UJS9JrFDuRo**

The Power of Habit: Charles Duhigg, Pulitzer Prize-winning writer talks to TEDx: **www.youtube.com/watch?v=OMbsGBIpP30**

The World's Most Talent-Ready Countries 2014: Global Talent Competitiveness Index authors talk at INSEAD: **www.youtube.com/ watch?v=4EdN0L54Qmc**

What Great Leaders Do. In this lecture that parallels his book Good Boss, Bad Boss, Stanford professor Bob Sutton unpacks the best habits of beloved and effective managers, and details the worst habits of those who fail to lead: **http://ecorner.stanford.edu/authorMaterialInfo.html?mid=2564**

Online video case studies

Bocconi: International Leadership and Organizational Behavior, by Franz Wohlgezogen of the Università Bocconi (**www.coursera.org/course/ intorb**). In this course – together with a team of Bocconi expert faculty and Bocconi alumni – the theory and practice of international and intercultural leadership and organizational behaviour is explored. Contributors include Julie Bellani, Chief HR Officer, BT Global Services,

London, Giovanni Ciserani, Group President, Procter & Gamble, Geneva; Kristin Engvig, Founder & CEO of Womens International Network, Geneva; Luca Mignini, President International, Campbell Soup Company, New York; Matteo Pellegrini, President Asia, Philip Morris International, Hong Kong and Maria Pierdicchi, Managing Director – Head of Southern Europe, Standard and Poor's, Milan.

Hewlett Packard: Leadership and Capability: Carly Fiorina (Former CEO, HP) talks at Stanford: **http://ecorner.stanford.edu/ authorMaterialInfo.html?mid=1719**

LinkedIn: CEO Jeff Weiner and LinkedIn's SVP of Global Solutions Mike Gamson discuss people strategies: **www.youtube.com/ watch?v=oU8BoQmgTp8**

Steve Jobs talks about managing people: **www.youtube.com/ watch?v=f60dheI4ARg**

Tesco: Dave Lewis, the new chief executive of Tesco, has said the culture of the company must change. Bloomberg: Can Tesco account for its problems: **www.bloomberg.com/news/videos/b/d02eb538-54d8-48ad-9b0d-f7e1dd108652**

Selecting and maintaining global strategic partners

8

- Why most mergers miscarry.
- Why some don't.
- Planning an acquisition strategy.
- Valuing businesses.
- Making the venture relationship work.

Acquisitions, mergers and joint ventures are the key tools used by international businesses, or those keen to become so, that an MBA is almost certain to encounter them early in their career. On some MBA programmes there may well be some unique content contained in specialized electives. For example at the London Business School there is an elective on Financial Analysis of Mergers, Acquisitions and Other Complex Corporate Restructurings and the partially related subject Dealing with Financial Crime is on offer at Cass Business School.

Before we look at this strategic option in a little more detail it would be as well to be clear on what each term means.

- An acquisition occurs when one company buys another – more often than not in a 'friendly' deal, but sometimes events are not so harmonious. After the acquisition only the parent company usually exists in any real legal sense and the top management of the 'victim' usually depart quickly.

- Mergers are friendly bids where companies join forces and the separate identities of the businesses of the companies concerned continue after the deal is consummated.

- Joint ventures occur when two or more companies decide to set up a separate third business to exploit something together. There may be no attempt to harmonize the whole of the two parent businesses, and the joint venture may be disbanded when the reasons they joined forces in the first place disappear. Carlos Ghosn's alliance forged with Nissan – who also have an alliance with Renault – is an example of a successful joint venture. These companies have joint purchasing and share engineering know-how. Both companies have separate joint ventures with other parties. Nissan has a joint venture with Dongfeng Motor Corporation, an important Chinese car maker. Nissan also has a 25 per cent stake in Avtovaz, a big Russian car manufacturer in need of all the help it can get. Renault has a three-way joint venture with Nissan since it brought Daimler, a German truck and luxury-car firm into their fold, after that company failed to negotiate a deal with Volkswagen.

Despite the semantic differences in practice the fates of the parties to any of these routes to global relationships are inexorably linked, as the BP case clearly demonstrates.

CASE STUDY BP partners fall out fast

In the spring of 2015 BP was ranked as the 69th most valuable brand in the world, just behind Boeing and well ahead of Aldi. This was up from the 89th spot it held the previous year. But that was still way short of its brand position back in 2009, when it was the 8th most valuable brand in the UK and the world's most valuable fuel brand ahead of its arch rival, Shell. In September 2010 Interbrand, one of the companies that assesses brand value concluded that the 'majority of the company's brand value has been destroyed' by the Gulf of Mexico disaster.

BP's Deepwater Horizon disaster in the Gulf of Mexico in 2010 is a good example of the range of complex relationships that can be involved in international business ventures and how different parties react when problems arise. Anadarko Petroleum Corp, the Texas oil company, owned a quarter of BP plc's blown-out oil well. Anadarko itself had no employees on the well and was a non-operating partner in the project. A subsidiary of Mitsui & Co Ltd of Japan had a 10 per cent stake and the rig was owned by Transocean Ltd of Switzerland and operated by BP. Following a suggestion by local politicians that Anadarko should help pay for the massive cleanup and spill-related claims, Anadarko Chairman and CEO Jim Hackett blasted BP's 'reckless decisions and actions' that led to the well's explosion. He went on to state that BP had a duty to perform the drilling 'in a good and workmanlike manner and to comply with all applicable laws and regulations'. The contract also holds BP responsible to its co-owners for damages 'caused by its gross negligence or wilful misconduct'. He went on to state that: 'The mounting evidence clearly demonstrates that this tragedy was preventable and the direct result of BP's reckless decisions and actions: whilst we recognize that ultimately we have obligations under federal law related to the oil spill, we will look to BP to continue to pay all legitimate claims as they have repeatedly stated that they will do.' Anadarko had little option but to turn on its partner as it was coming under severe financial pressure itself. Moody's Investors Service downgraded Anadarko's long-term debt rating to non-investment grade, dropping it to Ba1 from Baa3, with further reductions possible. As well as signalling credit concerns the company's $12.9 billion of rated debt securities became much more expensive at a stroke.

Although M & A are popular with CEOs the research literature produces, at best, inconclusive evidence to support the hypothesis that M & As generally create increased shareholder value for the owners of the acquiring firm.

Since Kitching's seminal work 'Why do mergers miscarry?' (*Harvard Business Review*, 1967, November–December, pp 84–101) there has been a big question mark over the subject of acquisitions and shareholder value. Porter ('From competitive advantage to corporate strategy', *Harvard Business Review*, 1987, 65(3), pp 43–59) concluded that 'acquisitions have been largely unsuccessful, when one considers that over half were subsequently divested'. A clear majority of the academic studies published over the past 50 years come down on the side of the doubters.

So why, you might wonder, do acquisitions capture so much of top management's attention. That arrogance plays a major part in this process is supported by the way that most corporate acquisitions are carried by relatively inexperienced individuals operating almost alone. This quotation from *The Wall Street Journal*, 'a struggle between a few ambitious men using public companies in which they owned a fractional share, for their own gain', captures the dominance of ego and arrogance in the merger process. A light-hearted, but statistically sound study conducted by two academics from Columbia University, found a way of confirming what we all knew already: there is a link between the premiums paid by bosses and their own inflated self-esteem. They measured such factors as the boss's salary relative to his peers and the acres of flattering press coverage and proved that the higher the self-esteem the higher the premium they paid to acquire the business and consequently the less likely it was that they would create additional value for their shareholders.

The other factor that draws top management to M & A is the immediacy of the apparent reward. Most business strategies present few opportunities to produce clear winners and losers in a very short time-frame. But with an acquisition strategy the successful bidder is declared the 'winner' by employees, middle management, competitors, their industry and the financial community at large, all within a matter of weeks. And even if the bid fails, the business community sees their management as a virile aggressor. The consequences of failure take years, even decades to emerge. Time Warner's acquisition of AOL and eBay's of Skype are two such examples where nothing of much value to the acquirers has arisen save copious positive press coverage in the early weeks after the event.

Then of course the protagonists are invariably cheered on by their professional advisors who stand to make a healthy profit whatever the outcome.

There are, however a number of conditions that research shows are more likely to lead to success:

1 Size matters: Deals between equals in terms of size are more likely to work well than not. The converse is also true. Where the acquired business is much smaller the chances of success are low.

2 Experience counts: For example M & A is viewed as a cornerstone of the strategy of Cisco whose top management have made such a study of the subject that management consultants from around the globe take their advice. In the United States, which has the greatest experience base of every type of merger and acquisition, buyers are more sophisticated and are less likely to overpay for their acquisitions than are Europeans, for example. In the United States, the medium control premium paid for a public company has been dropping steadily over the past decade from 58 per cent to just 26 per cent. In Europe by contrast, the average premium increased from 31 per cent to 37 per cent.

3 Cash is king: One much-vaunted reason for medium-sized firms to go public is the opportunity to use paper to fund acquisitions. But much academic research suggests that both bidders and targets lose in stock-financed deals, as opposed to those financed by cash. The reasons for this are:

   – Cash deals are quicker and less costly to implement than share deals.

   – A stock offer opens up the bidding to a wider group (ie any firm with or without cash). This in turn increases the competitiveness, which tends to be a disadvantage to the bidder.

   – Issuing new stock can be viewed negatively by the capital markets, leading to a drop in the share price of the bidder. This in turn can make the deal more expensive for the acquiring firm.

4 Avoid firms where the management owns a large slice of the business: It seems reasonable to assume that increased managerial share ownership, through options and the like, encourages managers to maximize shareholder value rather than simply to pursue aggrandizement strategies for their own sake. Giving managers a share of ownership requires them to bear a higher part of the cost of poor decisions. At the same time greater ownership gives company managers greater control of the company, a power that can then be used to resist acquisitions. Managers often resist bids, even when the bid looks likely to create greater shareholder value. Research bears these views out conclusively.

5 Cross-border deals work well: It seems that when firms expand into a new geographic market the shareholders of the acquiring firm are highly likely to experience significant increases in shareholder wealth, but not if they try to repeat the process in the same market. One interesting study (J Doukas and NG Travlos, 1988, 'The effects of corporate multinationalism on shareholder's wealth: Evidence from international acquisitions', *Journal of Finance*, **43**, pp 1161–75) found that US bidders going abroad for the first time made significant positive abnormal gains. Those making further acquisitions in the overseas countries in which they were operating did not fare so well. They made either zero or insignificant gains from second and subsequent acquisitions.

Going on the acquisition trail

M & A strategies are often messy, and in hostile bids there can be blood on the carpet. But just because they may end up messy – that is almost in-evitable in corporate warfare – they don't have to start off that way. Getting information on public companies is relatively easy. They are required by the rules of the stock exchange they are listed on to provide comprehensive and current – usually quarterly – information on performance. If any major event occurs, for example a serious profit warning, a legal dispute or any-thing that could materially affect the current profit forecast, that would have to be disclosed immediately. Searching out private companies will call for a bit more digging.

Look back to 'Desk (or secondary) research' in Chapter 3, where you will see how to find information on companies and markets around the globe.

The following are some steps you can advise to be taken to improve the chances of making a successful acquisition, merger or joint venture.

Know why you want to buy

Ideally the reasons to buy a business need to be practical and down-to-earth and embedded in the firm's core strategy. Sound reasons for acquisitions include the following:

- to increase market share and eliminate a troublesome competitor;
- to broaden your product range or give you access to new markets;
- to diversify into new markets, acquiring the necessary management, marketing or technical skills to enable you to capture a reasonable slice of the market, relatively quickly;
- to get into another country or region;
- to protect an important source of supply that could be under threat from a competitor;
- to acquire additional staff, factory space, warehousing, distribution channels, or to get access to additional major customers more quickly than by starting up yourself.

Your company should produce a written statement explaining the rationale behind your reason to buy – before you start looking for companies to buy – otherwise you could end up pursuing a bargain just because it seems cheap but which has absolutely nothing to do with your previously defined commercial goals. It is also worth remembering that companies available at knockdown prices are likely to need drastic surgery. So unless you fancy your chances as a company doctor, stay well away.

Decide what you want to buy

It can take over one man-year of work, on average, to find and buy a business. The more accurately you describe your ideal purchase the simpler, quicker and cheaper your search will be. Just imagine trying to buy a house without any idea where you wanted to live, how much you wanted to spend, how many bedrooms were needed, whether you wanted a new house or a listed building, or if you wanted a garden. The search would be near impossible to organize, it could take forever, and the resultant purchase would almost certainly please no one. The same problem is present when buying a company. The definition of what you want to buy should explain:

- the business area/products/service the company is in;
- the location;
- the price range and the cash you have available;
- the management depth and the management style you are looking for;
- the minimum profitability and return on capital employed you could accept;

- the image compatibility between your company and any target;
- scope for integration and cost savings;
- the tax status – for example a business nursing a substantial loss could be worth looking at if that can be offset against your company's profits and so reduce tax due.

Outside the factors listed above, you may have vital reasons that, if not met, would make the acquisition a poor bet. For example, if you want to iron out major cash flow or plant capacity cycles, there is little point in going for a business similar to your own. That will only make the peaks and troughs more pronounced.

Investigate and approach

Once you have your shopping list of prospective purchases you need to arm yourself with everything you can find out about them. Get their literature; get samples, copies of their advertising, press comment and, of course, their accounts. Then get out and see their premises and as much of their operation as it is possible to see. If you cannot get in, get one of your salespeople in to look the business over for you. This investigation will help you both to shorten your shopping list and to put it into order of priority. Now you are ready for the approach. Although you are technically buying, psychologically you would be well advised to think of acquiring a company as a selling job. As such you cannot afford to have any approach rejected either too early or without a determined effort.

You have three options as to how to make the initial approach and each has its merits. You can telephone, giving only the broadest reason for your approach – saying, perhaps, that you wish to discuss areas of common interest. You could write and be a little more specific on your purpose, following that up with a phone call to arrange a meeting, perhaps over lunch. Finally, you could use a third party such as an accountant or consultant (reasons of secrecy could make this method desirable) or a corporate finance house: if executive time is at a premium, there may be no other practicable way. The first meeting is crucial and you need to achieve two objectives. Firstly, you must establish mutual respect, trust and rapport. Nothing worthwhile will follow without these. Then you need to establish in principle that both parties are seriously interested. Time scale, price, methods of integration etc, can all be side-stepped until later, except in the most general sense.

Valuing a target

There are two special situations that make an initial valuation relatively easy, at least in theory.

Public companies: If your target is already floated on a stock market its value is measured by buyers and sellers every day, or perhaps more often in turbulent times. For example, during the banking meltdown in the autumn of 2008 HBOS's shares oscillated by as much as 40 per cent on an almost daily basis. They were not alone in seeing violent swings and indeed some stock markets, most prominently the Russian main market, actually had to shut down as both the volume of selling orders and the spread of prices was too great to comprehend, yet alone manage. Nevertheless the market set the value of every business on a stock exchange for every transaction. This market price is not necessarily the price that the owners will get for their shares, but in more normal times it is a reasonably close approximation.

Asset sale: Ongoing businesses are all valued by some measure of future expected profits. In fact the accounts don't even attempt to put a value on the assets. Fixed assets, except for freehold property, is recorded as the cost at date of purchase, reduced by a notional depreciation amount the sole purpose of which is to allocate costs over an asset's working life. The asset itself could be of virtually no value at all, such as, say, second-hand office furniture. But that would not be revealed in the balance sheet, whose purpose in this respect is only to show where money has come from and what has been done with that money. The exception to this rule is if a business is not going to continue trading; for example if no buyer can be found. In those circumstances the assets now all have to be valued and sold off piecemeal.

Price/Earnings rules

The simplest and most usual way for businesses to be valued is using a formula known as the Price/Earnings ratio. The P/E ratio is calculated by dividing the share price into the amount of profit earned for each share. For example, if a business makes £100,000 profit and has 1,000 shares, the profit per share is £100. If the share price of that company is £10, then its P/E ratio is 10 (100/10). So much for the science, now for the art: P/E ratios vary both with the business sector and current market sentiment for that sector. For example, the high-tech sector may have a P/E ratio of 30 or more at times – Google had a P/E of 100 at one point. That means that shareholders were prepared to pay £100 for every £1 of profit the company was making. For Barclays Bank, however, they were only paying £10 for every £1 of profits and in the market mayhem of 2008 the banking sector slipped well below that. The market as a whole trades with P/Es between 10 and 20.

P/E ratios are published alongside share price information in the financial press. You can get more detailed information on P/E ratios by sector and over time by using a business reference library such as that of the ICAEW (Institute of Chartered Accountants in England and Wales). Your employer may have access or can provide you with a letter of introduction from your accountants, in which case using the library's resources is free. Otherwise you can pay a daily or weekly fee, currently set at £15+VAT per day and

£50+VAT for the week. Visit **www.icaew.com/en/library/subject-gateways/ financial-markets/knowledge-guide-to-pe-ratios_**.

If you are investigating a company not listed on a stock market, termed a private company, you won't be able to find a P/E ratio easily. Also, they don't trade on as high a P/E multiple as their big brothers on the stock market do. So if a public company in your sector is on a P/E of 12, as a private company your prospective P/E would be around 8, or a third less. Why? Good question. The simplest answer is that whereas shares in your business are hard to dispose of, you can unload a public company every business day by making a phone call to your broker. In other words the premium is for liquidity.

BDO, the accountancy firm, produces a Private Company Price Index (PCPI) which tracks the relationship between the current FTSE price earnings ratio (P/E) and the P/Es currently being paid on the sale of private companies. Put simply, the PCPI lets a buyer know what a company without a stock market listing could reasonably be expected to sell for now. Visit **www.bdo.co.uk/news/private-company-price-index-pcpi**.

Discounting future earnings

A valuation technique popular with the venture capital community is to discount future earnings. We know intuitively that getting cash in sooner is better than getting it in later. In other words a pound received now is worth more than a pound that will arrive in one, two or more years in the future because of what we could do with that money ourselves, or because of what we ourselves have to pay out to have use of that money. So anyone buying your business will need to ascribe a value to a future stream of earnings to arrive at what is known as the present value. If we know we could earn 20 per cent on any money, we then know the maximum we would be prepared to pay now for a pound coming in one year hence would be around 80p. If we were to pay one pound now to get a pound back in a year's time we would in effect be losing money.

The process is known as discounting and the technique is termed discounted cash flow (DCF). The residual discounted cash is called the net present value.

The first column in Table 8.1 shows the simple cash flow implications of an investment proposition; a surplus of $/€/£5,000 comes after five years from putting $/€/£20,000 into a project. But if we accept the proposition that future cash is worth less than current cash the only question we need to answer is how much less. If we assume an investor wants to make at least a 15 per cent return on their investment then that is the discount rate selected (this doesn't matter too much, as you will see in the paragraph below on internal rate of return).

The formula for calculating what a pound received at some future date is:

$$\text{Present Value (PV)} = \$/€/£P \times 1/(1 + r)^n$$

TABLE 8.1   Discounting a stream of future earnings

£	Cash flow A	Discount factor at 15% B	Discounted cash flow A × B
Initial cash cost NOW (Year 0)	20,000	1.00	20,000
Net cash flows			
Year 1	1,000	0.8695	870
Year 2	4,000	0.7561	3,024
Year 3	8,000	0.6575	5,260
Year 4	7,000	0.5717	4,002
Year 5	5,000	0.4972	2,486
Total	25,000		15,642
Cash surplus	5,000	Net Present Value	(4,358)

Where $/€/£P is the initial cash cost, r is the interest rate expressed in decimals and n is the year in which the cash will arrive. So if we decide on a discount rate of 15 per cent the present value of a pound received in one year's time is:

Present Value
$$= \$/€/£1 \times 1/(1 + 0.15)^1$$
$$= 0.87 \text{ (rounded to two decimal places)}$$

So we can see that our £1,000 arriving at the end of year one has a present value of $/€/£870; the $/€/£4,000 in year two has a present value of $/€/ £3,024 and by year five present value reduces cash flows to barely half their original figure. In fact, far from having a real payback in year four and generating a cash surplus of $/€/£5,000, this project will make us $/€/£4,358 worse off than we had hoped to be if we required to make a return of 15 per cent. The investment in buying this business fails to meet the criteria using DCF.

Internal rate of return (IRR): DCF is a useful starting point but does not give us any definitive information. For example, all we know about the above investment is that it doesn't make a return of 15 per cent. In order to know the actual rate of return we need to choose a discount rate that produces a net present value of the entire cash flow of zero, known as the internal rate of return. The maths is time-consuming but Spreadsheet.com has a useful template (**www.spreadsheetml.com/financialmodeling/free_ investment_financial_calculator_tvm_npv_irr.shtml**).

Aswath Damodaran, who teaches corporate finance and valuation on the MBA programme at the Stern School of Business at New York University, has a wide range of free spreadsheets for all aspects of finance including DCF and IRR (**http://pages.stern.nyu.edu/~adamodar/New_Home_Page/ spreadsh.htm**). You will see that the IRR for the project in question is slightly under 7 per cent, insufficient to warrant taking any risks for. Venture capital providers will be looking for an IRR of above 30 per cent.

Rules of thumb

Some business sectors have their own yardsticks for estimating the value of a business. For example, sales turnover is often used for computer mainte- nance businesses and mail order businesses; the number of customers for a mobile phone airtime provider; the number of outlets for an estate agency, restaurant or pub chain; and grocery shops are valued partly on their turnover and partly on the value of the stock they hold. BizStats (**www.bizstats.com/ reports/valuation-rule-thumb.php**) has a nifty table giving a list of these rules.

CASE STUDY City Flyer Express

Robert Wright, a Cranfield MBA who started up his airline venture, Connectair, immediately after completing his MBA, sold out to Harry Goodman, late of International Leisure fame for around £7 million. Not bad for just under five years' work. However, negotiations with Goodman took up nearly a year, and the opening offer was under £1 million. In the end the deal was valued on a multiple of landing slots, as Goodman planned to use these for his fleet of much larger planes and create value. Things didn't quite work out as planned and International Leisure went bust. Robert bought the business back from receivership for a nominal £1 and with £1 million of venture capital from 3i built the business up again, this time under the name City Flyer Express. A decade later he sold the business to British Airways for a healthy £75 million.

Robert was a Founder shareholder and former non-exec director (May 2004 – April 2011) at Wizzair, the Hungarian low-cost airline with its head office in Budapest.

Multiple models

Some valuation techniques, particularly those used by business brokers who help sell private companies, involve using a number of adjustments to the basic P/E method. Once such approach is based around the following formula:

Add-back profitability × Industry Sector P/E + Adjustment for assets and liabilities

The add-back profitability involves trying to arrive at what the profit might be in the hands of the acquiring company. In the case where the reported profit of a business for sale is say $/€/£500,000 it might be argued that the $/€/£50,000 of interest charges should be added back to the profits based on the fact that new owners would finance the company in a different way and would have access to these funds as disposable profits. The same argument could be made for the two directors who are paying themselves a hefty $/€/£300,000 a year, when in fact the business could be run with a divisional manager by the acquirer paying around $/€/£100,000 including a performance-related bonus. That would add a further $/€/£200,000 to the profits being available in the business. There could be deductions to profits too, if the acquiring firm doesn't expect to be able to retain the income stream post-purchase – specialist consultancy income from work done by one of the owners or the rental income arising from letting out part of the business premises, if that won't continue, for example. To carry on our example let's assume that this amounts to a deduction of $/€/£100,000. So the business's continuing profits would be assessed as:

$/€/£500,000 + $/€/£50,000 + $/€/£200,000 − $/€/£100,000
= $/€/£650,000

That figure would then be the basis from which to apply the P/E multiple. In the case where the sector P/E is 5 then the value would be $/€/£3.25 million rather than the $/€/£2.5 million that would otherwise have been assumed.

There is one further adjustment made in this valuation approach: an adjustment for assets and liabilities is made by calculating the net assets; that is the surplus of assets over liabilities. The argument for this is that it represents the current value of the owner's stake in the business. The P/E approach gives the value of future earnings. So adding one to the other gives the 'real' value. In practice, any valuation approach is just the starting point for negotiations.

Valuing minority shareholdings

If you are not buying an entire business but taking a minority stake, perhaps putting down a marker for a later bid, or as part of a strategic alliance strategy the rules on value are specialized. The value of their stake will not just be smaller because they have fewer shares, but by virtue of that fact a minority stake usually can neither force nor prevent the sale of a business. Discounts are applied to most share calculations for a lack of marketability.

EBITDA (Earnings before interest, tax, depreciation and amortization)

This measure of a company's operating efficiency is the one favoured by acquisitive firms as it strips out extraneous costs that may not continue post acquisition, or if they do continue they may not be of a similar proportion. Factors such as:

- Financing costs: Interest rates, for example, may not be the same for both parties to an acquisition and in the case of a cash- or share-based transaction there may be no residual debt post the event for interest to be paid on.

- Accounting practices: Such items as depreciation and amortization may be different if, for example, some assets were to be eliminated should the acquiring business not require them or have different accounting procedures.

- Tax. If the acquiring company operates in a country where tax rates are lower or higher than the business to be acquired it makes sense to remove them from consideration. This is particularly important where, as is typically the case, the acquiring company has more than one acquisition target in mind. If one of those targets operates in a country with a high tax rate they will appear less attractive as their net profits will appear lower, a factor that may not be relevant after the acquisition has been concluded.

EBITDA Adjustments

Look back to the components of EBITDA. Even having stripped out the elements of cost (interest, tax, depreciation and amortization) there are some other costs that can reasonably be expected to terminate when a business changes hands. Those costs, once added back, will have the effect of increasing profits and hence the potential value of the enterprise. Some such costs might be the rent of any property that won't be required to run the business going forward. That might well be the case if some functions are to be consolidated into the parent company.

It may also be that directors of the company being bought are being paid above the market rate; this is fairly common where the business founder is still in the business. There may also be some directors with very nominal roles but far from nominal pay cheques.

Limit the risks

Buying a business will always be risky. If you have done your homework and got the price right, with any luck the risks will be less. Here are some other things you can do to lessen the risks:

- Set conditional terms: for example, you could make part of the price conditional upon a certain level of profits being achieved.
- Handcuff key employees: if most of the assets you are buying are on two legs, get service contracts or consultancy arrangements in place before the deal is signed.
- Non-competitive clauses: make sure that neither the seller nor his key employees can set up in competition, taking all the goodwill you have just bought.
- Tax clearances: obviously you want to make sure any tax losses you are buying, or any tax implications in the purchase price, are approved by the Inland Revenue before committing yourself.
- Warranties and indemnities: if, after you have bought, you find there is a compulsory purchase order on the vendor's premises and the patent on his exciting new product is invalid, you would quite rightly be rather miffed. Warranties and indemnities set out those circumstances in which the seller will make good the buyer's financial loss. So you could try to include anything crucial that looks worrying under this heading. Not unnaturally, the seller will resist, but you need to be firm on key points.

Manage the acquisition/venture relationship

However well-negotiated the deal, most acquisitions and venture relationships that go wrong do so because of the human factor, often in the first few weeks and months after the deal is made public. Some important rules to follow are listed below. Have an outline plan for how to handle the merger and be prepared to be flexible. (Interestingly enough, only one buyer in five has a detailed operational plan of how to manage their acquisition; 67 per cent of those being bought believe the buyer has such a plan, so it is psychologically important.)

- Let business go on as usual for a few weeks, as you learn more about the internal workings of the company. Then you can make informed judgements on who or what should go or remain in post. This rule is followed by 90 per cent of successful acquisitions.
- Hold management and staff meetings on day one, to clear up as much misunderstanding as you can. This should be done by the CEO.
- Never announce takeovers on a Friday. Staff will have all weekend to spread rumours. Wednesdays are best: just enough time to clear up misunderstandings, followed by a useful weekend breathing space.

- Make cuts/redundancies a once-only affair. It is always best to cut deep, and then get on with running the business. Continuous sacking saps morale, and all the best people will leave before it is their turn.
- Set limits of authority and reporting relationships and put all banking relationships in the hands of your own accounts department, as quickly as possible.

But to be truly successful and achieve enduring cost savings there has to be something in it for both parties as the Röhm and BASF Coatings case study shows.

CASE STUDY   BASF Coatings AG and Röhm GmbH & Co KG

BASF Coatings AG, a major paint supplier, and its relationship with Röhm GmbH & Co. KG, an important supplier, is a case in point when it comes to holding stock on assignment. BASF can trace its roots back to 1903, when its parent company, Glasurit-Werke Max Winkelmann, started up in Münster-Hiltrup. With annual sales turnover of €2.5 billion (£2.2 billion/$3.63 billion) and strong market positions in Europe, North and South America, as well as the Asian-Pacific region, and with satellite companies in Australia, China, India, Japan and the Philippines, the company has a complex supply and stock chain. The situation has been exacerbated by having the motor industry as a major customer segment, who demand a high degree of flexibility from their suppliers and exert strong cost pressure, never more so than during major economic downturns.

Initially Röhm and BASF Coatings maintained a fairly traditional customer–supplier relationship. At the beginning of each year BASF Coatings would provide an approximate, non-binding estimate of requirements. Other than that no further information was provided so production planning at Röhm was based almost entirely on past experience. The result was that both parties had problems. BASF experienced frequent stock shortages when demand accelerated and Röhm had idle capacity when the reverse occurred.

To overcome these supply problems, BASF Coatings initiated a project called PROGRESS (process integrated supply) and invited core suppliers, Röhm among them, to collaborate in order to reduce costs, shorten process and production times and improve the quality of information and the level of service for all parties. As a result Röhm now maintains consignment depots for BASF Coatings at BASF's plants, taking on tank fillings and deliveries on the basis of live online data on stock, forecasts and planned withdrawals submitted by BASF Coatings. BASF

Coatings pays for the chemicals via credit (self-billing) as they are drawn off with the relevant documentation delivered on a common electronic platform. BASF and Röhm calculated a joint annual cost saving in excess of €500,000 (£439,000/$726,000).

Clear the regulators

You may have one further hurdle to face before signing off on an acquisition. If the combination looks like creating a monopoly (this is covered in Chapter 2) you may need to get regulatory clearance. It is not always obvious what is likely to create a monopolistic situation. Europe's long-running battle with Microsoft over its domination of the operating system market and Google's stranglehold of search engines seem reasonable areas for the regulator to question. But quite why the Competition and Markets Authority, the UK's monopoly regulator, announced on 9 April 2015 that 'the anticipated acquisition by Poundland plc of 99p Stores Limited will be referred for an in-depth investigation by the CMA' is less clear. The regulator case revolves around their claim that these two stores operate in a unique market with a distinctive price sensitive group of customers selling at a 'single price point.'

The Poundland deal is for a fairly modest £55 million ($80/€75 million), hardly likely to cause a ripple in a retail market worth billions. The company's chief executive, Jim McCarthy told the *Daily Telegraph* that he was 'particularly frustrated that the CMA considered the deal on the basis that the retailer's only main rival was 99p and its other competitors were B&M, Home Bargains, Wilko and Poundstretcher. He, on the other hand, believes it competes against a wide collection of retailers, including the major super-market chains.

Online video courses and lectures

Developing a Successful Acquisition Strategy: Positioning Your Business for Growth. Georgetown University Alumni Career Services, John Dearing (MBA '96), Managing Director at Capstone Strategic: **www.youtube.com/watch?v=NtbwR48FmjM**

Enterprise Value: Khan Academy: **www.khanacademy.org/economics-finance-domain/core-finance/stock-and-bonds/valuation-and-investing/v/enterprise-value**

Price to Earnings Ratio (or P/E ratio): Khan Academy: **www.khanacademy.org/economics-finance-domain/core-finance/stock-and-bonds/valuation-and-investing/v/introduction-to-the-price-to-earnings-ratio**

Review of Enterprise Value and Comparing it to EBITDA: Khan Academy: **www.khanacademy.org/economics-finance-domain/core-finance/ stock-and-bonds/valuation-and-investing/v/ebitd**

The Stock Market Is Not Rational: A History of Risk, Reward, and Delusion on Wall Street (2009), Justin Fox, Time Magazine: **www.youtube.com/watch?v=XEN0Hwm-Eos**

Online video case studies

Apple's acquisition strategy: CNBC's Josh Lipton and USA Today San Francisco Bureau Chief Jon Swartz discuss what Apple's acquisition plans say about its hardware business: **http://video.cnbc.com/ gallery/?video=3000296348**

Is Facebook's acquisition strategy successful? Scott Redler, Chief Strategic Officer at T3live.com, describes how the tech giant is using acquisitions to penetrate the market: **http://video.cnbc.com/ gallery/?video=3000259684**

What's Behind Alibaba's Acquisition Strategy? GGV Capital Managing Partner Glenn Solomon discusses Alibaba's acquisition strategy and possible Apple partnership on 'Bloomberg West.': **www.bloomberg.com/ news/videos/2014-11-04/whats-behind-alibabas-acquisition-strategy**

Walmart Case Study – Strategic Marketing. Rod McNealy, Johnson & Johnson Marketing Executive, Wharton Lecturer, presenting the Walmart Case Study on Strategic Marketing to Princeton audience: **www.youtube.com/watch?v=cFhfOj36s4l**

Warren Buffett on How to Buy a Business: Private Companies vs. Stock Market, Investing: CNBC: **www.youtube.com/watch?v=UsCHutekxuQ**

9 Ethics and social responsibility in the global marketplace

- Owners vs directors.
- Stakeholder groupings.
- Ethical and responsible strategies.
- Whistle-blowing.
- Green pays off.
- Corruption revealed.

This subject is perhaps the most controversial and disputed in terms of the teaching methodology and content used in business schools. A recent survey on Corporate Social Responsibility Education in Europe found that while most business schools had some content in this area, only a quarter had a specific topic, module or elective covering the ground. In 2015 courses in corporate social responsibility (CSR), ethics, sustainability or business and society are now a requirement for 68 per cent of MBAs, up from 45 per cent in 2003 and 34 per cent in 2001. Most had the subject embedded in various other subject areas; for example under titles such as a combination of 'Accounting, Corporate Governance, Law and Public Governance' or 'Stakeholder Management'. Others had ethics and social responsibility covered in the context of specific disciplines – ethical accounting systems or marketing and ethics. Georgia Tech College of Management's MBA set as a business ethics paper the task 'Analyse Sarbanes-Oxley from both conceptual and implementation perspectives', which is largely a single issue of directors' responsibilities to investors.

There is widespread use of practitioner speakers from business or NGOs as well as case studies from industry, and these methods dwarf the more academic methods (lectures, tutorials) used in other subject areas. Tuck School of Business at Dartmouth, for example, teach a 'brief mini-course' based on discussions of ethical issues encountered by their faculty in cases involving their experience 'particularly on the functional areas of business as exercised in both the United States and the global marketplace, where different local practices and cultural norms seem to muddy the ethical water'. The academics, however, are on the march! Nottingham University Business School has an International Centre for Corporate Social Responsibility and a Professor of CSR (Corporate Social Responsibility). INSEAD has a chaired professor of Business Ethics and Corporate Responsibility, although the focus there appears to be very much around ethical consumerism, deception in marketing and marketing ethics. But the University of Chicago Graduate School of Business leads the field in raising the bar on teaching in this field. It's the only Business School anywhere to have a Nobel laureate – Robert Fogel, winner of the 1993 Nobel Prize in Economics – teaching 'A Guide to Business Ethics'.

However, Jonathan P Doh and Peter Tashman, in their research findings on how the top 50 business schools taught social responsibility concluded: 'Our results suggest that the institutionalization of CSR, sustainability and sustainable development is far from extensive. These subjects do appear to be diffusing through the business school curricula, but with uneven records of adoption and diverse methods of implementation by faculty.' (Doh, J P and Tashman, P (2014) Half a world away: The integration and assimilation of corporate social responsibility, sustainability, and sustainable development in business school curricula, *Corporate Social Responsibility and Environmental Management*, 21 (3), pp 131–42)

Ethics and social responsibility defined

Actions for which a person or group of people can be held accountable and so commended or blamed, disciplined or rewarded, are those said to lie within their sphere of responsibility. Anything that lies outside our control also lies beyond the scope of our responsibilities. Ethics, known in academic circles as moral philosophy, is concerned with classifying, defending and proposing concepts of right and wrong behaviour in the way in which we discharge our responsibilities. While many responsibilities lie within the scope of the law – shareholders' protection, discrimination at work, misleading advertising and so forth – both in those areas and the grey area that surrounds them lies the province of ethics and social responsibility. Right and wrong in themselves are often not too difficult to separate out. The problem usually stems from competing 'rights' – giving shareholders a better return vs saving the planet, for example, and the inherent selfishness of humans. Many, if not all, of our actions are triggered by self-interest. In fact much of the justification for capitalism's attraction lies in the 'invisible hand' theory advanced by Adam Smith in his defining book *The Wealth of Nations*:

> Every individual... generally, indeed, neither intends to promote the public interest, nor knows how much he is promoting it. By preferring the support of domestic to that of foreign industry he intends only his own security; and by directing that industry in such a manner as its produce may be of the greatest value, he intends only his own gain, and he is in this, as in many other cases, led by an invisible hand to promote an end which was no part of his intention.

Unfortunately the invisible hand suggests only that businesses and consumers in being selfish may by accident do good, not that their actions are made ethical in the process. Many purely selfish actions, say operating a cartel to rip off consumers, or adopting a polluting production process purely to boost the bottom line, fall firmly into the unethical bracket. Even overtly ethical actions, for example when a business gives to charity, or supports a 'not for profit' event such as Coca-Cola's sponsorship of the Olympic Games over an 80-year period, can prove ethically questionable. In the first place Coca-Cola, McDonald's, Samsung and the other Olympic sponsors hope for a share of the huge marketing benefits that accrue from such association. Secondly, supporting the Games may be the 'right' thing to do, but supporting the host country, China, a regime with a questionable human-rights track record may well be 'wrong'.

Business ethics defines the categories of duty for which we are morally responsible. Lists of moral duties and rights can be lengthy and overlapping. The duty-based theory advanced by British philosopher WD Ross (1877–1971), provides a short list of duties that he believed reflects our actual moral convictions:

- Fidelity: the duty to keep promises.
- Reparation: the duty to compensate others when we harm them.
- Gratitude: the duty to thank those who help us.
- Justice: the duty to recognize merit.
- Beneficence: the duty to improve the conditions of others.
- Self-improvement: the duty to improve our virtue and intelligence.
- Non-maleficence: the duty to not injure others.

Ross recognized that there will be occasions when we must choose between two conflicting duties. For example, should your business be involved in any way with products that facilitate abortions? On one side of that moral argument lies beneficence in improving the conditions of women and on the other non-maleficence in not doing injury to the unborn child. You can find out more about the theoretical aspects of ethics on the Internet Encyclopedia of Philosophy (**www.iep.utm.edu/e/ethics.htm**) and on related business issues on the Free Management Library website (**www.managementhelp.org/ethics/ethxgde.htm**).

CASE STUDY Bayer AG of Germany

On 4 April 2015 Marijn Dekkers, chairman of Bayer AG since 2010, announced that the company's net profit had jumped by almost a third the previous year to €3.19 billion ($4.35/£3 billion) on record high sales. Aside from growing profits, both the company and its chairman were on top of their respective games. Dekkers was appointed to the Board of Directors of General Electric in the United States and effective from September 2014, he took over the two-year presidency of the German Chemical Industry Association (VCI). The company had barely taken the acquisition of US-based Merck & Co's consumer-care division under its belt than the quest for innovation moved on with the launch of five new blockbuster drugs. When Dekkers took over from his predecessor, Werner Wenning, Bayer had just been awarded the German Future Prize, the most important accolade in Germany for innovation, for the development of Xarelto, a drug for the prevention of venous thromboembolism following elective hip- or knee-replacement surgery.

The company, best known in consumer markets for aspirin, is one of the world's largest and oldest chemical and health-care products companies. Their mission statement 'Bayer: Science For A Better Life' conceals a much more complex organization with a range of goals beyond the short-term balance sheet.

Bayer had been successful for some decades with a conventional organizational structure departmentalized by function. But now the company aimed to occupy leading positions in all their markets worldwide and be in a position to continue developing these businesses successfully over the long term. They are the third-largest company in the German stock index DAX, with 108,000 employees worldwide.

With their international growth goals in mind the company committed to the biggest reorganization in Bayer's history. They separated the strategic management of the group from the day-to-day running of the business, established clear lines of responsibility and focused their businesses more closely on their respective markets.

The company set out to devise a structure that would enable it to:

1 shift management control from the German parent company to its foreign divisions;

2 restructure business divisions to more clearly define their activities;

3 flatten the organization, empower lower level managers and free up top executives so they could devote more time to strategic thinking.

Headquartered in Leverkusen, Germany, is the strategic management holding company for the Bayer Group. Business activities are conducted by three operating strategic business units, HealthCare, CropScience and MaterialScience subgroups, supported by the service companies Bayer Business Services, Bayer Technology Services and Currenta.

Nothing in Bayer's quest for international growth deflected them from being conscious of their responsibilities as a business with global aspirations. The company has invested heavily in burnishing a wide range of softer credentials. In 2000 they became a founding member of the UN Global Compact and in so doing made a clear commitment to 10 principles relating to human rights, employment standards, environmental protection and the fight against corruption. In 2004 they became the first company to partner with the United Nations Environment Programme in the area of youth and environment. The development of the Bayer Climate Program, launched in 2006, was a milestone in their commitment to sustainable development. As well as substantially reducing their greenhouse gas emissions they have set themselves further ambitious targets. Bayer were the only European company in the chemical and pharmaceutical industry to be listed for the fifth time in succession in the world's first global climate index and in 2009 they were rated as the world's best company in the 'Carbon Disclosure Leadership Index'. The Bayer Science & Education Foundation supports innovative school projects in Germany that make science lessons more attractive. Each year they provide a total of about €45 million in funding for the 300 projects they support as part of their social commitment.

Bayer also take their responsibility toward their employees very seriously, even in difficult times. In December 2009 they reached an agreement with the employee representatives on a comprehensive pact for safeguarding employment through 2012, despite facing a highly uncertain economic environment. The company even has a staff function at corporate HQ to head up 'Environment and Sustainability'.

FIGURE 9.1   Bayer's organization structure

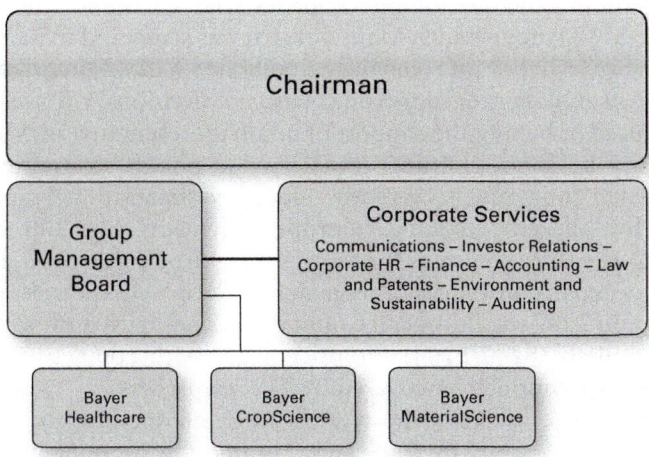

Corruption – the international perspective

Transparency International (**www.transparency.org**) who interview over 70,000 people each year and produce an international corruption league table, reckon that more than 1 in 10 people interviewed reported having paid a bribe in the previous 12 months. Countries are scored on a variety of factors and are rated between 1 (very corrupt) and 10 (very ethical). Unsurprisingly, countries such as Denmark, New Zealand, Sweden, Singapore and Finland appear in the list of least corrupt countries with scores above 9. Afghanistan, Iraq, Haiti, Somalia and Myanmar are bottom of the list with scores of 1.5 or less, indicating high levels of corruption throughout their economies.

TI's (Transparency International) studies regularly show that the level of corruption remains disturbingly high. They assert that it is far from uncommon for multinationals to pay bribes to secure public procurement contracts, often with the willing cooperation of civil servants, many of whom may be underpaid and hence struggling to make ends meet. In developing and transition countries alone, corrupt politicians and government officials receive bribes believed to total between $20 (£13.3bn/€16.16bn) and 40 billion (£26.6/€32.32), which equates between a fifth and two-fifths of total development.

Corruption makes it possible for companies to evade local regulations, with consequences ranging from water shortages in Spain, unfair work conditions in China, illegal logging in Indonesia, unsafe medicines in Nigeria and poorly constructed buildings in Turkey that collapse with deadly consequences. More than 283 private international cartels were uncovered between

1990 and 2005 whose aggregate sales of some $1.2 trillion caused consumers to be overcharged by over $300 billion.

But it is not just in developing countries that corruption flourishes. Volkswagen's (VW) labour leader, Klaus Volkert, was sentenced to 33 months in prison in February 2008 for receiving €2 million ($3/£2.43) in bribes from VW executives in exchange for supporting managers' decisions. VW's managers were also accused of buying the support of union representatives with secret bonuses, luxury holidays, clothing, jewellery and phoney consulting fees. Alstom, a French company, is currently under investigation in France and Switzerland for allegedly making improper payments of $200 million (£133/€161.6) to secure contracts for Brazil's Itá hydroelectric plant, for São Paulo's subway expansion and for other major works in Venezuela, Singapore and Indonesia. In 2007 the European Commission's antitrust authority fined Alstom €65 million ($247/£164) for price-fixing with competitors. Such cases and more are routinely uncovered by TI's researchers.

The United States, as befits the world's most prosperous country has corruption on a mega scale. In 2006 Jack Abramoff, a prominent lobbyist with close ties to Republican administration officials and legislators, was sentenced to four years after being alleged to have offered bribes as part of his lobbying efforts. In March 2009, Bernard Madoff pleaded guilty to turning his wealth-management business into a massive Ponzi scheme that defrauded thousands of investors of billions of dollars. In fact, no country is wholly exempt from corruption.

Transparency International comments on the United States, for example: 'Although the United States has an effective anti-money laundering framework, experts are concerned about various legislative and regulatory weaknesses... Furthermore, there are loopholes that allow entities and persons to use shell companies as well as trusts to hide and launder proceeds from illegal activities.' (**www.transparency.org/country#USA**). For the UK, it focuses its attention on political corruption: 'Conflict of interests between public office and the private sector continues to undermine trust in government. Notable MP scandals raise further doubts about the 'revolving door' between government and the private sector.' (**www.transparency.org/country#GBR**). Still, those comments pale beside their take on the Russian Federation where they claim their research shows that 26 per cent of the population has paid a bribe in the past year and 53 per cent think corruption is on the rise.

Owners vs directors: the start of the ethical tug of war

Directors are appointed by the owners of a business to control the business and look after their interests in their absence. When enterprises were small and local this was an expediency rarely invoked as owners more often than not were the directors and where they were not it was usual to ensure at least some family oversight. Now where nearly two-thirds of all business activity is conducted by giant global enterprises this separation of ownership from control has become both necessary and commonplace. Also, such businesses have replaced 'owners' with 'shareholders'. The difference is subtle but it is the key to understanding the requirement for including business ethics and social responsibility on the business school curriculum.

Shareholders only rarely own more than a small fraction of any one business, they have no special reason to identify with the founders' vision or code of behaviour and they are preoccupied with relatively simple outcomes such as growth in earnings per share. If they become unhappy in that respect they just swap their holding in that business for a similar stake in another. In fact, even if such shareholders are satisfied with financial performance, when a sector is out of 'favour', say as retailers may be during a recession, they may well sell their holding in any case. The main holders of large shareholdings in businesses now are fund managers and pension funds and arguably these have an even greater imperative to focus their attention on earnings. True, they exert pressure from time to time but that is usually when they see too much control moving into the hands of one director, say when there is an attempt to combine the roles of chairman and chief executive. Also, when directors are trying to pay themselves more than they may be worth or are trying to improve their lot in some other way at the expense of shareholders, a fund manager may step in. Fund managers are not always honest brokers with regard to looking after shareholder interest. For example, during a takeover there is a good chance a fund manager will find themselves with holdings in both buyer and seller.

The board of directors has in effect replaced the 'owner' as the custodian of the moral tone and in setting standards of behaviour towards everyone the business has dealings with. They are in some ways encouraged by legal constraints placed on them to take a narrow view of those responsibilities. They are required 'to act in good faith in the interests of the company'; 'not to deceive shareholders and to appoint auditors to oversee the accounting records'; 'not to carry on the business of the company with intent to defraud creditors or for any fraudulent purpose'; and 'to have regard for the interests of employees in general'. (See Chapter 6 for more on the responsibilities of directors.)

Directors and managers also have responsibilities to protect their customers when using their products or services or when visiting company premises and to follow rules inhibiting pollution in the operating processes. But it is only relatively recently that companies have been required to take a wider view of their responsibilities to other 'stakeholder' groups. Enlightened managers, or those that are particularly astute, depending on your level of cynicism, have often taken on broader responsibilities; sponsoring charities, funding social amenities such as play areas or providing low-cost housing. These initiatives are often spurred on by enlightened self-interest, say, to help with recruiting and retaining employees, with getting favourable PR, or in the case of low-cost housing, providing amenities is a usual requirement in getting planning consent for a property development or a site for a supermarket for instance.

CASE STUDY Unilever – embedding ethics

In 2015, when Unilever published their accounts for the preceding year, the chairman stated, 'Our growth model is based on a leaner, more agile Unilever.' Reporting turnover at €48.4 billion with their operating profit margin up 0.4 per cent to 14.5 per cent, the chairman continued, 'Our business is growing ahead of our markets... the consistency of our delivery is underlined by the fact that our average growth over the last five years is 4.9 per cent, making us one of the most reliable performers in our industry.'

Unilever is no stranger to growth.

In 1887 William Hesketh Lever, already a highly successful soap manufacturer, was looking for a new site for his factory to allow him to expand. The site also needed to be near to a river for importing raw materials, and a railway line for transporting the finished products. The 56 acres of unused marshy land at the site that became Port Sunlight, named after his soap, was far more than he needed simply for manufacturing purposes. Lever had something more all-embracing in mind. His stated aims were to create an environment that allowed his workers 'to socialise and Christianise business relations and get back to that close family brotherhood that existed in the good old days of hand labour'. His intention was to extend his responsibilities beyond making money for himself and to share that, albeit on his own terms, with everyone who worked for him. Between 1899 and 1914 Lever built some 800 houses, taking an active part in the design himself. The community's population of 3,500 enjoyed shared allotments, public buildings including the Lady Lever Art Gallery, schools, a concert hall, open air swimming pool, church, and a temperance hotel. His cottage hospital, built in 1907, continued until the introduction of the National Health Service in 1948. He also introduced schemes for welfare, education and the entertainment of his workers, and encouraged recreation and organizations that promoted art, literature, science or music.

Unilever, as the company is now known, has carried the Lever values and vision on into corporate life. The company's behaviour in all affairs is governed by a set of clear, stated and communicated guidelines. Starting with their core value, 'As a multi-local multinational we aim to play our part in addressing global environmental and social concerns through our own actions, and working in partnership with stakeholders at local, national and international levels', the company has developed a comprehensive set of principles to guide their behaviour in all aspects of their work. The guidelines they expect employees to work to include always working with integrity with 'the highest standards of corporate behaviour towards everyone we work with, the communities we touch, and the environment on which we have an impact'. The full value statement can be seen on their website at this link (**www.unilever.com/ourvalues**).

Understanding stakeholders

As we've seen, directors and by extension the managers of an organization first saw their primary, and often their only, responsibility was to look after the shareholders' interests. Measures were, and still are, taken to attempt to ally their interests; for example, linking bonuses to share price or profits. For the most part these attempts have failed, as the case of Enron showed, where shareholders were systematically deceived. Also, in the whole sub-prime debacle, bankers were rewarded for systematically repackaging toxic loans, spreading them in near-undetectable layers around the globe, to the eventual detriment of their shareholders and the taxpaying public at large who had to pick up the bill. But even if it is possible to ally directors' interests with those of shareholders that leaves a myriad of other interested parties effectively disenfranchized, except in so far as they are expressly protected by laws.

The idea that businesses had a responsibility other than to shareholders was brought to popular attention in Howard R Bowen's book *Social Responsibilities of the Businessman* (1953, New York, Harper and Brothers), but it was a decade later before the term 'stakeholder' was coined in an internal memorandum at the Stanford Research Institute in 1963. Over the next two decades the term stakeholder was debated and defined until Edward Freeman, a professor at the Darden School of Business (**www.darden.virginia.edu**), University of Virginia, in his book *Strategic Management: A stakeholder approach* (1984, United States, Pitman Bowen) set out simple guidelines that anyone in an organization could understand and follow. Freeman's stakeholders were defined as 'any group or individual who can affect or is affected by the achievement of the organisation's objectives'.

Mapping out the stakeholders

Freeman divided stakeholders into six distinct categories – owners, employees, customers, suppliers, communities, and governments – with which an organization has varying responsibilities or 'social contracts'. The first step in the process of developing an ethical strategy is to identify all the people, institutions and agencies that your organization is likely to impinge on in the normal course of its activities.

Figure 9.2 below gives an example of a stakeholder map. It shows how stakeholders move outwards from the individual at the centre, to internal groups including their immediate work environment, colleagues, team, peers and on to external groups, suppliers, customers, shareholders and eventually on to ever-distant publics and organizations.

Assessing obligations

Not all stakeholders will be affected by any one particular strategy or course of action, nor will those that are be affected to the same degree. So the next step in the process is to see which stakeholders will be affected and to what degree. This can be done using a stakeholder relevance matrix, as in Table 9.1. This shows which stakeholder groups will be affected by the decision to relocate a production unit to a new lower-cost country.

The next step in the process is to analyse the specific interests/expectations, rights/responsibilities of each affected stakeholder group. Following through with the example of relocating a factory we can see in Table 9.2 the different expectations and rights of the three stakeholder groups seen to be most relevant to this decision.

FIGURE 9.2   Stakeholder mapping

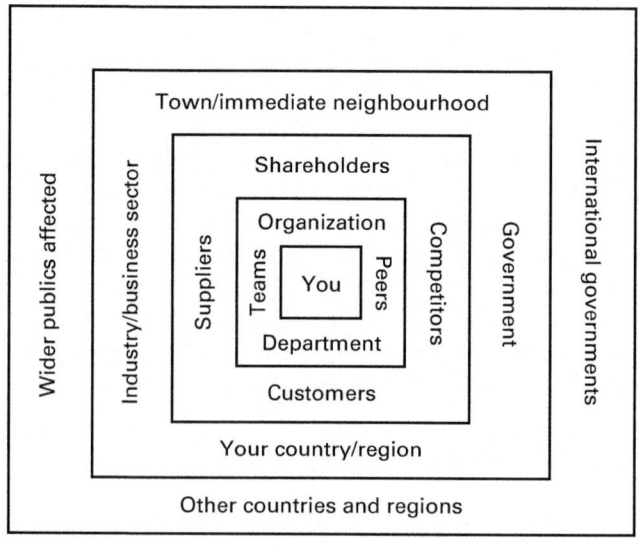

TABLE 9.1 Stakeholder relevance matrix

Proposed strategy: Move production to lower-cost country	Positively affected	Adversely affected
Directly affected	Employment created in new country New community in new country	Existing workforce Existing community in existing country Local subcontractors will lose work
Indirectly affected	Shareholder returns improved	Home government gets less tax Management will have to travel more

TABLE 9.2 Stakeholder rights and expectations grid

	Stakeholders		
	Customers	Shareholders	Employees
Rights	Be given information on all factors concerning new production source	To be informed in the annual report and accounts or sooner if the implications will cause public discussion	To statutory redundancy payments
Expectations	Any change should be seamlessly implemented	That the company will treat employees properly That the move is in the long-term best interest of the organization	To be consulted and given help with job search

Stakeholder strategies

Having identified the stakeholders and weighed up their rights and expectations an organization has basically three possible ethical stances it can take:

- Immoral business – make decisions that are clearly unethical to large groups of stakeholders. The Mafia and organized crime in general certainly fit into this category, as in many respects do the sex industry, large tracts of the gambling industry and arguably the tobacco and drinks industry, too. These last three are accepted as being a customer's inalienable right to free choice, aided by being major employers and taxpayers.

- Amoral business – make decisions without considering their ethical implications either through carelessness, indifference or the mistaken belief that business is there to make profit only. Such businesses see governments and their laws as the only ethical or moral constraint they need concern themselves with.
- Moral business – all decisions are made considering what is ethical, fair and just.

There is a growing feeling that multinationals have a special obligation to their 'home' country, though the exact definition of 'home' is far from clear. Governments take the simplistic view that home is where your company is registered as a corporation or company and it is to that country a business owes its loyalty, especially when it comes to paying tax. But unlike countries with specific and relatively rigid boundaries, international businesses have fluid boundaries and shifting loyalties.

CASE STUDY Taxing Times for Internationals

Amazon, Apple, Facebook, Google and Starbucks are finding out whether staying strictly within the law is sufficient to be ethical. Google, Amazon and Starbucks, three US companies with a widespread global presence got the answer to that question on 12 November 2012 when they appeared before a select committee in the House of Commons, the UK's parliament. The committee were told that Amazon had paid an effective UK tax rate of 2.5 per cent on 2011 earnings of £309 billion. Google paid 0.4 per cent on £2.5 billion. Starbucks paid nothing, though its UK earnings were £365 million. Starbucks has achieved this position by using a number of tax reduction strategies including paying royalties on intellectual property and using the 'buying expertise' of its 40 staff in Switzerland. Starbucks' Swiss business trades coffee and charges the UK arm a premium of 20 per cent for the privilege. That allows Starbucks to pay 12 per cent Swiss corporation tax, rather than the UK's 20 per cent, despite the UK being the company's main operation in Europe with some 6,600 employees.

By using a registered base in Luxembourg, Amazon was able to generate £3.3 billion of sales in the UK while paying no corporation tax at all. The same location strategy allowed it to get away with paying just three per cent VAT on UK book sales, a fraction of the UK's rate of 20 per cent. Amazon employs 15,000 people in the UK and operates all its warehouses there, yet drives all its sales out of Luxemburg, a country with a population of 517,000.

All of these companies use legal tax avoidance strategies, channelling much of their business outside of the United States through subsidiaries in tax-friendly countries including Ireland where the corporation tax is about half the UK level. Other ploys include paying royalty on intellectual property, commissions and fees with the aim of moving any profit to a low- or no-tax regime, including Caribbean tax havens.

Margaret Hodge, the Commons Committee's chair, summed the situation up with this sentence: 'We are not accusing you of being illegal; we are accusing you of being immoral.' The problem for these companies may be more immediate as the UK press has been quick to suggest that UK customers vote with their wallets. For example, going to Costa, owned by Whitbread who paid £15 million in corporation tax, rather than companies such as Starbucks and Caffe Nero, would be more patriotic.

Implementing ethical and responsible strategies

Ethics and values play a central role in shaping a company's identity and reputation, building its brands, earning the trust of customers, suppliers or other business partners. While honesty, fairness and responsibility are crucial for building a good reputation, an organization that is looking for pre-eminence in its field needs to go beyond just meeting stakeholders' needs. It has to emphasize the message that it is attractive as a business partner and as a good corporate citizen. To achieve this status the following steps need to be pursued:

- acknowledge and monitor all stakeholders who have a valid claim on your attentions;
- communicate regularly with stakeholders, listening to their interests and concerns;
- actively cooperate with stakeholders to minimize risks;
- always avoid actions that endanger lives;
- use processes that are sensitive to stakeholders' needs;
- recognize the danger that the managers' convenience and the needs of most other stakeholder groups will almost always be in conflict;
- resolve stakeholder conflicts speedily and fairly.

Resolving conflict

Unfortunately, however ethical and socially responsible an organization is, it will at some stage, perhaps even frequently, find itself pursuing a strategy that upsets other stakeholder groups, usually in another country. A recent example of one such conflict was Shell's decision to pull out of the London Array wind farm. This £2 billion ($3/€2.43) project for 341 turbines capable of producing 1,000 megawatts of power was a key part of the UK government's strategy to produce 15 per cent of UK energy needs from renewable sources by 2015, with an aspiration to raise that to 20 per cent by 2020. Given that in 2008 renewable energy accounted for only 2 per cent of output in the UK the London Array was seen as important, perhaps vital, to achieving those goals. But Shell had to weigh up the consequences of upsetting the UK government, Friends of the Earth and its other German and Dutch partners in the project, with other concerns. Shell's view was that the cost of wind farms was simply spiralling out of control with steel prices rising with increased world demand from such countries as China and India. In any event world turbine production was booked up years in advance. Shell already had stakes in 11 wind farms producing over 1,100 megawatts and reckoned as a company they could make the same contribution to the environment at a much lower cost to their shareholders, but probably on another continent and in another technology.

Resolving stakeholder conflicts calls for tact and communication and the recognition that while you can't please everyone, you can still be ethical. About 1 per cent of Shell's investments are in green projects. For example, a company subsidiary, Shell Solar, has played a major role in the development of first-generation CIS (copper indium diselenide) thin-film technology. This they believe to be the most commercially viable form of photovoltaic solar technology to generate electricity from the sun's energy. Together with their joint venture partner in this project, Saint Gobain, they have a pilot plant under construction in Saxony, Germany that will produce sufficient solar panels to save 14,000 tonnes of CO_2 per year. Therefore, stakeholders such as the UK government and Denmark's DONG Energy in the London Array project had to be weighed up against Saint Gobain, with the German government being party to both strategies through the participation of that country's energy giant, E.ON. All the while Shell was under pressure to match its historic profit growth. Authenticity Consulting (**www.authenticityconsulting.com/misc/long.pdf**) has a useful checklist to help with decisions about resolving stakeholder conflict.

Whistleblowers – an ethical longstop

Not surprisingly the people most likely to know about unethical or socially irresponsible behaviour are those working in the organization itself. Governments around the world have adopted measures to encourage a flow of information on ethical problems and fraud from whistleblowers – ie anyone employed or recently employed by a public body, business organization or charity who reveals evidence of wrongdoing. Whistleblowers have also been given a measure of legal protection. In the United States the Lloyd-La Follette Act of 1912 started the ball rolling giving federal employees the right to provide Congress with information, to be followed by a patchwork of laws covering such fields as water pollution, the environment, the Sarbanes-Oxley Act (2002) to deal with corporate fraud and the Whistleblower Protection Enhancement Act (2007). In the UK the Public Interest Disclosure Act (1998) and various laws enacted by the European Union and other governments provide a framework of legal protection for individuals who disclose information.

Many firms, too, have established ways to attract information on frauds being committed against them including 24-hour hotlines and corporate ethics offices. For example, Vodafone's 'Speak Up' programme – launched in 2006/07 – provided suppliers and employees working in their supply chain with a means of reporting any ethical concerns to an independent third party.

These organizations can provide further background on the subject:

- The National Whistleblowers Centre (**www.whistleblowers.org**): Focuses on exposing government and corporate misconduct, promoting ethical standards and protecting the jobs and careers of whistleblowers.
- Wikileaks (**www.wikileaks.org**): Their primary interest is in exposing oppressive regimes but they offer an avenue for anyone who wishes to reveal unethical behaviour in their governments and corporations, with a degree of anonymity.

Does being ethical pay off?

There is plenty of anecdotal evidence that ethical and socially responsible organizations are better places to work. At the very least being ethical provides an organization with an insurance policy limiting its exposure to a range of legal liabilities for faulty products, misleading advertising, price fixing and discrimination at work, for example. But evidence on whether being ethical helps a business organization to become and stay more profitable is less clear. One study in Consulting News published in November 2013 (**www.consultant-news.com/article_display.aspx?id=10798**) showed clear water between the performance of ethical companies and the rest, but went on to suggest that the size of the ethical business sample was probably too small to be statistically significant. See 'Causal relationships', Chapter 12, for more on this subject.

But that still begs the question of what constitutes 'good'. The FTSE4Good Index (**www.ftse.com/products/indices/FTSE4Good**) sets out to measure the performance of companies that meet globally recognized corporate responsibility standards. For inclusion a company must be:

- working towards environmental sustainability;
- developing positive relationships with stakeholders;
- upholding and supporting universal human rights;
- ensuring good supply-chain labour standards;
- countering bribery.

They also exclude companies that have been identified as having business interests in these industries:

- tobacco production;
- companies manufacturing either whole, strategic parts, or platforms for nuclear weapon systems;
- companies manufacturing whole weapons systems;
- owners or operators of nuclear power stations;
- companies involved in the extraction or processing of uranium.

This only serves to highlight the problem of deciding what is ethical and what is not. For example, is mining uranium for nuclear power really more harmful than, say, switching to biofuels, which aside from probably releasing between two and nine times more carbon gases over the next 30 years than fossil fuels, will almost certainly cause food prices to stay high, particularly in the developing world. Or is the motor industry, whose products kill more people every year than the armaments industry, a more ethical and socially responsible sector?

However, a small but growing band of business schools believe there is enough mileage in social responsibility and ethics to launch 'Green MBA programmes that emphasize a triple bottom line, also known as 'TBL' or '3BL' – profit, people, planet'.

Corporate Knights, The Magazine for Clean Capitalism, now produces a ranking for green and sustainable MBA programmes and for the most Green business schools. Two Canadian business schools come out top and the UK's Exeter Business School (which hosts the sustainability-focused One Planet MBA Programme) is third. The full list is published at **www.corporateknights.com/reports/2013-sustainable-mba**.

Princeton Review and *Entrepreneur Magazine* do their own ranking – the top 16 green MBA programmes in the United States – a list that includes the usual suspects Columbia University, Duke University, Stanford University, and New York University. Visit **www.entrepreneur.com/article/219236**.

'Social Responsibility' took something of a knock in September 2015 when Volkswagen fell from grace. Recently ranked as the 11th best in the world for its CSR (Corporate Social Responsibility) work by The Reputation

Institute, in 2014, it collected the "Gold Medal Award for Sustainable Development" from the non-profit World Environment Center and its own sustainability report runs to 156 pages. There is a view gaining ground that CSR departments are simply providing an insurance policy allowing companies to take risk with their own internal standards.

Online video courses and lectures

Corporate Governance – What do shareholders really value? Prof Lynn Stout, the Paul Hastings Distinguished Professor of Corporate and Securities Law at UCLA: **www.youtube.com/watch?v=s5Eoy988728**

Corporate Social Responsibility: Delivered by the Study Academy. Their fees start from $50 a month, but come with a five day free trial: **http://study.com/academy/lesson/business-ethics-corporate-social-responsibility.html**

IBM Study: Corporate Social Responsibility: a survey based on responses from top executives at more than 250 companies worldwide: **www.youtube.com/watch?v=PdkYieDuVvY**

Practical Ethics: run occasionally by Peter Singer, a professor at Princetown University: **www.coursera.org/course/practicalethics**

Social Responsibility Perspectives: The Shareholder and Stakeholder Approach: Alanis Business Academy: **www.youtube.com/watch?v=vD9XJKZmXEs**

'Stakeholders vs. Shareholders': Haas faculty debate 'Whom exactly should business serve?' At Berkeley-Haas in this Oxford-style debate, Professors Ernesto Dal Bó and Dean Rich Lyons speak from the stakeholder point of view; Professors Hayne Leland and David Vogel champion shareholders: **www.youtube.com/watch?v=yQ1x8jKLWDg**

What is Corporate Social Responsibility (CSR)? Professor Thomas Beschorner, University of St. Gallen, Switzerland: **www.youtube.com/watch?v=E0NkGtNU_9w**

Online video case studies

Body Shop: Corporate Responsibility? **www.globalissues.org/video/733/anita-roddick-corporate-social-responsibility**

Coca Cola: Corporate Social Responsibility: **www.youtube.com/watch?v=B7dDSHwFgKk**

Nike and Corporate Responsibility: Claire Anderson, Global Justice Final Project: **www.youtube.com/watch?v=xTB4thqyo5Q**

Nike Sweatshops: Behind the Swoosh. Using Nike as a case study, the film documents first-hand the widespread and oppressive and exploitative labour practices in the developing world: **www.youtube.com/ watch?v=M5uYCWVfuPQ**

PepsiCo: Defining sustainability: **www.youtube.com/watch?v=n_ykvWuYADc**

Primark on the racks: BBC Trust: **www.youtube.com/ watch?v=OWio7NVOnaI**

Primark responds to the BBC Trust's Panorama verdict: **www.youtube.com/watch?v=hUSsG_tDDY0**

Starbucks: Being a Responsible Company: **www.starbucks.co.uk/ responsibility**

Starbucks: Building a Future with Farmers: Committed to 100% Ethically Sourced: **www.starbucks.com/responsibility/sourcing/coffee**

Entrepreneurship 10

- Entrepreneur vs intrapreneur.
- Social entrepreneurs.
- Creative destruction, the spur.
- Why we need entrepreneurs.
- Money for business plans.
- Getting into an incubator.
- Family businesses.

Entrepreneurship is one of the newest disciplines in the business school armoury and in many schools the subject is still not taught. In some it is a topic within economics, which is considered appropriate as JB Say, a French economist in circa 1800, first coined the term entrepreneur using it to describe 'someone who shifts resources out of an area of lower and into an area of higher productivity and greater yield'. The most common practice is to reduce the subject to a basic 'start your own business' project culminating in a business plan presentation, with a handful of MBAs going the whole hog and launching a venture.

There is rather more to the subject than just starting a business, though that in itself is a worthy outcome. Governments are fixated with entrepreneurship, secondary schools are teaching it, one in 15 people in work run a business and over half the world work for and report directly to an entrepreneur.

The worthiness of teaching entrepreneurship in business schools on the international stage can be seen in two initiatives launched in the summer of 2010. The US government and the Institute of Business Administration (IBA) in Karachi, Pakistan, a business school set up in 1955 with technical help from the Wharton School of Finance, University of Pennsylvania, established a centre for entrepreneurship. Babson College, another world-class business school is helping IBA develop and teach the curriculum. Wharton graduated the first students on its Women's Entrepreneurship and Leadership Programme, run in conjunction with the American University in Cairo, Egypt with financial backing from Goldman Sachs. Goldman support similar programmes in business schools around the world including: American

University of Afghanistan; American University of Beirut, Lebanon; Indian School of Business; Pan-African University, Nigeria; School of Finance and Banking, Rwanda; United States International University, Kenya; University of Cape Town Graduate School of Business, South Africa; University of Dar es Salaam, Tanzania; Fundação Getulio Vargas Escola de Administração de Empresas de Sao Paulo in Brazil; and Zhejiang University in China.

The global entrepreneurship environment

The Global Entrepreneurial Index (GEI), run from The Global Entrepreneurship and Development Institute (GEDI) in Washington DC, sets out to measure the quality and the scale of the entrepreneurial process in 130 countries around the world.

The institute was founded by entrepreneurship scholars from the George Mason University, University of Pécs and Imperial College London. The GEI uses an academically rigorous process that measures the 'quality and dynamics of entrepreneurship ecosystems at a national and regional level.' While the Index 'recognizes that entrepreneurship can mean very different things in different economic and institutional contexts. A local horticultural venture, for example, would have different economic consequences for the Kenyan economy than a social media start-up in Silicon Valley', they nevertheless end up with a single composite figure measurement, a percentage, which for the United States at number one position is 85 per cent in 2015 and for Bangladesh, the last of the 130 countries studied, 14.4 per cent.

The Index is based on what they call the 'The 14 Pillars of Entrepreneurship.' The first five pillars are based around Entrepreneurial Attitude – Opportunity Perception, Start-Up Skills, Risk Acceptance, Networking and Cultural Support. Next comes Entrepreneurial Ability where Opportunity Start-Up, Technology Absorption, Human Capital and Competition are considered. Finally Entrepreneurial Aspiration comprising Product Innovation, Process Innovation, High Growth, Internationalization and Risk Capital is brought into play. The last pillar alone would give the top handful of countries a head start on the rest, but that is what creative destruction is all about.

The Global Entrepreneurship Monitor (GEM) with Babson College, Wellesley, Massachusetts as a founding institution and lead sponsor, also studies the relative entrepreneurial conditions around the world. Alongside Universidad del Desarrollo, one of the top three private universities in Chile, Universiti Tun Abdul Razakn (UNIRAZAK), Malaysia and Tecnológico de Monterrey, Mexico they harness the collective effort of more than 500 researchers to conduct the annual GEM survey. They question over 200,000 adults around the world anonymously and use some 4,000 national experts 'who provided their thoughts on the entrepreneurship ecosystem.' GEM is into their 17th year, whilst GEDI, a relative newcomer, has been working for five years.

TABLE 10.1   Top and bottom ten most entrepreneurial countries according to Global Entrepreneurship Index 2015

Top 10	Bottom 10
1. United States	130. Bangladesh
2. Canada	129. Uganda
3. Australia	128. Malawi
4. United Kingdom	127. Guyana
5. Sweden	126. Chad
6. Denmark	125. Ethiopia
7. Iceland	124. Burundi
8. Taiwan	123. Pakistan
9. Switzerland	122. Guatemala
10. Singapore	121. Suriname

SOURCE: http://thegedi.org/2015-global-entrepreneurship-index/

GEM looks at entrepreneurial activities by using the 'organizational life-cycle approach' whilst 'gender and age descriptors are used to emphasize some distinctive patterns.'

For early-stage Entrepreneurial Activity (TEA) which examines individuals in the process of starting a venture and those running a new business less than three and a half years old they found the highest TEA rates in Qatar (16.4 per cent TEA), Trinidad & Tobago (14.6 per cent), the United States (13.8 per cent), Australia (13.1 per cent) and Canada (13 per cent). Japan, with 3.8 per cent TEA, and Italy, with 4.4 per cent, has the lowest share of early-stage entrepreneurs among their respective adult populations. Part of the reasoning for the counterintuitive position of some of these countries lies in the higher proportion of 'necessity-driven entrepreneurs', who have no other realistic option to earn a living.

GEM dices the data so many ways that every country can show a positive take on entrepreneurship. So for Uganda for example GEM sites an initiative that gives youth groups the equivalent of $10,000 if their business proposal meets certain criteria, representing a sizeable sum in that region. Global

Entrepreneurship Index confines its information to a position one up from the bottom of their 130 nation study. (**www.gemconsortium.org/**).

Whatever the intentions or practice of entrepreneurs and would-be business starters, the environment in which they operate varies greatly from country to country. The World Bank's annual survey published in their Doing Business report (**www.doingbusiness.org**) reveals some stark statistics on the ease of doing business. New Zealand, Canada and Singapore are relatively easy places to set up your business, as, surprisingly, are Georgia and Belarus. Chad, Eritrea and Haiti, on the other hand tie would-be entrepreneurs in knots before they start. In Chad there are nine procedures taking 60 days to complete. Still, that's better than in 2012, when there were 19 procedures that took 75 days to complete before a business could open its doors. In Canada there is only one form to fill in and you can be launched in five days. In New Zealand the process takes just one day.

Why entrepreneurship matters

You might be surprised at the number of people and organizations that appear keen to give entrepreneurs a helping hand. *Dragons' Den* panellists, bankers and government ministers all seem eager to lend a helping hand. None of these would-be helpers is particularly altruistic. The primary reasons entrepreneurs are essential are as follows.

Job creation

Governments need a constant injection of new businesses as they create most of the new jobs in any economy; a fact uncovered by David Birch, a researcher at MIT (Massachusetts Institute of Technology) back in 1979 (*The Job Generation Process*, MIT) and corroborated by dozens of other studies since then. Also of course you will pay tax on your profits and become an unpaid tax collector for VAT or Sales Tax on behalf of government agencies.

Creative Destruction and the innovative spur

Creative Destruction is a term attributed to Joseph Schumpeter. Born in 1883, at 26 he became the youngest professor in the Austrian Empire and finance minister at 36 only to be dismissed after presiding over a period of hyperinflation. A brief spell as president of a small Viennese bank was followed, after its failure, by a return to academia, first in Bonn then in 1932 at Harvard. He is remembered for two books in particular: *Theory of Economic Development* (1911), where he first outlined his thoughts on entrepreneurship; and *Capitalism, Socialism, and Democracy* (1942) when he detailed how the entrepreneurial process worked and why it mattered. His view was that the fundamental impulse that sets and keeps the capitalist engine in motion comes from 'the new consumers, goods, the new methods of production or transportation, the new markets, the new forms of industrial organization that capitalist enterprise creates'. He pointed out that entrepreneurs innovate and develop new products, services or ways of doing business and in the process destroy those organizations who can't adapt or who have been effectively made redundant. Schumpeter believed that capitalism has to create short-term losers alongside its short- and long-term winners in order for the economy to grow and prosper: 'Without innovations, no entrepreneurs; without entrepreneurial achievement, no capitalist... propulsion. The atmosphere of industrial revolutions... is the only one in which capitalism can survive.' He went rather further than this by arguing that the more countries that try to mitigate the possibilities of business failing, the worse their economic performance would be. Picking up the pieces through social insurance is fine; propping up failing businesses or declining business sectors is not.

In a thoughtful article 'Why big companies can't innovate', published in February 2013, the author, Steve Blank, argues convincingly that big firms spend most of their energy buying up competitors and perfecting their existing business model. Small firms have to innovate their way into business in the first place. (**http://steveblank.com/2013/02/23/why-big-companies-cant-innovate/**). Fast Company's latest study of the most innovative companies (**www.fastcompany.com/section/most-innovative-companies-2014**) is dominated by new businesses. Though Google tops their 2014 list of the Most Innovative Companies in business, the company is only 16 years old. This is the second time that Google has earned the No. 1 spot. The last time was in 2008. The No.2 slot went to the Chinese consumer-electronics company, Xiaomi. Just three years old, the company released four new smartphones last year and sold almost 19 million units, up more than 150 per cent from 2012. Its low-cost, feature-rich devices sold out its initial run of 100,000 units in less than two minutes. Then came Airbnb, a start-up from 2007 that enables users to rent out their spare rooms or vacant homes to strangers. In 2015 they surpassed 12 million stays on their platform and doubled their listings to 650,000 (in 194 countries). They are now the world's largest hotel chain – without operating a single hotel (**www.fastcompany.com/most-innovative-companies/2014/airbnb**).

Who makes a good entrepreneur?

There are absolutely no reliable characteristics that predispose people to become entrepreneurs. Despite diligent research Durham University's General Enterprise Tendency (GET) Test with 12 questions measuring need for achievement, 12 to assess internal locus of control, 12 to determine creativity, 12 to gauge calculated risk taking, and 6 to measure need for autonomy, has failed to gain recognition. Peter Drucker, the international business guru probably got it right with this description: 'Some are eccentrics, others painfully correct conformists; some are fat and some are lean; some are worriers, some relaxed; some drink quite heavily, others are total abstainers; some are men of great charm and warmth, some have no more personality than a frozen mackerel.' Entrepreneurs do have one distinguishing characteristic in common, however. They put independence and doing their own thing above everything, including getting rich. That doesn't mean they don't want to succeed; it's just that success is not all about money. Research carried out at Cass Business School found that 20 per cent of entrepreneurs in their sample (250 entrepreneurs and 250 managers) were dyslexic whereas managers reflected the UK national dyslexia incidence level of 4 per cent.

Lord Sugar, Anita Roddick, Richard Branson, Jamie Oliver and Ikea founder Ingvar Kamprad are amongst star dyslexic entrepreneurs. Julie Logan, emeritus Professor of entrepreneurship at Cass Business School, who carried out the study, states 'people with dyslexia tend to compensate for things they can't do well by developing excellence in other areas: oral communication, delegation (because they must learn to trust other people with tasks they can't do from an early age), as well as problem-solving and people management.' (**www.cassknowledge.com/research/article/unusual-talent-study-successful-leadership-and-delegation-dyslexic-entrepreneurs**).

Research into entrepreneurship carried out jointly at The Department of Twin Research and Genetic Epidemiology at Kings College, London and the Department of Entrepreneurial Studies at Case Western Reserve University in Ohio came up with these findings in 2015:

- 37 to 48 per cent of the tendency to be an entrepreneur is genetic;
- the tendency to identify new business opportunities is in your genes;
- personality traits such as extroversion and openness, important characteristics for entrepreneurs, have a genetic component.

Although it is perhaps comforting to know that dyslexia, or even not completing schooling or university because of it, is no bar to entrepreneurship, it is not something you can do much about.

What can be said with certainty is that there are an awful lot of entrepreneurs everywhere and from every walk of life. It also seems likely that entrepreneurs are as likely to be made as born. There are over 50 million people running their own business in the developed world alone. That is double the number of just two decades or so ago.

Research from various organizations including GEM (see above), Lloyds Bank, NatWest and the Institute for Small Business Enterprise shed further light on the small business population and demographics. No section of the public appears to be excluded from the small business world. One in seven businesses are started by people over 50; just over a third of business proprietors are women; one in 10 left school early and barely a quarter have a degree; immigrants are as likely to work for themselves as others; and interestingly enough those who start their business in their teens or early 20s are no more likely to fail than those in their 40s and 50s with a career in big business under their belt.

Would you make a good entrepreneur?

All too often, people believe themselves to be the right sort of person to set up a business. Unfortunately, the capacity for self-deception is enormous. When a random sample of male adults were asked recently to rank themselves on leadership ability, 70 per cent rated themselves in the top 25 per cent; only 2 per cent felt they were below average as leaders. In an area in which self-deception ought to be difficult, 60 per cent said they were well above average in athletic ability and only 6 per cent said they were below.

A common mistake made in assessing entrepreneurial talent is to assume that success in big business management will automatically guarantee success in starting your own business. However, a study of the occupation of Cranfield School of Management's MBAs 15 years after graduation revealed that 18 per cent were working for themselves. Not all of these are entrepreneurs, of course, with many operating as consultants or specialists in accounting, finance and IT.

Rate yourself against the characteristics in Table 10.2 and see how you stack up as a potential business starter. A score of over 30 suggests you have

TABLE 10.2   Business starter attribute check

Attribute	Score (0–5, where 0 indicates having none of the attribute and 5 rating highly)
Self-confident all rounder	
Ability to bounce back	
Innovative skills	
Results-orientated	
Professional risk taker	
Total commitment	
Self-sufficient	
Self-disciplined	

what it takes and less than 20 should be treated as a warning signal. Get a couple of people who know you well to rate you too, so you get an unbiased opinion.

You can find out more about whether or not entrepreneurship would be right for you by taking one or more of the many online entrepreneurial IQ-type tests. For example:

- *Entrepreneurs*, What's Your Entrepreneurial IQ? (**www.entrepreneur.com/greatminds/quiz**)
- Canada's business development bank (**www.bdc.ca/en** > Articles and tools > Entrepreneur's toolkit > Business assessments > Entrepreneurial potential self-assessment)

Entrepreneurial categories

Entrepreneurs are usually associated with successful businesses such as those run by Alan Sugar, Richard Branson, Bill Gates or Roman Abramovich. There are, however, several different types of entrepreneurial ventures, not all associated either with making money or with charismatic leadership. These are the main subsidiary categories of entrepreneurial organization.

Social entrepreneurs

A social entrepreneur is concerned primarily with achieving sustainable social change, though in many respects the strategies they employ to achieve those goals are similar to those employed in most organizations. The idea of social business is fast becoming mainstream. There is an annual Queen's Award for Industry for Sustainable Development, an ACCA Award for the Best Social Accounts and a School for Social Entrepreneurs (**www.sse.org.uk**) that helps would-be social entrepreneurs to get started. The Schwab Foundation (**www.schwabfound.org**) covers much the same ground in the United States. Columbia Business School's MBA programme has an elective course on Social Entrepreneurship as part of their Research Initiative on Social Entrepreneurship (**www.riseproject.org/**). Students complete projects where they shadow leading social entrepreneurs and social investors for a semester and details of all their case studies are published on their website. Stanford Graduate School of Business (**www.gsb.stanford.edu/programs/social-innovation/executive-program-social-entrepreneurship**) with its Executive Program in Social Entrepreneurship, Harvard's Social Enterprise Initiative (**www.hbs.edu/socialenterprise/**) which has supported research and written over 800 social enterprise books, cases and teaching notes since 1993, and Said Business School, Oxford which has its Skoll Centre for Social Entrepreneurship (**www.sbs.ox.ac.uk/ideas-impact/skoll/about-skoll-centre-social-entrepreneurship**), which offers a scholarship that provides tuition for entrepreneurs who have set up or have been working in entrepreneurial ventures with a social purpose, take the subject to the heart of mainstream business education.

The primary motivation for social entrepreneurs is to build an ethical venture that is of benefit to the wider community. As one social entrepreneur put it, 'I am trying to build a little part of the world in which I would like to live.' Money is important, but getting rich is not. However the motivations and characteristics of social entrepreneurs are complex. GEM (see above) has examined the sector in detail. As an aid to better understanding, GEM developed a typology with four broad groups, derived from three different features of a social enterprise:

1 prominence of social (or environmental) goals with respect to economic goals;

2 reliance on an earned-income strategy and its contribution with respect to total revenues of the organization;

3 presence of innovation.

This resulted in GEM classifying social entrepreneurs into four categories:

1 Traditional NGOs (high levels of social/environment goals; not-for-profit status).

2 Not-for-profit SE (high levels of social/environmental goals; not-for-profit status; innovation).

3 Hybrid SE (high levels of social/environmental goals; earned-income strategy 'integrated' or 'complementary' to the mission).

4 For-profit SE (high but not exclusively social/environmental goals; earned-income strategy).

GEM's study shows the distribution of the four general categories of social enterprise (SE) plus the overlap for each participating country. Across all countries, the order of prevalence was Not-for-profit SE (24 per cent), Hybrid SE (23 per cent), For-profit SEs (12 per cent) and traditional NGOs (8 per cent). However, the Hybrid SE was most popular in the Scandinavian countries of Finland and Iceland, as well as in Algeria, Uganda, Dominican Republic, Hungary, Latvia, Malaysia, Belgium, France, the Netherlands, Slovenia and Switzerland. The For-profit SE model is most favoured by the United Arab Emirates, Venezuela and Romania.

One significant finding from the GEM study is that a sizeable minority of social entrepreneurs, particularly in developing countries, appear to want to have their cake and eat it, making money from doing good. Having a profitable business that at the same time addresses social issues, such as green energy, waste management and health, is perhaps the fastest-growing global category of social entrepreneur. In the developing world this is usually the only option, as other funding options are in scarce supply.

Intrapreneur

The Economist of 25 December 1976 carried a survey called 'The coming entrepreneurial revolution' in which Norman Macrae, the magazine's deputy editor, who is considered by many as one of the world's best economic forecasters, contended 'methods of operation in business were going to change radically in the next few decades'. The world, Macrae argued, was probably drawing to the end of the era of big business corporations; it would soon be nonsense to have hierarchical managements sitting in skyscrapers trying to arrange how brainworkers (who in future would be most workers) could best use their imaginations. The main increases in employment would henceforth come either in small firms or in those bigger firms that managed to split themselves into smaller and smaller profit centres that in turn would need to become more and more entrepreneurial.

Two years later in an article titled, 'Intra-corporate entrepreneurship: Some thoughts stirred up by attending Robert Schwartz's School for Entrepreneurs', Gifford Pinchot III and his wife Elizabeth S Pinchot began the process that would lead to their coining the word Intrapreneuring. Their organization, Pinchot & Company (**www.pinchot.com**), based around the proposition that you don't have to leave the corporation to become an entrepreneur, advanced the idea that the way for big business to adapt was to create an environment where managers could behave as though they were entrepreneurs, but within the business and using its resources. By 1992 the term intrapreneur had been added to the third edition of *The American Dictionary of the English Language*. 3M's Post-it Note, a product of an entrepreneurial team 'bootlegging' company resources, is an example from one of Pinochet's list of Fortune 500 clients. Others include Apple, DuPont, Cable and Wireless, Nabisco and Procter & Gamble.

Intrapreneurs, unlike entrepreneurs, don't have 'doing their own thing' at the top of their list of motivators. They feel happier in a comfort zone afforded by a corporate structure and the resources and respectability which that provides.

GEM's research shows a tentative positive correlation between intrapreneurship and GDP per capita. So it appears that entrepreneurial activities by employees are, as one might expect, more prevalent in more advanced phases of economic development. For example, the incidence of social entrepreneurship in Norway and the Netherlands is three times the level than in Ecuador and Iran.

Two sources of further information are:

● The 5th Intrapreneurship Conference, which was run in London in 2015. The conference was previously held in Brussels, Paris, Barcelona and Eindhoven. The latter event saw 100 people in the room, and featured intrapreneurs from Johnson & Johnson, Grundfos, DSM, Rabobank, Boehringer Ingelheim and Deutsche Telekom.

- The Academy for Corporate Entrepreneurship (AfCE) enables entrepreneurship to take off within established organizations by leveraging their know-how from having trained over 600 corporate start-up teams. (**www.afce.co**)

CASE STUDY Pret A Manger: Corporate venturing entrepreneur

Pret A Manger, the quick-serve restaurant and coffee shop, extended its business in two directions in April 2015. Following a conventional path they opened up Pret's 39th New York City shop at New York Penn Station on 10 April. In the last 30 years some 350 Prets have opened worldwide with shops in the UK, United States, Paris, Hong Kong and Shanghai, serving more than 300,000 customers every day. The other expansion was into a new time zone. 'Good Evenings' also known as the first Pret restaurant, opened on a trial basis at its 88 Strand branch in London. Run as a normal sandwich shop by day, after 6pm the ambiance changes subtly. Lights dim, candles are lit and real cutlery is set out with a menu offering Korean BBQ pulled pork quinoa hotpot, craft beer, salt beef toasty and prosciutto-topped macaroni cheese. Nothing exceeds the £7 ($10/€9.70) mark, Pret's pricing proposition point. This is only a pop-up for now, but if successful could be the shape of things to come.

Pret's success in striding across the international stage is quite an achievement when you look back to their modest beginnings. Sinclair Beecham and Julian Metcalfe started with a £17,000 loan ($26,656.59) and a name borrowed from a boarded-up shop and went on to found Pret A Manger; they were not entrepreneurs who were content with doing their own thing. They had global ambitions and it was only by cutting in McDonald's the burger giant, that they could see any realistic way to dominate the world. They sold a 33 per cent stake for £25 million ($39,205,307) in 2001 to McDonald's Ventures, LLC, a wholly owned subsidiary of McDonald's Corporation, the arm of McDonald's that looks after its corporate venturing activities. They joined forces with the corporate venturing arm of a big firm. They could also have considered Cisco, Apple Computers, IBM and Microsoft who also all have corporate venturing arms. Other corporate ventures include Deutsche Bank who set up DB eVentures to get a window on the 'Digital Revolution'; Reuters Greenhouse has stakes in 85 companies and even the late and unlamented Enron 22 had venture investments (totalling $110m). For an entrepreneur this approach can provide a 'friendly customer' and help open doors. For the 'parent' it provides a privileged ringside seat as a business grows and the opportunity to decide if the area is worth plunging into more deeply, or at the least provides valuable insights into new technologies or business processes.

Recent research into corporate venturing by Ashridge (**www.ashridge.org. uk**> Research and Faculty) Business School concluded that less than 5 per cent of corporate venturing units created new businesses that were taken up by the parent company. Moreover, many failed to make any positive contribution whatsoever. There are some success stories, however. McDonald's offloaded its Pret A Manger stake in 2008 to a private equity firm, Bridgepoint, who bought a majority stake including McDonald's 33 per cent shareholding, for £345 million ($540,971,884). That would suggest that McDonald's at least quadrupled the value of its initial stake. Nokia Venture Partners (NVP) who make significant minority investments in start-ups in the wireless Internet space, had as its biggest success to date the Initial Public Offering of PayPal, in 2002. At a conference in July 1999, they and Deutsche Bank used Paypal's, (then called Confinnity) encryption technology to send founders Peter Thiel and Max Levchin $3 million in venture capital via a Palm Pilot as their initial stake.

Corporate venturing entrepreneurs think big and are happy to cut others in on the deal who have cash, if it will help make them rich. Independence for independence's sake is not a high priority.

Entrepreneurship in practice

Business schools usually teach entrepreneurship using the 'Action Learning' approach. This generally takes the form of having back a handful of inspiring alumni entrepreneurs to talk about how they got started. At Cranfield the stars would include a couple of big hitters; Karan (now Lord) Billimoria of Cobra Beer fame, for example. Cass wheels out Stelios Haji-Iannou, founder of easyJet and London Business School has Tony Wheeler who graduated in 1972 and together with his wife Maureen founded Lonely Planet Publications. Then a cross-section of those entrepreneurs who have interesting stories to tell, say about raising money, hiring and firing or selling up; or who are recent leavers that switched career paths from perhaps big corporate lives to small business. At IMD, in Lausanne on Lake Geneva in Switzerland, the emphasis is on Family Business, and Warren Buffett, whose son looks set to take over at Berkshire Hathaway, is typical of the speakers there.

The teaching is based around preparing a business plan to be presented to a panel along the lines of *Dragons' Den*, often with similar outcomes in that the business gets funding. It would be incorrect to suggest droves of MBAs rush off to found ventures straight off, but perhaps three or four in a hundred do. Within a decade that will have risen to around 40 per cent according to research carried out for Top MBA (**www.topmba.com**).

Aside from getting funding and marks towards their MBA grade, the most successful business plans are usually entered into one of a number of Business Plan Competitions. You can see some of these competitions in action in the online video section at the end of this chapter.

Business incubators

Science Parks, Technology Innovation Centres and various permutations of the words Business, Incubator, Venture, Research and Programme are all in use to describe the process of incubation. An innovation centre is essentially an interaction between the research community and the business community. Here there is an important openness as to what is happening in the wider environment in the form of new techniques and potentially applicable research acquired through technology scans or in the form of market needs. For the business incubation approach, the key factor is the entrepreneur and the direction that individual wants to take in the development of the business start-up. Countries such as Korea and Japan have emphasized science parks as the approach to increasing research-related activities. Here, research takes priority over any business or jobs that may be created and those that are should be directly related to the science park itself. Countries such as China, the Philippines, Trinidad and Tobago, and Nigeria, with the assistance of the United Nations Fund for Science and Technology Development have moved into the business incubation approach. With this approach job and business creation is paramount. Germany, Taiwan, Singapore, the Netherlands, Ireland and the Scandinavian countries have plumped for the innovation centre route. In this approach, a dynamic relationship is the goal, and entrepreneurs are sought out who may be able to commercialize the output of university or government research. Once again jobs and business are created, but the main aim is to recover monies spent and to provide a war chest for future research.

A short history of business incubators

Tempting though it might be to believe that business incubators are an Internet phenomenon, their history stretches a good bit further back than that. The first serious attempt at incubation is credited to a near-derelict building near New York and the name came into common usage more by way of a joke than as a serious description of the task in hand. In 1959 the heirs to a prominent family business, Charles Manusco & Son, had just bought another building. The Manuscos owned a wide range of local business in Western New York, where they regularly increased their real estate holdings and investments. Their latest acquisition was a huge multi-storey structure amounting to 850,000 square feet. The building dated from 1882 and had originally housed John Harvester and later Massey Ferguson, which manufactured combine harvesters. Along with the building came 30 acres of land. The building, unsurprisingly, had been vacant for a few years, and much of its massive roof needed replacing. The cost of restoring the property was to dwarf the $180,00 purchase price.

Joseph Manusco, the family member assigned to look after the project, quickly concluded that the property would be impossible to rent to a single tenant. He decided on what was at the time a revolutionary strategy. He would partition the building and lease it out in small pieces hoping to find enough tenants to turn a potential white elephant into a money-making proposition.

His first tenant, a sign painter, took 2,000 square feet and by the end of the first year he had 20 to 30 tenants taking 9,000 square feet. Not exactly a wildfire success, but at least the building was paying its way and the capital appreciation was building up as a sweetener for the family firm's coffers. Manusco, who has been credited with inventing the term 'incubator', stumbled on the name by accident. One of his early tenants, a company from Connecticut, incubated chickens. Pretty soon after the firm's arrival Manusco would joke that he was incubating chickens, when asked what he was doing with his building. From there it was but a short leap before his venture was known as a business incubator.

Today the business is known as the Batavia Industrial Center, with 1,000 people working in the building. Some of the early tenants are still in the building and the centre's philosophy is that while it continues to encourage new businesses to start up, anyone can lease space and stay as long as they like.

Several waves of accelerators followed this inauspicious start and by the 1980s several hundred such facilities were scattered around the United States, Canada, Europe and Australia. Later, incubator progressions took in the developing economies and the Internet variation, which came into being in the mid-1990s, swept across the United States, Europe, India, China, Malaysia, Singapore, the Philippines, and elsewhere, bringing the total to date to some 5,000 facilities worldwide.

Business incubator aims and purpose

Varieties of accelerators and incubators now co-exist in the market, with radically different aims and objectives. Some, such as those founded by entrepreneurs, venture capital firms, the 'for profit' variety, only want to get rich, by helping entrepreneurs to get rich. That goal at least has the merit of transparency. Some have revenue models that can make the incubator rich without necessarily benefiting anyone else that much. Governments and local governments are more concerned with job creation than wealth, and universities, another major player, want jobs for the students and funding for faculty research, rather than riches themselves. Big corporate firms run private incubators to encourage firms who might buy their products or services or create career opportunities for their more entrepreneurial and potentially less fickle employees.

These incubators are havens for entrepreneurs with innovative or technology-based business ideas that need more help than most to be brought to fruition. Such ventures usually have more potential than other business starters, but they are also more risky. No one knows how many entrepreneurs graduate from these incubators each year. But it's a reasonable supposition that each of the estimated 5,000 incubators has two or three graduates each year. So 15,000 or so 'eggs' are hatched in a safe environment each year. That's not a big number in terms of business start-ups. Across Europe and the United States somewhere between 3 and 4 million new businesses get going in most years. But for the entrepreneurs, some of them at any rate, who get into an incubator, their chances of success are better than if they went it alone.

Finding an incubator

The National Business Incubator Association (**www.nbia.org/links_to_member _incubators/index.php**) maintains a directory of some 2,100 incubators in over 60 countries. They also maintain a directory of international incubation associations (**www.nbia.org/links_to_member_incubators/international.php**).

Family business

Family firms make up around 70 per cent of businesses worldwide and account for a substantial proportion of GDP. Many of the world's leading corporations originated as family firms and retain cultural distinctiveness as a result. According to Nigel Nicholson, who runs the Family Business elective at the London Business School (LBS), the financial crisis has illustrated, 'with their long time scales, adaptive cultures and vision-led leadership many are much better fitted to prosper in turbulent times than many PLCs.'

PricewaterhouseCooper's 7th Family Business survey saw 2,484 interviews conducted with key decision makers in family businesses in over 40 countries worldwide. (**www.pwc.com/us/en/private-company-services/publications/ 2015-family-business-survey.jhtml**)

Their findings show some significant difference between countries.

- 65 per cent of family businesses reported growth in the last 12 months and 15 per cent are aiming to grow aggressively over the next five years compared with 12 per cent in 2012. Just under three quarters of the businesses interviewed expect to see steady growth.

- 70 per cent of family businesses in the United States have grown in the last 12 months and 95 per cent are aiming to grow over the next five years.

- 61 per cent of family businesses in Germany have experienced sales growth over the last 12 months while 88 per cent are looking to grow over the next five years, but only 5 per cent are aiming to grow quickly and aggressively.

- 52 per cent of Italian family businesses experienced sales growth in the past 12 months, down from 60 per cent in the last FBS.

You can find a directory of the oldest family businesses by country at Family Business United (**www.familybusinessunited.com/resources/oldest-family-business/**)

CASE STUDY Ford Motor Company

'2014 was a successful step forward in furthering our One Ford plan to deliver profitable growth for all. Despite a challenging environment, particularly in South America and Russia,' going on to note that it was 'the company's fifth consecutive year of pre-tax profit and positive automotive operating-related cash flow.'

This statement in front of Ford's 2014 Annual Report demonstrated clearly how the company has weathered turmoil in its markets (**http://corporate.ford.com/investors/reports-and-filings/annual-reports.html#/undefined**).

Ford Motor Company is the second-largest car manufacturer in the United States and one of the biggest family businesses of all time. Ford's history begins with its legendary founder, Henry Ford, who once said, 'a business that makes nothing but money is a poor kind of business'. Ford had some practice at not making dollars. His first car, finished in 1896, was built in his garden. Mounted on bicycle wheels the two-cylinder car had neither reverse gear nor brakes. While hardly a show stopper, this helped Ford to get some outside investors to back him. By 1899 Ford had raised and spent $86,000 without producing a car that could be sold. Based on a successful appearance at the Grosse Pointe Blue Ribbon track at Detroit, Ford pulled in more investors, this time selling 6,000 $10 dollar shares in a new company. This venture too was a failure but nothing daunted him; in June 1903, he found 12 more investors who between them put up $28,000 in Ford's third shot at building a successful motor company.

The Model A, Ford's first production car sold well and by 1907 he broke the $1 million profit barrier. The Ford Model T, available 'in any colour so long as it's black', is generally considered the most significant vehicle in automobile history.

When the Model T (or 'Tin Lizzie') rolled off the assembly line in 1908, Henry Ford had achieved his dream of building 'a motorcar for the great multitude'. Unlike other car manufacturers Ford didn't focus his dream solely on performance, but on popularity. Before the Model T, cars were the ultimate playthings for the very rich. What Ford managed to do with the Model T (after 19 previous experimental models, from A to S) was to turn the car into a vehicle for the masses.

Ford's success was based on radical economics. Instead of making money by raising the cost of the product, and therefore raising profit margins, Ford realized he could make more money by increasing sales volume and lowering prices and profit margins. At this time Frederick Winslow Taylor, a professor at Dartmouth College, was developing his Principles of Scientific Management, showing how by a close examination of manufacturing tasks work could be streamlined and made much more efficient. Ford built this information and research into his manufacturing processes.

But what differentiates Ford from its competitors is continuity of ownership and management philosophy. For more than 100 years, the Ford family has maintained control of the business and shaped its future. The founder's great-grandson, William Clay Ford, Jr, currently serves as the executive chairman and two other family members sit on the board. Despite reporting losses of $14.6 billion during the 2008–2012 financial crisis, Ford alone of US car makers declined the US government's auto bail-out cash offered at the peak of the banking crisis of 2008. While both Chrysler and GM reported sales drops, Ford's sales rose 33.5 per cent.

Online video courses and lectures

Stanford Graduate School believes that entrepreneurs are made rather than born and are the result of a specific process of experience, education and encouragement. Their course relies heavily on case studies of business success and failure, starting a real venture in a team and working with practicing industry experts to breathe life into their venture. All the subjects of a conventional MBA are distilled to uncover the essence of what is needed for a start-up to succeed. Faculty facilitate as much as teach. The success of their method is made clear by the sheer scale of the success of their alumni. Yahoo, Google, Hewlett Packard. Instagram and Dropbox are just a handful of stars that Stanford can lay claim to playing some role in their achievement.

In March 2015 Stanford announced that it was bringing its teaching model to London. Stanford Ignite, as the London scheme is known, takes in 50 participants each year, each paying £6,000 for the privilege of what has a good chance of being a passport to success. Stanford runs its Ignite programme in these locations as well as in London: Bangalore, Beijing, New York City, Santiago and São Paulo (**www.gsb.stanford.edu/programs/ stanford-ignite**)

Below is a cross-section of the video sessions made available by the School, with running times of between 10 minutes and an hour. You can find details of all the entrepreneurship teaching material under the heading, 'Knowledge and inspiration, one entrepreneur at a time.' (**http://ecorner. stanford.edu/index.html**)

The Art of Teaching Entrepreneurship and Innovation delivered by Stanford Technology Ventures Program's Executive Director Tina Seelig: **http://ecorner.stanford.edu/authorMaterialInfo.html?mid=2266**

Creating Enchantment: Guy Kawasaki, entrepreneur and business advisors whose clients include Apple, Nike, Gartner, Audi, Google, Microsoft, and Breitling: **http://ecorner.stanford.edu/ authorMaterialInfo.html?mid=2669**

Five Biggest Mistakes That Entrepreneurs Make: Jerry Kaplan, serial entrepreneur: **http://ecorner.stanford.edu/ authorMaterialInfo.html?mid=364**

Five Critical Skills That Entrepreneurs Need: Jerry Kaplan, serial entrepreneur: **http://ecorner.stanford.edu/ authorMaterialInfo.html?mid=366**

The Power of Curiosity and Inspiration: Square and Twitter Co-Founder Jack Dorsey: **http://ecorner.stanford.edu/ authorMaterialInfo.html?mid=2635**

Social Entrepreneurship: Part of 2010 Conference on Entrepreneurship with two social entrepreneurs and two investors: **www.youtube.com/ watch?v=SkCUaIVWiW0**

Timing is Important: The Same Idea Can Have Different Fates: Jerry Kaplan, serial entrepreneur: **http://ecorner.stanford.edu/ authorMaterialInfo.html?mid=369**

Tips for the Entrepreneur: Google co-founder Larry Page provides several tips for entrepreneurs: **http://ecorner.stanford.edu/ authorMaterialInfo.html?mid=1076**

Types of Risks: Jerry Kaplan, serial entrepreneur: **http://ecorner.stanford.edu/authorMaterialInfo.html?mid=370**

Unlearn Your MBA: David Heineimeier Hansson, the creator of Ruby on Rails and partner at 37signals in Chicago: **http://ecorner.stanford.edu/ authorMaterialInfo.html?mid=2351**

The Wave of Social Entrepreneurship: Jeff Church, founder of Nika Water, a thriving social enterprise that supports clean water projects in impoverished countries: **http://ecorner.stanford.edu/ authorMaterialInfo.html?mid=2933**

What Is Creativity? Using Play-Doh and the Apple iPod as examples, Robert Sutton, Co-Director of the Center for Work, Technology, and Organization at Stanford University, explains that often creativity is simply making new things out of old ones: **http://ecorner.stanford.edu/authorMaterialInfo.html?mid=1187**

Duke University – The Fuqua School of Business: Intrapreneurship Symposium: Corporate Careers that Harness the Entrepreneurial Spirit: **www.youtube.com/watch?v=c1AzfwN_Ywo**

Wharton, University of Pennsylvania: Exploring the Next Iteration of Social Entrepreneurship: Diana Ayton-Shenker, first Nazarian Social Innovator in Residence at Wharton. **http://knowledge.wharton.upenn.edu/article/exploring-the-next-iteration-of-social-entrepreneurship/**

Online video case studies

Apple Computers: Heartfelt talk by Steve Jobs All Things at Wall Street Journal D8 Conference 2010: **www.youtube.com/watch?v=qkXxFILYwPc**

Dropbox: Finding Your Way as an Entrepreneur. Co-Founder Drew Houston shares personal moments from starting the cloud-based file storage service Dropbox: **http://ecorner.stanford.edu/authorMaterialInfo.html?mid=2983**

Facebook: Mark Zuckerberg, founder of Facebook, gives an example to demonstrate product development and experience at Facebook and talks about how their product has evolved with the company. **http://ecorner.stanford.edu/authorMaterialInfo.html?mid=1499**

Instagram: Co-Founders Kevin Systrom and Mike Krieger challenge many of the myths surrounding startups and the lives of entrepreneurs: **http://ecorner.stanford.edu/authorMaterialInfo.html?mid=2735**

Microsoft – The Bill Gates Story, The Biography Channel: **www.youtube.com/watch?v=UnTuFsmsc1**

Steve Jobs and Bill Gates at Wall Street Journal D5 Conference, 2007: **www.youtube.com/watch?v=NfAfZbTq8ow**

Ray Krok and the McDonald's story: Business Mastery: Case Studies from the World's Most Successful Entrepreneurs: **www.youtube.com/watch?v=j-8SzTMwkEo**

Starbucks: Howard Schultz, CEO of Starbucks at Daniels College of Business, University of Denver: **www.youtube.com/watch?v=dUJ0d7xUMLQ**

Walmart: The Sam Walton Biography. The History Channel: **www.youtube.com/watch?v=jP3PnOw9p1c**

11 Preparing the international business growth plan budget

- Establishing objectives.
- Tools for planning growth.
- Preparing budgets.
- Analysing performance against budget.

There is one word that the MBA will hear most frequently, be most involved in helping to achieve and in its successful achievement ultimately be measured against – GROWTH. Business schools from The Massachusetts Institute of Technology (MIT) and Harvard (Owner/President Management) in the United States, through to Cranfield, Warwick and Henley in the UK and Curtin Business School (CBS) in Australia, all have electives or programmes dedicated to the subject of business growth. IMD in Switzerland has a Professor of Sustainable Business Growth sponsored by Shell and the School of Business and Economics, University of Jyväskylä, Finland has a Professor of Growth Venturing.

So business growth, once a peripheral subject at best is now mainstream teaching on the MBA curricula, in one guise or another. That's just as well because striding the world stage with any stature requires a business to grow and keep growing. METRO GROUP, one of the most important international retailing companies with 300,000 employees from 150 nations working at over 2,100 outlets in 33 countries in Europe, Africa and Asia, is typical in this respect. METRO GROUP's goal, as stated on their website, is to provide for the long-term appreciation of its corporate value through profitable and sustained growth. The company's credo includes a shared commitment to profitable growth and the pursuit of market leadership in each segment of the markets in which they operate. The other leaders in their sector – Wal-Mart Stores lnc, Carrefour Group, The Home Depot lnc, Royal Ahold, Tesco and the like – all run global operations. The only top-tier firm in this sector operating in just one market is the Kroger Co. Headquartered in Cincinnati, Ohio, Kroger (NYSE:KR) is no slouch with sales of $76.7 billion, operating 2,468 grocery retail stores in 31 states. But the US domestic market is a microcosm of the international business world in any event.

The starting point for preparing the international growth plan comes in the form of a clear steer from the top. Taking METRO as an illustration again – 'All sales brands of the METRO GROUP take leading market positions in their respective segment' – leaves the operating managers heading their wholesale, food retail, non-food speciality stores and department stores in no doubt as to the direction of travel.

Leadership – setting international goals and objectives

However great the employees are, unless a business has effective leadership nothing of great value can be made to happen. While the boss may have a pretty clear idea of what the business is all about and what makes it special and different, it may not be so clear to those who work further down. Employees often just keep their heads down and get on with the task in hand. Although that's a useful trait it is not sufficient to make a business grow into a successful international enterprise. To make that happen, the CEO has to have a precise idea of where the business is heading and use their leadership skills to achieve results.

Tasks

Leaders have three major tasks: to determine the direction; chart the course; and set the goals. The direction of a business has a number of components that can be best understood if thought of as being parts of a pyramid (see Figure 11.1).

FIGURE 11.1   The purpose pyramid

Vision

A vision is about stretching the organization's reach beyond its grasp. Few can immediately see how the vision can be achieved, but can see that it would be great if it could be.

Microsoft's vision of a computer in every home, formed when few offices had one, is one example of a vision that has nearly been reached. As a mission statement in 1990 it might have raised a wry smile. After all it was only a few decades before then that IBM had estimated the entire world demand for its computers as seven!

Mission

A mission is a direction statement, intended to focus your attention on the essentials that encapsulate your specific competence(s) in relation to the market/customers you plan to serve. Firstly, the mission should be narrow enough to give direction and guidance to everyone in the business. This concentration is the key to business success because it is only by focusing on specific needs that a business can differentiate itself from its competitors. Nothing kills off a business faster than trying to do too many different things too soon. Google's mission when it started out in 1998 was 'to organize the world's information and make it universally accessible and useful'. Secondly, the mission should open up a large enough market to allow the business to grow and realize its potential. Google managed to grow a multi-billion-dollar business striding the globe without moving an inch from the parameters of its initial mission. Google by 2010 had added advertising, e-mail and mobile phones to its product offerings, some way from its original mission but well within newly acquired competences.

In summary, the mission statement should explain:

- what business you are in and your purpose;
- what you want to achieve over the next one to three years, ie your strategic goal;
- how, ie your ethics, values and standards.

Above all, mission statements must be realistic, achievable – and brief.

Objectives

The milestones on the way to realizing the vision and mission are measured by the achievement of business objectives. These objectives 'cascade' through the organization from the top where they are measures of profit, through to measures such as output, quality, reject rates, absenteeism and so forth.

Objective setting is a primary process in which clear performance measures are agreed with every employee. The achievement of specific objectives is the ultimate measure of effective leadership.

CASE STUDY TomTom

In February 2015 TomTom's Chief Executive Officer Harold Goddijn stated that the company was well on track to fully replacing their map-making system with a transaction-based platform that will enable near real-time maps in the second half of 2015. The preceding year saw TomTom claim to have 52 per cent of the European market for PNDs (Portable Navigation Devices), a market the company assessed as nearly 7 million units a year. With revenue approaching £1 billion per year, the company has come a long way since 1991, when TomTom was founded and began a journey that would change the way people drive forever.

Harold Goddijn and Corinne Vigreux, married for more than two decades, are the co-founders of the satellite navigation device that has come to define the sector. Vigreux studied at a Paris business school, starting her working life at a French games firm before moving to the UK to Psion, then an FTSE 100 technology company famed for its handheld PDA (Personal Digital Assistant). Goddijn read economics at Amsterdam University and whilst working for a venture capital firm came across some of Psion's handheld computers and organizers and was impressed. He approached Psion suggesting a joint distribution venture selling the company's products in the Netherlands. Vigreux was sent to the Netherlands to negotiate with Goddijn, the first time the pair had met. They married in 1991 and Vigreux resigned from Psion and moved to Amsterdam.

A brief spell working for a Dutch dairy co-operative saw Vigreux suffering from technology withdrawal symptoms. With software wizards Peter-Frans Pauwels and Pieter Geelen, she started Palmtop Software, later to become TomTom, designing software such as dictionaries, accounting packages and diet books that could be loaded on to Palm Pilots and Pocket PCs. In late 1998 Goddijn and Vigreux saw a navigation system built for a computer and gradually the idea took shape. Three years and €4 million later the quartet had created the TomTom, launching it at €799. Even at this price it was far cheaper than existing products and superior in that it featured a touch screen, a first for the sector.

The year after launch the company floated, selling 50 per cent of the business to fund the growth and acquisition. But 2008 saw them hit turbulence. The credit crunch, market saturation, a high level of debt, and Google starting to offer maps for free represented more serious problems in a single year than many face in a lifetime. The company restructured, reduced debt and now generate half their revenue from selling licences to their maps, constructing in-built systems for the car industry, and telematics. TomTom Telematics is now recognized as a leading provider of telematics solutions with over 350,000 subscriptions worldwide. In 2013 TomTom launched its own branded GPS sport watches to help runners, cyclists and swimmers keep moving towards their fitness goals, by providing essential performance information at a glance. The company now employs 3,600 people and is a globally recognized brand.

Shaping business growth – tools and techniques

While Porter's five-forces approach to marketing strategy formulation (see Chapter 3) is, at least as far as business schools are concerned, the standard starting point, there are also a number of other tools that an MBA needs to be familiar with to help to turn strategy into detailed marketing plans.

These are the main tools and techniques an MBA in an international business will be expected to know and understand.

Ansoff's Growth Matrix

Igor Ansoff, while Professor of Industrial Administration in the Graduate School at Carnegie Mellon University published his landmark book, *Corporate Strategy* (1965), where he explained a way of categorizing strategies as an aid to understanding the nature of the risks involved. He invited his students to consider growth options as a square matrix divided into four segments. The axes are labelled with products and services running along the 'x' axis, starting with 'present' and 'new'; and markets on the 'y' axis are similarly labelled.

Ansoff then went on to assign titles to each type of strategy, in an ascending scale of risk (see Table 11.1).

- Market Penetration, which involves selling more of your existing products and services to existing customers – the lowest risk strategy.

- Product/Service Development, which involves creating extensions to your existing products or new products to sell to your existing customer base. This is more risky than market penetration, but less risky than entering a new market where you will face new competitors and may not understand the customers as well as you do your current ones. At one end of this spectrum are truly new and innovative products, high risk in nature. Steve Job's NeXT workstation, generally recognized as being technologically superb, was launched into a market already dominated by Sun Microsystems and Hewlett-Packard and failed to capture a worthwhile slice of the action. At the other end are relatively modest product or service line extensions. Amazon's music and video/DVD business could be seen as a product line extension. Their tools and hardware operation looks more like a new product, but is only new to them, of course, not to the thousands of other businesses in that sector. Most new product launches by big businesses don't succeed and in the grocery business the failure rate is over 75 per cent. Although that figure may sound alarming you have to offset against that the cost of development, which if low may not be a problem, and the rewards of success. Google's two dozen new product launches in the four years to 2006, including Google Talk and Google Finance, have yet to become serious players, ranking around 40th in their respective markets with no more than 2 per cent shares. Google's strategy of launching early and often mean that glitches are accepted; but their aim is to encourage their geeks to take risks and stay creative knowing that the pay-off when they get a winner will be colossal.

- Market Development involves entering new market segments or completely new markets either in your home country or abroad. So, for example, Motley Fool's entry into the German market involved only a modest change, mostly in translating text, in a well-proven product, as for its entry to the British, French and Italian markets all executed over a four-year period. When Merrill Lynch launched its online investment service they aimed it at a market of younger Internet-literate potential clients, quite a different market segment from their then existing customer base who were generally older people who preferred a more personal service.

- Diversification is selling new products into new markets; the most risky strategy as both are relative unknowns. Avoid unless all other strategies have been exhausted. Diversification can be further subdivided into four categories of increasing risk profile:

  - horizontal diversification (entirely new product into current market);
  - vertical diversification (move backwards into firm's suppliers or forward into customer's business);
  - concentric diversification (new product closely related to current products either in terms of technology or marketing presence but into a new market);
  - conglomerate diversification (completely new product into a new market).

TABLE 11.1   Ansoff's growth matrix

	Existing products	New products
Existing markets	**Market penetration**	**Product development**
New markets	**Market development**	**Diversification** Horizontal Vertical Concentric Conglomerate

Boston matrix

Developed in 1969 by the Boston Consulting Group, this tool can be used in conjunction with the life cycle concept (see Chapter 4, 'Product/service life cycle' section) to plan a portfolio of product/service offers. The thinking behind the matrix is that a company's products and services should be classified according to their cash-generating or consumption ability against two dimensions; the market growth rate and the company's market share. Cash is used as the measure rather than profit as that is the real resource used to invest in new offers. The objective then is to use the positive cash flow generated from 'cash cows', usually mature products that no longer need heavy marketing support budgets, to invest in 'stars', that is fast-growing, usually newer products, positioned in markets in which the company already has a high market share – usually newer markets. 'Dogs' should be disinvested and 'question marks' limited in number and watched carefully to see if they are more likely to become stars or dogs (see Figure 11.2 below).

FIGURE 11.2 The Boston matrix

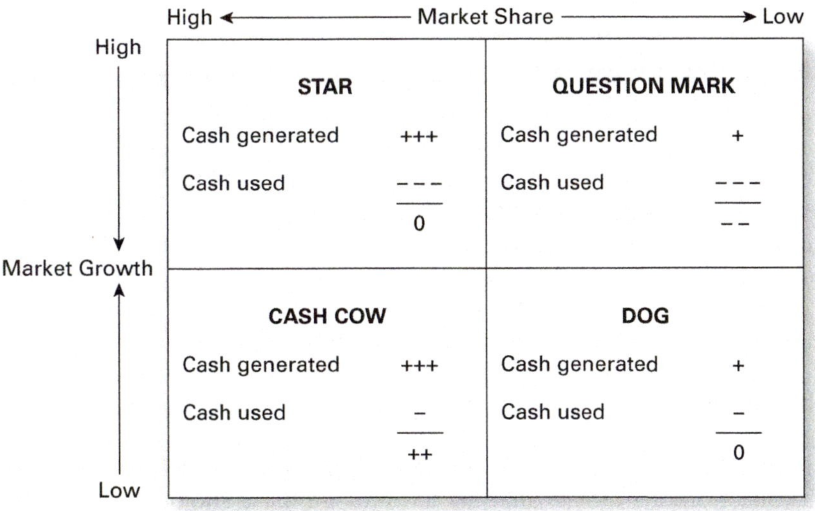

High
Market Share
Low
High
Market Growth
Low
STAR
Cash generated +++
Cash used – – –
0
QUESTION MARK
Cash generated +
Cash used – – –
– –
CASH COW
Cash generated +++
Cash used –
++
DOG
Cash generated +
Cash used –
0

The GE–McKinsey directional policy matrix

General Electric was much taken by the visual aspect of the Boston matrix and was using it to enhance its own performance using another consulting firm, McKinsey and Company to help. Between them in 1971 they came up with a variant and, in some ways, an improvement by substituting business strength and industry attractiveness for market share and market growth rate (Figure 11.3). The logic being that although these are subjective measures they are more accessible than market growth and share, as these are hard to

FIGURE 11.3 The GE–McKinsey directional policy matrix

Business strength
High
Medium
Low
Low
Medium
High
Industry attractiveness

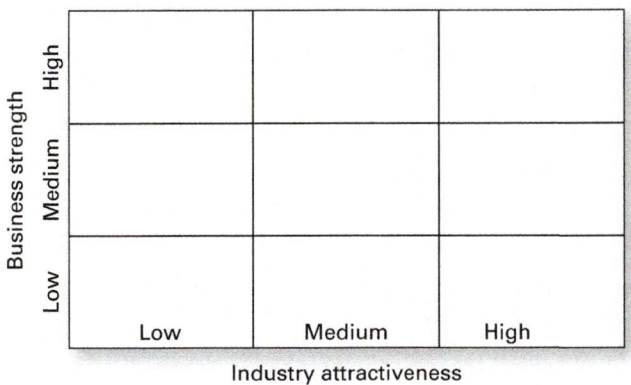

establish and in any event the figures are themselves largely subjective suppositions based mostly on opinions.

Other matrix variations

A dozen or so other similar matrices are in use each with their own strengths and weaknesses. Arthur D Little Inc, a management consultancy founded in 1886 based in Cambridge Massachusetts, came up with its own matrix in the late 1970s using competitive position and industry maturity as the directions. Two business school professors, Gary Hamel (London Business School) and CK Prahalad (University of Michigan) developed a matrix in 1994 as an aid in setting specific acquisition and deployment goals. Other academics – in the United States (Charles W Hofer and Dan Schendel) and in the UK (Cranfield colleagues Malcolm McDonald and Cliff Bowman) – as well as companies such as Shell have all added twists to the basic matrix strategy tool.

Mind Tools (**www.mindtools.com/pages/main/newMN_STR.htm**), provides a collection of strategic analysis tutorials on these and other matrices.

The long-run return pyramid

Another helpful marketing planning tool is the long-run return pyramid, which is in effect a checklist of growth options. None of the options are mutually exclusive and the tool does not provide for any form of evaluation. Nevertheless it can be a valuable aide-memoire to ensure that no stone has been left unturned during the strategic review process. The pyramid's pedigree is unknown, but it is loosely based on the DuPont's return on investment pyramid used to trace all the performance ratios that influenced return on investment. The pyramid in the form shown in Figure 11.4 is attributed to Robert Brown, a senior academic at Cranfield School of Management.

FIGURE 11.4 The long-run return pyramid

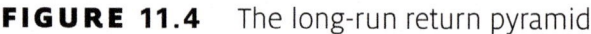
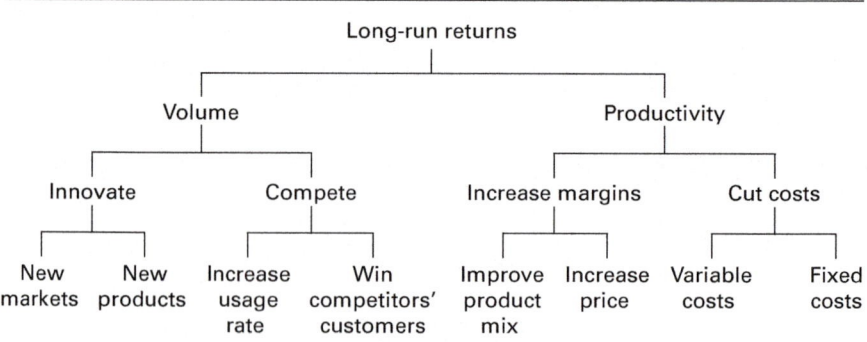

FIGURE 11.5 The balanced scorecard

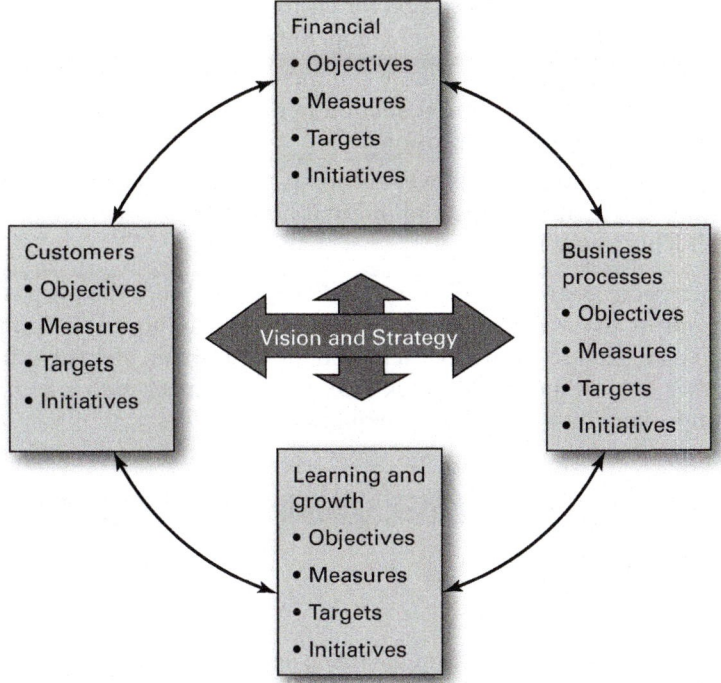

Balanced scorecard

The balanced scorecard (see Figure 11.5), developed by Robert Kaplan and David Norton and published in a *Harvard Business Review* article in 1992, is a management process that sets out to align business activities to the vision and strategy of the organization, improve internal and external communication, and monitor organization performance against strategic goals. Its uniqueness was to add non-financial performance measures to traditional financial targets to give managers and directors a more 'balanced' view of organizational performance.

Although Kaplan and Norton are credited with coining the phrase, the idea of a balanced scorecard originated with General Electric's work on performance measurement reporting in the 1950s, and the work of French process engineers (who created the tableau de bord – literally, a 'dashboard' of performance measures) in the early part of the 20th century.

Four perspectives are included in the management process, which in effect extends the range of management by objectives and value-based management into areas beyond purely financial target setting. A number of objectives, measures, targets and initiatives can be set to achieve specific Key Performance Indicators (KPIs) for each perspective:

- Financial: these include KPIs for return on investment, cash flow, profit margins and shareholder value.
- Customers: here the KPIs can be for customer retention rates, satisfaction levels, referrals and complaints.
- Internal business processes: these can include stock turn, accident rates, defects in production, reduction in the number of processes and improvements in communication.
- Learning and growth: employee turnover, morale levels, training and development achievements and internal promotions vs new recruits are all KPIs to use here.

The four perspectives are linked by a double feedback loop, the purpose of which is to ensure that KPIs are not in conflict with one another. For example, if customer satisfaction could be achieved by improving delivery times, achieving that by, say, increasing stock levels might conflict with a financial target of improving return on capital employed.

CASE STUDY Alpharma

As well as having a clutch of MBAs at operating levels throughout the company, recent chairmen and CEOs of Alpharma also have MBAs. Gert W Munthe (1994–2000) has an MBA from Columbia and Peter G Tombros, chairman and a member of Alpharma's Board of Directors since 1995, received his MBA from the University of Pennsylvania in 1968. Other members of the top team with MBAs include Michael J Nestor, initially as president of the pharmaceutical business and later as president of the branded specialty pharmaceutical business where he established Alpharma's pain franchise. He has a Bachelor of Business Administration degree from Middle Tennessee State University and an MBA from Pepperdine University.

Alpharma's journey began in 1903, when a group of Norwegian pharmacists formed the A/S Apothekernes Laboratorium for Specialpræparater (Alpharma). The company grew rapidly as a manufacturer of pharmaceutical products and, in the years leading up to the First World War, production increased rapidly. By 1939 Alpharma was an important manufacturer of bandages and adhesive plasters, products considered vital to the Norwegian war effort. The next two decades saw a flurry of acquisitions leading to them becoming the largest manufacturer of bacitracin in the world, a strategy that laid the foundation for expansion into the United States.

In 1983 Alpharma acquired its biggest competitor, the Danish company A/S Dumex, financing the transaction through a public offer of shares in New York.

This was the first time a US subsidiary of a European organization was listed in New York and with access to the largest capital market in the world they set about on an acquisition blitz. In 1987, they bought US company Barre-National, Inc., the largest manufacturer in the United States, and possibly the world, of liquid generic pharmaceuticals. The following year they bought the US pharmaceutical company NMC Laboratories, Inc., which specialized in generic medicinal ointments and creams. In May 2000, Alpharma acquired Roche's Medicinal Feed Additives business and in 2001 they acquired the American company, Purepac Pharmaceutical Co Ltd, owned by Australian company F H Faulding. Purepac manufactured generics in tablet and capsule form for the North American market.

A few years earlier, around 1997 according to company sources, the pressure to meet shareholders' requirements for ever increasing returns in a business with many different divisions serving diverse markets led to a need to monitor every company activity that impacted on EBIT (Earnings Before Interest and Tax). Believing that the company could not meet shareholders' expectations with the management tools on hand the search was on for new ones. It was at this point that the company's chief executive officer, who had an extensive network of contacts with external consulting firms began considering the Balanced Scorecard. Its simplicity, its function as a strategy evaluator and the ability to use non-financial indicators in addition to the financial ones was particularly attractive to a business whose culture was steeped in medical communications.

Once decided on, a project team of four from the company's Internal Control department was assembled to see how best to implement BSC. They formulated their findings in a handbook that was distributed company-wide at the end of June 1998, setting out company policy on all matters relating to the scorecard. Initially subsidiary divisions were encouraged to develop a scorecard, but the use of the concept was not compulsory until January 2001 when, for the first time, scorecard reporting was officially required in the strategic planning process.

Kaplan and Norton suggest that it takes about 25 to 26 months for a company to make the BSC a routine part of the management process and deliver value. By 2003 Alpharma Inc. had become a global pharmaceutical company with operations in 27 counties generating sales of $654 million a year.

On 29 December 2008, Alpharma, Inc finally agreed to King Pharmaceuticals Inc's $1.6 billion cash takeover offer, ending the drug makers' months-long battle. That day King agreed to pay $37 a share for Alpharma, representing a 54 per cent premium to the Bridgewater, New Jersey company's stock price on 21 Aug, the last trading day before King's initial $33-per-share bid.

International business plans

All the thinking that goes into devising and shaping business plans for an international organization has to be set out in a form that will ensure that it can be successfully implemented. That form is a marketing plan, which itself is part of a wider plan for the business as a whole, setting out in detail the role each part of the organization has to play for the next three to five years. That period is needed because recognizing an opportunity, developing a product or service to exploit that opportunity and bringing that product to market all takes time and the plan has to encompass all these stages to be of any value. The dichotomy here is that while strategy takes time for the results to show, the world in which the business is implementing its plans is changing. As one military strategist succinctly put it – all plans disintegrate on contact with the enemy. So three- to five-year business plans need to be reviewed fundamentally each year and progress monitored at least quarterly.

Preparing business plans is a task that MBAs are invariably expected to be able to carry out, so this section describes the total structure of plan within which the marketing function plays a key role. Exactly how large that role is will depend on the organization structure adopted (see Chapter 6). If the marketing organization is a strategic business unit with full profit accountability then there will in effect be no difference between the business and marketing plans.

Preparing these plans calls for a broad level of understanding of all aspects of the business – cash flow, profit margins, funding issues, marketing and selling, staffing and structures, production, operations, research and development, supply chain etc – that few others in the organization are likely to have. It is an opportunity for an MBA to broaden and deepen their relationships with all key executives as well as the board of directors. So often tedious and always time-consuming, the task of preparing business plans should be welcomed as a career progression opportunity par excellence.

Structure of the business plan

The plan is in essence the route map from where the business is to where it wants to go and how it will go about getting to its destination; the roles and responsibilities of key players, the resources required in terms of money, people and materials and so forth. Although there is much debate about exactly what should go into the business plan and how it should be laid out, there is no doubt that it is the essential tool for ensuring that a well-thought-out marketing strategy is executed successfully too.

This is the suggested general layout for a business plan as used on the MBA programme at Cranfield; and from observation at international business plan competitions it seems to be fairly universal.

Executive summary

This is the most important part of the plan and will form the heart of any presentation to the board, shareholders or prospective investors. Written last this should be punchy, short – ideally one page but never more than two – and should enthuse any reader. Its primary purpose is to excite and inspire an audience to want to read the rest of the business plan.

The executive summary should start with a succinct table showing past performance in key areas and future objectives. This will give readers a clear view of the business's capacity to perform as well as the scale of the task ahead.

TABLE 11.2 Executive summary – history and projections

Last year	This year	Business area	Year 1	Year 2	Year 3 etc
		Sales turnover by product/service And by market segment 1. 2. etc Total sales			
		Gross profit % Operating profit % Total staff nos			
		Sales staff nos Capital employed Return on capital employed %			

The executive summary should then continue with sections covering the following areas:

- What the primary products/services are and why they are better or different from what is around now.
- Which markets/customer groups will most need what you plan to offer and why.
- How close you are to being ready to sell your product/service and what if anything remains to be done.
- Why your organization has the skills and expertise to execute this strategy and if new or additional people are required, who they are, or how you will recruit them.

- Financial projections showing in summary the sales, profit, margins and cash position over the next three to five years.
- How the business will operate, sketching out the key steps from buying in any raw materials, through to selling, delivering and getting paid.
- What physical resources – equipment, premises – the plan calls for.

The contents – putting flesh on the bones

Unlike the executive summary, which is structured to reveal the essence of your business proposition, the plan itself should follow a logical sequence such as this:

- Vision: A vision's purpose is to stretch the organization's reach beyond its grasp. Generally, few people concerned with the company can now see how the vision is to be achieved, but all concerned agree that it would be great if it could be. Once your vision becomes reality it may be time for a new challenge, or perhaps even a new business.
- Mission: A mission statement explains concisely what you do, who you do it for and why you are better or different from others operating in your market. It should be narrow enough to give focus yet leave enough room for growth. Above all it should be believable to all concerned.
- Objectives: These are the big-picture numbers, such as market share, profit, return on investment that are to be achieved by successfully executing the chosen strategy.
- Operations: This covers any processes such as manufacture, assembly, purchasing, stock holding, delivery/fulfilment and the website.
- Financial projections: Detailed information on sales and cash flow for the period of the plan showing how much money is needed, for what, by when and what would be the most appropriate source of those funds; long- or short-term borrowings, equity, factoring or leasing finance, for example.
- Premises: What space and equipment will be needed and how your home will accommodate the business while staying within the law.
- People: What skills and experience do you have on board that will help run this business and implement the chosen strategy; what other people will you need and where will you find them?
- Administrative matters: Do you have any IP (intellectual property) on your product or service; what insurance will you need; what changes if any will be needed to the accounting and control and record systems?
- Milestone timetable: This should show the key actions you have still to take to be ready to achieve major objectives and the date these will be completed.

- Appendices: Use these for any bulky information such as market studies, competitors' leaflets, customer endorsements, technical data, patents, CVs and the like that you refer to in your business plan.

The marketing plan – in detail

Above is a basic summary of the contents of the business plan, each section of which will be in rather more detail. For the marketing department that detail will include:

- market projections and forecasts by product, market and market segment;
- competitor analysis – SWOT (see Chapter 3 for more on strengths, weaknesses, opportunities and threats as well as other tools for analysing competitors);
- specific growth objectives by product/service category using Ansoff and Boston matrices (see earlier in this chapter);
- major new product/service launches and new market entry goals;
- advertising and promotion actions and schedules;
- distribution and channel to market routes;
- detailed pricing by product/service and market segment, including discounts and offers;
- customer retention methods and goals;
- sales force size, structure and incentives;
- market research tasks and programmes.

All these topics are covered in this book and by using the Index and Contents pages you can find your way to them quickly.

Using planning software

There are a number of free software packages that will help you through the process of writing a business plan. Those listed below include some useful resources, spreadsheets and tips that may speed up the process, but are not substitutes for finding out the basic facts about your market, customers and competitors.

A good place to start is with BizPlanIt's free virtual business plan (**www.bizplanit.com/virtual-business-plan/**). There is a menu to explore each section or topic you are interested in learning more about, covering 14 areas ranging from the Executive Summary through to the Appendices; a good foundation, or refresher to the subject. They offer a consultancy service to help you write a custom business plan, priced at $1975 (£1,300) and taking between three and five weeks.

Budgets and variances

Budgeting is the principle interface between the marketing department and the finance department. As a staff function (see Chapter 6 for more on line and staff functions) the finance department will assist managers in preparing a detailed budget for the year ahead for every area of the organization and is in effect the first year of the marketing plan. MBAs are invariably expected to play a role in facilitating the process within their department. Budgets are usually reviewed at least half way through the year and often quarterly. At that review a further quarter or half year can be added to the budget to maintain a one-year budget horizon. This is known as a 'rolling quarterly (half yearly) budget'.

Budget guidelines

Budgets should adhere to the following general principles:

- The budget must be based on realistic but challenging goals. Those goals are arrived at by both a top-down 'aspiration' of senior management and a bottom-up forecast of what the department concerned see as possible.
- The budget should be prepared by those responsible for delivering the results – the salespeople should prepare the sales budget and the advertising and promotion people the A&P budget. Senior managers must maintain the communication process so that everyone knows what other parties are planning for.
- Agreement to the budget should be explicit. During the budgeting process, several versions of a particular budget should be discussed. For example, the boss may want a sales figure of $/€/£2 million, but the sales team's initial forecast is for $/€/£1.75 million. After some debate, $/€/£1.9 million may be the figure agreed upon. Once a figure is agreed, a virtual contract exists that declares a commitment from employees to achieve the target and commitments from the employer to be satisfied with the target and to supply resources in order to achieve it. It makes sense for this contract to be in writing.
- The budget needs to be finalized at least a month before the start of the year and not weeks or months into the year.
- The budget should undergo fundamental reviews periodically throughout the year to make sure all the basic assumptions that underpin it still hold good.
- Accurate information reviewing performance against budgets should be available 7 to 10 working days before the month's end.

Variance analysis

Explaining variances is also an MBA-type task so performance needs to be carefully monitored and compared against the budget as the year proceeds, and corrective action must be taken where necessary. This has to be done on a monthly basis (or using shorter time intervals if required), showing both the company's performance during the month in question and throughout the year so far.

Looking at Table 11.3 we can see at a glance that the business is behind on sales for this month, but ahead on the yearly target. The convention is to put all unfavourable variations in brackets. Hence, a higher-than-budgeted sales figure does not have brackets, while a higher materials cost does. We can also see that, while profit is running ahead of budget, the profit margin is slightly behind (−0.30 per cent).

This is partly because other direct costs, such as labour and distribution in this example, are running well ahead of budget.

Flexing the budget

A budget is based on a particular set of sales goals, few of which are likely to be exactly met in practice. Table 11.3 shows a company that has used £762,000 more materials than budgeted. As more has been sold, this is hardly surprising. The way to manage this situation is to flex the budget to show what, given the sales that actually occurred, would be expected to

TABLE 11.3   The fixed budget

Heading	Month			Year to date		
	Budget	Actual	Variance	Budget	Actual	Variance
Sales	805*	753	(52)	6,358	7,314	956
Materials	627	567	60	4,942	5,704	(762)
Materials margin	178	186	8	1,416	1,610	194
Direct costs	74	79	(5)	595	689	(94)
Gross profit	104	107	3	820	921	101
Percentage	**12.92**	**14.21**	**1.29**	**12.90**	**12.60**	**(0.30)**

* Figures indicate thousands of pounds

TABLE 11.4   The flexed budget

Heading	Month			Year to date		
	Budget	Actual	Variance	Budget	Actual	Variance
Sales	753*	753	–	7,314	7,314	–
Materials	587	567	20	5,685	5,704	(19)
Materials margin	166	186	20	1,629	1,610	(19)
Direct costs	69	79	(10)	685	689	(4)
Gross profit	97	107	10	944	921	(23)
Percentage	**12.92**	**14.21**	**1.29**	**12.90**	**12.60**	**(0.30)**

* Figures indicate thousands of pounds

happen to expenses. Applying the budget ratios to the actual data does this. For example, materials were planned to be 22.11 per cent of sales in the budget. By applying that to the actual month's sales, a materials cost of £587,000 is arrived at.

Looking at the flexed budget in Table 11.4 we can see that the company has spent £19,000 more than expected on the materials given the level of sales actually achieved, rather than the £762,000 overspend shown in the fixed budget.

The same principle holds for other direct costs, which appear to be running £94,000 over budget for the year. When we take into account the extra sales shown in the flexed budget, we can see that the company has actually spent £4,000 over budget on direct costs. Although this is serious, it is not as serious as the fixed budget suggests.

The flexed budget allows you to concentrate your efforts on dealing with true variances in performance.

The Annual Marketing Budget Template (**www.score.org/resources/annual-marketing-budget-template**) can help you to estimate your annual marketing expenses. This spreadsheet provides space for market research, communications, sales and event support, marketing travel, advertising, and online marketing. The template can be modified as needed to fit your business needs.

Seasonality and trends

The figures shown for each period of the budget are not the same. For example, a sales budget of £1.2 million for the year does not translate to £100,000 a month. The exact figure depends on two factors:

1 The projected trend may forecast that, while sales at the start of the year are £80,000 a month, they will change to £120,000 a month by the end of the year. The average would be £100,000.

2 By virtue of seasonal factors, each month may also be adjusted up or down from the underlying trend. You could expect the sales of heating oil, for example, to peak in the autumn and tail off in the late spring.

Estimating your break-even point

The stage at which income exceeds cost is the break-even point and the period of time taken to reach that point is when any growth strategy is at greatest risk. Your business plan should show how long it will take you to reach break-even. As a rule of thumb anything longer than 18 months would be a concern to backers as a lot can happen over that time. New competitors could enter the market, better products and services could come along or the market may turn sour.

First we need to distinguish between different types of costs. Some costs don't change however much you sell; rent, rates and general utilities, for example. On the other hand, the cost of making the products you are selling such as raw materials, distribution and sales commission are all dependent on volume. The more you sell, the more it 'costs' to buy stock. The former of these costs is called 'fixed' and the latter, 'variable', and you cannot add them together to arrive at total costs until you have made some assumptions about sales.

Figure 11.6 shows the factors that govern how break-even is achieved. The vertical axis shows the value of sales and costs in £000 and the horizontal axis the number of 'units' sold.

In this elementary example a business plans to sell only one product and has only one fixed cost, the annual rent and business rates, a total of £10,000. That is shown on the figure as a horizontal line above the axis. The angled line running from the top of the fixed costs line is the variable costs. In this example we plan to buy in at £3 per unit, so every unit we sell adds that much to our costs so that line also represents our total costs.

Only one element is needed to calculate the break-even point – the sales line. That is the line moving up at an angle from the bottom left-hand corner of the chart. We plan to sell out at £5 per unit, so this line is calculated by multiplying the units sold by that price.

FIGURE 11.6 Break-even graph

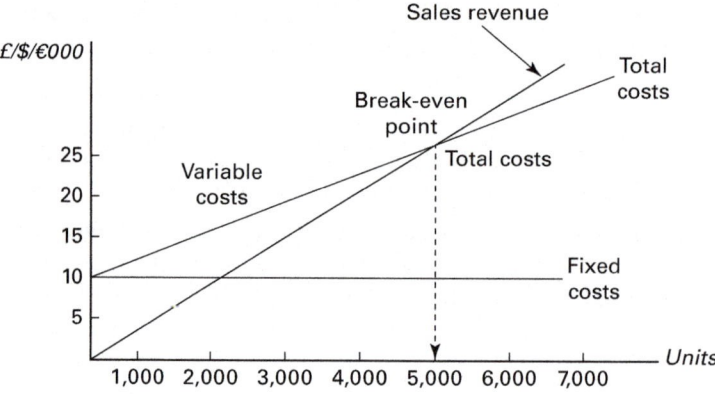

The break-even point is the stage at which a business starts to make a profit. That is when the sales revenue begins to exceed both the fixed and variable costs. The chart shows our example break-even point as 5,000 units.

A formula, deduced from the chart, will save time for your own calculations.

$$\text{Break-even point} = \frac{\text{Fixed costs}}{\text{Selling price} - \text{Unit variable cost}}$$

Therefore:

$$\frac{10,000}{\pounds 5 - \pounds 3} = 5,000 \text{ units}$$

The next and perhaps the most important calculation from a business planning perspective is to estimate when we will reach our break-even point. If our plan indicates that we will sell around 1,000 units a month, then it will take five months to reach break-even.

To complete the break-even picture we need to add one further dimension – your profit objective. In this example £4,000 is used.

The new equation to include your 'desired' profit will look like this:

$$\text{Break-even profit point} \atop (\text{BEPP}) = \frac{\text{Fixed costs} + \text{Profit objective}}{\text{Selling price} - \text{Unit variable cost}}$$

Therefore:

$$= \frac{10,000 + 4,000}{5 - 3} = 7,000 \text{ units}$$

We know that to reach our objective we must sell 7,000 units at £5 each and have no more than £10,000 tied up in fixed costs.

Online video courses and lectures

Break Even Analysis Formulas Chart & Plotting Break Even Point On Chart: At the excelisfun Channel at YouTube: **www.youtube.com/watch?v=7MxlVMzRxa8**

Evaluating a Business Idea: This lecture at Stanford Graduate School of Business by Russ Siegelman, a former vice president of Microsoft and venture capitalist at Kleiner Perkins Caufield & Byers, covers the general areas that an entrepreneur should evaluate when considering a new business idea: **www.youtube.com/watch?v=y9ClKzMq3n0**

Forecasting – Time series models – Simple Exponential smoothing: Prof G Srinivasan, Department of Management Studies, IIT Madras: **www.youtube.com/watch?v=k9dhcflyOFc**

From Business Plan to Business Model: Alex Osterwalder talks at Aaltoes Summer of Startups Finnish start-up accelerator programme: **www.youtube.com/watch?v=jMxHApgcmoU**

How the Boston Consulting Group (BCG) Growth-Share Matrix Works: Alanis Business Academy: **www.youtube.com/watch?v=lc36fK38pLA**

How to Create a Marketing Plan – A Step by Step Guide: Business Training Made Simple, part of the Made Simple Group is a London based training company: **www.youtube.com/watch?v=YlFpM1UAEaE**

How to Write a Business Plan: VC's and an entrepreneur's perspective on business plans addressing the nuts and bolts detail of what is important in a plan at Berkeley-Haas: **www.youtube.com/watch?v=QwlClWaR7Dl**

Introduction to the Balanced Scorecard: Alanis Business Academy: **www.youtube.com/watch?v=l-jt8zySe8E**

A MIT Nuts & Bolts: Business Plans – Refining and Presenting your Venture Idea: Joe Hadzima, Senior Lecturer at MIT Sloan School of Management: **www.youtube.com/watch?v=AdI-E-_InCl**

Online video case studies

Alice + Olivia: Deanna Berkeley, President, discusses her journey into the fashion world and how she has grown this contemporary clothing line to 800 points of sale in more than 50 countries since 2002. Under Ms Berkeley's leadership, the company recently made a major entree into the Greater China and Southeast Asia market through a strategic partnership with Asia's leading retail brand management and distribution company, ImagineX group. This talk was part of the Dean's Speaker Series at Berkeley-Haas on 16 October 2014: **www.youtube.com/watch?v=hUsn2tXhE14**

Airbnb: Nathan Blecharczyk – CTO and Co-founder talks about their strategy to reach customers located in 192 different countries: **www.akamai.com/html/customers/testimonials/airbnb.html**

Boden: Johnnie Boden, founder of this British clothing retailer selling womenswear, menswear and children's wear online and by mail order talks about his plans and omissions: **www.high50.com/startup/johnnie-boden-entrepreneur-interview-i-dismissed-online-shopping-now-i-own-a-global-brand**

The Branson Business Plan – work hard, play hard: Richard Branson talks to Global Conversation: **www.youtube.com/watch?v=g7fbe-oV-X0**

UC Berkeley Business Plan Competition Finalist Presentations and Awards Ceremony. The Haas School of Business presents the eight finalist teams from a record-breaking 110 entries. The finalists were competing for $45,000 in prizes: **www.youtube.com/watch?v=k4NlDNmAaGM**

UW Business Plan Competition 2012 Final Round Presentation – from Foster School of Business: **https://vimeo.com/43505531**

Other central subjects

- Understanding accounting reports.
- Interpreting financial data.
- Getting to grips with behaviour.
- Dealing with decisions.
- Appreciating the basics of statistics.

Every MBA student, whether they take a general programme or one that specializes in a particular discipline, as this book does, will be required to study the same general disciplines. These contain the basic tools that an MBA will use or need to refer to more or less every working day and comprise:

- **Understanding and interpreting key accounting reports.**
  The construction of the key accounting reports – profit and loss, cash flow and balance sheet. The principles that underpin the recording of accounting information and the tools required to assess a business's financial health and performance.

- **Statistics and decision-making tools.** This is where it all began. Fredrick Winslow Tailor, author of *The Principles of Scientific Management* (1911) set out to 'measure each and every task and establish a system of work'. The first person to have on his business card the title 'Consultant to Business', he was the pioneer of the school of 'getting at the facts'. This is also where many business schools started out. Cranfield School of Management was born out of the Work Study Department, itself part of the School of Production.

- **Forecasting.** Understanding the elements of projection – underlying trends, cyclical patterns and random movements.

This chapter contains the essential tools within each of those disciplines to enable an MBA international student, currently inhibited by a lack of fundamental business knowledge, to bring their skills to bear and play a more rounded role in shaping and implementing the direction of the organization in which they work.

Understanding and interpreting key accounting reports

The financial data that an MBA will rely on to measure performance will be contained in three different reports; cash flow, the income statement (profit and loss), and balance sheet. Having an appreciation of the rules governing the construction of these reports is essential to making sense of the facts they seek to convey, bearing in mind that there may be variations in those rules from country to country around the globe. Those facts once uncovered have to be interpreted to reveal and interpret their meaning and this involves using some standard measurement tools.

Cash flow

There is a saying in business that profit is vanity and cash flow is sanity. Both are necessary, but in the short term – and often that is all that matters in business as it struggles to get a foothold in the shifting sands of trading – cash flow is life or death. The rules on what constitutes cash are very simple – it has to be just that, or negotiable securities designated as being as good as cash. Cash flow is looked at in two distinct and important ways.

- as a projection of future expected cash flows;
- as an analysis of where cash came from and went to in an accounting period and the resultant increase or decrease in cash available.

The future is impossible to predict with great accuracy but it is possible to anticipate likely outcomes and be prepared to deal with events by building in a margin of safety. The starting point for making a projection is to make some assumptions about what you want to achieve and testing those for reasonableness.

Take the situation of High Note, a business being established to sell sheet music, small instruments and CDs to schools and colleges, who will expect trade credit and members of the public who will pay cash. The owner plans to invest \$/£/€10,000 and to borrow \$/£/€10,000 from a bank on a long-term basis. The business will require \$/£/€11,500 for fixtures and fittings. A further \$/£/€1,000 will be needed for a computer, software and a printer. That should leave around $/£/€7,500 to meet immediate trading expenses such as buying in stock and spending $/£/€1,500 on initial advertising. Hopefully, customers' payments will start to come in quickly to cover other expenses such as some wages for bookkeeping, administration and fulfilling orders. Sales in the first six months are expected to be $/£/€60,000 based on negotiations already in hand, plus some cash sales that always seem to turn up. The rule of thumb in the industry seems to be that stock is marked up by 100 per cent; so $/£/€30,000 of bought-in goods sell on for $/£/€60,000.

On the basis of the above assumptions it is possible to make the cash flow forecast set out in Table 12.1. It has been simplified and some elements such as VAT and tax have been omitted for ease of understanding.

The maths in the table is straightforward; the cash receipts from various sources are totalled, as are the payments. Taking one from the other leaves a cash surplus or deficit for the month in question. The bottom row shows the cumulative position. So, for example, while the business had $/£/€2,450 cash left at the end of April, taking the cash deficit of $/£/€1,500 in May into account, by the end of May only $/£/€950 ($/£/€2,450 – $/£/€1,500) cash remains.

Cash flow spreadsheet

Entrepreneur has a calculator to help you in an analysis of factors that impact your net cash flow and produce projections of future cash flows based on various alternative financial planning decisions as to profit margins, stock levels and the amount of credit given to customers.
(**www.entrepreneur.com/calculators/cashflowcalculator.html**)

Statement of cash flows for the year

A cash flow statement summarizes exactly where cash came from and how it was spent during the year. At first glance it seems to draw on a mixture of transactions included in the profit and loss account and balance sheet for the same period end, but this is not the whole story. Because there is a time lag on many cash transactions – for example, tax and dividend payments – the statement is a mixture of some previous year and some current year transactions; the remaining current year transactions go into the following year's cash flow statement during which the cash actually changes hands. Similarly, the realization and accrual conventions relating to sales and purchases respectively result in cash transactions having a different timing from when they were entered in the profit and loss account.

TABLE 12.1   High Note six-month cash flow forecast

Month	April $/£/€	May $/£/€	June $/£/€	July $/£/€	Aug $/£/€	Sept $/£/€	Total $/£/€
Receipts							
Sales	4,000	5,000	5,000	7,000	12,000	15,000	
Owners' cash	10,000						
Bank loan	10,000						
Total cash in	*24,000*	*5,000*	*5,000*	*7,000*	*12,000*	*15,000*	*48,000*
Payments							
Purchases	5,500	2,950	4,220	7,416	9,332	9,690	39,108
Rates, electricity, heat, telephone, internet etc	1,000	1,000	1,000	1,000	1,000	1,000	
Wages	1,000	1,000	1,000	1,000	1,000	1,000	
Advertising	1,550	1,550	1,550	1,550	1,550	1,550	
Fixtures/fittings	11,500						
Computer etc	1,000						
Total cash out	*21,550*	*6,500*	*7,770*	*10,966*	*12,882*	*13,240*	
Monthly cash							
Surplus/deficit(–)	2,450	(1,500)	(2,770)	(3,966)	(882)	1,760	
Cumulative cash balance	2,450	950	(1,820)	(5,786)	(6,668)	(4,908)	

Example

A company had sales of $/£/€5 million this year and $/£/€4 million last year and these figures appeared in the profit and loss accounts of those years. Debtors at the end of this year were $/£/€1 million and at the end of the previous year were $/£/€0.8 million. The cash inflow arising from sales this year is $/£/€4.8 million ($/£/€0.8 million + $/£/€5 million – $/£/€1 million) whereas the sales figure in the profit and loss account is $/£/€5 million.

For these reasons it is not possible to look at just this year's profit and loss account and balance sheet to find all the cash flows, you need the previous year's accounts too. The balance sheet will show the cash balance at the period end but will not easily disclose all the ways in which it was achieved. Compiling a cash flow statement is quite a technical job and some training plus inside information is needed to complete the task. Nevertheless, the bulk of the items can be identified from an examination of the other two accounting statements for both the current and previous years.

From an MBA perspective it is understanding the requirement for a cash flow statement as well as the other two accounts that is important, as well as being able to interpret the significance of the cash movements themselves.

Straight plc

An un-audited condensed cash flow statement for Straight plc, established in 1993 as a supplier of container solutions for source-separated waste, is shown below in Table 12.2. Initially one man and a desk, the company grew to become the UK's leading supplier of kerbside recycling boxes as well as a key supplier of other types of waste and recycling container solutions. Turnover by 2008 was running at over £30 million a year with operating profit in excess of £1m.

The three columns represent the cash activities for two equivalent six-month periods and for the whole of the preceding year. The cash of £2.126 million generated to 31 December 2006 (bottom of the right-hand column) is carried over to the start of the June 2007 six-month period (second figure from bottom of left-hand column). By adding the net increase (or decrease) in cash generated in this period we arrive at the closing cash position.

The cash flow statement then gives us a complete picture of how cash movements came about: from normal sales activities; the purchase or disposal of assets; or from financing activities. This is an expansion of the sparse single figure in the company's closing balance sheet stating that cash in current assets is £3.751 million.

The profit and loss account (income statement)

If you look back to the financial situation in the High Note example you will see a good example of the difference between cash and profit. The

TABLE 12.2 Un-audited condensed cash flow statement for Straight plc (for the 6 months ended 30 June 2007)

	Half year to 30 June 2007 $/£/€'000	Half year to 30 June 2006 $/£/€'000	Year 31 Dec 2006 $/£/€'000
Net cash flows from operating activities	2,242	3,879	1,171
Cash flows from investing activities			
Purchases of property, plant and equipment	(603)	(464)	(701)
Proceeds from sale of property, plant and equipment	345	–	–
Purchase of intangible assets	(55)	(87)	(193)
Purchase of investments	(35)	–	–
Interest received	28	58	107
Net cash used in investing activities	(320)	(493)	(787)
Cash flows from financing activities			
Dividends paid	(310)	(283)	(422)
Proceeds from issue of shares	13	–	128
Net cash used in financing activities	(297)	(283)	(294)
Net increase in cash and cash equivalents	1,625	3,103	90
Cash and cash equivalents at beginning of period	2,126	2,036	2,036
Cash and cash equivalents at the end of period	3,751	5,139	2,126

business has sold $/£/€60,000 worth of goods that it only paid $/£/€30,000 for, so it has a substantial profit margin to play with. While $/£/€39,108 has been paid to suppliers only $/£/€30,000 of goods at cost have been sold meaning that £9,108 worth of instruments, sheet music and CDs are still in stock. A similar situation exists with sales. They have billed for $/£/€60,000 but only been paid for $/£/€48,000; the balance is owed by debtors. The bald figure at the end of the cash flow projection showing High Note to be in the red to the tune of $/£/€4,908 seems to be missing some important facts.

The difference between profit and cash

Cash is immediate and takes account of nothing else. Profit, however, is a measurement of economic activity that considers other factors that can be assigned a value or cost. The accounting principle that governs profit is known as the 'matching principle', which means that income and expenditure are matched to the time period in which they occur.

So for High Note the profit and loss account for the first six months would be as shown in Table 12.3.

TABLE 12.3 Profit and loss account for High Note for the six months April to September

	$/£/€	$/£/€
Sales		60,000
Less cost of goods to be sold		30,000
Gross profit		30,000
Less expenses:		
Heat, electric, telephone, internet, etc	6,000	
Wages	6,000	
Advertising	9,300	
Total expenses		21,300
Profit before tax, interest and depreciation charges		8,700

The structure of the profit and loss statement

This account is set out in more detail for a business in order to make it more useful when it comes to understanding how a business is performing. For example, although the profit shown in our worked example is $/£/€8,700 in fact it would be rather lower. As money has been borrowed to finance cash flow there would be interest due, as there would be on the longer-term loan of $/£/€10,000.

In practice we have four levels of profit:

- gross profit is the profit left after all costs related to making what you sell are deducted from income;
- operating profit is what's left after you take away the operating expenses from the gross profit;
- profit before tax is what is left after deducting any financing costs;

- profit after tax is what is left for the owners to spend or reinvest in the business.

For High Note this could look much as set out in Table 12.4.

TABLE 12.4   High Note extended profit and loss account

	$/£/€s
Sales	60,000
Less the cost of goods to be sold	30,000
Gross profit	30,000
Less operating expenses	21,300
Operating profit	8,700
Less interest on bank loan and overdraft	600
Profit before tax	8,100
Less tax	1,827
Profit after tax	6,723

A more substantial business than High Note would have taken on a wide range of commitments. For example, as well as the owner's money, there may be a long-term loan to be serviced (interest and capital repayments); parts of the workshop or offices may be sublet generating 'non-operating income'; and there will certainly be some depreciation expense to deduct. Like any accounting report it should be prepared in the best form for the user, bearing in mind the requirements of the regulatory authorities. The elements to be included are:

1 Sales (and any other revenues from operations).
2 Cost of sales (or cost of goods sold).
3 Gross profit – the difference between sales and cost of sales.
4 Operating expenses – selling, administration, depreciation and other general costs.
5 Operating profit – the difference between gross profit and operating expenses.
6 Non-operating revenues – other revenues, including interest, rent etc.
7 Non-operating expenses – financial costs and other expenses not directly related to the running of the business.
8 Profit before income tax.

9 Provision for income tax.

10 Net income (or profit or loss).

Profit and loss spreadsheet

There is an online free Excel profit and loss spreadsheet on *Entrepreneur's* website at (**www.entrepreneur.com/formnet/form/939**) with 25 expense columns and four income streams built in, which you can add, subtract or edit to suit your needs.

The balance sheet

A balance sheet is a snapshot picture at a moment in time. On the one hand it shows the value of assets (possessions) owned by the business and, on the other, it shows who provided the funds with which to finance those assets and to whom the business is ultimately liable.

Assets are of two main types and are classified under the headings of either fixed assets or current assets. Fixed assets come in three forms. Firstly there is the hardware or physical things used by the business itself and which are not for sale to customers. Examples of fixed assets include buildings, plant, machinery, vehicles, furniture and fittings. Next comes intangible fixed assets, such as goodwill, intellectual property etc, and these are also shown under the general heading 'fixed assets'. Finally there are investments in other businesses. Other assets in the process of eventually being turned into cash from customers are called current assets, and include stocks, work-in-progress, money owed by customers and cash itself.

$$\text{Total assets} = \text{Fixed assets} + \text{Current assets}$$

Assets can only be bought with funds provided by the owners or borrowed from someone else; for example, bankers or creditors. Owners provide funds by directly investing in the business (eg when they buy shares issued by the company) or indirectly by allowing the company to retain some of the profits in reserves. These sources of money are known collectively as liabilities.

$$\text{Total liabilities} =$$
$$\text{Share capital and reserves} + \text{Borrowings and other creditors}$$

Borrowed capital can take the form of a long-term loan at a fixed rate of interest or a short-term loan, such as a bank overdraft, usually at a variable rate of interest. All short-term liabilities owed by a business and due for payment within 12 months are referred to as creditors falling due within one year, and long-term indebtedness is called creditors falling due after one year.

So far in our High Note example the money spent on 'capital' items such as the $/£/€12,500 spent on a computer and fixtures and fittings have been ignored as has the $/£/€9,108 worth of sheet music etc remaining in stock waiting to be sold and the $/£/€12,000 of money owed by customers who have yet to pay up. An assumption has to be made about where the cash deficit will be made up and the most logical short-term source is a bank overdraft.

For High Note at the end of September the balance sheet is set out in Table 12.5.

TABLE 12.5   High Note balance sheet at 30 September

	$/£/€	$/£/€
Assets		
Fixed assets		
Fixtures, fitting, equipment	11,500	
Computer	1,000	
Total fixed assets		12,500
Working capital		
Current assets		
Stock	9,108	
Debtors	12,000	
Cash	0	
	21,108	
Less current liabilities (creditors falling due within one year)		
Overdraft	4,908	
Due to suppliers	0	
	4,908	
Net current assets [Working capital (CA-CL)]		16,200
Total assets less current liabilities		28,700
Less creditors falling due after one year		
Long-term bank loan		10,000
Net total assets		18,700
Capital and reserves		
Owner's capital introduced	10,000	
Profit retained (from P&L account)	8,700	
Total capital and reserves		18,700

Balance sheet and other online tools

You can find further guidance on all matters relating to balance sheets and the other accounting reports at Accounting Coach. This was set up by Harold Averkamp, CPA, MBA, to 'to utilize the Internet for communicating a more clear explanation of accounting concepts to people in all parts of the world and at a low cost.' (**www.accountingcoach.com/accounting-topics**). The basic information is free, which may be sufficient to get a good feel for the subject. The Pro version costs £33 ($49) and includes a series of short videos, lecture notes and exams in the main financial topics. The 'Dictionary of Terms' tab on this website will take you to a definition and explanation of most terms in the field.

Package of accounts

The cash flow statement, the profit and loss account and the balance sheet between them constitute a set of accounts, but conventionally two balance sheets, the opening and closing one, are provided to make a 'package'. By including these balance sheets we can see the full picture of what has happened to the owner's investment in the business.

Table 12.6 shows a simplified package of accounts. We can see from these that over the year the business has made $/£/€600 of profit after tax,

TABLE 12.6   A package of accounts

Balance sheet at 31 Dec 2010 ($/£/€)		P & L for year to 31 Dec 2011 ($/£/€)		Balance sheet at 2011 ($/£/€)	
Fixed assets	1,000	Sales	10,000	Fixed assets	1,200
Working capital	1,000	less cost of sales	6,000	Working capital	1,400
	2,000	Gross profit	4,000		2,600
		less expenses	3,000		
Financed by		Profit before tax	1,000	Financed by	
Owner's equity	2,000	Tax	400	Owner's equity	2,000
		Profit after tax	600	Reserves	600
					2,600

invested that in \$/£/€200 of additional fixed assets, \$/£/€400 of working capital such as stock and debtors, balancing that off with the \$/£/€600 put into reserves from the year's profits.

Accounting is certainly not an exact science. Even the most enthusiastic member of the profession would not make that claim. There is considerable scope for interpretation and educated guesswork as all the facts are rarely available when the accounts are drawn up. For example we may not know for certain that a particular customer will actually pay up, yet unless we have firm evidence that they won't – for example if their business is failing – then the value of the money owed will appear in the accounts.

Obviously, if accountants and managers had complete freedom to interpret events as they will, no one inside or outside the business would place any reliance on the figures, so certain ground rules have been laid down by the profession to help get a level of consistency into accounting information.

Fundamental conventions

These are the enduring principles that govern the way in which the accounting profession assemble and present financial information.

Money measurement

In accounting, a record is kept only of the facts that can be expressed in money terms. For example, the state of the managing director's health and the news that your main competitor is opening up right opposite in a more attractive outlet are important business facts. No accounting record of them is made, however, and they do not show up on the balance sheet, simply because no objective monetary value can be assigned to these facts.

Expressing business facts in money terms has the great advantage of providing a common denominator. Just imagine trying to add computer equipment and vehicles, together with a 4,000 sq m office, and then arriving at a total. You need a common term to be able to carry out the basic arithmetical functions, and to compare one set of accounts with another.

Business entity

The accounts are kept for the business itself, rather than for the owner(s), bankers or anyone else associated with the firm. The concept states that assets and liabilities are always defined from the business's viewpoint. So, for example, if a business owner were to lend his business money it would appear in the accounts as a liability, although in effect he might see it as his own money. Anything done with that money, eg buying equipment, would appear in the accounts as an asset of the business. The owner's stake is accounted for only by the increase or decrease in net worth of the enterprise as a whole.

Cost concept

Assets are usually entered into the accounts as the cost at date of purchase. For a variety of reasons, the real 'worth' of an asset will probably change over time. The worth, or value, of an asset is a subjective estimate that no two people are likely to agree on. This is made even more complex, and artificial, because the assets themselves are usually not for sale.

So in the search for objectivity, the accountants have settled for cost as the figure to record. It does mean that a balance sheet does not show the current worth or value of a business. That is not its intention. Nor does it mean that the 'cost' figure remains unchanged forever. For example, a motor vehicle costing £/$/€6,000 may end up looking like the example in Table 12.7 after two years.

TABLE 12.7 Example of the changing 'worth' of an asset

	Year 1	Year 2
Fixed assets	$/£/€	$/£/€
Vehicle	6,000	6,000
Less cumulative depreciation	1,500	3,000
Net asset	4,500	3,000

The depreciation is how we show the asset being 'consumed' over its working life. It is simply a bookkeeping record to allow us to allocate some of the cost of an asset to the appropriate time period.

The time period will be determined by factors such as the working life of the asset. The tax authorities do not allow depreciation as a business expense, so this figure can't be manipulated to reduce tax liability, for example. A tax relief on the capital expenditure known as 'writing down' is allowed, using a formula set by government that varies from time to time dependent on current economic goals; for example, to stimulate capital expenditure.

Other assets, such as freehold land and buildings, will be revalued from time to time, and stock will be entered at cost, or market value, whichever is the lower, in line with the principle of conservatism (see later in this chapter).

Other methods for recording assets

Although cost at date of purchase is the norm for accounting for assets in conventional enterprises there are certain types of businesses and certain situations when other methods of recording a monetary figure are used:

- Market value: This is usually used when an asset is actually to be sold and there is an established market for that particular type of asset. This could arise when a business or part of a business is to be closed down.
- Fair value: This is described as the estimated price at which an asset could be exchanged between knowledgeable but unrelated willing parties who have not and may not actually exchange. This basis is often used in the due diligence process where because of particular synergies a price higher than market value (resulting in goodwill) could reasonably be set.
- Market to market: This is where market value is calculated on a daily basis, usually by financial institutions such as banks and stockbrokers. This can result in dramatic changes in value in turbulent market conditions requiring additional assets, including cash, to be found to cover a fall in market price. This approach is blamed for helping to create liquidity 'black holes' by forcing banks to sell assets to meet liquidity targets, which in turn forces prices lower, requiring yet more assets to be sold.

Going concern

Accounting reports always assume that a business will continue trading indefinitely into the future – unless there is good evidence to the contrary. This means that the assets of the business are looked at simply as profit generators and not as being available for sale. Look again at the motor vehicle example above. In year two, the net asset figure in the accounts, prepared on a 'going concern' basis, is \$/£/€3,000. If we knew that the business was to close down in a few weeks, then we would be more interested in the car's resale value than its 'book' value: the car might fetch only \$/£/€2,000, which is quite a different figure.

Once a business stops trading, we cannot realistically look at the assets in the same way. They are no longer being used in the business to help generate sales and profits. The most objective figure is what they might realize in the marketplace.

In practice the directors and auditors have to believe a company will be viable for at least the next twelve months otherwise they have an obligation to draw attention to the danger that the company may not be a going concern. History shows that more companies experience going concern difficulties towards the end of a recession. In the early spring of 2010, for example, EMI, the holding company for the music group, and Vantis, an AIM-listed professional advisory group, were among a host of firms whose auditors raised such uncertainties. The general view is that a company has a better chance of survival if it is up-front about liquidity problems, rather than letting the market find out about difficulties and, in an atmosphere of mistrust, exaggerate the situation beyond that which is warranted by the facts.

Dual aspect

To keep a complete record of any business transaction we need to know both where money came from and what has been done with it. It is not enough simply to say, for example, that a bank has lent a business $/£/€1m; we have to show how that money has been used, for example to buy a property, increase stock levels, or in some other way. You can think of it as the accounting equivalent of Newton's third law: 'For every force there is an equal and opposite reaction.' Dual aspect is the basis of double-entry book-keeping (see below).

The realization concept

A particularly prudent sales manager once said that an order was not an order until the customer's cheque had cleared, he or she had consumed the product, had not died as a result, and, finally, had shown every indication of wanting to buy again. Most of us know quite different salespeople who can 'anticipate' the most unlikely volume of sales. In accounting, income is usually recognized as having been earned when the goods (or services) are dispatched and the invoice sent out. This has nothing to do with when an order is received, how firm an order is or how likely a customer is to pay up promptly. It is also possible that some of the products dispatched may be returned at some later date – perhaps for quality reasons. This means that income, and consequently profit, can be brought into the business in one period, and have to be removed later on.

Obviously, if these returns can be estimated accurately, then an adjustment can be made to income at the time. So the 'sales income' figure that is seen at the top of a profit and loss account is the value of the goods dispatched and invoiced to customers in the period in question.

The accrual concept

The profit and loss account sets out to 'match' income and expenditure to the appropriate time period. It is only in this way that the profit for the period can be realistically calculated. Suppose, for example, that you are calculating one month's profits when the quarterly telephone bill comes in. The picture might look like Table 12.8.

This is clearly wrong. In the first place, three months' telephone charges have been 'matched' against one month's sales. Equally wrong is charging anything other than January's telephone bill against January's income. Unfortunately, bills such as this are rarely to hand when you want the accounts, so in practice the telephone bill is 'accrued' for. The figure (which may even be absolutely correct if you have a meter) is put in as a provision to meet this liability when it becomes due.

TABLE 12.8   Example of a badly matched profit and loss account

Profit and loss account for January, year_____	
	$/£/€
Sales income for January	4,000
Less telephone bill (last quarter)	800
Profit before other expenses	3,200

Accounting conventions

These concepts provide a useful set of ground rules, but they are open to a range of possible interpretations. Over time, a generally accepted approach to how the concepts are applied has been arrived at. This approach hinges on the use of three conventions: conservatism, materiality and consistency.

Conservatism

Accountants are often viewed as merchants of gloom, always prone to take a pessimistic point of view. The fact that a point of view has to be taken at all is the root of the problem. The convention of conservatism means that, given a choice, the accountant takes the figure that will result in a lower end profit. This might mean, for example, taking the higher of two possible expense figures. Few people are upset if the profit figure at the end of the day is higher than earlier estimates. The converse is never true.

Materiality

A strict interpretation of depreciation (see above) could lead to all sorts of trivial paperwork. For example, pencil sharpeners, staplers and paperclips, all theoretically items of fixed assets, should be depreciated over their working lives. This is obviously a useless exercise and in practice these items are written-off when they are bought.

Clearly, the level of 'materiality' is not the same for all businesses. A multinational may not keep meticulous records of every item of machinery under £1,000. For a small business this may represent all the machinery it has.

Consistency

Even with the help of those concepts and conventions, there is a fair degree of latitude in how you can record and interpret financial information. You should choose the methods that give the fairest picture of how the firm is performing and stick with them. It is very difficult to keep track of events in a business that is always changing its accounting methods. This does not mean that you are stuck with one method forever. Any change, however, is an important step.

Analysing accounts

The main analytical approach is to examine the relationship of pairs of figures extracted from the accounts. A pair may be taken from the same statement, or one figure from each of the profit and loss account and balance sheet statements. When brought together, the two figures are called ratios. Miles per gallon, for example, is a useful ratio for drivers checking one aspect of a vehicle's performance. Some financial ratios are meaningful in themselves, but their value mainly lies in their comparison with the equivalent ratio last year, a target ratio, or a competitor's ratio.

Accounting ratios

Ratios used in analysing company accounts are clustered under five headings and are usually referred to as 'tests'.

- Tests of profitability.
- Tests of liquidity.
- Tests of solvency.
- Tests of growth.
- Market tests.

The profit and loss account and balance sheet in the tables earlier in this section will be used, where possible, to illustrate these ratios.

You can quickly see the consequences of decisions on business performance. For example, extending credit terms and so taking longer to get paid or developing products that fail to sell as forecasted will lead to reduced profitability and declining liquidity. Neither of these is a desirable consequence and as such the MBA International Business needs to have a grasp of the tools required to analyse performance and anticipate the consequences.

Tests of profitability

There are six ratios used to measure profit performance. The first four profit ratios are arrived at using only the profit and loss account and the other two use information from both that account and the balance sheet.

Gross profit This is calculated by dividing the gross profit by sales and multiplying by 100. In this example the sum is $30,000/60,000 \times 100 = 50$ per cent. This is a measure of the value we are adding to the bought-in materials and services we need to 'make' our product or service; the higher the figure the better.

Operating profit This is calculated by dividing the operating profit by sales and multiplying by 100. In this example the sum is 8,700/60,000 × 100 = 14.5 per cent. This is a measure of how efficiently we are running the business, before taking account of financing costs and tax. These are excluded as interest and tax rates change periodically and are outside our direct control. Excluding them makes it easier to compare one period with another or with another business. Once again the rule here is the higher the figure the better.

Net profit before and after tax Dividing the net profit before and after tax by the sales and multiplying by 100 calculates these next two ratios. In this example the sums are 8,100/60,000 × 100 = 13.5 per cent and 6,723/60,000 × 100 = 11.21 per cent. This is a measure of how efficiently we are running the business, after taking account of financing costs and tax. The last figure shows how successful we are at creating additional money to either invest back in the business or distribute to the owner(s) as either drawings or dividends. Once again the rule here is the higher the figure the better.

Return on equity This ratio is usually expressed as a percentage in the way we might think of the return on any personal financial investment. Taking the owner's viewpoint, their concern is with the profit earned for them relative to the amount of funds they have invested in the business. The relevant profit here is after interest and tax (and any preference dividends) have been deducted. This is expressed as a percentage of the equity that comprises ordinary share capital and reserves. So in this example the sum is: return on equity = 6,723/18,700 × 100 = 36 per cent.

Return on capital employed This takes a wider view of company performance than return on equity by expressing profit before interest, tax and dividend deductions as a percentage of the total capital employed, irrespective of whether this capital is borrowed or provided by the owners.

Capital employed is defined as share capital plus reserves plus long-term borrowings. Where, say, a bank overdraft is included in current liabilities every year and in effect becomes a source of capital, this may be regarded as part of capital employed. If the bank overdraft varies considerably from year to year, a more reliable ratio could be calculated by averaging the start- and end-year figures. There is no one precise definition used by companies for capital employed. In this example the sum is: return on capital employed = 8,700/18,700 + 10,000 × 100 = 30 per cent.

Tests of liquidity

In order to survive, companies must also watch their liquidity position, by which is meant keeping enough short-term assets to pay short-term debts. Companies go out of business compulsorily when they fail to pay money due to employees, bankers or suppliers.

The liquid money tied up in day-to-day activities is known as working capital, the sum of which is arrived at by subtracting the current liabilities from the current assets. In the case of High Note we have £21,108 in current assets and £4,908 in current liabilities, so the working capital is £16,200.

Current ratio As a figure the working capital doesn't tell us much. It is rather as if you knew your car had used 20 gallons of petrol but had no idea how far you had travelled. It would be more helpful to know how much larger the current assets are than the current liabilities. That would give us some idea if the funds would be available to pay bills for stock, the tax liability and any other short-term liabilities that may arise. The current ratio, which is arrived at by dividing the current assets by the current liabilities is the measure used. For High Note this is 21,108/4,908 = 4.30. The convention is to express this as 4.30:1 and the aim here is to have a ratio of between 1.5:1 and 2:1. Any lower and bills can't be met easily and much higher and money is being tied up unnecessarily.

Quick ratio (acid test) This is a belt and braces ratio used to ensure a business has sufficient ready cash or near cash to meet all its current liabilities. Items such as stock are stripped out, as although these are assets the money involved is not immediately available to pay bills. In effect the only liquid assets a business has are cash, debtors and any short-term investment such as bank deposits or government securities. For High Note this ratio is 12,000/4,908 = 2.44:1. The ratio should be greater than 1:1 for a business to be sufficiently liquid.

Average collection period We can see that High Note's current ratio is high, which is an indication that some elements of working capital are being used inefficiently. The business has $/£/€12,000 owed by customers on sales of $/£/€60,000 over a six-month period. The average period it takes High Note to collect money owed is calculated by dividing the sales made on credit by the money owed (debtors) and multiplying it by the time period in days; in this case the sum is as follows: 12,000/60,000 × 182.5 = 36.5 days.

If the credit terms are cash with order or seven days, then something is going seriously wrong. If it is net 30 days then it is probably about right. In this example it has been assumed that all the sales were made on credit.

Average payment period This ratio shows how long a company is taking on average to pay its suppliers. The calculation is as for average collection period, but substituting creditors for debtors and purchase for sales.

Days stock held High Note is carrying $/£/€9,108 of stock of sheet music, CDs etc and over the period it sold $/£/€30,000 of stock at cost (the cost of sales is $/£/€30,000 to support $/£/€60,000 of invoiced sales as the mark-up in this case is 100 per cent). Using a similar sum as with average collection period we can calculate that the stock being held is sufficient to support

55.41 days' sales (9,108/10,000 × 182.5). If High Note's suppliers can make weekly deliveries then this is almost certainly too high a stock figure to hold. Cutting stock back from nearly eight weeks (55.41 days) to one week (seven days) would trim 48.41 days or $/£/€7,957.38 worth of stock out of working capital. This in turn would bring the current ratio down to 2.68:1

Circulation of working capital This is a measure used to evaluate the overall efficiency with which working capital is being used; ie the sales divided by the working capital (current assets – current liabilities). In this example that sum is: 60,000/16,420 = 3.65 times. In other words we are turning over the working capital more than three-and-a-half times each year. There are no hard and fast rules as to what is an acceptable ratio. Clearly the more times working capital is turned over – stock sold, for example – the more chance a business has to make a profit on that activity.

Tests of solvency

These measures see how a company is managing its long-term liabilities. There are two principal ratios used here.

Gearing (or leverage) This measures as a percentage the proportion of all borrowing, including long-term loans and bank overdrafts, to the total of shareholders' funds – share capital and all reserves. The gearing ratio is sometimes also known as the debt/equity ratio. For High Note this is: (4,908 + 10,000)/18,800 = 14,908/18,800 = 0.79:1. In other words for every $/£/€1 the shareholders have invested in High Note they have borrowed a further 79c/p/c. This ratio is usually not expected to exceed 1:1 for long periods.

Interest cover This is a measure of the proportion of profit taken up by interest payments and can be found by dividing the annual interest payment into the annual profit before interest, tax and dividend payments. The greater the number, the less vulnerable the company will be to any setback in profits, or rise in interest rates on variable loans. The smaller the number, then the more risk that level of borrowing represents to the company. A figure of between two and five times would be considered acceptable.

Tests of growth

Growth is inevitably regarded as a measure of marketing virility. These ratios are arrived at by comparing one year with another, usually for elements of the profit and loss account such as sales and profit. So, for example, if next year High Note achieved sales of $/£/€100,000 and operating profits of $/£/€16,000 the growth ratios would be 67 per cent, that is $/£/€40,000 of extra sales as a proportion of the first year's sales of $/£/€60,000; and 84 per cent, that is $/£/€7,300 of extra operating profit as a percentage of the first year's operating profit of $/£/€8,700.

Some additional information can be gleaned from these two ratios. In this example we can see that profits are growing faster than sales, which indicates a more healthy trend than if the situation were reversed.

Market tests

This is the name given to stock market measures of performance. Four key ratios here are:

$$\text{Earnings per Share} = \text{Net Profit} : \text{Shares Outstanding}$$

The after tax profit made by a company divided by the number of ordinary shares it has issued.

$$\text{Price Earnings Ratio} = \text{Market Price per Share} : \text{Earnings per Share}$$

The market price of an ordinary share divided by the earnings per share. The PE Ratio expresses the market value placed on the expectation of future earnings, ie the number of years required to earn the price paid for the shares out of profits at the current rate.

$$\text{Yield} = \text{Dividends per Share} : \text{Price per Share}$$

The percentage return a shareholder gets on the 'opportunity' or current value of their investment.

$$\text{Dividend Cover} = \text{Net Income} : \text{Dividend}$$

The number of times the profit exceeds the dividend, the higher the ratio, the more retained profit to finance future growth.

Other ratios

There are a very large number of other ratios that businesses use for measuring aspects of their marketing performance in particular, such as:

- sales per £ invested in fixed assets – a measure of the use of those fixed assets;
- sales per employee – showing if your headcount is exceeding your sales growth;
- profit per employee;
- sales per manager, per support staff and so on – showing the effectiveness of overhead spending.

Combined ratios

No one would use a single ratio to decide whether one vehicle was a better or worse buy than another. MPG, MPH, annual depreciation percentage and residual value proportion are just a handful of the ratios that would need to be reviewed. So it is with a business. A combination of ratios can be used to form an opinion on the financial state of affairs at any one time.

The best-known of these combination ratios is the Altman Z-Score (**www.creditguru.com/CalcAltZ.shtml**) that uses a combined set of five financial ratios derived from eight variables from a company's financial statements linked to some statistical techniques to predict a company's probability of failure. Entering the figures into the onscreen template at this website produces a score and an explanatory narrative giving a view on the business's financial strengths and weaknesses.

Statistics and decision-making tools

International executives collect an inordinate amount of data, usually supported by an IT (Information Technology) department that processes it. However, it falls to the application of analysis techniques, usually carried out by MBAs, to interpret the data and explain its significance or otherwise. Bald information on its own is rarely of much use. If sales people start leaving in large numbers, customers start complaining and debtor payment delinquencies start to rise; however, these facts on their own may tell you very little. Are these figures close to average, or should it be the mean or the weighted average that will reveal their true importance? Even if the figures are bad you need to know if they are outside the range you might reasonably expect to occur in any event.

Rotterdam School of Management, Erasmus University (**www.rsm.nl/mba/international-full-time-mba/curriculum/teaching**), for example, runs an elective, Quantitative Platform for Business, where students investigate the whole range of quantitative methods available for problem solving. This business school considers the subject important enough to put it into Term 1 in their Foundations of Management subjects. EM Lyon (**www.em-lyon.com/english**) confines its teaching to Business Statistics covering 'the essential quantitative skills that will be required of you throughout the programme'. MIT Sloan School of Management (**http://mitsloan.mit.edu/mba/program/firstsem.php**) has a teaching module, Data, Models, and Decision in its first semester that 'Introduces students to the basic tools in using data to make informed management decisions'.

But before you can even get into a top business school such as Wharton, Harvard or Chicago in the United States; INSEAD, London Business School or Cranfield in Europe; or to Nanyang Business School (Singapore) and Ipade (Mexico) you need to take the Graduate Management Admissions Test (GMAT) or the very similar Graduate Record Examinations (GRE) which became a serious alternative in 2005 when Stanford decided to accept it for MBA admissions. In some 1,800 business schools worldwide, the GMAT has been recognized for over 50 years as a proven and reliable measurement to assess candidates' skills and predict their success on MBA programmes. The test itself takes 2½ hours and comprises tests in three areas; analytical writing (analysis of an issue and of an argument); quantitative section (problem solving and data sufficiency); and verbal (reading comprehension, critical reasoning and sentence correction). The average score is currently around 500. Less prestigious business schools look for a GMAT score of 550 and a score upwards of 660 will make you a competitive candidate at most business schools. You are up against everyone else taking the test so as the average scores move up so does the required score.

A lot of MBA candidates flunk the maths element of this test and even some who get through need remedial work in this area. Dartmouth's Tuck School of Business MBA programme runs a pre-orientation math-refresher programme, familiarly known as maths camp, which is in effect a crash course in MBA maths skills. MIT's Sloan, Stanford and Penn's Wharton, run similar refreshers and Professor Peter Regan who started the Tuck programme runs MBAmath.com, a for-profit venture online maths course available to anyone on a subscriber basis.

To perform to the standard expected of an MBA you will need a good grounding in statistics and what follows should be seen as the minimum. It is an area where with a modicum of application an MBA can demonstrate skills that will make them stand out from the crowd.

Statistics

Statistics is the set of tools that we use to help us assess the truth or otherwise of something we observe. For example, if the last 10 phone calls a company received were all cancelling orders, does that signal that a business has a problem, or is that event within the bounds of possibility? If it is within the bounds of possibility what are the odds that we could still be wrong and really have a problem? A further issue is that usually we can't easily examine the entire population so we have to make inferences from samples and unless those samples are representative of the population we are interested in and of sufficient size we could still be very wrong in our interpretation of the evidence. At the time of writing there was much debate as to how much of a surveillance society Britain had become. The figure of 4.2 million cameras, one for every 14 people, was the accepted statistic. However, a diligent journalist tracked down the evidence to find that extrapolating a survey of a single street in a single town arrived at that figure!

Central tendency

The most common way statistics are considered is around a single figure that purports in some way to be representative of a population at large. There are three principle ways of measuring tendency and these are the most often confused and frequently misrepresented set of numbers in the whole field of statistics.

To analyse anything in statistics you first need a 'data set' such as that in Table 12.9.

TABLE 12.9   The selling prices of a company's products

Product	Selling Price $/£/€
1	30
2	40
3	10
4	15
5	10

The mean (or average)

This is the most common tendency measure and is used as a rough and ready check for many types of data. In the example above, adding up the prices ($/£/€105) and dividing by the number of products (5) you arrive at a mean, or average selling price of $/£/€21.

The median

The median is the value occurring at the centre of a data set. Recasting the figures in the table above puts product 4's selling price of $/£/€15 in that position, with two higher and two lower prices. The median comes into its own in situations where the outlying values in a data set are extreme, as they are in our example, where in fact most of the products sell for well below $/£/€21. In this case the median would be a better measure of the central tendency. You should always use the median when the distribution is skewed. You can use either the mean or the median when the population is symmetrical as they will give very similar results.

The mode

The mode is the observation in a data set appearing the most; in this example it is $/£/€10. So if we were surveying a sample of the customers of the company in this example we would expect more of them to say they were paying $/£/€10 for their products, though as we know the average price is $/£/€21.

Variability

As well as measuring how values cluster around a central value, to make full use of the data set we need to establish how much those values could vary. The two most common methods employed are range and deviation from the mean.

Range The range is calculated as the maximum figure minus the minimum figure. In the example being used here that is $/£/€40 – $/£/€10 = $/£/€30. This figure gives us an idea of how dispersed the data is and so how meaningful, say, the average figure alone might be.

Standard deviation from the mean This is a rather more complicated concept as you need first to grasp the central limit theorem, which states that the mean of a sample of a large population will approach 'normal' as the sample gets bigger. The most valuable feature here is that even quite small samples are normal. The Bell Curve, also called the Gaussian distribution, named after Johann Carl Friedrich Gauss (1777–1855) a German mathematician and scientist, shows how far values are distributed around a mean. The distribution, referred to as the standard deviation, is what makes it possible to state how accurate a sample is likely to be. When you hear the results of opinion polls predicting elections based on samples as small as 1,000 are usually reliable within four percentage points, 19 times out of 20, you have a measure of how much reliance you can place on that information. (You can get free tutorials on this and other aspects of statistics at Web Interface for Statistics Education (**http://wise.cgu.edu**).

Figure 12.1 is a normal distribution that shows that 68.2 per cent of the observations of a normal population will be found within 1 standard deviation of the mean; 95.5 per cent within 2 standard deviations; while 99.7 per cent within 3 standard deviations. So almost 100 per cent of the observations will be observed in a span of six standard deviations, three below the mean and three above the mean. The standard deviation is an amount calculated from the values in the sample. Use this calculator

FIGURE 12.1 Normal distribution curve (bell) showing standard deviation

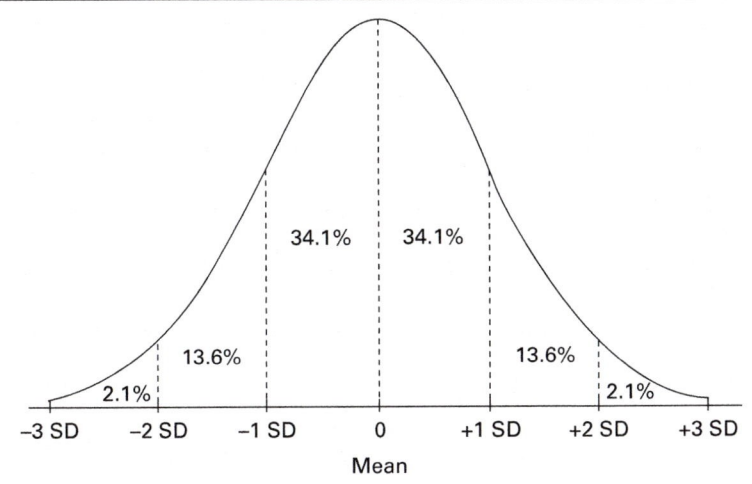

(**www.easycalculation.com/statistics/standard-deviation.php**) to work out the standard deviation by entering the numbers in your sample.

Decision theory

Blaise Pascal (1623–62), the French mathematician and philosopher who with others laid the foundations for the theory of probability, is credited with inaugurating decision theory or decision making under conditions of uncertainty. Until Pascal's time the outcome of events was considered to be largely in the hands of the gods; however, he instigated a method for using mathematical analysis to evaluate the cost and residual value of various alternatives so as to be able to choose the best decision when all the relevant information is not available.

Decision trees

Decision trees are a visual and valuable way to organize data so as to help make a choice between several options with different chances of occurring and different results if they do occur. Trees (see Figure 12.2 below) were first used in business in the 1960s but became seriously popular from 1970 onwards when algorithms were devised to generate decision trees and automatically reduce them to a manageable size.

FIGURE 12.2 Example decision tree

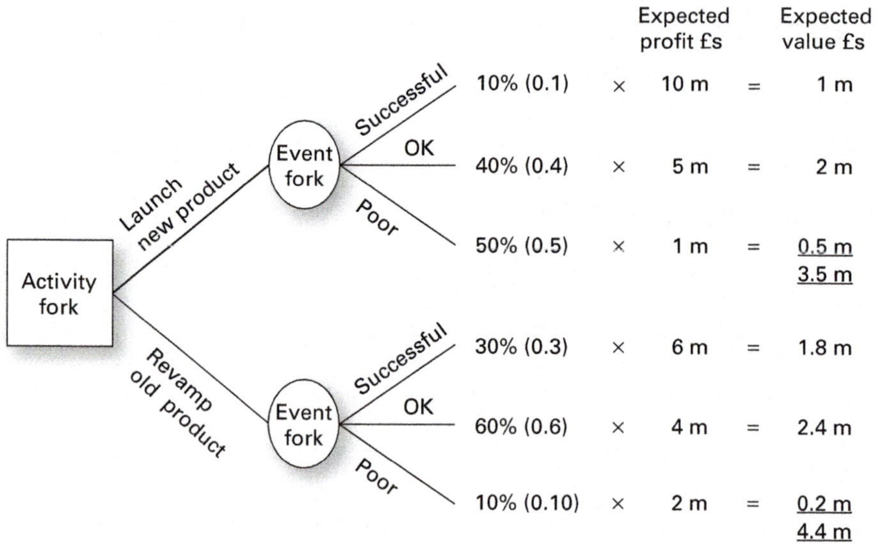
Expected profit £s
Expected value £s
Activity fork
Launch new product
Revamp old product
Event fork
Successful
OK
Poor
Event fork
Successful
OK
Poor
10% (0.1) × 10 m = 1 m
40% (0.4) × 5 m = 2 m
50% (0.5) × 1 m = 0.5 m
3.5 m
30% (0.3) × 6 m = 1.8 m
60% (0.6) × 4 m = 2.4 m
10% (0.10) × 2 m = 0.2 m
4.4 m

Making a decision tree requires these steps to be carried out initially from which the diagram can be drawn:

- establish all the alternatives;
- estimate the financial consequences of each alternative;
- assign the risk in terms of uncertainty allied with each alternative.

Figure 12.2 shows an example decision tree. The convention is that squares represent decisions and circles represent uncertain outcomes. In this example the problem being decided on is whether to launch a new product or revamp an existing one. The uncertain outcomes are whether the result of the decision will be successful (£10 million profit), just ok (£5 million profit) or poor (£1 million). In the case of launching a new product, the management's best estimate is that there is a 10 per cent (0.1 in decimals) chance of success, a 40 per cent chance it will be ok and a 50 per cent chance it will result in poor sales. Multiplying the expected profit arising from each possible outcome by the probability of its occurring gives what is termed as an 'expected value'. Adding up the expected values of all the possible outcomes for each decision suggests in this case that revamping an old product will produce the most profit.

The example is a very simple one and in practice decisions are much more complex. We may have intermediate decisions to make, such as should we invest heavily and bring the new product to market quickly, or should we spend money on test marketing? This will introduce more decisions and more uncertain outcomes represented by a growing number of 'nodes', the points at which new branches in the tree are formed.

Forecasting

Sales drive much of a business's activities; they determine cash flow, stock levels, production capacity and ultimately how profitable or otherwise a business will be, so unsurprisingly much effort goes into attempting to predict future sales. A sales forecast is not the same as a sales objective. An objective is what you want to achieve and will shape a strategy to do so. A forecast is the most likely future outcome given what has happened in the past and the momentum that provides for the business.

The components of any forecast are made up of three components and to get an accurate forecast you need to decompose the historic data to better understand the impact of each on the end result.

- Underlying Trend: This is the general direction, up, flat or down, over the longer term, showing the rate of change.
- Cyclical Factors: These are the short-term influences that regularly superimpose themselves on the trend. For example, in the summer months you would expect sales of certain products – swimming

wear, ice creams and suntan lotion, for example – to be higher than in the winter. Ski equipment would probably follow a reverse pattern.

- Random Movements: These are irregular, random spikes up, or down, caused by unusual and unexplained factors.

Using averages

The simplest forecasting method is to assume that the future will be more or less the same as the recent past. The two most common techniques that use this approach are:

- Moving average: This takes a series of data from the past, say the last six months' sales, adds them up, divides by the number of months and uses that figure as being the most likely forecast of what will happen in month seven. This method works well in a static, mature marketplace where change happens slowly, if at all.

- Weighted moving average: This method gives the most recent data more significance than the earlier data since it gives a better representation of current business conditions. So before adding up the series of data each figure is weighted by multiplying it by an increasingly higher factor as you get closer to the most recent data.

Exponential smoothing and advanced forecasting techniques

Exponential smoothing is a sophisticated averaging technique that gives exponentially decreasing weights as the data gets older and, conversely, more recent data is given relatively more weight in making the forecasting. Double and triple exponential smoothing can be used to help with different types of trend. More sophisticated still are Holt's and Brown's linear exponential smoothing models and the Box–Jenkins method, named after two statisticians of those names, which apply autoregressive moving to average models to find the best fit of a time series.

Fortunately, all an MBA needs to know is that these and other statistical forecasting methods exist. The choice of which is the best forecasting technique to use is usually down to trial and error. Various software programs will calculate the best-fitting forecast by applying each technique to the historic data you enter. Then wait and see what actually happens and use the technique with the forecast closest to the actual outcome. Professor Hossein Arsham of the University of Baltimore (**http://home.ubalt.edu/ntsbarsh/Business-stat/stat-data/forecast.htm**) provides a useful tool that allows you to enter data and see how different forecasting techniques perform. Duke University's Fuqua School of Business, consistently ranked among the top 10 US business schools in every single functional area, provides this helpful link (**www.duke.edu/~rnau/411home.htm**) to all their lecture material on forecasting.

Causal relationships

Often when looking at data sets it will be apparent that there is a relationship between certain factors. Look at Figure 12.3, which is a chart showing the monthly sales of barbeques and the average temperature in the preceding month for the past eight months.

It's not too hard to see that there appears, as we might expect, a relationship between temperature and sales, in this case. By drawing the line that most accurately represents the slope, called the line of best fit, we can have a useful tool for estimating what sales might be next month, given the temperature that occurred this month (see Figure 12.4).

FIGURE 12.3   Scatter diagram example

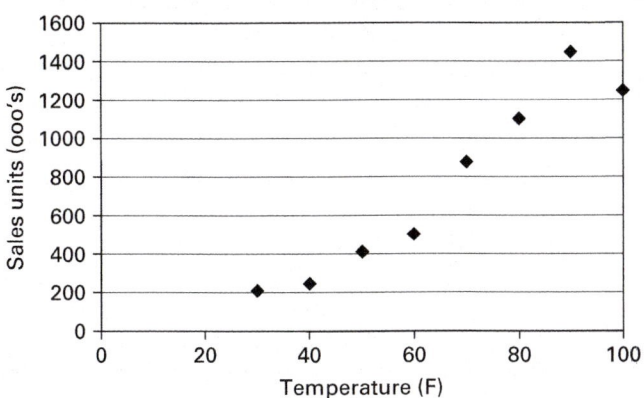

FIGURE 12.4   Scatter diagram – the line of best fit

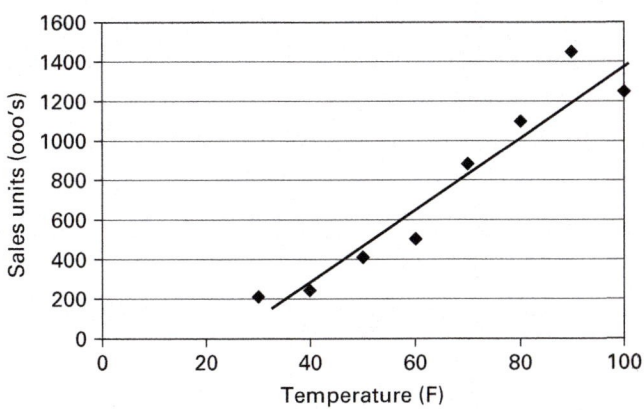

The example used is a simple one and the relationship obvious and strong. In real life there is likely to be much more data and it will be harder to see if there is a relationship between the 'independent variable', in this case temperature, and the 'dependent variable', sales volume. Fortunately there is an algebraic formula known as 'linear regression' that will calculate the line of best fit for you.

There are then a couple of calculations needed to test if the relationship is strong (it can be strongly positive or even if strongly negative it will still be useful for predictive purposes) and significant. The tests are known as R-Squared and the Students t-test, and all an MBA needs to know is that they exist and you can probably already find the software to calculate them on your computer. Otherwise you can use Web-Enabled Scientific Services & Applications (**www.wessa.net/slr.wasp**) software, which covers almost every type of statistic calculation. The software is free online and provided through a joint research project with K.U.Leuven Association, a network of 13 institutions of higher education in Flanders.

For help in understanding these statistical techniques read Gerard E Dallal of Tufts' book *The Little Handbook of Statistical Practice* available free online (**www.jerrydallal.com/LHSP/LHSP.htm**) and at Princeton's website (**http://dss.princeton.edu/online_help/analysis/interpreting_regression.htm**) you can find a tutorial and lecture notes on the subject as taught to their Master of International Business students.

Surveys and sample size

Surveys are the most common research method used in organizations to get a handle on almost every aspect of performance from measuring sales force morale, assessing customer satisfaction to getting the views of almost any stakeholder group on almost any issue. MBAs will certainly have to know how to get surveys done and if working in a small organization they may well have to do it themselves.

The size of the survey undertaken is vital to its accuracy. You frequently hear of political opinion polls taken on samples of 1,500–2,000 voters. This is because the accuracy of your survey clearly increases with the size of sample, as the following table shows:

With a random sample of ...	95 per cent of surveys are right within ... percentage points
250	6.2
500	4.4
750	3.6
1,000	3.1
2,000	2.2
6,000	1.2

So, if on a sample size of 600, your survey showed that 40 per cent of women in the town drove cars, the true proportion would probably lie between 36 and 44 per cent. A sample of 250 completed replies is about the minimum to provide meaningful information on which reliance can be placed.

Creative Research Systems survey software provide this Sample Size Calculator as a public service together with some information on the terms that you need to know (**www.surveysystem.com/sscalc.htm**).

Online video courses and lectures

Accounting: Dr Ray Gregg, Oral Roberts University, Tulsa, OK. A series of 37 lectures from the basics of debits and credits to capital budgets and investments: **www.youtube.com/playlist?list=PL31FC5F69A409A706**

Capital Structures in Major Corporations: Discussion at Columbia Business School by visitors and faculty: **www7.gsb.columbia.edu/video/v/node/1363?page=1**

Corporate Finance Essentials: Prof Javier Estrada of IESE Business School offers this course each year. It consists of six sessions requiring no previous knowledge or preparation. Each session will consist of a video lecture of around 45–60 minutes and one or two recommended readings. **www.coursera.org/course/corpfinance**

The Debt To Equity Ratio: Investopedia: **www.investopedia.com/video/play/debt-to-equity-ratio/**

Finance Fundamentals: Taught by Jim Stice and Kay Stice, professors at Marriott School of Management, Brigham Young University (US). You can watch this 3 hour 27 minute course as an introductory free trial at Lynda.com: **www.lynda.com/Business-Accounting-tutorials/Finance-Fundamentals/174917-2.html**

Forecasting – Time series models – Simple Exponential smoothing: Prof G Srinivasan, Department of Management Studies, IIT Madras: **www.youtube.com/watch?v=k9dhcflyOFc**

Introduction to Financial Accounting: Contents include an introduction to the balance sheet, the income statement, cash flows and working capital assets and how to read an annual report. This course is presented as a combination of lecture videos, quizzes and discussion. The only required math knowledge is addition, subtraction, multiplication, and division. Delivered four times a year by Wharton's faculty: **www.coursera.org/course/whartonaccounting**

Introduction to Probability and Statistics: MIT Open Courseware: **http://ocw.mit.edu/courses/mathematics/18-05-introduction-to-probability-and-statistics-spring-2014/this-course-at-mit/#Video**

Measures of Central Tendency and Dispersion: Alanis Business Academy: **www.youtube.com/watch?v=DgC3DdnBtE4**

Population and Sample Means: Alanis Business Academy: **www.youtube.com/watch?v=E25i4FHFe2U**

Online video case studies

Adobe: Marketing by the numbers: How Adobe puts the data back into its marketing: **http://tv.adobe.com/watch/adobe-summit-2014-emea/marketing-by-the-numbers-how-adobe-puts-the-data-back-into-its-marketing/**

Carson Dellosa: Steve Griffin, Carson Dellosa's CTO describes how Mariner and Carson Dellosa, a publisher of educational books and tools, improved the ability to analyze point of sale data beginning with a pilot project and then moving into building a complete business intelligence framework: **www.youtube.com/watch?v=LmdmHfPaVbg**

How we helped IT contractor Ronan Moriarty understand his income: Crunch Accounting: **www.youtube.com/watch?v=cCja3dEpsXY&list=PLY1w7ViHqCO359V9apwhwoCPLFjwYCHBz&index=4**

How we're brightening up Greyworld's finances: Crunch Accounting: **www.youtube.com/watch?v=9NfghzMKXZQ&list=PLY1w7ViHqCO359V9apwhwoCPLFjwYCHBz&index=1**

What Sherlock Holmes Can Teach Us About Decision Making: Maria Konnikova at the RSA: **www.youtube.com/watch?v=JfZd2oLlIMw**

INDEX